Q33 "states appeared when one died"
Q34 "rulers sought to control discourse about power. sequence
94 "writing at invention of cities."
98 strong gods represent "unusual powers of nature"
98 strong kings control "crude gods", puppets & used by specialists under their control
100 evolution of autonomous elites"
102 — thousands of years before states became storage enough to "engineer rivers
103 — 300 years before Hammurabi, promise not to pour out deeds &
explain to the powerful

Myths of the Archaic State

In this ground-breaking work, Norman Yoffee challenges prevailing myths underpinning our understanding of the evolution of the earliest cities, states, and civilizations. He counters the emphasis in traditional scholarship that the earliest states were large and despotically controlled and their evolution can be adequately modeled by ethnographic analogies. By illuminating the creation and changes in social roles – not simply of male leaders but also of slaves and soldiers, priests and priestesses, peasants and prostitutes, merchants and craftsmen – Yoffee depicts an evolutionary process centered on the concerns of everyday life. Drawing on evidence from ancient Mesopotamia as well as from Egypt, South Asia, China, Mesoamerica, and South America, the author explores the changes in human societies that created the world we live in. This book offers a bold new interpretation of social evolutionary theory, and as such it is essential reading for any student or scholar with an interest in the emergence of complex society.

112 – "councils of Egypt towns" & "elders of guilds" decide disputes in Babylon

NORMAN YOFFEE is Professor of Near Eastern Studies and Anthropology at the University of Michigan. His various publications include *Archaeological Theory: Who Sets the Agenda?* (co-editor with Andrew Sherratt, Cambridge University Press, 1993) and *The Collapse of Ancient States and Civilizations* (co-editor with George L. Cowgill, University of Arizona Press, 1988). He is editor of the *Journal of the Economic and Social History of the Orient* and *Cambridge World Archaeology*.

116 – collapse of hyper-bureaucratic state in Mesopotamia.
132 collapse. "a good deal of bungling, at best, not understood
134-5 Hammurabi. "hyper-centralized" "the worst of evils"
160 – Hammurabi – no bureaucrat – propagandist!

MYTHS OF THE ARCHAIC STATE

Evolution of the Earliest Cities, States, and Civilizations

NORMAN YOFFEE

CAMBRIDGE
UNIVERSITY PRESS

CAMBRIDGE UNIVERSITY PRESS
Cambridge, New York, Melbourne, Madrid, Cape Town, Singapore, São Paulo, Delhi

Cambridge University Press
The Edinburgh Building, Cambridge CB2 8RU, UK

Published in the United States of America by Cambridge University Press, New York

www.cambridge.org
Information on this title: www.cambridge.org/9780521521567

First published 2005
Reprinted with corrections 2006
Third printing 2007

A catalogue record for this publication is available from the British Library

Library of Congress Cataloguing in Publication data
Yoffee, Norman.
Myths of the archaic state : evolution of the earliest cities, states, and civilizations /
Norman Yoffee.
   p. cm.
Includes bibliographical references and index.
ISBN 0 521 81837 0 – ISBN 0 521 52156 4 (pbk.)
1. State, The.   2. Cities and towns, Ancient.   3. Civilization, Ancient.   I. Title.
JC51.Y64   2004
320.1′09′01 – dc22   2004052683

ISBN 978-0-521-81837-7 hardback
ISBN 978-0-521-52156-7 paperback

Transferred to digital printing 2009

For Barbara

Contents

List of figures   *page* x
List of tables   xiii

INTRODUCTION   1

1   THE EVOLUTION OF A FACTOID   4
    An introduction to social evolutionary mythology   5
    Types, rules, and factoids   6
    Neo-evolutionism evolving   8
    States and civilizations: beyond heuristics   15

2   DIMENSIONS OF POWER IN THE EARLIEST STATES   22
    The pursuit of the wily chiefdom   22
    Neo-evolutionism and new social evolutionary theory: back
        to the future   31
    The evolution of power and its distribution in the earliest states   33
    Dimensions of power in social evolutionary theory   34
    States as states of mind   38
    What neo-evolutionism cannot explain   41

3   THE MEANING OF CITIES IN THE EARLIEST STATES
    AND CIVILIZATIONS   42
    City-states and chimeras   44

Cities and states   45
Mesopotamian city-states and Mesopotamian civilization   53
Cities and city-states in social evolutionary perspective   59

4   WHEN COMPLEXITY WAS SIMPLIFIED   91
Simplifying the path to power in early Chinese states   94
Law and order in ancient Mesopotamia   100
    The context of Mesopotamian law   102
    The context and function of the code of Hammurabi   104
    The complexities of legal simplification: decision-making in Mesopotamia 109

5   IDENTITY AND AGENCY IN EARLY STATES: CASE STUDIES   113
A peculiar institution in Old Babylonian Mesopotamia   116
Imagining sex in an early state   121
Conclusion: Encounters with women in early states   128

6   THE COLLAPSE OF ANCIENT STATES AND CIVILIZATIONS   131
Theorizing collapse   132
    Neo-evolutionism and collapse   134
    Collapse as the drastic restructuring of social institutions   138
The collapse of ancient Mesopotamian states and civilization   140
    The Old Akkadian state   142
    The Third Dynasty of Ur   144
    The Old Babylonian and Old Assyrian states   147
The end of the cycle?   151
    Collapse as the mutation of social identity and suffocation of cultural memory 153
    The collapse of Mesopotamian civilization and its regeneration   159

7   SOCIAL EVOLUTIONARY TRAJECTORIES   161
Evolutionary history of the Chaco "rituality"   162
Non-normative thinking in social evolutionary theory   171
Southwest and Southeast   173
Towards a history of social evolutionary trajectories   177

8   NEW RULES OF THE GAME   180
The game of archaeological neologisms   181
    The engineering of archaeological theory: mining and bridging   182

How archaeologists lost their innocence 183

Levels of archaeological theory 185

Sources of analogy in archaeological theory 188

Analogy and the comparative method 192

9 ALTERED STATES: THE EVOLUTION OF HISTORY 196

An essay on the evolution of Mesopotamian states and civilization 198

Initial conditions and emergent properties 200

Interaction and identity 204

The formation of Mesopotamian civilization and Mesopotamian city-states 209

Evolutionary histories of the earliest cities, states, and civilizations 228

Acknowledgments 233

References 236

Index 268

LIST OF FIGURES

1.1	Neo-evolutionist step-ladder model of stages	*page* 18
1.2	Myth of "our contemporary ancestors"	19
2.1	"Real" stratification	30
2.2	Hypothetical potential stratification	30
3.1	Earliest states and civilizations	63
3.2	Egypt	63
3.3	Hierakonpolis	64
3.4	Memphis (Early Dynastic and Old Kingdom)	65
3.5	Thebes	66
3.6	Amarna	66
3.7	Amarna – workmen's village	67
3.8	Mesoamerica	68
3.9	Teotihuacan	68
3.10	Teotihuacan, urban growth	69
3.11	North China	70
3.12	Erlitou	70
3.13	Zhengzhou	71
3.14	Anyang	71
3.15	Indus Valley/Harappan sites	72
3.16	Mohenjo-Daro	73
3.17	Mohenjo-Daro – DK-G area	74
3.18	Harappa	74
3.19	North coast of Peru and Central Andes	75

3.20   Moche   76
3.21   Tiwanaku   76
3.22a Wari   77
3.22b Wari, aerial view   77
3.23   Wari, urban growth   78
3.24   Maya region   79
3.25   El Mirador   79
3.26a Tikal, greater city   80
3.26b Tikal, urban core   81
3.27   Copán   81
3.28   Selected Mesopotamian cities   82
3.29   Mesopotamian settlement pattern in the late Uruk period   82
3.30   Mesopotamian settlement pattern in the Early Dynastic II
       and III periods   83
3.31   Uruk   84
3.32   Nagar/Tell Brak   85
3.33   Kish   85
3.34   Lagash city-state   86
3.35   Comparison of some ancient cities   87
3.36   Comparison of some modern urban places on the scale of the
       earliest cities   88
       a. Amsterdam, 1936
       b. Leiden, 1936
       c. Ann Arbor, Michigan, 2003
       d. University of Michigan, Central Campus, Ann Arbor
       e. Hong Kong Island
       f. New Orleans (Métropole de La Nouvelle Orléans, 1765)
4.1   Chinese potters' marks   95
4.2   Mesopotamian tokens   95
4.3   Shang period bronze   97
4.4   Shang period oracle bone   99
4.5   Code of Hammurabi   105
7.1   Northern Southwest   163
7.2   Chaco, outliers, roads   164
7.3   Great house sites of Chaco Canyon   165
7.4   Shapes of great houses   166
7.5   Pueblo Bonito   166
7.6   Mississippian sites   175

7.7	Cahokia	176
7.8	Examples of some evolutionary trajectories discussed in the text	178
8.1	Structure of archaeological theory	187
8.2	Valley of Oaxaca	190
8.3	Monte Albán	191
9.1	Selected Mesopotamian sites from various periods	215
9.2	Selected early Holocene and Neolithic sites	215
9.3	Selected Hassuna and Samarra sites	216
9.4	Yarim Tepe I	216
9.5	Hassuna ceramics	217
9.6	Samarra ceramics	218
9.7	Tell es-Sawwan, levels III and IV	219
9.8	Selected Halaf sites	220
9.9	Halaf ceramics	220
9.10	Tell Arpachiyah burnt house	221
9.11	Eridu, temple VII	221
9.12	Tepe Gawra, acropolis, level XIII	222
9.13	Tell Madhhur house	222
9.14	Tell Abada village	223
9.15	Eanna precinct, Uruk	224
9.16	White temple, Anu ziggurat, Uruk	225
9.17	Beveled-rim bowls	225
9.18	Archaic tablet scribal exercises	226
9.19	Archaic tablet list of professions with later copies	226
9.20	Uruk expansion sites	227
9.21	Some southern Mesopotamian city-states in the early third millennium BC	227

LIST OF TABLES

3.1   Area and population size estimates of the earliest cities mentioned
in the text   *page* 43

9.1   Chronological table of selected periods in Mesopotamia   199

Introduction

The evolution of the earliest cities, states, and civilizations is an enormous topic and writing about it is made no easier by my discomfort with the term "evolution" itself. Although I criticize "neo-evolutionary" theory – that is, the attempt to create categories of human progress, which in anthropology stems from the nineteenth-century work of Edward Tylor and Lewis Henry Morgan and which was revivified in the mid-twentieth century by Leslie White and Julian Steward and others – I do not reject the term evolution or social evolution.

Economically stratified and socially differentiated societies developed all over the world from societies that were little stratified and relatively undifferentiated; large and densely populated cities developed from small habitation sites and villages; social classes developed from societies that were structured by kin-relations which functioned as frameworks for production, and so forth. These changes must be explained, and archaeologists have been doing the job with remarkable success for more than a century, with the pace of research quickening in the last decades. As I discuss throughout this book, it doesn't much matter what we call things, as long as we explain clearly what we mean, and as long as our categories further research, rather than force data into analytical blocks that are self-fulfilling prophecies.

This book is about the earliest states, particularly the constellations of power in them, and also about their evolution, that is, where varieties of power came from. I also discuss certain other features of the evolution of the earliest states, for example their "collapses," as well as what happens after collapse. Archaeologists traditionally group these and related phenomena and try to explain them by building what they call social evolutionary theory. I do not intend to break from this tradition.

As Thomas Carlyle said of the lady who told him that she accepted the universe, "By God, she'd better."

The central myth of this book is not that there was no social evolution (but see further in Chapter 1), but the claim that the earliest states were basically the same sort of thing: large territorial systems ruled by totalitarian despots who controlled the flow of goods, services, and information and imposed true law and order on their subjects. If myth can be defined (in at least one respect) as "a thing spoken of as though existing," we find that much of what has been said of the earliest states, both in the professorial literature as well as in popular writings, is not only factually wrong but also is implausible in the logic of social evolutionary theory.

Indeed, much of the literature on the evolution of ancient states focuses nearly exclusively on political systems and has tended to reduce the earliest states to a series of myths about godly and heroic (male) leaders who planned and built prodigious monuments and cities, conquering their neighbors and making them powerless subjects of the ruling elites. Little has been written about the roles of slaves and soldiers, priests and priestesses, peasants and prostitutes, merchants and craftsmen, who are characteristic actors in the earliest states. No one should conclude, however, from my discussions of the limitations on the power of rulers, and because I am interested in the "bottom-up" aspects of power, that I regard the nature of rule in the earliest states as anything other than repressive and exploitative.

There are many things I do not even hope to cover in this book. I do little more than glance at biological or astrophysical conceptions of evolution. These evolutions may or may not provide interesting and useful ideas for the study of social change, but the mechanisms and scales of biological change or of stellar ontogeny (themselves different kinds of evolution) are different from those pertinent to the study of change in human social organizations. I do not intend this book as a rebuttal to all the ideas of social evolutionary change with which I happen to disagree, and I have tried not to clutter the book with copious references to theories and data. Some readers may still find the number of citations daunting and the narrative thereby occluded.

Although I am a Mesopotamianist and provide my lengthiest examples from Mesopotamia, a large part of my project is to illustrate the varieties of social systems and modes of power that existed in many of the earliest states. If "social evolution," in the end, seems to some onlookers as "world history," I shall shed no tear.

This book deals with the theories that have been used to understand the evolution of the earliest states and also why such theories have been invented and in which academic environments (in Chapters 1 and 2). I describe the variety of trajectories towards ancient cities and states (in Chapter 3) and the "evolution of simplicity" in them (in Chapter 4). I consider certain roles of Mesopotamian women, as elites and as prostitutes (in Chapter 5), as examples of how people constructed their social lives within cultural circumstances, and I discuss the "collapse" of the earliest states and civilizations (in Chapter 6) as studies in "social memory" and "identity." I meditate on "constraints on growth" (in Chapter 7) – that is, why states did not appear in some areas of the world, especially in the American Southwest – and on the use and abuse of analogy and the comparative method by archaeologists (in Chapter 8). I conclude with a sketch of the evolution of Mesopotamian states and civilization (in Chapter 9), borrowing the language and some of the reasoning of "complex adaptive systems" theorists.

By means of case-studies that survey the world-landscape of emerging states, I depict an evolutionary process in which social roles were transformed into relations of power and domination. Stratified and differentiated social groups were recombined under new kinds of central leadership, and new ideologies were created that insisted that such leadership was not only possible, but the only possibility. I center social evolutionary theory in the concerns of how people came to understand their lives in the earliest cities and states, how the new ideology of states was instituted in everyday life, and how leaders of previously autonomous social groups in states negotiated with rulers and/or contested their domination.

Some may say that such a project can have no successful conclusion, for its scale is too large. They may be right. I am buoyed, I think, only by a comment attributed to John Kenneth Galbraith: "The surest means for attaining immortality is to commit an act of spectacular failure."

This is not a book of reprinted essays, although I have drawn from journal articles and book chapters that I have written. Some of these, for example on specific Mesopotamian institutions, appeared in small-circulation journals, Festschriften, and other out-of-the-way publications that will not be familiar to archaeologists and historians. I have updated and altered already published material considerably, added new data and discussions, and connected the chapters so as to form a narrative. Although I express a variety of critiques of existing theory and advance new perspectives on theory, I adhere throughout to Ludwig Wittgenstein's dictum, "A book should consist of examples." No one can write a book with the scope of this one, however, without the help of many friends, whom I thank individually in the acknowledgments at the end of this book. I want to express my gratitude for their expertise and collegiality collectively also at its beginning.

1

THE EVOLUTION OF
A FACTOID

Definierbar ist nur Das, was keine Geschichte hat. (You can only define things that
have no history.)

FRIEDRICH NIETZSCHE

There is an irony in beginning a book on the "evolution of the earliest states and
civilizations" with an apology for using the term "evolution." Nevertheless, it is far
from unusual for archaeologists (e.g. Hegmon 2003) to eschew the term in favor
of discussing "social change," "social development," or the like. Critics have argued
that social evolution presents a theory of how history is a continuation of biological evolution, in which societies advance from lower to higher forms. Such "neo-
evolutionary" theory has been used to justify racism, the exploitation of colonized
peoples, and Occidental contempt towards other cultures (Godelier 1986:3). Social
evolution has, not entirely unfairly, been characterized as an illusion of history, as
a Hegelian prophecy of a rational process that culminated in the modern bour-
geois state, capitalist economies, and technological advance. Such criticisms are
by no means new, and exuberant schools of disenchantment that are today common in anthropology and other faculties disdain the idea of social evolution in
all its forms. Little wonder that many archaeologists are uncomfortable with the
term.

Although I criticize neo-evolutionary theory as it has been used in archaeology
and anthropology, that is, the attempt to create categories of human progress and
to fit prehistoric and modern "traditional" societies into them (which stems from

the nineteenth-century founders Lewis Henry Morgan and Edward Tylor[1] and was represented in the mid-twentieth century by Leslie White and Julian Steward and others), I find "evolution" an appropriate term for investigating the kinds of social change depicted in this book. Class-stratified societies with many different social orientations and occupations and with internally specialized political systems developed from societies in which kin-relations functioned to allocate labor and access to resources; large and densely populated urban systems emerged over time from small habitation sites and villages; ideologies that espoused egalitarian principles[2] gave way to belief systems in which the accumulation of wealth and high status was regarded as normal and natural, as were economic subordination and slavery. These changes occurred across the globe, mostly independently and about the same time (especially if time is calculated in each region from the onset of the first agricultural communities). Archaeologists have the resources to explain these and many other kinds of change, and the term evolution is the only one I know that can enfold the various theories needed for the job.

AN INTRODUCTION TO SOCIAL EVOLUTIONARY MYTHOLOGY

I contest a variety of myths of the evolution and nature of the earliest states, or "archaic states," as some have curiously called them.[3] These include: (1) the earliest states were basically all the same kind of thing (whereas bands, tribes, and chiefdoms all varied within their types considerably); (2) ancient states were totalitarian regimes, ruled by despots who monopolized the flow of goods, services, and information and imposed "true" law and order on their powerless citizens; (3) the earliest states enclosed large regions and were territorially integrated; (4) typologies should and can be devised in order to measure societies in a ladder of progressiveness; (5) prehistoric representatives of these social types can be correlated, by analogy, with modern societies reported by ethnographers; and (6) structural changes in political and economic

---

[1] For discussions of the history of social evolution, which, depending on the commentator, stretches hundreds or thousands of years before Tylor and Morgan, see Patterson (2003), M. Harris (1968), Skinner (1978), Lovejoy and Boas (1965), and Meek (1976).

[2] I do not imply "egalitarianism" is a basic human social form, and much egalitarianism in the ethnographic record might itself be an evolved form of organization from earlier, different social organizations.

[3] The term "archaic states" was used by Talcott Parsons (Sanderson 1990:110) and others (also see Trigger 2003). The working title of the recent book now called *Archaic States* (Feinman and Marcus 1998) was *The Archaic State*.

systems were the engines for, and are hence necessary and sufficient conditions that explain, the evolution of the earliest states.

In this book I question the image of the earliest states as totalities (as in such phrases as "Teotihuacan did this or that") within which political competition and social conflict were rare, and I critique "types" of societies as essentially content-free, abstract models that say little about how people lived or understood their lives. I want to contribute to the rehabilitation of social evolutionary theory as a means for investigating how the emergence of new and differentiated social roles and new relations of power in early agricultural societies occurred and how differentiated groups were recombined by means of the development of new ideologies of order and hierarchy. These ideologies are at the core of what we call ancient states. I begin by reviewing how the theory of neo-evolutionism, the "factoid" that I refer to in the title of this chapter, took hold of archaeologists' imaginations in the period roughly 1960–90 and in what academic circumstances.

TYPES, RULES, AND FACTOIDS

It has taken archaeologists many decades to reject the neo-evolutionist proposition that modern ethnographic examples represent prehistoric stages in the development of ancient states.[4] Defining "types" of societies (e.g. bands, tribes, chiefdoms, states), establishing putative commonalities within a type, and postulating simple lines (or even a single line) of evolutionary development had led archaeologists to strip away most of what is interesting (such as belief systems) and important (such as the multifaceted struggle for power) in ancient societies and consigned those modern societies that are not states to the scrap-heap of history. I review why most archaeologists have now explicitly discarded, or just ignore, these "old rules of the game" of social evolutionary theory, even to the extent of excising the word "evolution" from their analysis of social change. This is not simply an exercise in the history of social thought, because the task of building the "new rules of the game" for understanding the evolution of ancient states depends on the self-conscious examination of the failures of neo-evolutionary theory.

The "rules of the game" – old and new – consist in two domains or sets of rules. First (but not necessarily chronologically prior) are the substantive rules of how archaeologists recover and analyze data, and how they build models that interpret, explain, and represent the past. Second are the academic rules governing why

---

[4] Not all archaeologists have rejected neo-evolutionist stages (see Billman 2003).

archaeologists take up certain problems and look for and often find particular kinds of data, and how they convince their colleagues of the plausibility and relevance of their interpretations. No one will be surprised to learn that the two sets of rules are inextricably interlinked. Of course, the substantive rules are themselves hardly theory-neutral, because the process of observing, analyzing, reporting, and drawing inferences from data cannot be kept separate from the reasons for which data are sought and the manner in which they are studied. No archaeologist doubts this, although there are many disputes, for example, about how recovered data are "resistant" to some interpretations and better fit others (Wylie 2002), and how one actually goes about deciding between rival claims to knowledge. I return to these substantive rules later.

I first consider the rules of academic behavior, namely the reasons archaeologists have been attracted to certain theories of the evolution of ancient states. These academic rules – the domain of the sociology of science – are those that guide academic success, since jobs, promotions, and status depend on learning the governing substantive rules, and how practitioners can convincingly amend, emend, or replace them with new rules. American academic archaeologists, who normally find employment in departments of anthropology, or were trained in these departments, have not unnaturally attempted to model prehistoric societies after one or another modern ethnographic or "traditional" society studied by their social anthropological colleagues. Social evolution was inevitably thought to proceed from one "type" of society to another. Archaeologists, who thus "found" ethnographic types in prehistory, could thereby claim to be genuine anthropologists. At least, this was the process invented in the 1950s and 1960s, when some social anthropologists (such as Leslie White and Julian Steward, Morton Fried and Elman Service) were defining and arguing about ethnological types of societies. It continued for another two decades in archaeological circles, although social anthropologists were progressively turning their interests from anything that might be called social evolutionary theory.[5] Why did archaeologists embrace neo-evolutionary theory, the theory of ethnographic types that were projected into the past and marched towards statedom, so wholeheartedly?

In the introduction to his photo-biography of Marilyn Monroe, Norman Mailer (1973) coined the term "factoid." A factoid is a speculation or guess that has been repeated so often it is eventually taken for hard fact. Factoids have a particularly insidious quality – and one that is spectacularly unbiological – in that they tend

[5] Marshall Sahlins, whose views of 40 years ago I discuss below, has said, "I'm still an evolutionist, but I've evolved."

to get stronger the longer they live. Unlike "facts," factoids are difficult to evaluate because, although they often begin as well-intended hypotheses and tentative clarifications, they become received wisdom by dint of repetition by authorities. The history of neo-evolutionary theory in archaeology is the evolution of a factoid. Neo-evolutionism advocated a "new taxonomic innovation" that could "arbitrarily rip cultures out of context of time and history and place them, just as arbitrarily, in categories of lower and higher development" (Sahlins 1960:32). "Any representative of a given stage is inherently as good as any other, whether the representative be contemporaneous and ethnographic or *only archaeological*" (Sahlins 1960:33, my emphasis). Once the factoidal nature of neo-evolutionism has been exposed, we can see that its deployment by archaeologists resulted in circular reasoning about the nature of ancient societies and the process of social change.

NEO-EVOLUTIONISM EVOLVING[6]

Neo-evolutionary theory was revivified, beginning in the 1940s, harkening back to its earliest proponents, the founders of the discipline of anthropology. Leslie White, the hero of the movement, in fact disclaimed the title of "neo-evolutionist" because "the theory of evolution set forth . . . does not differ one whit in principle from that expressed in Tylor's *Anthropology* in 1881" (White 1959a:ix). White, in his first essay on the subject in 1943, in his last in 1960, and in several in-between, was fond of citing a remark of B. Laufer, exhumed from a 1918 review, which White considered exemplary of the low regard into which social evolutionary studies had fallen in the early twentieth century: "The theory of cultural evolution[7] [is] to my mind the most inane, sterile, and pernicious theory ever conceived in the history of science" (Laufer 1918:90). In 1943 White predicted that the "time will come . . . when the theory of evolution will again prevail in the science of culture" (1943:356) and nearly two decades later he was gratified to report that "antievolutionism has run its course . . . The concept of evolution has proved itself to be too fundamental and fruitful to be ignored" (1960:vii).

---

[6] This section is based on an earlier essay (Yoffee 1979). There aren't many new discussions of neo-evolutionism. Jonathan Haas (2001) presents a slight review of the subject; Thomas Patterson (2003) considers the ideas of White, Steward, and others within the development of social theory in anthropology and archaeology. I include this updated discussion here as a prologue to new concerns of archaeologists with the evolution of power and ideology, which hardly played a role in the writings of the neo-evolutionists.

[7] I use the terms cultural evolution, social evolution, and sociocultural evolution – and also the terms cultural anthropology, social anthropology, and sociocultural anthropology – interchangeably.

If Tylor and Morgan and other nineteenth-century anthropologists were reacting against the supernatural in history (Kaplan and Manners 1972:39–40) and the creation theory of Judeo-Christian theology (White 1959a:1; Lesser 1952:135), White was reacting mainly against the errors of Boasian particularism. Boas and his group (those most frequently cited by White include Goldenweiser, Sapir, Lowie, Herskovits, Mead, and Benedict) were particularists and relativists, refusing to set up stages of development and asserting that any evaluation of cultures was chimerical and ethnocentric. Boasians and others ascribed social change to diffusion and borrowing, anti-evolutionary or non-evolutionary ideas, according to White (1959b:108).

Evolutionism in its most irreducible form was for White "a temporal sequence of forms" (1959a:vii), for "no stage of civilization comes into existence spontaneously, but grows or is developed out of the stage before it" (Tylor 1881:20, quoted by White 1959b:108). "Evolution is the name of a kind of relationship among things and events of the external world . . . [and] in the dynamic aspect, things and events related in this way constitute a process, an evolutionist process" (White 1959b:114). For archaeologists the relevance of studying process was not lost and the born-again archaeologists of the 1960s (mainly students at the University of Chicago of Lewis Binford, who had studied with White at the University of Michigan, and then students of the students of Binford) called themselves "processual archaeologists."[8] Since archaeologists study the history of artifacts and the people who made them, they perforce study change; it is thus no surprise that archaeologists of the time flocked under the banner of evolutionism.

For White the stream of evolution was the culture of humanity as a whole. There was no question of confusing individual culture histories, because the subject of the evolutionist sequence was all of human culture. Furthermore, the evolutionist process is irreversible and non-repetitive, and any appeal to a particular culture's ups-and-downs was ruled out of court since White was only interested in the evolution of human culture worldwide. The scale White used in evaluating the progress of human culture, for this was his aim, was based on the amount of energy utilized by a culture. According to the second law of thermodynamics, the universe is breaking down structurally and moving to a more uniform distribution of energy. Culture develops, then, as the efficiency of capturing energy increases and as the amount of goods and services produced per unit of labor increases (White 1959a:47; 1943:336). This, according to White, is *the* law of cultural evolution (1943:338). Since energy

---

[8] Joseph Caldwell called them "new archaeologists" (Patterson 2003), a term that Alison Wylie (1993) has shown to have been employed about every two decades since the early years of the twentieth century.

capture depends on technological advance, "social evolution is a consequence of technological evolution" (1943:347).

Armed with the evolutionist concept of development in human culture on a world-wide scale and the progressive utilization of energy through technological advance, White was able to describe a basic evolutionist trajectory in the development of human civilization. In agreement with Maine (1861) and Morgan (1889), he depicted the "great divide" (Service 1975:1) in human cultural evolution as the change from societies based on kinship, personal relations, and status (societas) to those based on territory, property relations, and contract (civitas). In the first type, relations of property are functions of relations among humans; in the second, relations among humans are functions of relations among items of property (White 1959a:329). This transformation occurs when ties of kinship wane and territorial factors wax. Further subdivision of evolutionist stages was left to White's students and colleagues.

A last element in this necessarily truncated appraisal of White's contribution to the conception and use of social evolutionist theory is a recurring motif of real concern to White, never directly stated, but nevertheless implicit throughout. In 1947 White stated that "Boas and his disciples . . . for reasons we cannot go into here . . . were definitely opposed to the theory of classical evolution as a matter of principle" (1947:191). In 1960 White was more forthcoming, contending that since "the capitalist-democratic system had matured and established itself securely . . . evolution was no longer a popular concept . . . On the contrary, the dominant note was 'maintain the status quo'" (1960:vi). White's point demonstrably was that antievolutionism was opposed to social progress in the Third World and to "the communist revolution which is spreading throughout much of the world" (1960:vi) and which constituted the next stage in social evolution. This was the reason the theory was opposed by Boas and his disciples. Marvin Harris (1968:640, following Barnes 1960:xxvi) traced White's conversion to "evolutionism" to his 1929 tour of the Soviet Union but dismissed his understanding of the subject, describing White by Engels's pejorative term, "a mechanical materialist." Maurice Godelier (1977:42) and Jonathan Friedman (1974) replied in kind, describing Harris's "cultural materialism" as "vulgar materialism." This point is relevant only insofar as it sheds light on White's earnestness concerning the subject of evolutionism and on a possible agenda in his "objective evaluation of cultures." These issues are not mentioned as an indictment, but rather as a justification for considering White's ideas as largely formulated in the context of other anthropological schools and political currents of the day.

The second source for the revival of social evolutionary theory in anthropology was the work of Julian Steward (see especially Steward 1955:11–29; cf. Patterson 2003; Harris 1968:642–3). Steward regarded social evolution as "multilinear," since divergent lines of evolution were occasioned by distinctive local environments and subsistence patterns. In this he opposed White, who simply disregarded local eco-logical situations: "If one wishes to discover how cultural systems are structured and how they function as cultural systems," wrote White, "then one does not need to consider the natural habitat at all" (1959a:51). Since White was talking about Cul-ture, not cultures, there could be no limits according to local conditions. Steward rejected White's universal evolution precisely because the theory wasn't relevant in explaining any particular cultural development: "The postulated cultural sequences are so general that they are neither very arguable nor very useful and cannot explain particular features of particular cultures" (Steward 1955:17). White countered expect-edly by pointing out that "a generalization is not a particularization," but this does not answer Steward's criticism of the lack of utility of the universal theory. As Harris aptly remarked, "If a generalization tells us nothing about particulars, it can scarcely enjoy the status of an empirical proposition" (Harris 1968:649).

Steward's framework did agree with and further articulate White's view that social evolution involved "development levels . . . marked by the appearance of qualita-tively distinctive patterns or types of organization . . . wholly new kinds of overall integration" (1955:13). If social evolution, however, is mainly divergent, "the attribute of progress" means that there are also genuine parallels "in historically independent sequences of cultural traditions." These parallels can be explained "by the indepen-dent operation of identical causality in each case" (1955:14). "Multilinear evolution" attempts to identify these parallel cases and underline the "cultural laws" that caused the parallels. These cultural laws are rooted in "cultural-ecological adaptations – the adaptive processes through which a historically derived culture is modified in a partic-ular environment" (1955:21). Steward then delineated "culture types," constellations of diagnostic features that had identical functional interrelations in each culture as sociopolitical structures were produced in environmentally similar situations. Steward was especially infatuated by Karl Wittfogel's "hydraulic hypothesis" (1957) that held that parallel trajectories to ancient states were determined by the need to manage scarce water resources.

Steward's essay, *Cultural Causality and Laws: A Trial Formulation of the Develop-ment of Early Civilizations* (1955), held that in arid lands (Mesopotamia being the prime example) production, population growth, and sociopolitical development were related to irrigation on a large scale. Initially, "irrigation was undertaken only on a small, local scale," and "the sociopolitical unit was a small house cluster, which probably consisted of a kin group or lineage" (1955:200–1). Population grew as irri-gation works were developed until "the flood plains became densely settled and . . . collaboration on irrigation projects under some co-ordinating authority became necessary" (1955:201). A theocratic ruling class emerged to manage irrigation, extending its control until finally forming a multicommunity state. Empires were created from competition over resources, population pressure, and the threat of hostile nomads. "Irrigation works were increased to the limits of water supply and population," after which peak the empires collapsed, "irrigation works were neglected and population decreased" (1955:204).

This explanatory scheme can now be refuted in almost every particular, as I shall discuss in subsequent chapters (see also Trigger 2003). However, as Steward himself elegantly noted, it is all too easy for specialists to produce new material and to point out inconsistencies in the "facts." As he put it: "Facts exist only as they are related to theories, and theories are not destroyed by facts – they are replaced by new theories which better explain the facts. Therefore, criticisms of this paper which concern facts alone and which fail to offer better formulations are of no interest" (1955:209).

I agree with Steward and, although I consider his "facts" to be wrong, my central point of dispute is with the theory used to explain the facts. The theory is, of course, social evolutionism, with its postulation of taxonomic units, Steward's "qualitatively distinctive patterns of organization . . . wholly new kinds of social integration." In this statement, Steward remained in substantive agreement with White's principle of evolutionist development through a series of stages.

The final element in the history of the development of evolutionist concepts in anthropology, and the most forceful and explicit appeal to archaeologists, was the putative compromise of White's and Steward's positions put forth by Sahlins and Service. Emphasizing the two-fold nature of the evolutionist process, Sahlins and Service (1960:4) harkened unto Tylor's view on the subject: on the one hand, evolution consisted in the "general development through which culture as a whole has passed 'stage by stage'"; while on the other hand it also lay in the study of "particular 'evolution along its many lines'." They coined the terms "general evolution" and "specific evolution" to describe this dual nature of the beast. Specific evolution, namely Steward's multilinear conception, accounts for the process whereby new forms differentiated from old ones, while general evolution refers to the process whereby higher forms arise from and surpass lower ones (Sahlins 1960:13). Specific evolutionary sequences can result in parallelism, "the consequences of similar adaptation to similar environment" (1960:28). The general evolutionist argument is, however, ineffably more powerful – essentially because it is general. It "is the central, inclusive, organizing outlook of anthropology, comparable in its theoretical power to evolutionism in biology" (1960:44).

To clarify the utility of the terms general and specific evolution, Sahlins presented the example of European feudalism. Feudalism is not "the general stage of evolution antecedent to high (modern) civilization"; rather it "is a stage only in a specific sense," part of a particular line of development (1960:31, 32). In general terms the stage preceding modern nation-states is represented by such classical civilizations as Rome, China, Sumer, and the Inca empire. Feudalism is thus a backward form representing "a lower level of *general* development than the civilizations of China, ancient Egypt, or Mesopotamia, although it arose later than these civilizations and happened to lead to a form still higher than any of them" (1960:33, my emphasis).

By extracting cultures from their historical contexts, Sahlins and Service (and their colleagues) could delineate the successive evolutionist stages of bands, tribes, chiefdoms, archaic states – which could be either contemporaneous and ethnographic or prehistoric – and nation-states. Service went on to explain how feudalism, a lower level of general development than ancient China or Sumer, could lead to a higher form than any archaic state, according to the "law of evolutionary potential": "The more specialized and adapted a form in a given evolutionary stage, the smaller the potential for passing to the next stage" (Service 1960:97). Furthermore, "an advanced form does not normally beget the next stage of advance" since "the next stage begins in a different line" and "if successive stages of progress are not likely to go from one species to its next descendant, they are not likely to occur in the same locality" (1960:98–9).

It is tempting to pause to critique the odd example of European feudalism, which itself is a complicated mix of the "collapse" of the Roman empire and the transformation of local "European" traditions, and the theory of social change that finds that collapse is due either to overspecialization and narrow adaptation or to the rise of superior competitors who have been stimulated by the now inferior society, and also why such terms as progress, superior, and inferior were used by Service. However, I defer critique to subsequent chapters and return to the story of how sociocultural anthropologists developed neo-evolutionist theory and why archaeologists adopted it so enthusiastically.

As White and Steward and others were advocating a return to social evolutionary theory in anthropology and establishing stages and levels of development, some social anthropologists entered into a classic debate over the mechanisms of change that resulted in the origin of states and civilizations. On one side, Elman Service (1975) saw the origin of civilization as contingent on the perceived benefits of good leadership. In times of danger from "nomadic raiding bands of predators" (1975:299), scarcity of resources, and unprecedented density of people, the enlightened, theocratic leadership in chiefdoms provided self-evident "blessings" (1975:294), "strengthening the coherence of a collectivity by making it plain to its members the benefits of being part of it" (1975:298). No coercive force is employed in the institutionalization of leadership and, indeed, for Service, "civilization" is a form of culture that was intermediate between the beneficent chiefdom and the coercive state (1975:305). The state is a "repressive institution based on secular force" (1975:306), and only when the "immense benefits" of a centralized redistributive system characteristic of chiefdoms become "evident" do "social inequalities . . . probably result" (1975:285) and states arise. In chiefdoms there are no serious socioeconomic differences and "stratification" is "mainly of two classes, the governors and the governed – political strata, not strata of ownership groups" (1975:285).

Morton Fried disputed Service's beneficent chiefdom scenario vehemently (Fried 1960, 1967; see also Wittfogel 1957; Carneiro 1970, 1981 among others). Fried contended that stratified society developed before the state and, in fact, the state evolved in order "to support the order of stratification" (1960:728). Once stratification existed, "the cause of stateship is implicit and the actual formation of the state is begun" (1960:728). Mechanisms leading to differential access to basic resources, economic power, and finally political control included population pressure on circumscribed land and warfare (as in Carneiro's view), the necessity of managing scarce water resources (the argument of Wittfogel), or simply endemic warfare (also see Johnson and Earle [1987] for the prime mover arguments of population pressure and war).

Obviously, this polarity of views was due in the main to the anthropologists' philosophical adherence to or rejection of larger theories of social change, especially orthodox Marxist ones. Although I do not attempt to dissect this situation further, one need not rigidly champion either a benefits or a conflicts/coercion model, since both forces must be assessed as dynamic parts of the theory of social change that I advocate. Although I discuss in the next chapter some of the archaeological reactions to benefits and conflicts models, I outline here the basic problems of both of them. I propose a quasi-dialectical resolution of this debate, that is, a model that incorporates aspects of the competing ones, which I rephrase in terms of ideology and power later on.

Service's interpretation of benefits (or consensus theory) states that power structures first institutionalize egalitarian exchange principles. That is, the economic interests of the governors are complementary with the interests of the governed. This theory, however, cannot account for the rise of repressive, economically riven states from beneficent, redistributive chiefdoms except under reductionist and mentalistic assumptions: everyone is at first merry with his and her prosperity, whether governor or governed, until the system's benefits become so large that the governors decide to hog all the goodies. *Amor pecuniae radix malorum est.*

Conflict theories, in contrast, tend to be highly deterministic, since the state is seen as the inevitable by-product of nascent stratification (Fried 1967:226). No account is taken of the fact that the problem posed by stratification may also lead to the breakdown of the system (Eisenstadt 1964:384). I devote a later chapter to the problem of collapse and also one to "the constraints on growth": there are plenty of instances of stratification and social differentiation that do not lead to states. Conflict models of change also untenably assume that a single power ("the state") organizes all of society; I show subsequently that in ancient states various subsystems – local community authorities, ethnic groups and their leaders, and social corporations of elites – aspire to their own autonomy, are at least partly independent of other parts of society, and compete for power according to accepted social rules. In other words, conflict models do not allow for the existence of endemic and legitimate struggle in ancient states.

In understanding the evolution of early states, then, we need to recast restrictive and exclusionary models within a social theory that incorporates patterns of both conflict and consensus. Internal differentiation within a state entails a "ubiquity of conflict" (Eisenstadt [with Curelaru] 1976:369–71), since dominant sociopolitical goals are never accepted by all the constituents of a society. Differentiation also requires that institutions of the center develop to cut across social divisions and recombine them in order to form a community whose borders may be harder or looser, politically defined and/or culturally manifested, as I illustrate by reference to various states and civilizations. Thus, ubiquity of conflict results in a partial, "consensual" resolution of conflict whereby a legitimacy of the order of differentiated subsystems and their goals is at least partly achieved (Parsons 1964).

STATES AND CIVILIZATIONS: BEYOND HEURISTICS

In the foregoing paragraphs I have used the terms state and civilization as if they were unproblematic and even interchangeable. Before returning (in Chapter 2) to the subject of why archaeologists adopted the agenda of neo-evolutionism, which, I stress, was created and debated in the 1950s and 1960s by sociocultural anthropologists, not archaeologists, I need to explain what the terms denote. First, although I insist that the terms state and civilization usefully refer to different kinds and scales of social phenomena, these phenomena are helix-like, in that one cannot discuss the evolution of civilizations without also investigating the evolution of states. Furthermore, whereas I argue that states and civilizations are different in critical institutional respects from non-states, they are not different from them in every respect. This Nietzschean approach of declining to define changing historical entities in absolute terms is quite foreign to archaeologists, who are trained to distinguish exactly between types of things. A lithic flake is either a biface or it isn't, a painted pot is either Show Low black-on-white or it isn't, and archaeologists have, not unreasonably, wanted to extend such analytical fineness to human social organizations.

The difficulty in separating states from non-states in the archaeological record has led some archaeologists to refer to "complex societies." "Complex social systems" differ from simple (or "complicated societies," in the sense of Hallpike [1986:278]), essentially in the degree and nature of social differentiation in them (e.g. Parsons 1964, but also in the tradition of Herbert Spencer [Patterson 2003]). Complex societies have institutionalized subsystems that perform diverse functions for their individual members and are organized as relatively specific and semiautonomous entities (Shils 1975; Eisenstadt 1964). Further differentiation, in normative social evolutionary thought, leads to problems of social order and to a need for generalized centers of political and economic administration that provide the linkages in these consequently functionally interrelated parts. I stress in this book both that these putative linkages are often quite weak in the earliest states and also that centrality is mainly concerned with the creation of new symbols of social identity, ideologies of power, and representations of history. Although centralization may "solve" some problems, it is the source of other ones (Paynter 1989).

In less complex societies major roles are allocated on an ascriptive basis and division of labor is based on family and kinship units. In complex societies a central authority develops in order to bring relatively autonomous subsystems within the contours of a larger institutional system. This central authority is structurally different from the subsystems that form the societal periphery (in the sense of Shils [1975]) in that key members are not recruited exclusively on the basis of some ascriptive status, but by reason of their competence. Their roles as officers of the center are differentiated largely from their other social roles, especially kinship roles. Over time, to summarize this process, at least provisionally, earlier rules of social relations lose their exclusivity and are transformed and/or replaced by other rules of incorporation.

Fried described this type of complex, differentiated system as the "organization of society on a supra-kin basis" (1960:728). So succinctly stated, however, the concept of a central authority in a stratified society remains imprecise. The entire social system in the earliest states was not organized without kinship rules; indeed, the ruling dynasty of most centralized political structures was usually constituted by a royal lineage. However, many members of the center were not chosen by virtue of their relations to that lineage.

In any event, kinship ties and their various functions in local production, distribution, and legal arrangements that characterized the organization of local communities did not disappear in states. The emergence of a political center depended on its ability to express the legitimacy of interaction among the differentiated elements. It did this by acting through a generalized structure of authority, making certain decisions in disputes between members of different groups, including kin groups, maintaining the central symbols of society, and undertaking the defense and expansion of the society. *It is this governmental center that I denominate as the "state," as well as the territory politically controlled by the governmental center.*

Since – as I argue in Chapter 3 – most early states are territorially small, indeed can be called city-states (or micro-states), and a number of such city-states share an ideology of government, *I refer to the larger social order and set of shared values in which states are culturally embedded as a "civilization."* Within a civilization the state serves as the focus and ideal of authority and maintains the offices that can be competed for by members of the social corporations that constitute the larger, civilizational order.

State and civilization are in a sense coeval since it is the emergence of the idea that there should be a state – a central authority, whose leaders have privileged access to wealth and to the gods – that must accompany the formation, legitimacy, and durability of a political center. The state as governmental center and its attendant hierarchy of officers and clients maintains features that are distinct from kinship, priestly, and other hierarchies, whose members interacted in a variety of ways with the government and were transformed by those interactions. The evolution of a new "civilizational" ideology, namely that there should be a state, was critical, because the state constituted and stipulated the orderly functioning of the cosmos, especially by requiring rulers to intercede with the gods and to represent the rest of society in such intercession.

State and civilization, inextricably intertwined, must be kept analytically distinct, because it is possible for there to be several states within the same "civilizational" umbrella. That is, several politically independent states – polities of modest territorial extent, each politically independent and with its own governmental center – can equally share the same ideological framework: there should be a state, the state should consist in a specific form, the states within this ideological confederation should interact in certain ways with respect to each other, and the symbols (both literary and material) that signify this common identity will be maintained, reproduced, and altered in concert.

Most neo-evolutionists, attempting to ascertain the essential qualities of evolutionist stages (band, tribes, chiefdoms, and states), ignored the concept of civilization (except for Service; see above and the critique by Patterson [2003]), which was for

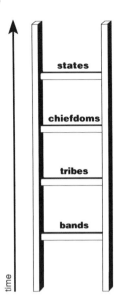

Figure 1.1   Neo-evolutionist step-ladder model of stages

them "vague and ambiguous" (Flannery 1972:400).[9] Failure to consider the development and nature of ancient civilizations and the ideational systems that bound the
earliest states into civilizations led to a fundamental misunderstanding about both
the size of ancient states and the rules of political struggle within them.

The neo-evolutionist model of stages and levels (Figure 1.1) leading to states was
characterized in the 1960s as *the* generalizing, basic cross-cultural tool of anthropology. Flannery's "Old Timer" (1982:269) observed, "There is no 'archaeological'
theory. There's only *anthropological* theory." Archaeologists embraced the model
of "our contemporary ancestors" (Service 1975:18; Figure 1.2) because it provided
archaeologists with a series of ready ethnographic analogies that could be introduced into the past. Such neo-evolutionary trees could be constructed without any
reservation that the ethnographic societies placed in a line of development did
not themselves lead to the next "higher" stage. The social evolutionists who had
constructed the model, after all, had advocated precisely that cultures should be
plucked from any context of time and history. One can see now, of course, that
the whole metaphysical arrangement of cultures was riddled with logical contradictions, and it channeled archaeological research into dangerous waters: modern

---

[9] Anthropologists today (e.g. Patterson 1997), as well as others, are offended by the term civilization,
   finding it reeking of the idea of progress and particularly of the superiority of Western civilization over
   "traditional" cultures. I intend that my use of the term conveys nothing about the values of one culture
   against another one.

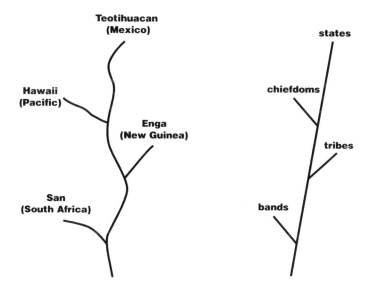

Figure 1.2   Myth of "our contemporary ancestors"

societies not having achieved "statehood" were "fossils," the relics of prehistoric underachievement, and the past itself was condemned to resemble some form of the present. I repeat: little wonder that many archaeologists today have rejected the term evolution.

In the 1960s and 1970s archaeologists engaged in neo-evolutionist research to identify and seriate sociocultural "types" in the material and ethnographic record. V. G. Childe (1950) was perhaps the first archaeologist to devise a trait-list to identify the common characteristics of urbanism and the state, but one or another of his ten traits were easily shown to be absent in some states. For example, Adams (1966) explored the developmental parallels between Aztec and Mesopotamian states, although the former had no system of writing and the latter did. If Carneiro (1968) could produce a Guttman-scale of types of societies, Feinman and Neitzel (1984) demonstrated that there were "too many types," since differences among societies are seldom whole differences, and the appearance of one trait or set of traits does not necessarily signal a totally new and different sociocultural form. The flaws in the neo-evolutionist classification that treated subsystemic linkages as fixed within classes and different between them were apparent.

Beyond all the fallacies in evolutionist logic, however, which I explore further in the next chapter, was the appeal of the theory to archaeologists seeking to model the organization of prehistoric societies from the residues they excavate. If one could posit a series of interlinked traits of one type and then identify one of those key traits in the material record, one could then flesh out the material sample by extrapolating the whole congeries of traits thought to characterize the type – no matter that these were completely absent in the record. For example, William Sanders (1974) determined, from his cross-cultural ethnographic surveys, that in chiefdoms a chief could mobilize significant labor on public buildings, especially temples, while he could not requisition similar amounts of manpower for the construction of his own residence. Thus, he reasoned, in the prehistoric sequence at Kaminaljuyu in Guatemala, there was a shift from the Terminal Formative times, when the amount of labor spent on the leader's residential platform was small compared with that devoted to the temple, to the Early Classic when there was "a much higher degree of centralization of construction activities." This leads Sanders to "very tentatively suggest that the shift from chiefdom to state level of organization" had occurred (Sanders 1974:111).

Similarly, in one of the most cited and important essays of the 1970s, Wright and Johnson (1975) identified the state as having minimally three levels of administrative hierarchy, which they correlated with site-size hierarchies and an administered flow of goods among the sites in the various levels. It is not my intention to explicate and value the analyses of these excellent archaeologists; rather I note that they (and many others of their time) were fundamentally concerned to identify a type of society in the archaeological record and then to place that type in the pre-ordained evolutionary ladder of development.

The very act of categorization turned researchers towards the goal of finding an ideal type in the material record – is it or is it not a chiefdom? – and to construct a shortcut for identifying an entire set of differences (as well as similarities) among prehistoric societies. Archaeological accounts of the rise of ancient states and civilizations thus retrojected ethnographic types (no matter that institutions varied exceedingly with a postulated type) into the prehistoric record and reconstructed social evolution as a series of holistic leaps from one stage to the next. The unavoidable conclusion was that archaeologists, in becoming true believers of neo-evolutionary theory, produced confirmations of revealed truth and had nothing new to contribute to social theory.

Merton (1949:7) has quoted Whitehead to the effect that disciplines in their infancy create grand evolutionary schemes that are ambitiously profound in their aims but trivial in their handling of details. This was certainly the case in archaeology. Having discarded the governing factoid of evolutionism in archaeology, archaeologists now have turned from questions of what prehistoric societies *are* and towards asking what (actors in) these societies *do*.

As anthropologists and historians we owe the neo-evolutionists of the mid-twentieth century and their archaeological acolytes great respect for having advanced the study of social change as a central goal in archaeology. Having acknowledged our debt, we now realize that the model of neo-evolutionism in its very comprehensiveness had buried the complexities of development under the single-minded aim of establishing an all-encompassing regularity, a teleology without a god. That model did little to advance our knowledge of social change and only offered an untestable dogma that fossilized, but once harmoniously adapted social systems are out there and only await identification and seriation. As Darwin famously observed, one must first see what the problems are that need solving before one can make progress in solving them. In the following chapters I discuss how archaeologists today can and do analyze the many trajectories of social change that are documented in the archaeological record and so explain the evolution of the earliest cities, states, and civilizations.

2

DIMENSIONS OF POWER IN
THE EARLIEST STATES

> The state drew its force, which was real enough, from its imaginative energies, its
> semiotic capacity to make inequality enchant.
>
> CLIFFORD GEERTZ (1980:123)

In this chapter I delineate what is not explained in "neo-evolutionary theory" and devise new means to investigate the evolution of ancient states and civilizations. Neo-evolutionary theory depicted the rise of states as a series of "punctuated" (that is, extremely rapid) and holistic changes from one stage (or type of society) to another. In each stage, all social institutions – politics, economy, social organization, belief system – were linked so that change had to occur in all institutions at the same time, at the same pace, and in the same direction. The prehistoric representations of these social types were modeled after "our contemporary ancestors," societies studied by ethnographers. This progression of ethnographic societies, however, was no more than a metaphysical construction, since San in southern Africa did not become Enga in New Guinea and Enga didn't become Hawaiians (see Figure 1.2).

THE PURSUIT OF THE WILY CHIEFDOM

One may see how archaeologists had implemented neo-evolutionary theory by reviewing why a mighty company of archaeological wallahs pursued the wily chiefdom so diligently. Colin Renfrew (1973) isolated twenty features of chiefdoms and determined that the builders of European megaliths were chiefs; William Sanders (1974) and colleagues (e.g. Michels 1979) identified chiefdoms among the prehistoric highland Maya; Winifred Creamer and Jonathan Haas (1985) found them in Central America, while Robert Drennan and Carlos Uribe (1987) located them everywhere in the Americas; Vernon J. Knight Jr. (1990) identified chiefdoms in the Southeast USA; George Milner did so in the Middle West (1998), as did David Doyel (1979) in the Southwest; Walter Fairservis (1989:217) argued that the Harappa culture was a chiefdom (and so did Gregory Possehl 1997, although he hedged his bets in 2002); for the Near East, Timothy Earle thought Ubaid and Uruk Mesopotamia were both chiefdoms (1987), and Gil Stein (1994) wrote about chiefdoms in the Ubaid, although Patty Jo Watson (1983) held that the preceding Halaf was a chiefdom; for Donald Henry (1989), the Natufian of the northern Levant was a "matrilineal chiefdom."

There is no great secret, of course, why the chiefdom was (and sometimes still is) so ubiquitous in the archaeological literature. First, something must precede states that is not even crypto-egalitarian, yet is not exactly state-like, and it requires a name. Second, anthropological archaeologists need a frame for cross-cultural comparison. "Primary" states arose independently in various parts of the world, and so similar pre-state entities must be identified in order to measure their distances from statehood. And third (as we have seen in Chapter 1), the received anthropological wisdom (created by social anthropologists in the 1960s) directed archaeologists to flesh out the fragmentary material record of an extinct social organization by means of an appropriate ethnographic analogy. The "archaeological" procedure was to correlate one or more central features of a favorite ethnographic type with some excavated material, then extrapolate all the rest of the characteristics of the type and so bring the not-directly-observable dimensions of an ancient society into view.

Archaeologists continued to search the past for chiefdoms into the 1990s (Earle 1991, 1997), although the task was becoming increasingly difficult, as the essential qualities of chiefdoms were themselves changing considerably. The chiefdom began life in the anthropological literature (Service 1962, 1975; Carneiro 1981) with several defining attributes: social organization consisted of branching kinship structures called ramages or conical clans, wherein all members are ranked pyramidally in terms of distance from real or putative founding ancestors. Chiefdoms are "kinship societies" (Service 1962:171) because status is largely determined through place in the generational hierarchy of groups and of individuals within the groups. In political terms, chiefdoms contain hereditary and usually endogamous leaders (sometimes called a nobility) and centralized direction, especially in matters of ceremony and ritual, but they have no formal machinery of forceful repression. Robert Netting (1972:221) summarized the chief's position:

The general pattern of the rights, duties, role, and status of the priest-chief is numbingly familiar to anthropological students of society. He is the famous *primus inter pares*, the essentially powerless figure who does not make independent decisions but voices the sense of the meeting. He leads by example or by persuasion. As chief he may have a title and an office, but his authority is circumscribed; he *is* something, but he *does* very little. As Sahlins (1968:21) remarks, "the Chieftain is usually spokesman of his group and master of its ceremonies, with otherwise little influence, few functions, and no privileges. One word from him and everyone does as he pleases."

Such chiefly authority in the classical view is correlated with religious authority (Service 1975:16). Therefore, chiefdoms are "theocracies," with authority distributed as of a religious congregation to a priest-chief. Service argued that chiefdoms did not contain any roots of economic differentiation, because production and consumption were governed by "sumptuary rules." The redistribution of goods is a central responsibility and perquisite of chiefly leadership, and it is through the success of such redistributive functions that the nature of leadership finally changes from (Service's) beneficent chief to wealthy and repressive kings.

To archaeologists the most appealing aspect of these classical attributes of chiefdoms was redistribution, which they correlated with Karl Polanyi's (1957) classification of dominant modes of exchange and their sequence, from reciprocal to redistributive to market forms. Timothy Earle (1977), however, effectively questioned whether redistribution – that is, the collection of goods from specialized producers into a center and from there the circulation of goods to members of an organically integrated society (Service 1962:144) – really occurred in classical chiefdoms such as Hawaii. He argued (Earle 1987, see also Johnson and Earle 1987, as did Peebles and Kus 1977) that local groups in chiefdoms were self-sufficient in staple goods, and goods given to chiefs supported chiefly led public feasts and fed the chief's attendants.

If redistribution was all but eliminated as a fundamental characteristic of chiefdoms, so also were considerations of economically egalitarian communities and powerless chiefs. For Earle, chiefly elites control strategic resources, mainly by achieving ownership of the best land and directing the labor of commoners who worked it as dependants. In short, the most important *social* characteristics of chiefdoms, the structure of conical clans and the related economic sumptuary rules that characterized chiefly economies, along with the function of the chief as a beneficent priest-chief, nearly disappeared from the archaeological literature. What replaced them was a conception of chiefly political organization.

In influential articles written by (then) young scholars who were associated as students or teachers in the Department of Anthropology, University of Michigan (the department of Leslie White), the basic point of the chiefdom was that it was a political unit (see Wright 1977, 1984; Peebles and Kus 1977; Steponaitis 1978, 1981; Spencer 1987, 1990; and joined significantly by Carneiro, e.g. 1981, who was a graduate student of White himself). That is, the chiefdom represented a breakthrough in social evolution in which local autonomy – which constituted 99 percent of all the societies that have existed, according to Robert Carneiro (1981:37) – gave way to a form of authority in which a paramount leader controlled a number of villages. Chiefs thus organized regional populations in the thousands or tens of thousands and controlled the production of staples and/or the acquisition of preciosities; the chiefdom was thus the stage preceding the rise of the state. For Carneiro, states were only quantitatively different from chiefdoms – larger, and with more powerful leaders.

Henry Wright (1984) differentiated between simple chiefdoms, which are the classically ascriptive sort, with ranks determined according to the distance from common ancestors, and the complex chiefdom in which there is a regional hierarchy with a paramount chief ruling over subsidiary chiefs. These paramount chiefs centralized decision-making authority, and they could (and did) mobilize resources to their seats, but they left local communities and sub-chiefs in place. As Wright put it, chiefdoms are externally specialized in order to get the goods from the various regions to the paramount's control, but they are not internally specialized (i.e. with a specialized bureaucracy) to accomplish the task. There was a rank difference between chiefs and commoners, with the chiefs forming a sort of "class" and competing with each other for leadership and control of the ritual institutions that could legitimize their status. However, such attempts at control of goods without a permanent, specialized coercive authority meant that rebellions, breakdowns, destruction of centers, and changes in symbolic orientation were part of what complex chiefdoms were about. This inherent tendency to break down caused chiefdoms to "cycle," a concept that was taken up by David Anderson (1990, 1994; and see below and in Chapter 7).

Charles Spencer (1990) has detected one point of schism in the analysis of complex chiefdoms and so of neo-evolutionary theory. According to Spencer, the single inconsistency in the position of the evolutionary typologists and their view of the chiefdom as a stage that precedes the state is the mistaken idea that social change is gradual (Earle 1987:221) and continuous (Wright 1984). Such a notion of change would reduce the distinction between the chiefdom and the state only to a quantitative difference and so render the neo-evolutionist stage model of little utility. For Spencer, the distinction between chiefdom and state had to be emphasized: chiefs, lacking internally specialized enforcement machinery, avoid delegating central authority and rely on the local power of sub-chiefs, while kings (in states) systematize and segment their power so as to undermine local authority. Thus, the transition from chiefdom to state proceeds transformationally (when it occurs – chiefdoms could also collapse, as Wright had argued). The key condition leading to transformation is population growth (which is Earle's mechanism for evolutionary change, too) and the consequent need to generate a greater surplus that requires an alteration in "regulatory strategies" (Spencer 1990:10) which transcend "the limitations of chiefly efficiency" (1990:11). For Spencer, the evolution of states is punctuational (in the language of Stephen Gould, meaning extremely rapid "speciational" change after long periods of stasis). States were created as centralized administrations with new administrative technologies and new political offices of the sort that did not exist in chiefdoms.

Students of chiefdoms themselves, including many of the participants in Earle's edited volume *Chiefdoms: Power, Economy, and Ideology* (1991) and Earle himself in *How Chiefs Come to Power: The Political Economy in Prehistory* (1997), became dissatisfied with the neo-evolutionary stress on politics in chiefdoms and the de-emphasis on social and economic institutions that were formerly their hallmarks. Arguments about the chiefdom as a specialized political system governing a large region or territory implied that political centralization must precede social stratification and economic differentiation. Although the aim was clearly to escape from Service's quandary – how do beneficent chiefs become repressive kings? – archaeologists were still left with the problems of how kinship systems of ranking that allocated access to resources and status could turn into class-riven states.

Some argued that chiefdoms might not become states, because internal contradictions in the kin-based structure of chiefdom societies sow the seeds of repeated organizational collapse (Anderson 1994). Failures to establish effective administrations outside the kinship system resulted in cycling from complex chiefdoms to simpler ones (see also Milner 1998). One way for chiefdoms to evolve into states was through conflict, with victorious chiefs attaining clients outside the system of kinship and institutionalizing new structures of government in the large territorial systems thus gained.[1]

The first published argument that chiefdoms might lie outside the evolutionary trajectory towards states was in an essay by William Sanders and David Webster (1978). In correlating environmental variables of climatic "risk" and "diversity" of resources, they considered that chiefdoms, which occurred in low-risk/high-diversity situations, were alternatives to state development. There could be a transition from chiefdom to state, but the process was one of contact from already developed states, which effected fundamental changes in the social and economic organization in chiefdoms. Although the archaeological neo-evolutionists had received their inspiration

---

[1] This argument was suggested by Carneiro (1970), who thought conflict was generated through geographical or other types of circumscription; Wright (1984) considered that conflict occurred among neighbors, with states emerging from the struggle between complex chiefdoms.

from sociocultural anthropologists, it is clear that by the 1980s (at the latest) that determining the essence of chiefdoms and their possible location in the great chain of becoming states was light-years from anything that sociocultural anthropologists were (and are) worried about.

Ethnologists in the 1970s themselves criticized neo-evolutionary explanations for the rise of chiefdoms. Thus, for Melanesia and Polynesia, the original example for Sahlins's (1963) distinction between big-man (or tribal) societies and chiefdoms, critics pointed out that some societies had the annoying habit of possessing traits of both types (Chowning 1979; Douglas 1979). The most absurd of situations occurred when Melanesian "chiefs," so defined according to their kin-ranking and inheritance of position, have as their foremost goal to become "big-men" (by achieving super-trader status [Lilley 1985]). Indeed, Sahlins's discussion of big-men and chiefs is simply a description of types, not a study of social change. Readers are left to imagine the unspecified evolutionary forces that would have transformed a big-man society into a chiefdom. In Patrick Kirch's archaeological study of the "evolution of Polynesian chiefdoms" (1984), there is no such transition from any putatively prior big-man society to a chiefdom, since chiefs existed before migrations to Polynesia (see most recently Kirch and Green 2001). The only "evolution" is that which is dependent on island geography – how the availability of certain kinds of land and resources and the proximity (or lack of it) to other islands affected the size and structure of various sorts of Polynesian chiefdoms.

In the neo-evolutionist movement from big-man societies to chiefdoms and then to states, there is something profoundly illogical: big-man societies are classically those in which leaders achieved status through their skills in hunting, warfare, oratory, and so forth, but in which such status cannot be inherited; in chiefdoms, classically, rank and status are ascribed through the kinship system and passed along intergenerationally. In states, it is again achievement – through the control of material resources in most accounts – that is the hallmark of social stratification, whereas kin-groups and ascribed relations play less important roles in social life. It would make more sense, perhaps, to derive states from achievement-oriented big-man societies than it would from ascriptively determined chiefdoms (if one were a neo-evolutionist).

Many archaeologists from the late 1970s onward criticized the archaeological obsession with chiefdoms as a stage in social evolution, mainly out of dissatisfaction with claims that social change proceeded holistically. Randall McGuire (1983) contended that the variables of "inequality" and "heterogeneity" needed to be kept separate and that one should not be a proxy for the other. His point was that a society could be very unequal vertically, as he considered was the case in the earliest states – think pyramids – but with a correspondingly small amount of heterogeneity, that is with few horizontally differentiated economic and social groups. Through time the amount of heterogeneity tended to increase. I elaborated my own criticism (1979) of holistic change, namely that change certainly did not occur in all institutions in instances of collapse (see Yoffee and Cowgill 1988 and, in this volume, Chapter 6). Political systems – governments – of early states could fall while other social and economic institutions continued to survive and even thrive. The continued existence of certain critical social groups, especially clear in the case of literati in dynastic China, provided the political ideology and bureaucratic infrastructure that generated the characteristic Chinese political system anew. Also, criticizing the neo-evolutionist scheme, Gary Feinman and Jill Neitzel (1984) observed that since prehistoric change was continuous (see Plog 1974), it was wholly arbitrary to break the sequence into discrete and distinct blocks. In reviewing books on Andean prehistory, Garth Bawden noted that even late pre-ceramic societies have been called "states" and that one finds "mixtures of characteristics that have been used to identify chiefdoms and states, ranked and stratified societies" (1989:331).

Robert Paynter (1989) argued that neo-evolutionist theory was inextricably linked to functionalist and adaptationist schools of thought. Stages of becoming implied a set of stable social formations, which were then beset by certain problems which, in the neo-evolutionary literature, usually were caused by population growth. Higher stages were pictured as problem-solvers, evolved into hierarchies so as to control efficiently larger numbers of people and to monitor larger amounts of information. For Paynter, however, more complex and bureaucratic political institutions were problem-creators, not problem-solvers, and culture is not simply a fitted-out machine to process resources, energy, and information. Coercive powers of the state led to intra-class tension, intra-elite struggle, and fierce attempts to maintain local autonomies in the face of integrative tendencies.

Such criticisms of the chiefdom also dispute (if mainly by implication) the analogy between social evolutionary stages and biological taxonomies in which types can be inductively classified. The assumptions of biological classification are that taxonomic "types" have content, that this content is imposed by evolutionary processes, and that classification is predictive (Simpson 1961:9). Thus, natural classes exist in the evolutionary record, can be traced to a common origin, and can be ranked into logically more and less complex forms according to genetic similarities and differences. In social evolutionary terms, such complexity has been ranked according to "progressively greater differentiation free[ing] the cybernetically higher factors from the narrow specifics of the lower-order conditioning factors, thus enabling the basic pattern of the cultural system to become more generalized, objectified, and stabilized" (Parsons 1966:112). Indeed, social evolution is the "process of increasing differentiation and complexity of organization which endows the . . . social system . . . with greater capacity to adapt to its environment so that it is in some sense more autonomous relative to its environment than were its less complex ancestors" (Bellah 1964:358).

Such statements, however, do not lead to an understanding of the rise of ancient states and civilizations and certainly do not explain cases of the "collapse" of ancient states (see Chapter 6), in which environments were altered by complex political systems to their detriment, not for their stability. Archaeologists document independent rates of change among loosely linked parts in societies and have been unable to determine any fixed set of "genetic" relationships of the "natural class" of chiefdoms or the "phylogenetic" distance of chiefdoms to other "natural classes."

There are two groups of archaeologists who often use the term chiefdom, and they must be kept distinct. First are the archaeologists studying the rise of ancient states. They use "chiefdom" in order to describe those prehistoric societies that directly precede the societies they call states (e.g. Stein 1994; Stein and Özbal 2001) but that are a lot more complicated than seems appropriate for "bands" or "tribes." They use the term "chiefdom" *without implying anything* about a kind of social organization and its ranking system, form of economic stratification, or amount of territory controlled by a simple or complex chief.

The second group of archaeologists includes those who study societies that were (arguably) *not part of a trajectory to statehood* at all, for example in the American Southeast or in Polynesia. These prehistoric societies were characterized by leadership structures that were calculated within the kinship system. Monumental structures were the scenes of ceremonies, which required goods to be submitted to the leaders and their ancestors, and leaders amassed not inconsiderable amounts of wealth. As I have already noted, some archaeologists studying these chiefdoms think that the contradictions of limited power along with duties of labor for the construction of ceremonial centers and the enactment of rituals resulted in a phenomenon of "cycling" in which more complex chiefdoms collapsed into simpler ones.[2]

One can diagram the hypothetical relation between those chiefdoms that might not actually lead to states and the so-called "chiefdoms" that simply denote societies that precede states and have been called chiefdoms for lack of a better word. In Figures 2.1 and 2.2, I illustrate two evolutionary trajectories, one of ethnographic

---

[2] Of course, no social cycle leaves off just where it began, and at the least there is a historical memory that is created in the process.

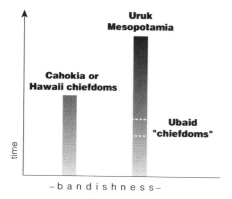

Figure 2.1   "Real" stratification

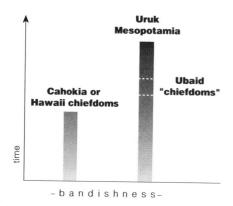

Figure 2.2   Hypothetical potential stratification

chiefdoms like Hawaii or prehistoric chiefdoms that did not become states, such as Cahokia, and one leading to states, with the example of Uruk-period Mesopotamia.[3]

Both chiefdoms have been described as societies in which leadership is ascribed in the kinship system, with paramount chiefs controlling a region in which local authority was vested in sub-chiefs (Earle 1987; Withrow 1990; Milner 1998). These chiefdoms arose from certain initial conditions, for example a pre-migration social organization in the case of Hawaii or a "formative" phase that preceded the Mississippian chiefdom at Cahokia. In Figure 2.1, the amount of "real stratification" in Cahokia (or Hawaii) is depicted as much less than in Uruk Mesopotamia, but much greater

---

[3] I elaborate this argument in Chapter 7. For now, it is important to note that Cahokia, which collapsed before European contact, was different from Hawaii, which had not become a state (although this is debated) by the time of European contact.

than the Ubaid "chiefdoms" that precede the Uruk period. In Uruk Mesopotamia real stratification is seen in political offices, temple and palace estates, dependent laborers, and the like. In Ubaid villages, none greater than about ten hectares (see Figure 9.14 for a comparison of the large Ubaid village of Abada with the city of Uruk), there is no evidence of chiefly ascribed leadership, accumulated wealth of chiefs, large-scale ritual activities, redistribution or indeed anything that looks remotely like Cahokia or Hawaii.

In Figure 2.2 I diagram the hypothesis that "potential inequality" in Ubaid Mesopotamia, which is based on potential massive surpluses of irrigation agriculture, the long-term economic activities of craftspeople and traders, which led to the formation of interregional connections among co-evolving communities, and the appearance of new kinds of religious leaders could lead to a larger degree of social and economic stratification and political centralization than existed in Hawaii or Cahokia.[4]

The imputed significance of Figures 2.1 and 2.2 is that no formative stage of a state-level society can be simply modeled according to any whole ethnographic example or any prehistoric chiefdom, because the trajectories of development are (or might be) completely different. Ethnographic and prehistoric chiefdoms may not precede the development of the earliest states but represent alternative trajectories to it. In social evolutionary terms, the basis for cross-cultural comparison is trajectories of social change in societies that did become states (see Chapter 8), not the projection into the archaeological record of (questionable) ethnographic analogies that have been snatched out of time, place, and developmental sequence.

NEO-EVOLUTIONISM AND NEW SOCIAL EVOLUTIONARY THEORY: BACK TO THE FUTURE

What neo-evolutionism never was a theory of social change. Rather, it was a theory of classification, of identification of ideal types in the material record. "Is it or is it not a chiefdom?" was the sort of dreary question most often asked by neo-evolutionists. The attraction of neo-evolutionism was precisely its weakness: it was a shortcut for investigating varieties of more complex and simpler forms of sociopolitical integration. In a vague sort of way, mainly by talking about different adaptations

---

[4] I reiterate that Polynesian chiefdoms and Mississippian ones differ so much in their own developmental trajectories and nature of organization and politics that it is unfair to lump them into the same social category. I do so solely for the sake of comparing their trajectories with those towards state formation. I discuss the topic of constraints on the development of states in Chapter 7.

as if they were somehow like genetic differences, neo-evolutionists drew on the prestige of Darwin's theory and often proclaimed they had created a new science of social
evolution. However, neo-evolutionists could not explain change other than in holistic terms and were content to identify as evolutionary mechanisms – you can hear the
gears turning – climate change or/and population growth. They offered little explanation of differences within types except by appealing to different environmental
circumstances and arrogantly assigned modern non-state-level societies as failures
from the normal evolutionary trajectory leading to states.

From the detritus of neo-evolutionism, archaeologists studying the evolution of
the earliest states now investigate how new social roles and new forms of social
relations emerged alongside, and to an extent supplanted, exclusive kinship rules
(of marriage and the status of children) that also functioned as the framework
for relations of production. Leadership, exercised by shamans, expert hunters, and
charismatic individuals, gave way to formalized ideologies in which the accumulation
of wealth and high status were seen as rightfully belonging to leaders whose roles
were, among other things, to "make inequality enchant." As social relations were
transformed into relations of domination, new ideologies led to the acquiescence
of subjects in their own domination and the reproduction of their own subordination (Godelier 1986). The new ideologies of state, which were inextricable from the
changing social relations that gave them birth, thus depicted how dominant leaders
"served" those who daily and perpetually served them.

I begin the discussion of how this happened by reviewing the utility of terms long
familiar to archaeologists – back to the future! – namely, differentiation and integration. These terms, which have been submerged in neo-evolutionary typologies, are
critical for two reasons: first, archaeologists have successfully identified various forms
of differentiated social groups in the archaeological record; second, we can trace the
manner and mechanisms whereby these groups were recombined, or integrated, in
new ways.

"Differentiation" refers to the process through which social groups become dis-
sociated from one another, so that specific activities, roles, identities, and symbols become attached to them. "Integration" denotes the political process in which
differentiated social groups come to exist within an institutionalized framework
(Eisenstadt 1964:376).

Kinds and amounts of social differentiation and integration have been successfully gauged in the archaeological record. Differentiation can be vertical, horizontal,
or both, as measured by the unequal arrangement of goods and services both
within social groups and among them. Vertical differentiation denotes the uneven
distribution of the conditions of existence (more and better stuff), and it results in

stratification that can be calculated (again, in familiar, material terms) within the whole society as well as within its social components. Horizontal, or radial, differentiation refers to the uneven distribution of people in relation to one another (Black 1976). This differentiation can be observed in the morphology of residence groups within settlements and in the pattern of settlements that interact as part of a network. Although archaeologists are seldom able to reconstruct social systems comprehensively, they have learned to live with and even thrive within a basic paradox: social change can be identified and understood diachronically even if one lacks a reasonably detailed (synchronic) knowledge of the society that was doing the changing.

Integration can be measured in the number and nature of symbols of incorporation as well as in the tools of repression. It may surprise some that the symbols of integration are the more apparent. Such symbols include ritual spaces, temples, palaces, monuments, and artifacts that represent public identity. In states these symbols are produced and maintained by people who are specialized precisely in the ideologies that legitimize the order of stratification of differentiated groups and individuals. States have the power to disembed resources from the differentiated groups for their own ends and glorification, not least because symbols of incorporation are so critical in establishing the legitimacy of societies.

THE EVOLUTION OF POWER AND ITS DISTRIBUTION IN THE EARLIEST STATES

The distinctive and empirically evident features marking the evolution of ancient states, which I have denoted as the process of social differentiation and political integration, are generated through various forms of power and the changing relations of power. By power, I mean the real or potential ability to accomplish tasks, that is, to render some behaviors possible and others less possible or impossible (after Wolf 1990). Neo-evolutionists only vaguely discussed power, which they simply asserted was an inherent quality of a social type. For example, in chiefdoms power was possessed by leaders, but limited within the rules of kinship. Political struggle was constituted in the competition between chiefs for territory and labor. States appeared when one chief was able to conquer his rivals.

Power, however, is not an abstract quality of social types, but the means by which leaders attempt to control the production and distribution of goods and to manage labor. In the evolution of the earliest states, new groups were created to transform, create, and marshal the symbolic and ceremonial resources that allowed the recombination of the differentiated groups into a new societal collectivity. The earliest states, thus, consisted of a political center with its own leadership structure, specialized activities, and personnel, but also included numerous differentiated groups. These social groups continuously changed in their organization and membership in relation to the needs and goals, strengths and weaknesses of the political center.

New ideologies in the earliest states created explicit systems of meaning about social and economic relations and events and specifications about who has political power and what holders of political power must do to maintain it. Rulers sought thus to control the discourse about power – that is, how the rules of power were communicated to various social groups – especially through ceremonies that celebrated the role of rulers in relation to their subjects. Since the order of inequality in social and economic relations in social groups was situated in daily practices, local acts such as those that did not challenge the sovereignty of centralized power also provided support for it. Leaders and members of local groups owed allegiance and resources (in material and labor of their clients) to the rulers, who in turn served them.

In the earliest states, therefore, power was not simply imposed from the top downward. Social actors, who could be members of more than one group (including kin-groups and occupational groups), could also be employed by the political center. Members of these groups could thus exploit the ambiguities of multiple group membership, evaluate their options, including their social identities, and, as circumstances changed, could transfer their allegiance to new leaders and adopt new beliefs (as I show in Chapter 6).

DIMENSIONS OF POWER IN SOCIAL EVOLUTIONARY THEORY

The central concern in studying the evolution of the earliest states is not to identify an essentialized and reified political structure ("the state"), but to explain the mechanisms through which social units that were becoming progressively differentiated were reassembled. In these newer and larger structures, ideals of order, legitimacy, and wealth in society were created and/or redefined, as were the mechanisms for the transmission of such ideals (Baines and Yoffee 1998, 2000).

Control over the sources and distribution of subsistence and wealth, the segregation and maintenance of the symbols of social integration and incorporation, and the ability to impose obedience by force, both on the governmental level and also within local groups, together constitute the main dimensions of power in the earliest states (Runciman 1982; Mann 1986). These dimensions (or sources) of power – economic power, social power, and political power – reinforce one another, and the earliest states did not evolve unless all these forms of power were in place. The sources of power are overlapping and interpenetrating, in that actors come to have roles in more than one social corporation. The dimensions of power are not simply analytical constructs (although they are that, too), since differentiated groups and different lines of authority emerge from the various means of gaining power over people and resources. Carole Crumley has described societies with multiple hierarchies, each with different forms of hierarchical construction, as "heterarchical" (Crumley 2003 and see also Chapter 7 here). In evolutionary terms, we must now ask whence come these varieties of power, what is the nature of the resulting social differentiation, and what constrains differentiated groups into social coexistence?

First, economic power is created through a process of differentiation of tasks in the production of subsistence and in the storage and distribution of reliable surpluses. The means from agricultural production to economic power lies in the conversion of stored wealth to a system of dependencies arising from restricted access to land and labor. Eventually, organizations consisted of elites, managers, and dependants, including both craft specialists and laborers who have been attracted to, or forced into the security provided by, a land-owning and surplus-producing estate. Such estates arose from a variety of sources, including land-owning kin-groups, minor royalty, official military figures or warlords, titled officials who were awarded land by rulers, or entrepreneurially successful individuals who bought land. All trajectories towards states began in processes of agricultural production, and all states were largely dependent on the surplus produced in the countryside.

The second major source of economic power is through mercantile activity. Long-distance, regular networks of exchange are generally found to accompany the first inequalities in access to production in early agricultural societies. Not only does the acquisition of preciosities represent burgeoning economic status, but the process of acquisition also becomes an institution requiring organization and thus a means through which status is produced. Long-distance trade, when coupled with other instances of inequality, becomes a particularly important and visible institution in ancient societies precisely because economic "action at a distance" (Renfrew 1975) produces wealth and status outside the moral economy of sharing usually imposed by kinship systems.

Archaeologists measure trends towards economic inequality in production and exchange by looking at the differing size of residences, activity areas, the distribution of artifacts, features, and mortuary furnishings. No prehistoric trajectory to any state fails to contain indications of significant economic inequality or the potential of such inequality well before the appearance of anything that might be called a state.

Wealth is an essential feature of the earliest states. It is clear that the productive potential of societies that became states was multiplied in the creation and institutionalization of surpluses. Surpluses might be in labor or in goods and might be applied to a vast range of purposes. An emblem of many early states is the architectural provision of enormous or hugely extravagant storage spaces, both for this world and for the next. Another obvious emblem, visible more or less everywhere, is the display and consumption of vastly expensive and rare artifacts dedicated to the gods, the dead, the ruler, and the elite.

The public, and archaeologists too, tend to place great weight on the wealth generated in the evolution of ancient states and civilizations, its display, and the competition for resources. Models of this sort, however, may depend on unexamined assumptions. Just as wealth is important, it seems equally clear that its exploitation and display were often subject to strong controls, and its most extravagant forms may be realized in contexts where such control was – at least in theory – easiest (think pyramids, again). Wealth was not seen as an end in itself, but rather an essential enabling factor whose potential lay in the display of social order.

Wealth also tended to expose the weakness of the system, because it made visible the reason and means for change. The obvious example of wealth's disruptive character was in the extravagant discarding of wealth in most of the earliest states – in material perspective but not in that of the actors – in burial. The world's second-oldest profession may have been tomb robbery, a practice that threatened social order, for it allowed wealth to be recycled. Tomb robbery has obvious parallels in the looting of temple treasures and other practices, which demonstrated that ideologies and legitimations were not completely persuasive or coercive. Central symbols were open to reincorporation in other forms or to rejection.

Social power was created in the process by which a society became horizontally segmentated and thus entails a consideration of numbers of people and population growth. Such segmentation can be ascertained from material and historic records, for example of Mesopotamian ethnic groups, barrios at Teotihuacan, neighborhoods at Wari and Harappa, and so forth. Leaders of these groups formed elites, sometimes becoming officers of states but also maintaining sets of local powers that lay outside states. These local leaders were community elders and could constitute assemblies with powers of decision-making that kings and the court found it in their interest not to penetrate. Leaders of these local groups also maintained relations with relatives in the hinterland and could use their relations to advance their own claims to power. An examination of social power also shows that the lives and experiences of individuals were inscribed through their identities in gender, ethnicity, kinship, and beliefs. Social actors, however, could belong to more than one group, and so identities could be activated, negotiated, adopted, or rejected according to circumstances and structures.

One aspect of social power that became important during the evolution of urban complexes and of regional interconnections was the creation and/or adaptation of symbols of cultural commonality. As individuals became invested in this recondite knowledge, priests and literati became institutionalized in semi-autonomous cadres with leaders. These elites owned land and property and employed managers, craftspeople, and dependants of various sorts. Ceremonial buildings and artistic and literary representations linked diverse social units and their belief systems beyond roles that were assigned by kinship and conferred honor and prestige on those conducting ceremonies and maintaining these symbols of community. The people who had greater access to the gods and ancestors legitimized the order of inequality, incorporated rulers in their ceremonies, and commanded goods, ostensibly on behalf of the entire community, but especially for their own ends. Archaeologists study these hallmarks of cultural commonality, from great monuments to ceramic horizon-styles.

Political power in states commonly means the ability to impose force through specialized, permanent administrators, including a military organization. The administrators and other clients of the dominant estate occupy their offices through means of recruitment beyond the co-existing system of kinship in a society, although "patrimonial" aspects of bureaucracies are also characteristic in early states. The ideal system of political differentiation is seen in the earliest historic states of China, where literati served as state bureaucrats but were not kinsmen of the rulers themselves. Whereas political power is exercised in administrative decision-making, in settling disputes (especially those in which the parties were of different social groups and hence required third-party adjudication), and in defending the society in times of war, it is important to note that local social groups also maintained their traditional roles of decision-making (e.g. in family law) that did not affect the ruling estate.

In all early states – but not only in states – it was necessary to disembed local resources for the requirements of governments and ceremonies. It is striking in some early states that rulers founded new capitals, not to gain access to better land or more plentiful water, but because a formal separation from local elites allowed kings to require more wealth and labor to support their enterprises. Richard Blanton (1983) has so explained the founding of Monte Albán as a "disembedded capital" (but see Chapter 8); King David transformed Jerusalem in order to create a new political system; Sargon built Akkade, and Neo-Assyrian kings were continually founding new capitals in their attempts to disenfranchise the old landed aristocracy.

In concluding this section, it is worth reiterating that all three main dimensions of power and the different means of achieving power – the struggle for control of economic resources, control of knowledge, ceremonies, and symbols, and control of armed forces – need to be co-evolving for states to emerge, since these three sources of power all reinforce one another. Landowners and traders sought political power (or at least freedom from political power and taxation), while political leaders owned much land, managed personnel, and commissioned traders to secure valuables. Religious leaders also owned land and received massive donations from political leaders, since rulers played critical roles in ceremonies. Leaders of temple estates sometimes sought political power in their own right, usually in response to oppressive political leaders. Political leaders required legitimation from the cultic establishment.

This interplay among leaders of social groups generated the evolution of new, society-wide institutions, new forms of political leadership, and the new symbols of community boundary. This process did not happen overnight, although the evolution of cities (see Chapter 3) and the institutions within them was usually extremely rapid. In any case, the goal of finding the exact date of origin of the state is quixotic, since the state itself is not just one thing. Finally, it is obvious that social evolution does not end with the rise of the early states, since nothing is more normal for an ancient state than for it to "collapse." That is, the struggle for political and economic power among various types of elites that resulted in the formation of states could also lead to their failure. The earliest states (no less than modern ones) functioned with a good deal of bungling and conflict within themselves as well as with their neighbors. States were (and are) "at best half-understood by the various people who made them, maintained them, coped with them, and struggled against them" (Cowgill 1988:253–4).

STATES AS STATES OF MIND

How did the various earliest states evolve by integrating, if only incompletely, the variously differentiated groups, which were themselves organized according to different sources of power? Neo-evolutionists have overwhelmingly studied the rise of states as the development of progressive degrees of inequality in wealth and the origin of political systems as institutions that monopolized wealth from which they derived their power. Archaeologists have been especially successful in delineating the geographic transformation of a region in which a relatively dispersed settlement pattern becomes an urbanized one, and this evidence has been interpreted as reflecting the awesome new power of the state and its centralized political control. Some archaeologists, in describing the state's monolithic and efficient direction of the flow of goods, services, and information in society, seem to have borrowed their vocabulary from modern Western business schools' notions of how to run a firm.

It is ironic that these inferences about political power tend to de-privilege much of the most visible archaeological materials – the monumental art and architecture that are associated both in the public mind and by archaeologists with the appearance of the first states (Baines and Yoffee 1998). These grand materials are symbols of the new ideologies of states, that is, foremost, the idea that there should be a state, centralized leadership, elites and dependants, the powerful and the powerless. Kings are owed service because they are the guarantors of earthly law and order; since they communicate with the high gods to ensure the continuity of the cosmos, wealth must legitimately accrue to them and to an inner elite who create and preserve the overarching traditions that integrate a differentiated and stratified society. The symbols of this ideology are everywhere – in decorative arts, architecture, monuments, and buildings and in the very construction of space in sites. The new ideology is actively constituted in materials and in texts. They are not mystifications of the political and/or economic order but are the very stuff that allows us to talk about, for example, what makes Mesopotamia Mesopotamia (or the Maya Maya).

Ideologies of states are thus different in kind from earlier ideologies, and they must be communicated through tangible vehicles that constitute them. They embody a new order of social relations, which crucially includes the king as a special category and the governmental apparatus we call the state. The gods and the dead are also part of the new order, absorbing a large proportion of the surplus flowing to the state, but with the agent of transmission being the ruler. The gods and the dead also participate in the fabrication of "social memory," which is given from on high, but memory and social order are made present by human labor. However massive and durable the embodiments of order are, they create a distancing between ideal order and the present, calling attention to order's fragility and need of support.

States and civilizations attempt to structure the universe in different ways than do the social forms that precede them and often surround them. Order is expensive, and there are those who are at the harsh receiving end of its effects. It does not follow, however, that the order proclaimed at the center is contested or rejected by those outside. They may accept it as legitimate, or resist oppression under the rules of order, or simply have no alternative to it. In certain cases, order may bring with it a reduction in the level of violence in a civilization and hence overlap in a straightforward way with the everyday sense of the term, including the "order" imposed by totalitarian regimes. In most ancient states, however, such order was fragile and quickly led to breakdown, often into the constituent units that order attempted to bring together.

These social units might be kin-based structures, non-kin-based territorial organizations, ethnic groups, economic groups, and/or a variety of differently constituted social orientations, but all could be overarched by the ideology of common participation in a society. It is this definition of order in an ancient, differentiated and stratified society with a specialized governmental center that denotes a civilization. Order circumscribes a dominant way of meaning and becomes axiomatic in the socialization of members of society, working as much from the bottom upward as from the top downward. Civilizational order, of course, may weaken or may change subtly, and it may be abrogated and subsequently reaffirmed. For the earliest civilizations, the disappearance or replacement of a recognized style of order betokened their end.

The transformations embodied in the new ideologies in and of states include the institutionalization of people's acceptance of, involvement in, and contribution towards order. Order could not survive the frequent shocks it suffered if people were not able to construct the institutions of legitimacy and to determine the quality of illegitimacy. Legitimacy normally invokes the past as something that is absolute and that acts as a point of reference for the present, normally by transmuting the past into some form of the present. This is the fabrication of "social memory," reshaping the past (Van Dyke and Alcock 2003, and see also Chapter 9 in this book) so that the state is seen as natural and ever-present (or at least as a logical outcome of the past).

Legitimacy encompasses the society as a whole, offering to the elite themselves a rationale for inequality that goes beyond simple prestige. But that is not the chief force of legitimacy. Rather, the entire society must accept, however variably and with whatever degree of coercion, that its order is the only one and the right one, and must work to maintain that order or contest those who are delinquent in, or incapable of, preserving order.

The amassing, retention, and harnessing of wealth can be seen as a social and cultural phenomenon as well as an economic one. The scale of productive institutions, the extent to which labor was deployed, and the level of specialized training and expertise have profound implications for a civilization's character and need for legitimation. Wealth makes a reversion to what went before almost unthinkable. Wealth helps to celebrate and reenact an order that may not be fully itself without such celebration. In joyfully reaffirming order and legitimacy, rulers and elites use wealth to counter fragility, especially in celebrations and ceremonies that involve much of the wider society. Without celebration, order may be threatened; with it, everyone may internalize its significance.

WHAT NEO-EVOLUTIONISM CANNOT EXPLAIN

In this chapter I have delimited what neo-evolutionist theory did not try to explain and could not explain: the evolution of states included increasing degrees of social and economic differentiation that were recombined in a distinctive manner. Differentiated social groups in the earliest states came to include rural manorial estate holders and their dependants, guilds of traders, ethnic and other territorial and/or kin-groups in cities and in the countryside, nomads, temple-estates directed by clerics, and palace-estates led by the royal establishment. New specialists refined, preserved, and reproduced the new order in the earliest states. Rulers, who were the officiants in the rituals that celebrated the new order and who were also subject to its rules, came to possess an institutionalized "body" in addition to their human one (after Kantorowicz 1957), and thus became the chief symbols of the state's sovereignty.

Neo-evolutionists spent much time attempting to decide whether a complex society was a state or a chiefdom. In this chapter I have tried to show the futility of those arguments and the emptiness of their categories. However, for those who persist in this quixotic venture, I submit "Yoffee's Rule" about how to identify the ineffable presence (or absence) of the earliest states: "If you can argue whether a society is a state or isn't, then it isn't."

Modern archaeologists, as I have indicated in this chapter and shall provide examples subsequently, investigate how people came to live within a variety of differentiated social organizations and the nature of power within these organizations. The earliest states "integrated" these social organizations only loosely, and rulers and elites were constantly concerned to communicate a dominant way of meaning. Non-elites or peripheral elites accepted, negotiated their lives under, or struggled against these terms.

In the 1960s and for the next decades, archaeologists were obsessed with identifying states and developing methods for the purpose. In the 1990s, archaeologists, having rejected the neo-evolutionary project, asked not what states were but what they did. In the new millennium, archaeologists now rather study what states did *not* do. That is, what were the limits of power in early states? How did people construct their lives in the earliest states? The following chapters are investigations of these questions.

3

THE MEANING OF CITIES IN THE EARLIEST STATES AND CIVILIZATIONS

> Numbers, the Homeric gods, relations, chimeras, and four-dimensional space all
> have being, for if they were not entities of a kind, we could make no propositions
> about them.
>
> BERTRAND RUSSELL

In the last chapter I argued that the evolution of the earliest states and civilizations (Figure 3.1) was marked by the development of semi-autonomous social groups, in each of which there were patrons and clients organized in hierarchies, and that there were struggles for power within groups and among leaders of groups. States emerged as part of the process in which these differentiated and stratified social groups were recombined under new kinds of centralized leadership. New ideologies were created that insisted that such leadership was not only possible, but the only possibility. The earliest states were made natural, that is, legitimized, through central symbols, expensively supported and maintained by inner elites who constituted the cultural and administrative core of the state. Ideologies of statecraft also set the rules for how leaders and would-be leaders must guard these symbols and perpetuate the knowledge of how to maintain, display, and reproduce them. In this chapter I explore the evolution of cities as central arenas in which these processes of differentiation, integration, and social struggle occurred.

The figures in this chapter illustrate the enormous size in area of the earliest cities, and Table 3.1 presents estimates of the large number of people who lived in them. The emergence of the earliest cities occurred as an urban explosion from the

Table 3.1 Area and population size estimates of the earliest cities mentioned in the text

Region (date)	Approximate size (100 ha = 1 km^2)	Estimated population	Source
Egypt			
Hierakonpolis (Naqada II, ca. 3300 BC)	3 km^2	10,000	Friedman pc (= personal communication); Kemp 1989
Memphis (Early Dynastic-Old Kingdom, ca. 3200–2400 BC)	11 km^2 + 150 km^2 (metropolitan area)	30,000 + 30–60,000	Jeffreys pc; Kemp 1989
Thebes (New Kingdom, ca. 1400 BC)	3–4 km^2	50,000	Meskell 2002; Baines pc
Amarna (1350 BC)	3.3 km^2	30,000	Kemp 1989; Janssen 1983; Kemp and Garfi 1993; Meskell 2002
Mesopotamia			
Uruk (3200 BC)	2.5 km^2	20,000	Nissen 2001
Eanna temple precinct	9 ha		
Nagar/Tell Brak (3600 BC)	70 ha	10,000	Emberling et al. 1999; Emberling pc
Lagash (2500–2000 BC)	3,000 km^2 (city-state)	120,000	Beld 2002; de Maaijer 1998; Matthews 1997; Beld pc
al Hiba	4 km^2	75,000	
Tello (Girsu)	80 ha	15,000	
Kish (2500–2000 BC)	5.5 km^2	60,000	Moorey 1978; Gibson 1972
Indus Valley			
Mohenjo-Daro (2500–1900 BC)	2.5 km^2+	40,000+	Possehl 2002; Chakrabarti 1999; Kenoyer 1998, pc
Harappa (2500–1900 BC)	1.5 km^2+	40–80,000	Kenoyer 1998, pc
North China			
Erlitou (1900–1500 BC)	3 km^2	18–30,000	Liu and Chen 2003; Liu pc
Zhengzhou (1600–1400 BC)	3.25 km^2 (inner city) 25 km^2 (metropolitan area)	100,000	Liu and Chen 2003; Liu pc
Anyang/Yinxu (1250–1046 BC)	19 km^2	120,000	Liu pc; Yates 1997
Mesoamerica			
Teotihuacan (ca. AD 600)	20 km^2	100,000	Millon 1973
Maya			
El Mirador (50 BC)	1 km^2 (urban core) 4.5 km^2 (central district)	30,000	Dahlin 1984; Clark pc
Copan (AD 700)	100 ha (urban core) 3–4 km^2 (metropolitan area)	20,000	Webster 2002; Webster et al. 2000
Tikal (AD 700)	3–4 km^2 (urban core) 16 km^2 (central district) 120 km^2 (metropolitan area)	50–60,000	Webster 2002; Fry 2003
Peru/Central Andes			
Moche (AD 500)	1.35 km^2	5–10,000	Billman 1996; Chapdelaine 2000; van Gijseghem 2001
Tiwanaku (AD 900)	6 km^2	15–20,000	Janusek and Blom 2004; Kolata 2003
Wari (AD 900)	6 km^2 (urban core)	10–30,000	Schreiber 1992, 2001; Isbell and McEwan 1991

modest villages that preceded them. This evolution affected the lives not only of the inhabitants of the earliest cities but also the people who lived in the countryside, and it reformed the social landscapes in which cities were embedded.[1]

It is especially evident – in contradiction to the neo-evolutionist myth that the earliest states emerged from chiefdoms and were territorially extensive – that most of the first states were not large, but evolved as "peer-polities" (Renfrew 1986) and were part of larger cultural associations. For example, in early Mesopotamia or among the Maya, there were many relatively small states – city-states or micro-states – that were hardly ever politically unified but whose central symbols of statecraft were shared. This common ideology that stretched over politically independent states was marked in material culture and literature and played out in economic and political interactions among the independent city-states. It is for these reasons that one needs to distinguish between Maya civilization (or Mesopotamian civilization) and Maya (or Mesopotamian) states.

CITY-STATES AND CHIMERAS

In his critique (!) of the step-ladder of social development in neo-evolutionist theory, as famously portrayed in Lewis Henry Morgan's scheme of savagery – barbarism – civilization – decadence, Winston Churchill noted that the United States of America was the only example of a society that had gone from savagery to decadence without having passed through the intervening stage of civilization. In this chapter I carry forward my argument (prefigured by Sanders and Webster [1978], as noted above) that the evolution of ancient states was unlikely to have passed through a stage like chiefdoms (or even, as Churchill might have put it, that states simply skipped over chiefdoms). The meaning of cities in the evolution of states and civilizations requires that archaeologists build new social theory.

Perhaps because archaeologists are especially creative people, they are keen to develop new terms and are just as ready to jettison them in favor of newer ones. Some of these terms become "factoidal," being repeated so often they seem like facts. In the face of arguments against them, one often encounters claims that a term is "heuristic," which seems to mean that archaeologists have used the term so often that they are unwilling to give it up. Here I utilize an old term, "city-state," which was not created by archaeologists studying social evolutionary theory (see

---

[1] All the figures in this chapter, which are found at the end of the chapter, were drawn by Elisabeth Paymal on the same scale, mainly 1:25,000 (or 1:50,000 or 1:100,000) so that the sizes of cities can be easily compared.

Hansen 2000 and below for the history of the term). I employ it for purposes of investigating the scale of ancient states, the centrality of cities in their evolution, and the development of "civilizational" boundaries within which the earliest cities existed.

The Greeks were not the only ones who invented the term city-state to denote the political forms of early states. There are ancient Indian and Chinese writings on city-states (Kenoyer 1997 and Yates 1997 respectively). Mesopotamian city-states (or micro-states or statelets) are always described with the logogram or semantic indicator "city" or "place"; Harappan/Indus Valley city-states, early north China city-states, and Maya city-states are all commonly described as such in the archaeological literature of their areas. Teotihuacan was an extremely large city that controlled its region; according to Carla Sinopoli and Kathleen Morrison (1995), city-states became empires in medieval South Asia; Wari and Tiwanaku in the Andean Middle Horizon were also cities that became the centers of imperial organizations. Whereas neo-evolutionists seem to have regarded cities as place-holders at the top of settlement hierarchies they called states, I argue that cities were the transformative social environments in which states were themselves created.

Although I discuss the usefulness of the term city-state in the evolution of many of the earliest states, I do not seek to elevate the term as an intellectual fetish, designed to control the discourse about the evolution of ancient states. However evocative the label, I insist that in using the term we must always "unpack" it, since there is considerable variability among city-states. Also, there are early states that are not city-states. The most obvious of these is ancient Egypt, but cases have been made for "valley states" in the north coast of Peru as well. Since city-states are both empirically real and exist in many forms that must be explained, they are chimerical, in Bertrand Russell's sense of the term, an ideal type of classification that invites us to make propositions about them, but not an essence that archaeologists must try to find and display.

CITIES AND STATES

Two recent books on city-states are *The Archaeology of City-States: Cross Cultural Approaches*, edited by Deborah Nichols and Thomas Charlton (1997), and *A Comparative Study of Thirty City-State Cultures*, edited by Mogens Herman Hansen (2000, 2002). The former includes an introduction, conclusion, and thirteen essays on city-states, of which nine pertain to the earliest city-states. In the latter Hansen (2000) contributes an elegant introduction and conclusion; of thirty chapters only five concern the earliest city-states (whereas the others review a variety of medieval and later city-states in Europe, Africa, and Asia).

Nichols and Charlton (1997:1) recapitulate the traits of city-states listed in Robert Griffeth and Carol Thomas's edited volume on the subject (1981):

In general we understand city-states to be small, territorially based, politically independent state systems, characterized by a capital city or town, with an economically and socially adjacent hinterland. The whole unit, city plus hinterlands, is relatively self-sufficient economically and perceived as being ethnically distinct from other similar state systems. City-states frequently, but not inevitably, occur in groups of fairly evenly spaced units of approximately equivalent size.

For Hansen (2000:19):

A city-state is a highly institutionalized and highly centralized micro-state consisting of one town (often walled) with its immediate hinterland and settled with a stratified population, of whom some are citizens, some foreigners and, sometimes, slaves. Its territory is mostly so small that the urban center can be reached in a day's walk or less, and the politically privileged part of its population is so small that it does in fact constitute a face-to-face society. The population is ethnically affiliated with the population of neighbouring city-states, but political identity is focused on the city-state itself and based on differentiation from other city-states. A significantly large fraction of the population is settled in the town, the others are settled in the hinterland, either dispersed in farmsteads or nucleated in villages or both. The urban population implies specialization of function and division of labour to such an extent that the population has to satisfy a significant part of their daily needs by purchase in the city's market. The city-state is a self-governing but not necessarily an independent political unit.

Although Hansen notes that these characteristics of city-states are "a kind of Weberian ideal type," he privileges the classical Greek polis, from which his ideal is framed. Colin Renfew (1975), also basing his generalizations from the Aegean area, described "early state modules" as the characteristically small territories of the earliest states, in distinction to what Hansen calls "country states" or "macro-states." Critical for Hansen (and for me, too) is his insistence on the term "city-state culture." In Hansen's terms this is "a civilization which, politically, is organized as a system of city-states" (Hansen 2000:19). As I have already discussed, however, the term "civilization" does not connote a political system but, rather, the cultural boundary within which city-states (and their citizens) interact. This chapter provides the support for this assertion.

Since "ideal types" require close inspection and delineation of variations and exceptions to the rule, I begin with the example that seems to be the clearest exception to the ubiquity of city-states in antiquity, the case of ancient Egypt

(Figure 3.2). Towards the end of the fourth millennium BC, following rapidly upon the development of large cemeteries, in which aspects of social rank and status are observed, and the standardization of material culture along the entire Nile Valley from the First Cataract at Aswan to the Mediterranean, an Egyptian territorial state arose (T. Wilkinson 1999; Baines and Yoffee 1998; Wenke 1997). This state was politically centralized, marked by an extreme polarization of wealth, symbols of kingship over an Egypt perceived as a geographic and symbolic duality, the growth of mortuary architecture ensuring the continuing role to be played by kings in an ordered and decorous cosmos, characteristic elite art forms, and writing. Although John Wilson (1960) famously said that Egypt was a civilization without cities, new research shows clear urban developments at Hierakonpolis (Figure 3.3), at the first capital of unified Egypt at Memphis (Figure 3.4) in the late pre-dynastic period to the Old Kingdom, and in other cities of Upper Egypt, Abydos and Naqada. (Archaeologists have also explored later cities, for example at Thebes [Figure 3.5] and Amarna [Figures 3.6 and 3.7] – see e.g. Kemp 1989).[2] Although, in comparison with other of the earliest states, the establishment of the unified and centralized polity in Egypt can be characterized by its territorial extent as well as by the process of urbanization, the earliest phase of the Egyptian state was marked by rivalries among the growing cities of Hierakonpolis, Naqada, and Abydos.[3]

Ancient Egyptians defined the extent of the country (Liverani 1990), the political state and the congruent cultural limit of Egypt, from the Mediterranean in the north to its southern border in Nubia. Whereas in some periods Egypt conquered sections of the Middle Nile and Palestine and Syria, they were not held for long periods, and these territories were regarded as non-Egyptian. When defining their world, Egyptians were more interested in its frontiers than in its center (Baines and Yoffee 1998).

Strong territorial demarcation in Egypt was the result of evolutionary trends towards stratification in the ecologically uniform environment of the Nile Valley,

---

[2] Some Egyptian cities such as Thinis, for which Abydos was primarily a mortuary and religious center, and Buto and Sais in the Delta, are poorly preserved and little known.

[3] The site plans of ancient Egyptian cities are redrawn from Kemp 1989 (Hierakonpolis, p. 40, Figure 11; Memphis, p. 34, Figure 2.5 [also Trigger 2003:135]; Thebes, p. 203, Figure 71; Amarna, p. 271, Figure 89). Renée Friedman provided valuable information on Hierakonpolis (see www.hierakonpolis.org) and especially about the extent to which Hierakonpolis was maximally occupied in the late pre-dynastic period (Naqada II). The site consists of low desert occupations, an alluvial town, and various mortuary areas. I have depicted the extent of the later center of Memphis, although there is little knowledge of the earliest phases there. David Jeffreys has informed me about the difficulties of assigning dates to the various parts of the site. Not all of the maximal "metropolitan" area of the site was occupied at any one time. The site of Amarna is the best-known urban place in Egypt, and I have included it here for this reason. I thank John Baines and Lynn Meskell for their advice about the nature of urbanism in Egypt.

the concentration of the most important resources within Egypt's borders, and the excellent transport link provided by the Nile. The relatively small population of about a million people in the Old Kingdom and twice that in the New Kingdom (Baines and Eyre 1983; Hassan 1993) within this large, if linear, expanse (of about 34,000 km² [Baines and Málek 2000:16]) made urbanism a part of the trends towards territorial unification rather than a factor opposing such trends, as was the case elsewhere. Symbols of kingship and unification, including royal names, are found all over the country in the latest prehistoric period, and these motifs supply the principal evidence of a developing territorial ideology within which cities also existed.

The unified state commanded and managed the distribution of resources in which cities played special roles. Much of the structure of cities was dedicated to displays of royal power and religious ceremony (especially in mortuary displays), and administration in the cities was primarily concerned with managing these displays and the labor needed to build and maintain the edifices of royal and ritual power.

Teotihuacan (in Mesoamerica, Figure 3.8) is also an exception – but of a different kind than Egypt – to the "ideal-typical" model of city-states. Teotihuacan is certainly not small, covering an area over 20 km² and with an estimated population of at least 100,000 people (Cowgill 1997, Figure 3.9). More significantly, Teotihuacan violates the principle that city-states exist in groups, "peer-polities" or "early state modules." Although Teotihuacan may have had at least one "peer," prior to the disappearance of Cuicuilco, which was buried under a volcanic eruption as the two cities were developing, Teotihuacan came to dominate its region and was without serious rivals for centuries. It is an example of urban primacy, since its direct hinterland became relatively depopulated as urban growth absorbed nearby villages (Figure 3.10).[4]

Although Teotihuacan was a very large city that did not exist in a network of similar cities, and so is not really a city-state that is part of a "city-state culture," there is a difficulty in terming it a "capital" of a territorial state. Indeed, not much is known about how Teotihuacan administered its territory and, indeed, there is uncertainty about how the great city itself was administered. In Teotihuacan, there was (little or) no writing, which is odd, in that Teotihuacanos certainly knew about Maya writing, and there are few images of kings (Taube 2000). George Cowgill (1983) has argued that the ciudadela was the location of ceremonies of state, but was not itself a palace,

---

[4] The plan of the site does not extend to its entire occupation. The maps of urban growth at Teotihuacan are redrawn from those in Sanders, Parsons, and Santley 1979. Table 3.1 shows that Teotihuacan, the largest of the earliest cities in the New World, is comparable in size to the largest cities in the Old World.

and that the "Street-of-the-Dead Complex" fits better our notion of what a palace should look like. New research by Saburo Sugiyama and colleagues (1989, nd) has identified rich warrior burials in pyramids at Teotihuacan, and these must indicate a hierarchy of rulers, elites, and retainers. At the time of the collapse of Teotihuacan, it had no mighty enemies in rival cities or states, according to Rene Millon (1988), who thinks that the fiery destruction of the ritual and governmental center of the city should be ascribed to internal strife. After the "collapse" of the central ceremonial precinct, Teotihuacan eventually became part of a specialized economic zone for Aztecs and exists today, the ruins lying adjacent to modern San Juan Teotihuacan. Although Hansen does not classify Teotihuacan as a city-state, since it has no peers, I have no such compunction in doing so (although I do insist on specifying the kind of city-state it is).

Other ideals or putatively defining characteristics of the earliest city-states – political independence, economic self-sufficiency, and ethnic homogeneity – as delineated by Griffeth and Thomas and by Charlton and Nichols (above), cannot be found in many of the earliest city-states. Maya city-states and Mesopotamian ones, our clearest examples, did try to conquer other city-states and sometimes succeeded. The cities of Calakmul and Tikal often controlled a number of other cities and so formed evanescent territorial states before breaking down into their constituent parts (Grube 2000; Martin and Grube 2000). The earliest Mesopotamian city-states were also constantly at war (Cooper 1983; Van De Mieroop 2004).

In Mesopotamia the conceptions of economic self-sufficiency and ethnic homogeneity break down utterly. Long-distance trade can easily be traced in prehistoric periods, and for historic ones we can read about how trade was organized. In Old Assyrian Assur, during the nineteenth century BC, traders were entrepreneurs, circulating goods from where they were plentiful to where they were scarce and making large profits from those activities (Larsen 1976, 2003; Veenhof 1972, 1997; Michel 2001, 2003). In southern Mesopotamia at the same time entrepreneurs often contracted with temple and palace organizations to supply both luxury and subsistence goods (Van De Mieroop 1992).

Mesopotamian city-states were multiethnic communities. Sumerians, Akkadians, Amorites, Kassites, Hurrians, and many other named social groups – the names themselves refer to languages rather than ethnic groups, in the strict sense – lived together in Mesopotamian city-states. Although the city-states provided identifications of citizenship, ethnic relations that transcended city-state boundaries could be mobilized to advantage in the struggle for power within city-states (Emberling and Yoffee 1999). In ancient China there are similar cases of ethnic and linguistic diversity in early cities (Boltz 1999).

Given all the exceptions to the definitions and characteristics of the earliest city-states, why is it useful to maintain the term at all?

In Benedict Anderson's much-cited book (1983) on the origins of nation-states and nationalism, scarcely a word needed to be devoted to the issue of *modern* states as country states, macro-states, or territorial states. That is, Anderson took for granted that the process of molding national consciousness and state power through print languages took place in relatively large geographic regions. Clifford Geertz elegantly criticized European definitions of the modern state that empha-size the monopolization of violence (1980:122), and he showed the lack of fit of such definitions to the "theatre-state" of nineteenth-century Bali. Nevertheless, he could assume that the state in Bali covered a reasonably large and more-or-less easily demarcated territory. In the case of most of the earliest states, however, there is a conspicuous lack of governance of a large territory by a capital, a single seat of state administration.[5]

The earliest states and cities in China (Figure 3.11) antedate the Shang dynasty (Liu and Chen 2003). The site of Erlitou (1900–1500 BC) reached an extent of 375 hectares (Figure 3.12). From its palaces "the state controlled bronze production" (2003:13). Previously, towards the end of the Longshan, ca. 2000 BC, clusters of sites around large centers, three of which range from 200 to 300 hectares, had emerged, but with associated dispersed occupation areas with little population (Liu 1996a, 1996b). Liu Li has concluded that Erlitou and Zhengzhou developed precociously as a result of migration from the countryside that was experiencing severe flooding in the Yellow River drainage, with the Yellow River itself changing course.

This prehistoric development does much to explain the nature of late Shang capitals, each of which ruled in turn over a portion of the countryside. David Keightley (1983) described the Shang state as "not solid like tofu, but full of holes like Swiss cheese." Shang kings were traveling men, showing the flag over large distances and claiming thus to control the lands in which they moved with their army. None of the earlier capitals, such as Zhengzhou (Figure 3.13) or Anyang (Figure 3.14), lasted long (Liu and Chen 2003). Robin Yates (1997) explains that early China had its own model of city-states, and the struggle of the Shang and Zhou kings to "galacticize" (Tambiah 1985) the countryside – that is, to centralize ritual in a capital, with smaller versions being replicated in other cities – did not succeed until the Qin and Han dynasties established firm political control over much of China (Chang 1999; Bagley 1999; Keightley 1999). Although Liu Li regards Erlitou and Zhengzhou as capitals of states rather than as city-states, Jing Zhichun has written (personal communication, 2003):

---

[5] Bruce Trigger (1985, 1993, 2003) has also observed that many of the earliest states were city-states, although there were also macro-states. He includes China among the latter.

that a number of urban sites have been located and dated to the Zhengzhou phase. One of them, Yanshi, about 20 km east of Erlitou, is the same size (if not bigger) than Zhengzhou and also falls in the same period (if not a little earlier). . . . I see these as two competing powers in that period. I would not be surprised if more urban sites with similar size and data will be discovered at that period.

New research in north China will clarify the extent to which the early "capitals" of Erlitou and Zhengzhou might be described as city-states.[6]

Mark Kenoyer (1997, 1998), Dilip Chakrabarti (1995, 1999), and Gregory Possehl (2002) point to the impressive evidence for a Harappan (or Indus Valley) civiliza- tional commonality overlying the five or six (explored and certainly more) Harap- pan city-states (Figure 3.15). The best-known of these city-states, Mohenjo-Daro (Figures 3.16, 3.17) and Harappa (Figure 3.18), were about 250 and 150 hectares in size respectively and consisted of multimound components along with extensive lower towns. Kenoyer (1997) considers these mounds not as functionally distinct aspects of a systemic whole, but changing centers of power among elites and merchants. The evidence for this is that most of the mounds (at Harappa) are surrounded by walls, and the mounds were founded at different times and grew at different rates. Vacant areas between the mounds were intentionally maintained, and the "redundancy" of artifacts and inferred functions in the mounds indicates to Kenoyer that they were rival administrative centers.[7]

Kenoyer is partly inspired from later historical descriptions of types of South Asian city-states that describe the different kinds of elites, resident aliens, social classes, material wealth, crafts and industrial specializations, local assemblies, and ideologies for right action. He not only models Harappan city-states from the much later city-states but considers the later cases to be historical developments from the earlier Harappan culture.[8] Kenoyer suggests that the "authoritarian

---

[6] I have based the plans of the earliest cities in North China and owe much of my knowledge of these sites to the recent work of Liu Li (see especially Liu and Chen 2003). Note that the scale of Zhengzhou is four times greater than the 1:25,000 scale that I have used for most of the plans of the earliest cities. Liu considers that the population estimates in Table 3.1 for Zhengzhou (by Yang Shengnan) and for Anyang (by Yang Baocheng) as high. See also plans of these cities in Yates 1997. The latest research suggests that Yanshi is only 200 ha., whereas Zhengzhou is 13 sq. km. The outer city wall of Zhengzhou (Figure 3.13) is probably the outer limit of the city proper.

[7] I owe population estimates of Harappa and Mohenjo-Daro in Table 3.1 to information provided by Mark Kenoyer. The lower town of Mohenjo-Daro extends beyond the plan in the figure, as does the occupation of Harappa extend beyond its plan. For Mohenjo-Daro, see the splendid illustrations in Possehl 2002:11, 160, 268–9; for Harappa, see Kenoyer 1998:51; Possehl 2002:11.

[8] Shereen Ratnagar (2000) presents a comprehensive view of the collapse of Harappan civilization that is at odds with Kenoyer's direct historical linkage to later times. The argument of an unbroken connection of Harappan (or Indus Valley) civilization to later South Asian states has unfortunately been used by certain political parties in India to demonstrate a cultural and ethnic continuity from Harappan times to the present.

model" of Harappan city-states must give way to one of competing elites within city-states.

What is striking in the Harappan city-states is the extent to which each city-state used a common form of writing, chert weights for commerce and taxation, and a wide range of other artifacts indicating that the communities living in these city-states were integrated into a single cultural system (Kenoyer 1997). Chakrabarti calls the major cities "city-states" or "kingdoms," which, "considering the sheer extent of Harappan distribution," were not "under one rule" but were part of a "common ideology" (Chakrabarti 1999:199).

In South America (Figure 3.19) the earliest states on the north coast of Peru, such as Moche (of the Early Intermediate Period, ca. AD 500), have been called "valley states" by David Wilson (1997:243) because of the presumed small size of the ritual center of the site compared to the large number of people who lived in the rest of valley which was under control of the center. In any case, the urban sector at Moche was certainly not small (Chapdelaine 2000; Figure 3.20). Whereas Kolata (1997) has delineated the regal-ritual nature of the city (contemporary with Moche but in the Lake Titicaca basin), Tiwanaku (Figure 3.21) was also a large urban complex with a sprawling residential area (Janusek and Blom 2004; Janusek 2002; Stanish 2001); the regal-ritual core was only part of the larger city. It seems that Wari, another highland Andean city-state (partly contemporary with Tiwanaku and Moche), was even larger than Tiwanaku, with about 6 km² of architectural core, but with residential remains extending much further (Isbell and McEwan 1991; Schreiber 1992; Figure 3.22a and Figure 3.22b). As at Teotihuacan and Uruk (below), urban growth at Wari was accompanied by a reduction in village life, a process of "ruralization" (Figure 3.23). According to Katharina Schreiber (2001), Wari not only became the capital of a territorial state, but its growth was also related to its control of very distant regions.[9]

Although David Webster (2002:164) prefers such terms as "polity" or "kingdom" instead of city-state in the Maya region (Figure 3.24), he agrees that the term "city-state does convey the general pattern of a central place and its rural hinterland." The earliest Maya cities emerged in the pre-Classic, and El Mirador (200 BC–AD 150) was the site (Figure 3.25) of the largest pyramid ever built in the Maya

---

[9] Nicholas Tripcevich drew the basic map of urban growth at Wari and sent me the digital images of the site. The maps of Moche and Wari do not show the full extent of the sites beyond the main mounds. Katharina Schreiber (personal communication, 2003) writes that the urban explosion at Wari in which the site of Wari becomes completely dominant over its countryside is much more dramatic than is depicted in Figure 3.23, which is based on her earlier research.

region. Pre-Classic centers like El Mirador and Nakbe, which evolved from small villages and ceremonial centers, collapsed at about AD 150–200. The Classic city-states represented their identities through emblem-glyphs (which included the names or symbols of the cities), and they were independent until and unless they were conquered by other city-states, as I have noted already. It is hard to calculate the size of Maya city-states, since the population, as is typical of tropical cities (Scarborough 2003), may be so dispersed that it is hard to estimate which of the far-flung folk may or may not have been "residents" of the city. A ruler of Copan, whose core covered only 15 hectares (Webster 2002:155) (Figure 3.27), set up a series of stelas that delimited his rule over 25 to 30 km² (Webster 2002:164–5). The core of Tikal, perhaps the largest Maya city-state, covered 3–4 km² (Figure 3.26a), the central district 16 km², and the entire city-state (Figure 3.26b) 120 km.² Webster thinks the king of Tikal "might have had in the order of 50,000–60,000 subjects" (Webster 2002:165).

MESOPOTAMIAN CITY-STATES AND MESOPOTAMIAN CIVILIZATION

As an example of the relation between city-states and civilizations, I present a more extended case from Mesopotamia. Since this section about Mesopotamian cities is the first of my examples from Mesopotamia in this book, it also serves as an orientation to subsequent discussions of Mesopotamian history and archaeology.

Mesopotamian archaeologists and historians are well aware that the term "Mesopotamia" is by no means easy to define. In the political sense of the word, Mesopotamia even has the disconcerting ability to dematerialize entirely, since "Mesopotamia" existed predominantly as a cellular pattern of city-states that rarely (if ever) acted in political concert (Figure 3.28). Nevertheless, it can be demonstrated that a very specific and shared cultural sense of a Mesopotamian world was independent of the presence of a pan-Mesopotamian state. This cultural sense of Mesopotamia can be seen most clearly in its absence, that is, after the collapse of Mesopotamian (Assyrian and Babylonian) empires in the late seventh and sixth centuries BC. After this time the rulers of Mesopotamia did not think of themselves as "Mesopotamian," and the land between the two rivers existed as part of a larger and non-Mesopotamian institutional order in which it was firmly embedded.

Since I discuss the prehistory of Mesopotamian states and civilization in a later chapter, I depict here only the appearance and contours of the early Mesopotamian city-state network. Robert Adams (1981) has traced the process of urbanization in lower Mesopotamia in the late Uruk period (ca. 3400–3100 BC; see also Pollock 1999) in which small sites were dispersed along watercourses, with a few larger sites as centers of clusters. Over a period of about 500 years the big sites became even bigger and the countryside became relatively depopulated and "ruralized" (Figures 3.29, 3.30; Pollock 2001); lower Mesopotamia had become a region of urban enclaves with nearly 80 percent of the population living in cities (Nissen 1983, 1988).

This demographic implosion was occasioned by a number of factors: cities became nodal points for military protection from neighbors, for leaders to co-ordinate labor that traveled to a patchwork of fields (which were left fallow every second year), and for the construction of branching canals that irrigated the fields. Emerging city-states were also the locations of regionally important temples (evolving from shrines, like Eridu and Gawra in the preceding Ubaid period – see Chapter 9) that were also centers of exchange. Migrations, from central to southern Mesopotamia and also perhaps from further south, were also stimulated by changing environmental conditions (Nissen 1988; Pollock 1999).

At Uruk, the only one of the late Uruk period city-states that has been extensively excavated, one observes the creation of monumental architecture on an unprecedented scale, such as the temple complexes at Eanna and the Anu Temple (Figure 3.31; see also Figures 9.15 and 9.16). The Eanna precinct itself covered about 9 hectares and included several temples, a putative palace (the "four-hall building"), an ornately decorated sunken court, and other large structures. Record-keeping devices, such as cylinder seals, and beveled-rim bowls, most plausibly interpreted as ration containers, are characteristic artifacts of this extraordinarily specialized and differentiated society and economy (Pollock 1999).

Representational art further reflects and comments upon social distinctions, and cuneiform writing appears as an invention (Michalowski 1990, 1993a, 1993b; see also Nissen, Damerow, and Englund 1993; Englund 1998). The bulk of the earliest texts concern administrative activities, but there are also lists of professions and geographical names. Rather than serving a bureaucratic function per se, these lists were conscious attempts to organize the Mesopotamian world and to instruct future generations of scribes in the art of writing and associated values. The transformations in the division of labor within the late-fourth-millennium city-states in southern Mesopotamia had repercussions well beyond the south, as southern Mesopotamian colonized or otherwise occupied cities in Syria and southern Anatolia and on the Iranian plateau (Figure 9.21). This "Uruk expansion" (Stein 1999; Rothman 2001; Postgate 2002) is thought to denote southern Mesopotamian attempts to secure trade routes to important resources. It did not last long, and southern Mesopotamians/

Urukians, whose characteristic cultural markers are found well outside southern Mesopotamia, encountered an urban environment in the north that was at least as old as the cities in the south (e.g. at Tell Brak, Figure 3.32; see Emberling 2003; Emberling et al. 1999; Emberling and McDonald 2001, 2003).

The native historiographic tradition in Mesopotamia clearly expresses the importance of city-states in the land and also the ideal of political unity, an ideal that was especially significant in that it was hardly ever fulfilled. The "Sumerian King List" (the earliest copies of which date to the "Third Dynasty of Ur," ca. 2100–2000 BC), begins when "kingship descended from heaven" to five cities. Dynasties of kings from each of these cities ruled in order, kingship passing from one city to another. The earliest kings ruled for long periods of time, in some instances thousands of years, thus implying an unbroken continuity from the most distant Mesopotamian past. After kingship passed to the fifth city, there came the Flood. Afterward, kingship again descended to other cities in the same orderly succession. Kings now ruled, however, for largely credible numbers of years, and some of them can be identified in contemporary texts of the early third millennium BC (Michalowski 1983).

Inscriptions show that this orderly march of single, dominant cities ruling all Mesopotamia is no faithful reflection of historical events. Some dynasties listed sequentially were in fact contemporary, and some powerful cities were simply omitted from the list. In one of the latter cities, Lagash, scribes composed their own king list, which is interpreted by its modern editor as a satirical commentary on the spuriousness of the "canonical" version that had slighted it (Sollberger 1967).

Thorkild Jacobsen, the brilliant editor of the "Sumerian King List," had thought that the ideal of political unity in the "Sumerian King List" referred elliptically to the early (that is, early-third-millennium) existence of an "amphictyony," a confederacy of cities joined through worship of the paramount Sumerian deity, Enlil, at the seat of his worship, Nippur. Perhaps the most interesting line of argument in favor of this confederacy derives from the study of certain "city-seals," that is, sealings (found on panels of clay around door-sockets, on jars, and also on tablets), which are decorated with the names of various cities (along with other motifs). They are best known from Ur in the Early Dynastic II/III periods (ca. 2700–2500 BC). Henry Wright (1969) interpreted the city-names as demarcating the locations of storehouses from which goods were circulated; Hans Nissen (1988:142) thought they denoted trade associations. In his assemblage of all examples of the city-seals, however, Roger Matthews (1993) found no consistency of names or significant correlation of seals and transactions (based on the tablets that were sealed). Whereas he inferred "real and practical intercourse between cities," he could only tentatively suggest that the small quantities of foodstuffs noted on the tablets might have been symbolic transfers to a central depot at Ur (not Nippur, the pivot of Jacobsen's amphictyony). One may carry this argument of the symbolic nature of the city-seals further, however, to infer that the city-names may have conveyed a message of the cultural commonality of city-states (Yoffee 1993; Michalowski 1993b; for another view, see Steinkeller 2002).

If there was no political center in early Mesopotamia before the time of Sargon of Akkade (ca. 2350 BC), who first brought together Mesopotamian city-states into a regional state and then empire (Liverani 1993), city-seals and other evidence show that a native conception of a Mesopotamian cultural unity preceded this unification and lasted after its dissolution. This Mesopotamian cultural identity is evident in the early standardization of writing and numerical and mathematical systems in the Early Dynastic period, as well as in the standard repertory of material culture that spanned the independent Mesopotamian city-states. The expressions of the cultural boundaries and boundedness of Mesopotamia were remolded through time and across changing regional developments. Typically, such ideals of what constituted Mesopotamian culture were never directly stated (Machinist 1986). Nevertheless, the evolution of a "Standard Babylonian" literary language (in the mid-second millennium), the various systematizations of god-lists and the larger belief system, the epics in which the Assyrian national deity, Assur, was superimposed on the Babylonian model, and "the preservation, transmission, and revision of whole bodies of texts – or what Oppenheim called the 'stream of tradition' – which were assembled from all parts of Mesopotamia over many centuries" (Machinist 1986:2) demonstrate the existence of such cultural boundaries. The formation of such pan-Mesopotamian cultural institutions was the more remarkable precisely because the early city-states were not held together in a single political system.

The absence of such a political entity, however, did not preclude the conception that there should be a political domain to match and concretize the cultural ideal of a single Mesopotamian political system. In the "Sumerian King List" it was natural and proper to convey that ideal, that only one king from one pre-eminent city-state should rule over Mesopotamia at any one time. The fact of Sargon of Akkade's real conquest and union of Mesopotamian city-states confirmed and helped shape this ideal.

Before Sargon's conquest, in the latter part of the Early Dynastic period, ca. 2500–2350 BC, rulers of city-states competed with their neighbors for fertile agricultural land and for access to trade routes, especially along the rivers. Kings consolidated their power bases precisely as representatives of their city-states in war and defense. Some kings achieved hegemony over their neighbors (e.g. King Eanatum of Lagash, Mesilim in Kish, Enshakushana of Uruk, Lugalzagesi of Umma), forming evanescent coalitions and mini-territorial states for the first time in Mesopotamia. This endemic conflict among city-states was ended by Sargon. He founded a new capital city, Akkade, which was not part of the normal internecine rivalries in the land and so could symbolize a new regime. Sargon ("True King"), a nom d'usurpation, came from the area around Kish.[10]

Kish, like the southern city-states, was made up of multiple mounds (Gibson 1972; Moorey 1978; Figure 3.33). The two major mounds, Ingharra and Uhaimir (the ancient names were Kish and Hursagkalama), were originally independent villages that merged into the city-state – as was also the case in Uruk, whose major sections were called Uruk and Kullab. The entire area of Kish covered about 5.5 km², although not all parts of the city were occupied throughout the more than three millenniums of the city's history.

The city-state that we know most about from the mid-third millennium through the Ur III period is Lagash (Beld 2002; de Maaijer 1998). Lagash consisted of two main towns, Lagash (Tell al-Hiba) and Girsu (Telloh), which alternately became the capitals of the city-state whose overall name was Lagash (Figure 3.34). Telloh covers about 80 hectares and al-Hiba about 400 hectares. Second-order towns were Gu'aba, Sirara (or Nina), and Kinunir. From north to south, the territory of the city-state extended about 80 km, and from east to west about 40 km – that is, more than 3000 km² of territory. There are at least four third-order villages and many named farmsteads and relay-stations (which are all known from texts). The province of Lagash in the Ur III period (2100–2000 BC) was divided into districts for purposes of administration.[11] As is well known, however, in the middle of the third millennium Lagash was almost continually at war with the neighboring city-state of Umma, just to the west. The multicelled city-state of Lagash was named after its first capital and had a principal, patron deity, Ningirsu ("the lord of Girsu"). The southern Mesopotamian countryside in the third millennium was carved into many such city-states (or micro-states), which consisted of several cities, with a capital and then towns, villages, and hamlets forming the hinterland (see Figure 9.21).

---

[10] Piotr Steinkeller (1993) has argued that central Mesopotamia was a land of Akkadians, whose capital was Kish. He regards this political territory as contrasting with the city-state structure of the Sumerian south. For a critique of this view, see Yoffee (2001b).

[11] I have calculated the area of the city-state of Lagash from the map drawn by de Maaijer (1998:64), which is of the Ur III province of Lagash. Scott Beld (2002) states that the same villages and towns mentioned in the Ur III texts are also recorded in the late Early Dynastic period, and the city-state of Lagash at 2400 BC must have been about the same size as the province of Lagash at 2000.

About a hundred years after the collapse of the dynasty of Akkade, kings from the city-state of Ur – whose dynasty was mentioned for the third time in the "Sumerian King List," after which modern scholars call it "the Third Dynasty of Ur" or simply "Ur III" – reassembled city-states that had regained their autonomy after the collapse of Akkade. The Ur III political regime itself fell after about a century, and the city-states once again were independent. In the Old Babylonian period (2000–1600 BC), kings from Babylon in central Mesopotamia began to conquer neighbors in this region, while kings from Larsa in the south gradually were able to establish a southern regional state. Hammurabi of Babylon (1792–1750) conquered the south towards the end of his regime, but it broke free from Babylon's control in the reign of his son and successor.

In northern Mesopotamia at this time, the Old Assyrian city-state of Assur held sway over the countryside. Assyrian kings fought to keep open trade routes to the north and south (and probably to the east, too) so that long-distance traders could ply goods for enormous profits. These Assyrian family-firms also maintained merchant colonies in Anatolia, one of which, Kanesh, has supplied thousands of texts from which the trading system has been reconstructed. The Old Assyrian city-state government was composed not only of a royal estate but also of councils and a city-hall, in which the representatives of elite merchant families played a role (Larsen 1976).

The role of cities changed in the middle of the second millennium BC. In the Middle Babylonian period (ca. 1600–1150) in the south, a ruling dynasty of foreigners, Kassites, called their country "Karduniash." This term, whose meaning is unknown, is the only designation in the history of Mesopotamia for the territory that we generally term "Babylonia." In the Middle Assyrian period, the "land of Assur" referred to the territory ruled by kings of the city of Assur and/or the god Assur. A king called Tukulti-Ninurta I, in the attempt to disenfranchise the ancient nobility of the land, built a new city across the Tigris River from Assur and called it Port Tukulti-Ninurta. He was assassinated by the nobles, who disapproved of his hubris in building a new capital and also of his bad behavior in sacking Babylon (Machinist 1976).

In the first millennium BC in Mesopotamia, the Neo-Assyrian kings took advantage of the lack of competitors in Western Asia to build a genuine empire, expanding into territory to the west (Syria, Lebanon, ancient Israel, and briefly Egypt) and to the north (in Syria and southern Anatolia), and led expeditions into Iran and elsewhere. Several of the ancient kings harkened back to the policies of Sargon of Akkade and Tukulti-Ninurta I by founding new capitals that symbolized new imperial ventures which required new bureaucrats to administer the far-flung provinces. Assyrians also gradually came to rule Babylonia in the south directly. The Assyrian kings granted tax exemptions to citizens of the ancient Babylonian city-states, thus acknowledging the individual identities of these polities. After the collapse of the Assyrian empire and state, the Neo-Babylonian kings who ruled the entire south from Babylon still ratified the privileges of several of the most ancient cities.

In this historical sketch, we have seen that the earliest city-states were independent polities, and the earliest territorial states that were achieved by conquest were highly unstable and ephemeral. City-states, which were uncomfortably embedded in state and imperial structures under Akkade and Ur III, revolted whenever the occasion permitted, normally in the transition to new kings of the ruling dynasty. If the ideal, as represented in the "Sumerian King List," was that a single dominant city ruled Mesopotamia at any one time, the reality was that the earliest city-states succeeded in re-establishing their independence.

CITIES AND CITY-STATES IN SOCIAL EVOLUTIONARY PERSPECTIVE

I discuss in conclusion the relations among city-states in various regions and also how regional landscapes were changed in the process of urbanization. In order to give readers some familiar referents to the enormous size of the earliest cites, I offer some comparisons with modern cities (Figures 3.35 and 3.36[12]). Table 3.1 summarizes areal and population figures; Figures 9.7 and 9.14, examples from Mesopotamia, illustrate the explosive growth of the earliest cities.[13]

---

[12] In the central campus of the University of Michigan, about 70,000 students, faculty members, and support staff live and interact daily. The city of Ann Arbor has a population of about 125,000. Of course, modern cities include much more dispersed residential areas than in most early cities. The sizes of Amsterdam and Leiden are redrawn from a map of 1936, namely before the modern urban sprawl. Hong Kong Island (about the same size as Zhengzhou) has a population density of about 250,000 per square kilometer. I also include a colonial American city, the "métropole" of New Orleans in 1765, which had a population of about 5,000. New Orleans was then described as large and heterogeneous, so unruly as to defy French ideas of urban order (Dawdy 2003). The sizes of the earliest cities dwarf colonial New Orleans. I thank Tim Utter of the Map Collection of the University of Michigan Hatcher Library, who supplied these maps, and Jenny Brandon of Library Services, who scanned them into a format that Elisabeth Paymal could use.

[13] This table provides estimates by experts on the sizes of the earliest cities. Elisabeth Paymal has drawn the figures on the same 1:25,000 scale (except for the largest cities – Memphis, Thebes, Zhengzhou, greater Tikal, Teotihuacan and Amarna – and for the smaller residential areas of cities, e.g. at Amarna and Mohenjo-Daro). Although I have occasionally been able to indicate residential areas as distinguished from ceremonial districts, my aim is only to depict the sizes of the earliest cities. None of the earliest cities, whose enormous extents are apparent, has been more than partially excavated. Archaeologists have estimated the extent of some sites according to residential debris and sherd scatters. Although the populations are little more than best guesses, the earliest cities were densely occupied.

First, I revisit my earlier comparison between Mesopotamian and Maya city-states and then expand the stage. In both regions city-states were engaged in a more-or-less endemic struggle for dominion and/or independence (Yoffee 2003). Neither the Mesopotamian nor the Maya region existed as a unified pan-regional state. The earliest network of interacting and competing city-states (or micro-states) in the Indus Valley and in north China can be described in similar terms. As we can (and must) speak of Maya and Mesopotamian civilizations, we perceive the cultural boundaries that overarch political diversity in the Indus Valley and north China as the "Harappan tradition" (Kenoyer 1997) and "early Chinese civilization" (Bagley 1999:124). The cultural boundaries of these civilizations/traditions are palpable. Of course, these boundaries changed over time as states alternately incorporated or resisted foreign elements and changed over centuries or millenniums.

Although my survey of cities in Egypt, South America, and Teotihuacan refers to particular historical trajectories of these regions, it also shows that in every region of the world where the first states appeared, cities were the collecting basins in which long-term trends towards social differentiation and stratification crystallized. The earliest states, with the exception of Egypt, in which cities and the early competition among cities were also important, did not encompass large, nation-like territories.

Furthermore, from the worldwide perspective that I have pursued in this chapter, we observe that the social evolutionary trend that we normally call "urbanization" has often an equally important counterpart: "ruralization." That is, for many of the earliest cities, the urban demographic implosion was accompanied by an equally important creation of the countryside. This process of ruralization can be observed in two dimensions. First, existing towns and villages became networked to urban places. The social and economic roles of non-urban dwellers were tied to decisions made in the cities; specialized institutions of production and consumption in the countryside (e.g. T. J. Wilkinson 2003) were altered by the demands of urban rulers and elites, and ranks of urban officials were conceived precisely to carry out new activities. Second, countrysides became relatively depopulated as many people became incorporated in the new cities, as I depict in the rise of Wari (Figures 3.22a and 3.22b), Teotihuacan (Figure 3.9), and Uruk (Figures 3.29 to 3.31). Subsequently, new villages, towns, and hamlets arose in the backdraft of urbanization. This condition also led to the intensification of specialized activities, such as pastoralism and nomadism, which flourished not only to supply goods and services to cities but also served as refuges for urban flight.

The growth of cities is revolutionary, in the sense used by V. Gordon Childe and others: cities were not simply accretions on a stable rural base, and states were not thus "pyramidal," a higher level of specialized governmental institutions stacked on previous, stable social formations. In the evolution of states and civilizations, the landscapes of social life changed utterly. Cities and city-states were the products of long-term evolutionary trends, and the identities of people as citizens and their participation in local networks of social, economic, and political interactions were redefined in cities.

Although I have focused here on cities, in which archaeologists have done the most work and from which most written information comes, I want to reiterate and expand upon the importance of new countryside–city interactions in the earliest states. First, the countryside, consisting of towns, villages, and, in general, more mobile elements of a city-state or micro-state, supplied the alimentary needs of the city. It was also a hard-to-control power base for those who sought to resist the requirements of urban leaders. Furthermore, the process of ruralization fostered endemic conflict between those in the countryside and those in cities. The situation, however, was not simply one of peasants in the countryside and elites in cities.

City-dwellers often maintained large agricultural estates, some granted by rulers, but in effect private holdings with obligations to pay taxes to the rulers. Kathryn Keith (1999, 2003) has shown that urban dwellers in the Old Babylonian period also owned country properties and even houses in other cities, and these "urban" folk may have had their roots in the hinterland of cities.[14] Rural elites, traditional leaders of kin-groups or rural gentry, had roles in urban-based political-religious ceremonies. The stability of the state often lay in the balance between the status and legitimacy provided by these ceremonies to rural leaders and the tangible support in goods and labor that rural elites and their dependants had to provide to urban leaders. Rural elites could withhold contributions of food and labor in times of an urban leader's political weakness. The failures of military adventures and of harvests could be interpreted as a loss of divine favor to kings, or the entire cosmological system that connected cities to the countryside could be called into question.

Within Mesopotamian cities, local assemblies were constituted by community members and traditional leaders, often those who still maintained ties to the countryside. These assemblies exercised judicial privileges, settling disputes among community members (see Chapter 4), and could stand in opposition to the palace and royal court. Leaders in the countryside could ally themselves with their kinsmen in

---

[14] John Baines notes that in Egypt elites similarly had houses in towns and estates in the country (personal communication).

the cities by mobilizing traditional ties of group solidarity against the great institutions of the royal court and its retainers. Also, cadet kin-branches within the royal court could challenge rulers.

Within cities and city-states, interaction among different social groups (such as kin-groups, especially strong in the countryside), economic groups (such as merchants), military cadres, court retainers, and others was intensified. The rules of interaction were displayed prominently in the performance of rituals and ceremonies that commemorated royal achievements and recognized the status of courtiers and retainers. These ceremonies legitimized a changing world as being in harmony with an unchanging and given cosmos. Rulers conducted these ceremonies throughout their realms, enacting the drama of citizenship, and some ceremonies were conducted in other cities that shared the common belief system and so reinforced the common cultural currency that bound them and restricted this identity against others.

Cities were not simply "containers" for a new scale of social and economic and religious activities but were "generative" (Soja 2000; Smith 2003) of new offices and ranks, a new environment of buildings, streets, and monumental art of various sorts. The density of social interaction in cities was unprecedented from earlier times in most of the earliest civilizations.

Table 3.1 shows that the core[15] areas of many of the earliest cities were often about 150 hectares[16] or more. City-states could be 100 km² or much larger. Population estimates for the earliest cities in the world range from 10,000 to more than 100,000. Some readers will certainly criticize this table as implying that size is the only thing that counts. However, I only mean to imply by these figures that these new urban environments, with few exceptions in social evolutionary history, were supernovas that exploded from the environment of village life that preceded them. Although neo-evolutionist archaeologists tended to ignore the meaning of cities, cities re-routed the practical experiences of everyday life, in cities and beyond them, and incubated new ideologies in which economic and social differences and bases of power could be expressed and contested. In further studies, I intend to illustrate and discuss the internal structure of the earliest cities whose sizes I have depicted here.

In the next chapters I present examples of how people lived and understood their lives in the earliest cities and states, how early states attempted to "simplify" complexity, how order and law were conceived, how ideology was instituted in everyday life, and how local leaders negotiated with rulers and/or contested their domination.

---

[15] By "core" I mean the ceremonial area and central elite residential precincts.
[16] 100 hectares = 1 km² (0.386 mile²).

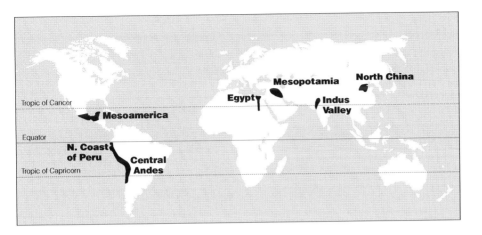

Figure 3.1   Earliest states and civilizations

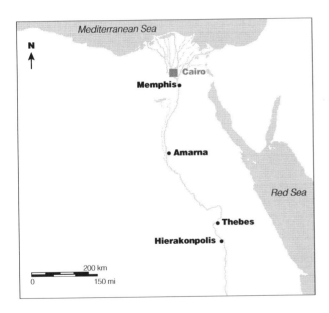

Figure 3.2   Egypt

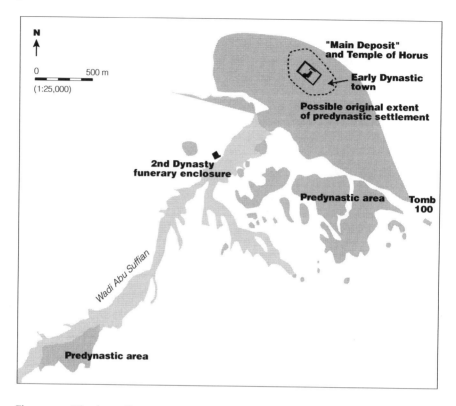

Figure 3.3   Hierakonpolis

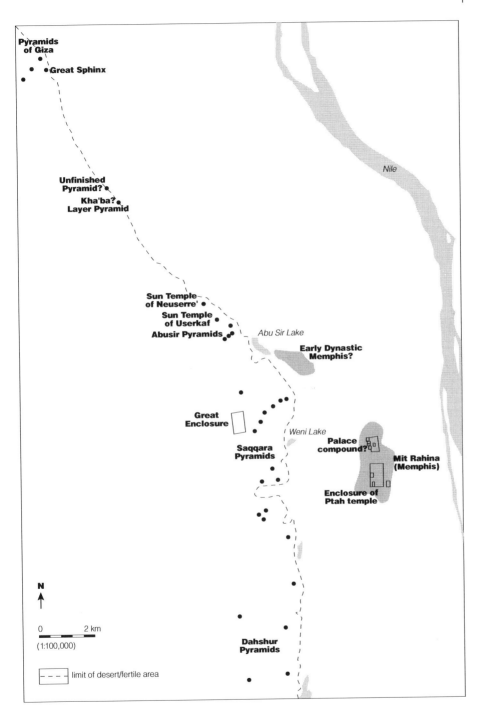

Figure 3.4 Memphis (Early Dynastic and Old Kingdom)

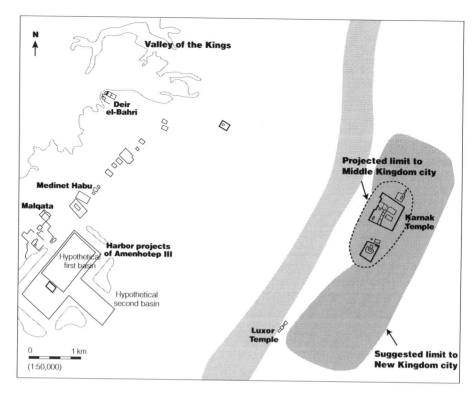

Figure 3.5   Thebes

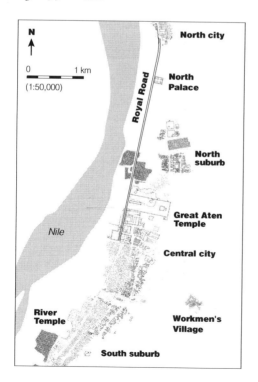

Figure 3.6   Amarna

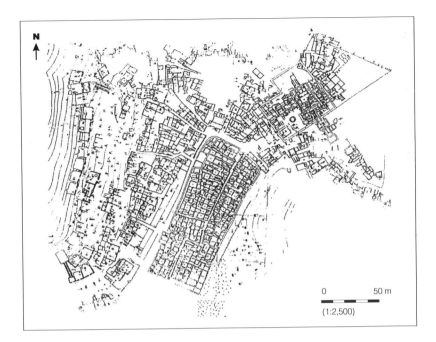

Figure 3.7 Amarna – workmen's village

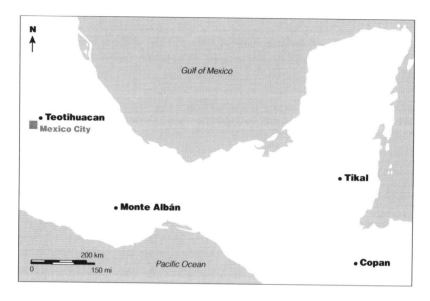

Figure 3.8   Mesoamerica

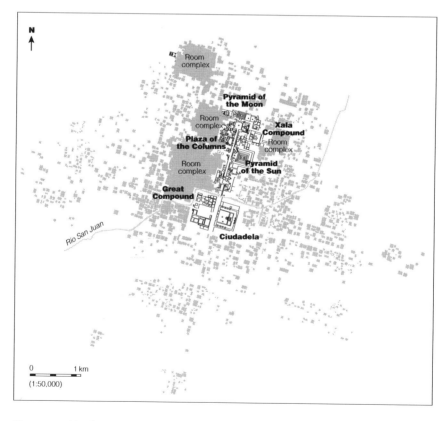

Figure 3.9   Teotihuacan

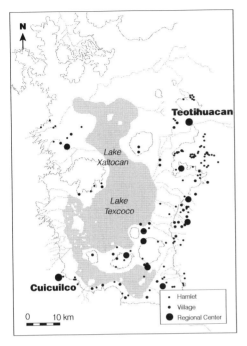

**Basin of Mexico
First Intermediate Phase Three
(300–100 BC)**

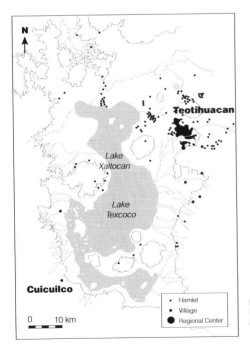

**Basin of Mexico
First Intermediate Phase Four
(100 BC–AD 100)**

Figure 3.10   Teotihuacan, urban growth

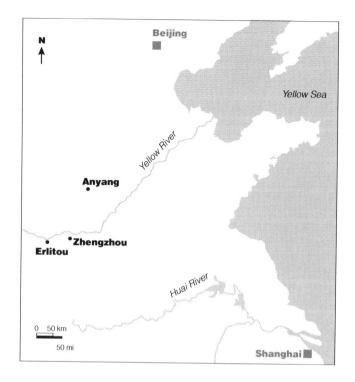

Figure 3.11   North China

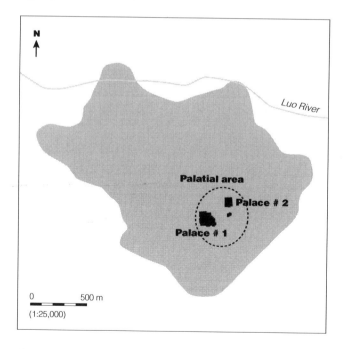

Figure 3.12   Erlitou

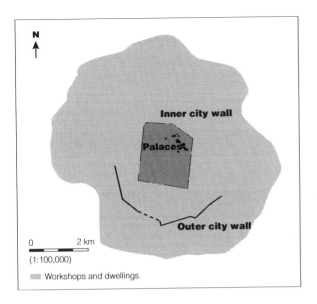

Figure 3.13   Zhengzhou

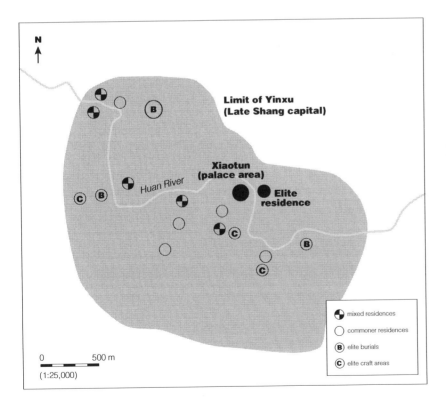

Figure 3.14   Anyang

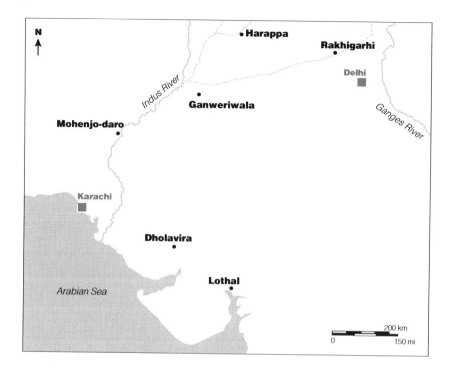

Figure 3.15   Indus Valley/Harappan sites

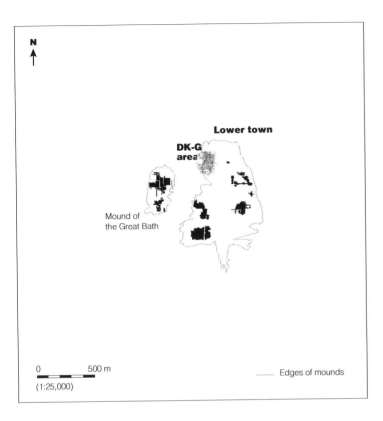

Figure 3.16   Mohenjo-Daro

Figure 3.17   Mohenjo-Daro – DK-G area

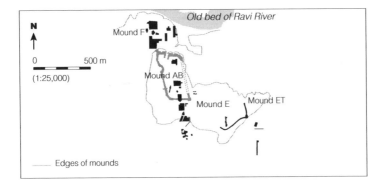

Figure 3.18   Harappa

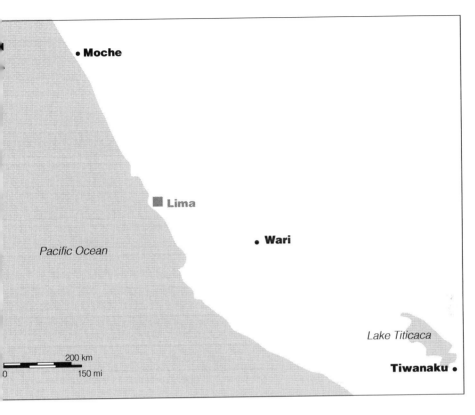

Figure 3.19   North coast of Peru and Central Andes

Figure 3.20   Moche

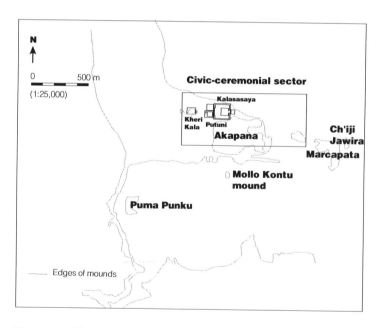

Figure 3.21   Tiwanaku

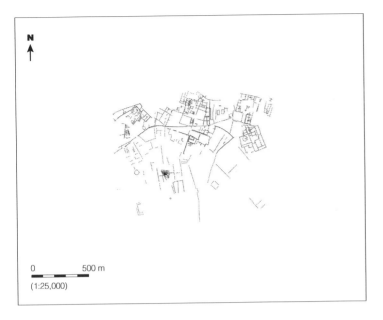

Figure 3.22a Wari

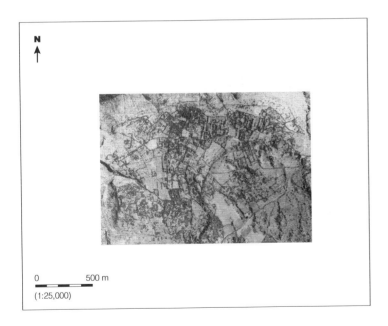

Figure 3.22b Wari, aerial view

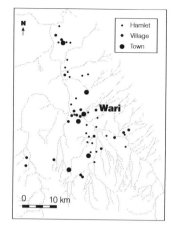

Ayacucho Basin sites
Early Intermediate period

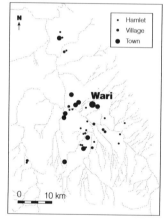

Ayacucho Basin sites
Middle Horizon 1

Figure 3.23   Wari, urban growth

Figure 3.24   Maya region

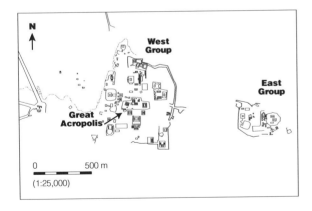

Figure 3.25   El Mirador

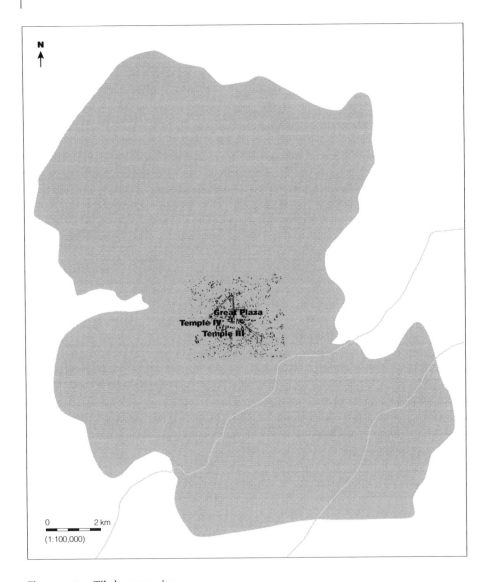

Figure 3.26a   Tikal, greater city

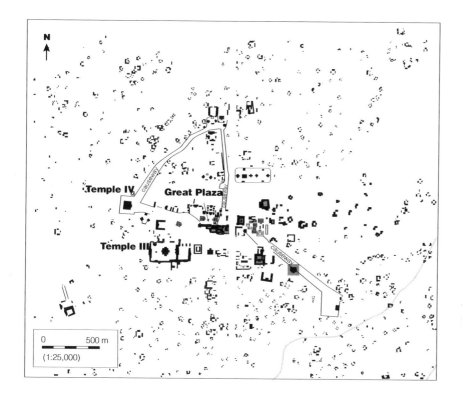

Figure 3.26b   Tikal, urban core

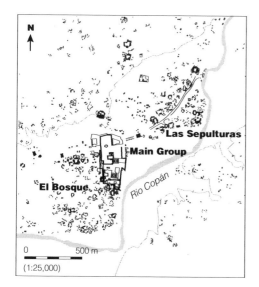

Figure 3.27   Copán

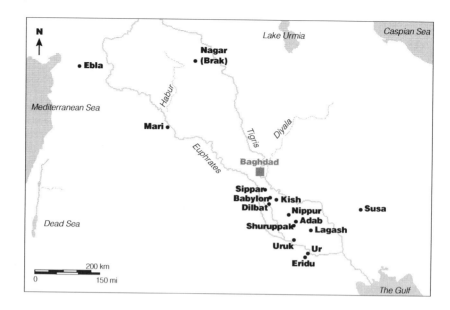

Figure 3.28   Selected Mesopotamian cities. After Pollock 1999

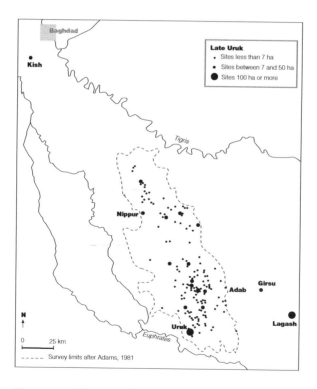

Figure 3.29   Mesopotamian settlement pattern in the late Uruk period. After Pollock 1999

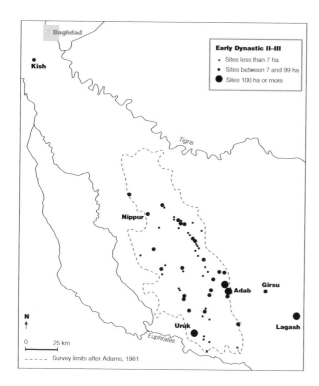

Figure 3.30 Mesopotamian settlement pattern in the Early Dynastic II and III periods. After Pollock 1999

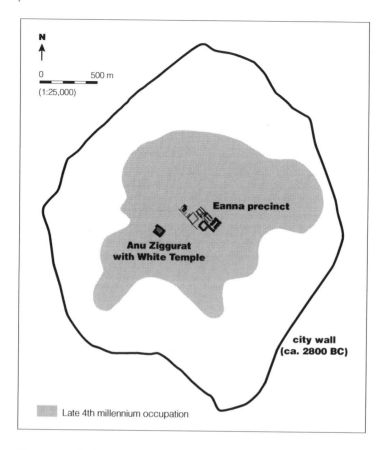

Figure 3.31 Uruk

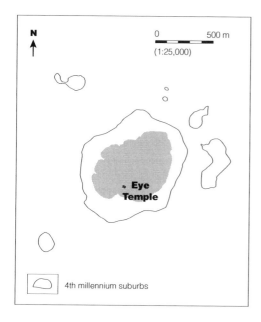

Figure 3.32   Nagar/Tell Brak

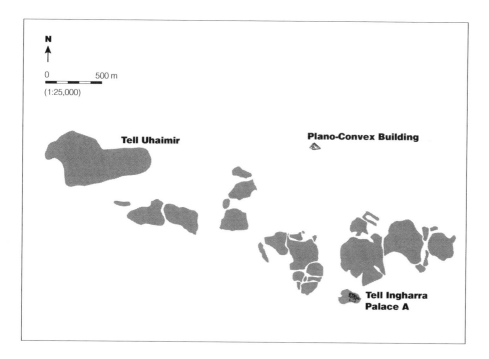

Figure 3.33   Kish

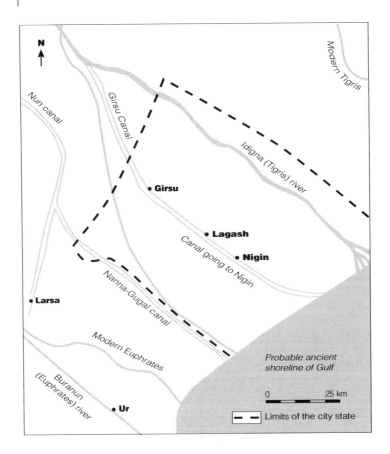

Figure 3.34   Lagash city-state

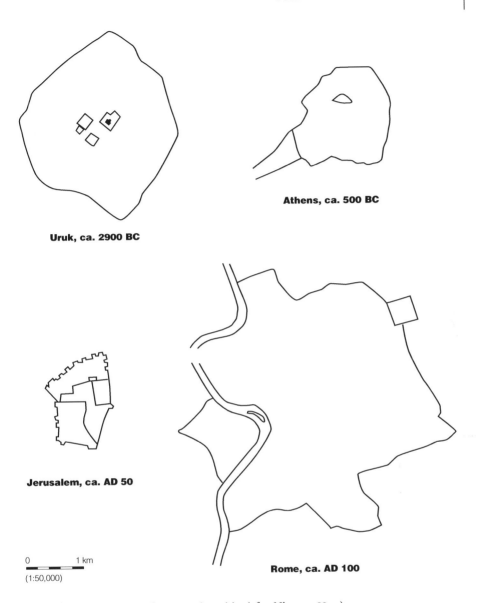

Uruk, ca. 2900 BC

Athens, ca. 500 BC

Jerusalem, ca. AD 50

0   1 km

(1:50,000)

Rome, ca. AD 100

Figure 3.35 Comparison of some ancient cities (after Nissen 1988:72)

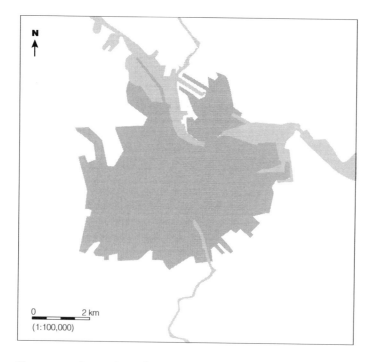

Figure 3.36 Comparison of some modern urban places on the scale of the earliest cities
(a) Amsterdam, 1936

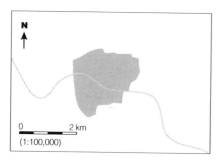

Figure 3.36b Leiden, 1936

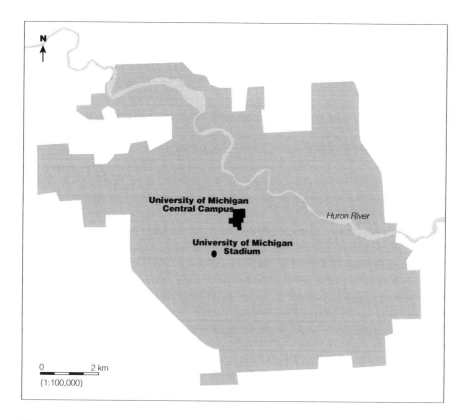

Figure 3.36c   Ann Arbor, Michigan, 2003

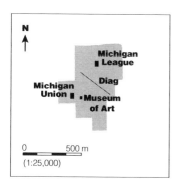

Figure 3.36d   University of Michigan, Central Campus, Ann Arbor

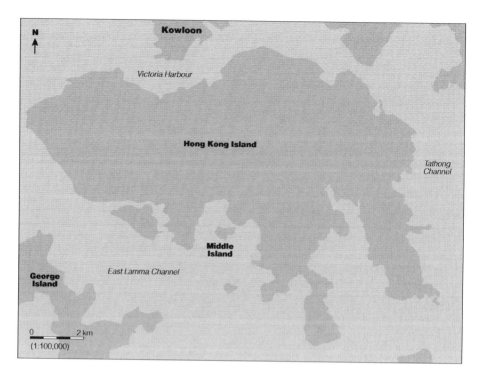

Figure 3.36e   Hong Kong Island

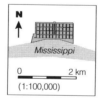

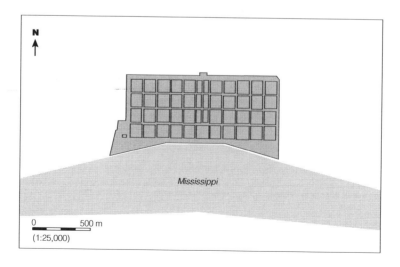

Figure 3.36f   New Orleans (Métropole de La Nouvelle Orléans, 1765)

4

WHEN COMPLEXITY WAS

SIMPLIFIED

A state evolves from agriculture to paradox.

E. M. CIORAN

In the early history of the first cities, states, and civilizations, differentiated social groups became recombined in cities. These cities were nodal points of pilgrimages, exchange, storage and redistribution, and centers for defense and warfare. In these cities, along with their associated and restructured countrysides, new identities as citizens were created but did not entirely supplant existing identities as members of economic, kin, and ethnic groups. Certain aspects of identity were also forged with citizens in other cities who shared a common, if created, heritage, and these were maintained and reproduced over time.

In the earliest cities, new rituals and ceremonies connected rulers with citizens and the gods. These displayed and justified the supremacy and legitimacy of kings and reaffirmed command over the social order. The social roles and practices of citizens were routinized within the urban layout of monumental constructions, streets and pathways, walls and courtyards. The built environment itself demonstrated the superior access to knowledge and planning held by rulers, ostensibly on behalf of all. Statecraft in the earliest cities involved providing an order to the present, which the rulers relentlessly proclaimed in literature and in a created landscape that overlay the unruliness of a society composed of many groups, each with its own interests and orientations.

Archaeologists commonly use the shorthand "complex society" to describe a society that encompasses numerous social groups and institutions of centralization. Also, some archaeologists use the term "complex society" to avoid the neo-evolutionary question of identifying a society as either a chiefdom or state. Both types of society were large, in the sense of being constituted in hierarchies, specialized activities, and ceremonial centers, and they also constitute a large archaeological problem in how to excavate significant portions of massive sites and monuments.

In this chapter I complicate complexity by showing that in the evolution of the earliest states it makes a great deal of sense to describe what states do as establishing simplicity. Indeed, one could say that one of the main trends in the evolution of states is the evolution of simplicity.

In his book *Seeing like a State: How Certain Schemes to Improve the Human Condition Have Failed* (1998), James C. Scott presents an intriguing analysis of how modern states attempt "to make a society legible," that is, to take ineffably complex and "illegible" local social practices and create a standard grid so that leaders and bureaucrats can record, monitor, and control them. "Legibility" is effected by the state, which mandates the formation of permanent last names, standardization of weights and measures, implementation of cadastral surveys, uniformity in legal discourse, and, not least, the promotion of a single official language. The environment is similarly rationalized and simplified by planners, engineers, and architects who implement a "high-modernist ideology" of scientific and technological progress towards a utopian goal.

Scott exemplifies this ideology by showing historically how modern states (that is, states of the eighteenth century AD and onwards) transformed forests from nature to natural resources, thereby reducing a complex of habitats for the sake of economic efficiency. Prussian foresters minimized the diversity of species, creating straight rows in large tracts, eliminated weeds and varmints, and in general facilitated the management of forests so that principles of commercial extraction could be inscribed and taught. These creators of monocultural forests, however, failed to recognize the symbiotic relation among soils, fungi, insects, and so forth, which made the forest resistant to disease and fire. The death of many forests from soil depletion and epidemics was the result of the abstract logic imposed to make forests governable.

High-modernist ideology was born in the late Renaissance and Enlightenment and intended to improve the human condition. The ability to transform the social and natural orders, however, had to wait until the twentieth century, when modern states acquired the power to set pervasive, industrialized planning projects in motion for the benefit of civil societies that were powerless to resist them. One villain in Scott's narrative is Le Corbusier, whose megaprojects of building and transforming cities were designed to eliminate waste, inefficiency, and disarray. Brasilia is discussed as the result of such ideas of scientific urban planning and judged by Scott an "inhuman" city, in which activities are functionally segregated and pedestrians are eliminated. Jane Jacobs is Scott's corresponding hero, because she has campaigned against artificial order and advocated cities of many mixed neighborhoods and lively social interaction.

For Scott, Lenin was the Le Corbusier of politics. His high-modernist views led to the technical rationality of modern production, the training of millions of workers, and the transformation of society into a smoothly humming machine. Soviet social engineers drew from the models of Frederick Taylor and Henry Ford in the West for the organization of large-scale agriculture. Collectivization, however, ignored the local knowledge of farmers, disempowered local elites, and created a peasantry dependent on the state for combines, tractors, fertilizers, and seeds.

In Tanzania in the early 1970s, Nyerere carried out a policy of "villagization," which settled pastoralists and brought in schools, clinics, and clean water, with the goal of improving rural life and encouraging socialist co-operation. Modern scientific agricultural techniques, however, mainly ignored actual topographic conditions, village sites were chosen from blanks on a map, and local knowledge about poly-cropping was, again, ignored. Attempts to regiment the peasantry economically and politically failed.

According to Scott, these high-modernist schemes, which simplified society and environment in order to apprehend and regulate them, were unable to recognize or incorporate ways of knowing created outside their paradigm. Standardizing agriculture in order to maximize productivity, for example, by selecting crops whose architecture was compatible with mechanization, often reaped unintended consequences. Monocropping (the word itself is now practically a pejorative [Smiley 1995:341]) and genetic uniformity regularly led to epidemics and infestations, while diversity is the enemy of diseases. Large-scale employment of commercial fertilizers, periodic applications of pesticides, and the mechanization of field preparation and harvesting led to the possibility of failure where none had existed before. The power and prestige of science and industrial technology led to visions of unparalleled agricultural productivity, but the concomitant contempt for practices of actual cultivators and what might be learned from them had tragic consequences.

Scott sees modern states, Western as well as Eastern, in the First as well as in the Third World, as hubristic, desiring to improve the human condition but lacking confidence in the ability of humans not versed in the laws of progress and scientific truth to lead productive, modern lives. High-modernist ideology goes wrong because it is abstract, laboratory science, removed from the experience of those who know best how to manage their environments and social relations (compare Netting 1993).

At the outset of his book, Scott notes that:

the *premodern* [my italics] state was, in many crucial respects, partially blind; it knew precious little about its subjects, their wealth, their landholders and yields, their location, their very identity. It lacked anything like a detailed "map" of its terrain and its people, a measure, metric, that would allow it to "translate" what it knew into a common standard necessary for a synoptic view. As a result, its interventions were often crude and self-defeating.

Although I agree that ancient states were certainly different from modern ones, they tried no less than modern states to refashion and simplify social arrangements and make them "legible." Indeed, the term "legibility" has considerable meaning in this context, because the first writing systems appeared in conjunction with the development of many (but not all) of the first states. I discuss first the evolution of critical policies and practices that were part of state-making in ancient China. I then offer a long example from Mesopotamia about the nature of legal systems there. Although many neo-evolutionist commentators have tried to define the state in part by its institution of "true law," I show that the "simplifying" regime of legal pronouncements in Mesopotamia was not only unsuccessful but was not even the intention of Mesopotamian rulers.

SIMPLIFYING THE PATH TO POWER IN EARLY CHINESE STATES

Mesopotamianists, who normally have to hear from on-lookers that the cuneiform writing system looks like "chicken-tracks" (see Figures 9.18, 9.19) may be interested to learn that Ts'ang Chieh's invention of writing in China was "inspired by the claw prints of birds" (Figure 4.1; Chang 1983:81). The precursors of writing in both China and Mesopotamia concerned the ownership of materials. In the Chinese case, Neolithic potters' marks seem to be emblems of families, lineages, or clans (Chang 1983:85), while in the Mesopotamian Neolithic some "tokens" (Figure 4.2) apparently denoted various commodities and numbers (Schmandt-Besserat 1977; Nissen 1986). Early systems of writing in both places, however lengthy their prehistory in kinds of notation, were inventions in the first cities (Michalowski 1990, 1993b, 1994; Boltz 1986, 1999).

In China, William Boltz (1986:432) considers that writing "appeared when someone realized that a graph or sign could stand for a word (or name or other meaningful unit of language)." When writing was invented in the two regions, there was

Figure 4.1 Chinese potters' marks (after Chang 1986:128)

Figure 4.2 Mesopotamian tokens (after Postgate 1992:52–3)

nothing rudimentary about its earliest forms. Boltz shows that both systems began as pictograms that soon became logograms (word-signs). In order to express abstractions, however, both systems utilized principles of homophony, in which words with different meanings but similar sounds could be written with the same graph, and polyphony, in which the same graph could stand for semantically congruent but phonetically distinct words. Boltz's example of how the sign for "mouth" could also stand for the verb "to call" fits Sumerian as well as Chinese. The invention of semantic and phonetic determinants as guides for the scribally perplexed also characterizes both systems of writing. Unlike the Chinese script, Mesopotamian writing underwent another stage of development to become syllabographic. The major impetus for such development, as Boltz notes, was contact with dissimilar languages in Mesopotamia and so the need to represent foreign names in a script that was not developed for these sounds. The social context of this language contact in Mesopotamia throws light on other contrasts between Mesopotamian and Chinese states and how they tried in different ways to simplify their universes.

The evolution of the first cities and states took place in north China as part of a process in which local cultures became embedded within a created "Chinese" sphere of interaction. That is, increasing amounts of trade, warfare (especially over access to resources), and migrations in the third millennium BC led to the formation of new material symbols that were shared by previously distinctive cultures (Liu and Chen 2003). In the first cities and states in the early second millennium, rulers wished to control access to the metals needed to make bronze and also to control the technology of constructing bronze ritual vessels. K. C. Chang argued that these vessels, which were in the shape of mythological beings that communicated with the spirit world, allowed rulers to claim privileged access to the ancestors. These symbols could "simplify" the path to authority in ancient China (Chang 1983).

The newest research into state development in China (Liu 2003; Liu and Chen 2003) traces the first cities to pre-Shang times (the Shang dynasty traditionally dates 1600–1046 BC). The city of Erlitou (ca. 1900–1500 BC), at about 300 hectares in area (Figure 3.12), contained a large temple/palace complex, craft production areas, and a concentration of population (estimated at 18,000–30,000 people [Liu, personal communication]. In terms of the "dynastic cycle" this was the "Xia" dynasty, although at this time and for a long time to come, China was far from unified under any dynast's control.

In the aftermath of the collapse of Erlitou, Zhengzhou, the center of Erligang culture, grew into a fortified city of 2,500 hectares, with an inner enclosed core of 300 hectares (Figure 3.13). This is early- and middle-Shang times (1600–1400 BC), when a number of cities and their leaders competed for control of land and resources (see also Chapter 3). In late Shang (ca. 1250–1046 BC), the site of Yinxu at Anyang (Figure 3.14) arose, with its famous royal burials, palaces, and residential quarters. New research has shown that many cities and small states existed, sometimes independently, at other times under the hegemony of neighbors, during much of the second millennium BC and into the Zhou dynasty of the first millennium. None of these states was very large; even late Shang was "a cultural sphere rather than a politically controlled territory" (Liu 2003).

K. C. Chang and David Keightley have asserted there was a unique path to the state in late Shang times, but this is one variation on the theme of how early states attempt

Figure 4.3   Shang period bronze (after Murowchick 1994:69)

to simplify their societies. Chang (1983) argued that wealth was the product of political power in Shang China, and that political power was derived through a "monopoly on high shamanism" (Chang 1984:2). Keightley insisted that Chinese society was one with few, if any, institutions that transcended kinship and that "the lineage was the source of authority in both government and religion . . . The organizing metaphors of Shang life were those of . . . ancestor worship" (Keightley 1983:555).

According to Keightley, late Shang kingship was highly itinerant. The king traveled constantly through the countryside, sacrificing to local spirits. Anyang itself, the last and greatest Shang capital, was a cult center and necropolis, as well as a seat of population and a royal capital. The purpose of the Shang royal road-show was to hold together a federation of lineages by the glue of the royal ancestor cult. Kinship alone could not sustain the Shang status hierarchy, and rulers had to earn their right to rule by demonstrating superior access to the ancestors and high gods. While kinship may have been an "organizing metaphor" for Shang rule, the "relative political status . . . could not be accomplished by genealogy alone" (Chang 1983:124). For Chang, political power was forged by manipulating lineage wealth and by restricting access to bronzes (Figure 4.3), which were the vehicles of shamans' communications to the ancestors. That is, monopolizing access to the gods and thus simplifying the pathway to the ancestors was the most important resource in constructing dependencies and so bringing diverse cities under the power of the Shang state.

But what kind of state was it in which such access to the gods was monopolized by Shang dynasts? "The Shang state was gruyère, filled with non-Shang holes, rather than tofu, solidly Shang throughout" (Keightley 1979–80:26). Further, if "l'état c'est moi was probably truer of the late Shang state of Wu Ting than of the French state of Louis XIV" (Keightley 1979–80:33), this is only an indication of the limits of Shang rule and its instability beyond the region occupied by the king. Wheatley (1971) called the Shang a "theocracy" because of the close connection of the king's political and ritual duties, but again this only denotes the restricted power of the king to conduct ceremonies that were designed in part to construct alliances and cement dependencies. Although Keightley described Shang government as a patrimonial state, an incipient state, an incipient dynastic state, or perhaps a chiefdom (Keightley 1983:558), I interpret the number of cities claiming to be the Shang capital over a relatively short period of time and which were in competition as a Shang network of city-states.

Benjamin Schwartz (1985) and Hsu Cho-yun (1986) have noted a trend in late Shang times in which the shamans, diviners, oracle bone scribes, and priests who conducted ceremonies were becoming bureaucratized and the process of divination was routinized. Further, Keightley saw these changes as reflecting "a shift from a religious or theocratic outlook to a more secular outlook" (cited in Schwartz 1985:39). This was still the period when the king was his most mobile highness and was attempting to introduce the royal ancestor cult of his urban center into the rural pantheon, which was mainly concerned with ensuring prosperity of the annual agricultural cycle.

Schwartz argued that the high gods of the Shang dynasty represented "numinous powers of nature," and the Shang kings interposed themselves into the relations between subjects and their own ancestors by demonstrating superior ability to reach the world of the gods and the ancestors of everyone. In this manner, the Shang kings attempted to simplify the channels of communication with the spirit world. One of the vehicles of communication controlled by the Shang kings was oracle bones (Figure 4.4), which were prepared and read by specialists under their control. These divination records were used to tell the future, especially that of kings (Keightley 1999). This reconfiguration of ideology, in which power accrued to those able to contact all ancestors most efficaciously through bronze vessels and writing, resulted in the creation of a class of what we may call "knowledgeables." The emergence of this class of officials specializing in the control and dissemination of ideology was critical in the evolution of the earliest cities and states in China. In the subsequent Zhou period the identity of intellectuals and the institutional nature of their

Figure 4.4 Shang period oracle bone (after Murowchick 1994:70)

service was transformed, and this set the stage for rule by the first territorial state in China.

As the Duke of Zhou related to his master, "Heaven instructed us, favored us, selected us, and gave us the Mandate of Tian (Heaven) to rule over your numerous regions" (Hsu 1986:308). Although Shang rulers attempted to universalize their divine patron into a supreme deity over all their subjects and so secure their own power, they also argued that their rule was merited because of the king's ability to communicate with the world of the gods. Inheriting the principle that kings merited the right to rule, the new Zhou rulers could justify their conquest of Shang by claiming that symbols of the Shang kings' power to reach the ancestor, especially through bronzes and oracle bones, were ineffective.

From the welter of petty kingdoms and independent cities that characterized the first phases of the Zhou "dynasty," the remnants of the earlier "knowledgeables" began to take new shape. Certain *shi* specialists, who were already attested in oracle bone inscriptions in the late Shang period and who were not kinsmen of the rulers (Schwartz 1985), became increasingly important over time. During the spring-and-autumn period (770–476 BC), as the pace of social and economic change accelerated in the wake of the Western Zhou collapse (Wheatley 1971), the *shi*, initially low-ranking warriors, received, in addition to military education, training in literary and ritual arts and assumed roles in the expanding domains of the civil service (Hsu 1986:7; 1999) As a by-product of endemic warfare in the Eastern Zhou and Warring States periods (519–222 BC), many *shi* were able to attach themselves to any larger court that could use their expertise. It was in this milieu that Confucius, himself of the *shi* class, lived and wrote. The history of the unification of China by the First Emperor of Qin (221 BC) and Han emperors (206 BC–AD 220) is also that of the Confucianization of the bureaucracy, in which standards of "moralized orthodoxy" were "welded together with political authority" (Hsu 1986:315–16; 1999). Qualifications that were required for entrance into governmental service were monopolized by the new "literati" who were "autonomous elites," so defined because their existence, recruitment, and legitimacy did not solely depend on the political establishment, or on traditional kinship ties, but on individual qualifications, especially intellectual ability. Their role was "to present a comprehensive view of the world, not merely of any particular group, and argue that the main task is to remake present reality, corrupt and imperfect as it is, in accordance with the dictates of a higher moral order" (Machinist 1986:183).

These literati redefined the Mandate of Heaven and how kings merited their positions by following the high principles of governance. They were carriers of dynastic legitimacy, and they safeguarded the form and structure of the state. When dynasties fell, as they inevitably did, they could be remade in accordance with the principles of Chinese statecraft that were interpreted by the literati.

Han literati created the idea of the dynastic cycle in China by simplifying the complex history of state formation. According to them, only one dynasty in China had ruled the land at any one time into the most distant times imaginable. Although archaeologists have demonstrated the contested nature of rule in pre-Shang and Shang city-states, it was the legacy of the Shang in establishing an ideology of statecraft that made the innovations of Han rule and the literati system possible.

LAW AND ORDER IN ANCIENT MESOPOTAMIA

One of the first goals of the first Mesopotamian states was to make their societies "legible" through the invention of writing. One of the specimens of Mesopotamian writing best known to the public is Mesopotamian law codes. Neo-evolutionary writers have interpreted these documents at face-value and have reified them as examples of how the first states were characterized by their establishment of "true law." In the following examples I illustrate how writing could be used to "simplify" the path to power in ancient Mesopotamia, although in a far different way than was the case in ancient China. Law codes in Mesopotamia can also be regarded as attempts to simplify social life there, but in a way and for a purpose not foreseen by the neo-evolutionists.

The first written texts in Mesopotamia occur in the city of Uruk and date to about 3200 BC. Whereas the large majority of the first texts were accounts of goods, some of the first texts were lists of people and things, the best-known of which is the list of professions (Nissen, Damerow, and Englund 1990; Englund 1998; and see Figure 9.19). These lists were products of scribal training and have been reconstructed from many fragments of clay tablets that were schoolboy exercises. Of course, it is unlikely that the idea of systematizing the universe began with the first writing, but it is the case that the first writing became part of a tradition that was reproduced and commented upon (in scribal schools) over the next 2,500 years (Civil 1969, 1995). The language of the first texts, Sumerian, itself became standardized as it was increasingly employed for all manner of inscriptions throughout the third millennium BC. Sumerian was written by many people whose spoken language was not Sumerian, and even for those who did speak Sumerian as their mother-tongue, the written language was artificial (Michalowski 1993b, 2004; Cooper 1999).

In the first Mesopotamian states, we observe not only the invention and progressive standardization of an official written language, but also new uniformities in the material culture assemblage. This simplification and standardization has been observed most strikingly in ceramics (Wengrow 2001). Decoration on bowls, jars, beakers, and dishes in the later Neolithic (the late Hassuna, Samarra, and Halaf wares, ca. 6500–4000 BC; see Chapter 9), namely the materials for the consumption of food and drink, became simplified in the late Ubaid as forms were less diverse and ornamentation was restricted to simple bands. In the subsequent Uruk period, the ubiquitous beveled-rim bowls (Figure 9.17) were crude, mass-produced containers of rations (Pollock 1999:94–5). The common experiences of eating and drinking, which were also vehicles for artistic expression and thus a way to know the world, were transformed into the bureaucratic management of the food supply, so that the everyday acts of production and consumption (in work gangs) were altered by the new state's desire to simplify and shape the universe that it was intending to create.

Standardizations of the calendric system and weights and measures (Powell 1989–90) ensued. There were also attempts by states to manage and regularize irrigation and field systems and even time itself (Postgate and Powell 1988, 1990; Potts 1997; Englund 1998). These simplifications are significant because they are cultural as well as economic, and there was no single-state power in Mesopotamia that could dictate such changes. Indeed, the power of kings and the state in Mesopotamia was much less than has been supposed. For example, the large irrigation systems that led to salinization in southern Iraq were built after thousands of years of Mesopotamian urbanism. New regional political powers of the Parthian-Sasanian and early Islamic periods of the first millennium AD were the first states strong enough to engineer ruin in the landscape of southern Iraq (Adams 1981; Powell 1985).

The context of Mesopotamian law

One of the most important attributes thought to be possessed by the earliest states, as I have noted, was its putative "monopoly on law" (Fried 1967; Flannery 1972). There is a variety of Mesopotamian legal data, and we can conveniently organize them according to Karl Llewellyn's and E. Adamson Hoebel's "three roads into the exploration of the law-stuff of a culture" (Hoebel 1954; Pospisil 1973). First are abstract rules, such as the Mesopotamian law codes, which appear to be formal principles of abstract jural behavior. Second is the observation of actual behavior of the members of a society, which in Mesopotamian terms encompasses the behavior recorded in thousands of contracts and letters. Principal actors, specific arrangements, oaths and statements that the contract will not be renounced, witnesses, and calendar dates are all detailed. The texts deal with marriages, divorces, adoptions, sales, rentals of movable and immovable property, and many other activities. Hoebel's criticism, that this second road concerns sociological rather than jural behavior, requires rather fine hairsplitting amongst the Mesopotamian data. Litigations are, in fact, drawn up in the form of contracts, with judges and court officers serving as witnesses. The decisions then functioned as contracts in succeeding stages of a complicated litigious process (e.g. Yoffee 2000). Furthermore, litigations usually arise from the non-compliance or non-performance of contractual situations or pre-existing obligations. In short, contracts are the stuff from which court cases are produced, and legal decisions are themselves contracts.

The third road, which was the one emphasized by Hoebel, under the influence of Llewellyn and the legal realists, is the analysis of trouble-cases: "Unless a dispute arises to test the principles of law in the crucible of litigation, there can be no certainty as to the precise rule of law for a particular situation, no matter what is said as to what will be or should be done" (Hoebel 1954:37). Following this principle, it is apparent that those abstract rules not enforced by courts cannot be regarded as legal. An understanding of Mesopotamian law codes in the anthropological perspective, therefore, must consider the context of these formal legal declarations and an investigation of their enforcement.

Before turning to the code of King Hammurabi of Babylon, which is the longest such document, and in the period when evidence of other legal material is greatest, it is important to realize that this code was by no means the first Mesopotamian law code (Roth 1995). At least three documents antedating Hammurabi's code contain the same prologue-laws-epilogue structure that characterizes Hammurabi's code. A still earlier forerunner of these documents is the "reforms of Urukagina" which are embedded in a building inscription (Cooper 1986) written in approximately 2400 BC in the city-state of Lagash. This text details certain "abuses" of previous rulers that were reformed in Urukagina's just reign. Following Diakonoff (1969), most interpreters consider that Urukagina, himself not of the ruling dynasty at Lagash, was no reformer at all. Indeed, by attempting to curb the encroachment of a secular authority at the expense of temple prerogatives, he was, if a modern term must be applied, a reactionary. Most of the "reforms" were intended to end specific royal taxes on, and the confiscation of, temple property. In addition to correcting these specific "abuses," however, Urukagina was careful to portray himself as the one "who will not pawn the widow or the orphan to the powerful." With such rhetoric Urukagina lays claim to be the legitimate ruler of Lagash, having been "grasped by the hand" of the god to rule the city-state. (That is to say, he was a usurper.)

The law code of Ur-Namma (ca. 2100 BC) prefigures Hammurabi's document by about 350 years. The code begins with a mythological introduction of how the gods gave him dominion in his city of Ur and includes Ur-Namma's claim to govern according to the principles of justice and truth and not to deliver the widow or the orphan to the rich or powerful. Following this prologue is a list of "if . . . then" statements, thus inaugurating the casuistic style in which the "laws" of subsequent law code were composed.

Another early law code is that of Lipit-Ishtar of Isin (ca. 1930 BC). The prologue and set of themes in the laws of this document are very much composed in the style of Ur-Namma's code. In the incompletely preserved epilogue Lipit-Ishtar claims to establish truth in the land and includes curses on any who would erase his words but blessings on those who heed them. The first preserved law code written in Akkadian was that of King Dadusha of Eshnunna, an earlier contemporary of Hammurabi. Although this code does not have a prologue, the laws echo themes of earlier codes, but with some new elements added, both in subject matter and in arrangement. Many of these themes, old and new, also appear in Hammurabi's code, although often greatly embellished. Suffice it to say that the code of Hammurabi was not at all unique in Mesopotamia. It was, however, the longest and most famous of these sets of rules in antiquity, as can be seen from the large number of tablets that excerpt sections of the laws or preserve only the prologue. Some of these date more than a millennium after Hammurabi's death (Driver and Miles 1952; Laessœ 1950).

The context and function of the code of Hammurabi

After the fall of the Third Dynasty of Ur (ca. 2000 BC), numerous city-states competed for power in southern Mesopotamia (Van De Mieroop 2004). From these competing rivalries, Hammurabi of Babylon extended his control from the core area around Babylon by defeating rivals from the east, west, and, most significantly, the heavily populated south. Economic policies in the conquered south were vigorously regulated by the crown in Babylon, often by the king himself. Vast quantities of subjugated land were bound to the Babylonian administration regardless of their prior ownership. Local political authority in the south was systematically bypassed, and resources were channeled by puppet administrators often to the distant capital. Although the empire of Hammurabi was established only in the last dozen years of his reign and did not survive that of his son and successor, for a brief time the ideal of political unification in Mesopotamia was matched by the creation of an imperial structure.

Fragments of the code of Hammurabi, which were found on tablets, were first studied in 1890 and throughout the following decade. Hence, it was not surprising, on one level, that in December 1901 and January 1902 excavators discovered in Susa three large diorite blocks that constituted the code (Driver and Miles 1952). The stela itself had been brought to Susa (in Iran) as part of the booty of Elamite raids on Babylonia from 1150–1145 BC. Actually, archaeologists recovered other blocks of diorite that were not part of the "original" stela: there were in fact several stelas. The major gap in the text, where the Elamite king Shutruk-nahhunte erased five to seven columns, apparently with a view to inserting his own inscription (which task was not completed), can largely be restored on the basis of duplicate stelas and numerous excerpt tablets from Hammurabi's time. The reconstructed stela is a cone-shaped monument (Figure 4.5) 2.25 m high. The prologue, laws, and epilogue were inscribed beneath an engraving of the sun god, the patron of justice, who is seated on a throne receiving the veneration of King Hammurabi (Figure 4.5). Although earlier commentators had thought that the code was written in Hammurabi's twenty-second year, which is named after the construction of a statue called "Hammurabi, King of Justice," the list of cities enumerated in the prologue that were conquered by Hammurabi show that the final edition of the law code was written in the latter years of Hammurabi's reign.

Figure 4.5   Code of Hammurabi (after Postgate 1992:288)

The prologue consists essentially of a hymn of glory to Hammurabi, announcing his divine election to kingship and praising his piety. Hammurabi, like earlier rulers, was concerned to establish equity in the land and to destroy the wicked and evil so that the strong do not oppress the weak. The prologue then recounts his beneficent accomplishments on behalf of the gods and the population of various cities under his control, and it portrays the prosperity that his rule will bring to all of Mesopotamia. Unconnected to this prologue in subject matter follow 281 rulings. These "laws" are stated in casuistic form, presenting a set of acts as having already occurred, with the circumstances considered as a protasis (if-clause) in a past tense, while the prescribed sanction is presented as an apodosis (then-clause) in a present-future tense. For example in the first ruling: "If a man has accused another man by lodging a charge of murder against him, but has been unable to prove it, his accuser shall be put to death."

The arrangement of the rules is by groups dealing with the same general topic. When a subject has been considered adequately treated, the transition to the next topic is effected by some suggestive similarity or common element between the first rule of the new subject and the preceding rule. For example, the last rule in a group of rules pertaining to family law (no. 195) concerns the punishment for a son who strikes his father. A transition is then made to the topic of assault and battery in general, which is treated in some detail (nos. 196–213).

The intent of the rulings is made clear in the epilogue to the code. The first words following the rulings are: "These are the equitable rules that Hammurabi, the able king, has established." The epilogue then goes on to proclaim that Hammurabi inscribed his "precious words" on the stela in order "to judge the cause of the people and to render the decisions of the land." In fact, though, there were only a limited number of new formulations in Hammurabi's laws, since many of the rules seem copied verbatim from earlier sets of laws that were part of the curriculum of Babylonian scribes. In light of this sort of contradiction, a lively debate has sprung up as to what the purpose of Hammurabi's laws was.

In one position, investigators consider that Hammurabi was a lawgiver and that the code represented a codification and a reform (Koschaker 1917:2). As an extension of this interpretation, Godfrey Driver and John Miles (1952:41) viewed the laws as a commentary on the common law of Babylon, "a series of amendments and restatements of parts of the law in force when he wrote." The laws "were something like the English case-law, which lays down a rule or norm of which the purpose is to be followed and regard is to be had to the spirit and not to the letter of the text. In fact, they set forth what Hammurabi recommended and desired as the law to be followed in his realm" (Driver and Miles 1952:52; see Westbrook 1989). In this tradition, the laws of Hammurabi were not necessarily statutes, but they did guide the manner and substance of decisions actually made in courts.

In the other position, "the great work of law-giving of the king [Hammurabi] remained only a representation and was never a legal reality" (Eilers 1932:8). Benno Landsberger (1939) pointed out that there was no word for law in Mesopotamia, that the laws of Hammurabi had no influence on Mesopotamian jural activity, and the laws formed no real codification. F. R. Kraus (1960) argued that the laws were similar in structure to products of scribal thinking. That is, the "if . . . then" form of the laws is the same as that found in Mesopotamian omens, especially the extispicy omens. (For example, "If a liver has a spot on the right lobe, the king will lose the battle.") These omens are in fact a mixture of real observations of the entrails of animals and academic systematizations designed to make the observations symmetrical, stylistically complete, and artistically elegant (Oppenheim 1977:206–7; Cooper 1980). According to Kraus, the laws of Hammurabi were similarly based on real cases that were then varied and expanded to present a more elegant expression of just action by the king. That the laws of Hammurabi were copied in Mesopotamian schools for over a millennium after Hammurabi's death attests to the literary success of the composition and has nothing to do with its juridical applicability.

J. J. Finkelstein (1968b) argued that when a rule found in Hammurabi's laws appears to coincide with a ruling in a documented court case, the appropriate conclusion must be that the statutory rule is a reflection of the prevailing practice, not the reverse. That is, the laws of Hammurabi are not made of whole cloth, but were composed on the basis of real Mesopotamian social behavior. However, it is equally clear that the various "codes" leave out a lot of instances that are the subject of court cases. Even if the laws echo certain customs, the so-called codes embroider on them and, more importantly, do not speak to the regulation of disputes and conflicts. There is no mention of the code of Hammurabi in the thousands of legal documents that date to his reign and those of his immediate successors. This is true even when the ruling in a case happens to coincide with a rule in the so-called code (R. Harris 1961). In sum, it may be inferred that Hammurabi never intended that his rules be accorded the status of practical law.

An example of literary embroidery in the cases is no. 21, which states that "If a man breaks into a house, they shall put him to death and hang him in front of that breach." Under Hammurabi's just rule all thieves who make breaches in houses will be caught, the evidence of their crimes will be unambiguous, and the penalty will be executed swiftly and serve as a reminder for all to see. Claus Wilcke (1992), however, has shown that in instances of theft in the time of Hammurabi, what robbed homeowners wanted was not the death of the thief but the restitution of their property.

The literary expression of how Mesopotamian kings must be just rulers, which is exemplified in the laws themselves, can be seen in the epilogue to the code of Hammurabi. There Hammurabi invites the aggrieved citizen of Babylon to approach the stela and have it read to him so that his case will become clear and that his heart will be set at ease. Naturally, the odds of finding such a case would be quite low considering the limited scope of the code and variety of circumstances that were, in fact, litigated in Babylon. Also, Hammurabi's words underscore that only a limited number of people in Mesopotamia could be expected to read anything, and these were the highly trained scribes, not common citizens and not even kings. But, Hammurabi goes on, once the citizen has found the particular legal point in question, he is then to appreciate the king's fine concern for justice and to utter a prayer to the patron deity of Babylon on the king's behalf. The stela naturally ends with a series of blessings on future kings who would abide by his rules, and with a row of curses on future kings who would flout them. It may be noted, however, that conspicuous by its absence in the 500-line epilogue is a word to the judges and officials of the realm, the only persons who would have been in a position to enforce the rules.

Who was, then, the audience of Hammurabi's code? Hammurabi says he was bestowed by Shamash, sun god and god of justice, not with laws but with "truth" (kittum), a word that is appropriate mainly in religious thought. We may translate it as "natural law"; that is, the law that transcends human creativity and whose suprahistorical ideals are those towards which lawmakers should strive. Hammurabi says in the opening lines to the prologue that his laws are "equitable rulings" (dīnāt mīšarim), decisions (dīnātum, singular dīnum) made by a judge or someone empowered to make such a decision. Dīnum also comes to mean the entire judicial proceeding, including the institution of a suit, the opponent in a suit, the trial, the decision, and the execution of the decision. Mīšarum is the quality of "equity" in human society, that which is achieved by the king's attempt to bring human affairs into balance with natural law (or truth). Kings issued mīšarum-edicts to restore economic balance in the land (Kraus 1984). Hammurabi saw himself thereby not as a legislator at all but as an executor, the divinely ordained shepherd of his people, representative of the higher powers to his land. His goal, in time-honored fashion, was to protect the weak and to cause everyone to prosper. On one level, therefore, the audience to whom Hammurabi addressed himself went beyond the general populace of Old Babylonian Mesopotamia to all of literate posterity and indeed to the great gods themselves (as Finkelstein [1968b] elegantly put it).

On another level, I argue, Hammurabi's code served a more immediate purpose. By carefully following traditional patterns of a legitimate king, he issued this law code in the attempt to portray Babylonian domination of conquered territory as quintessentially just. In the prologue to the code, the scribes of Hammurabi carefully listed twenty-one cities or regions, meticulously and reverently including both the area and its patron deity and most important shrine, for which Hammurabi will provide truth and justice (kittum and mīšarum). These cities and regions Hammurabi had conquered, sometimes having pillaged, burned, and destroyed them. By carefully following the venerable pronouncements of a legitimate king, Hammurabi (or, really, his scribes) justified the extirpation of his enemies from north to south; by ending war, he will ensure prosperity for the land and cause the people to be safe and fear none (as he says in the epilogue).

With these grandiose sentiments glorifying the infinite justice of the monarch and guaranteeing unparalleled prosperity under his rule, the famous law code of Hammurabi was designed, or perhaps better, adapted as a piece of political propaganda to win the hearts and minds of citizens of formerly autonomous city-states. Hammurabi's system of management, however, though greatly enriching the capital, was debilitating in the extreme to subject territories and could be maintained only at great cost to the royal administration. Although I shall pursue this story in subsequent chapters, let me note here that the constituent pieces of Hammurabi's empire were soon able to achieve their independence from the Babylonian menace.

We may conclude that the laws of Hammurabi represent homage to the notion of justice, but they say nothing about its implementation. The code was formulated on stereotypic lines of how rulers in early Mesopotamian states claimed to simplify the complex process of deciding disputes and instituting order. This does not mean that we must reject investigation of his casuistic formulations as reflections of actual legal activities, but it does require that Hammurabi's laws be examined in the context of the legal praxis of the land.

The complexities of legal simplification: decision-making in Mesopotamia

Recent studies by Eva Dombradi (1996) and John Fortner (1996) list about 350 legal cases with their decisions in the Old Babylonian period, ca. 1900–1600 BC, that is, the era of Hammurabi, his dynasty, contemporary kings, and his successors. From these trials, which are tantamount to Hoebel's third road into testing the principles of law in the crucible of litigation, we can see what cases actually came to court and trace the social tensions and grievances that led to dispute and how these were settled. Most cases were settled by "judges" or judges along with corporate groups: the city/town (ālum), the port-authority (kārum, literally quay or harbor), the assembly (puhrum), elders (šībūtum), elders of the city (šībūt ālim), and the "ward" (babtum), to cite the most common examples (Seri 2003). It is not clear whether a "judge" is a professional rank or whether judges were simply men of influence who had shown themselves able to weigh evidence and make sensible decisions.

A brief examination of ten court cases dealing with divorce[1] reveals an interesting picture of legal authority in the Old Babylonian period. In eight of the litigations the authorities who decide the actions or verify testimonies and/or written evidence

---

[1] These cases are drawn from Westbrook (1982) and represent all the cases of divorce known at the time of Westbrook's study.

are connected to the ward, the port-authority, or the town and its headman. The remaining cases, including one in which the trial concerned adultery and one in which the plaintiff was a high royal official, did not include local authorities in the settlement. On the basis of these limited data one may consider that when litigations concern aspects of family relations and the disputants are not part of public organizations (like the temple or palace), the cases are decided by local community authorities. In the case of adultery, it might be thought that the state – indeed in the relevant document it is the king himself – interceded either because of the status of the individuals or because the nature of the dispute extended beyond the precinct of any single local organization. If, indeed, a ward can be identified as a particular corporate group, perhaps even a lineage, as some evidence is inferred to indicate (Donbaz and Yoffee 1986:66–7), one would be able to predict that the law of the state would precisely be invoked when a dispute occurred between two such organizations or between members of two such groups. At any rate, the existence of a number of wards in a city in the Old Babylonian period seems secure on the basis of a famous text (Gelb 1968) in which five wards, each named after a particular person, appear.

The title "headman" (Seri 2003) appears in the Old Babylonian period as a community leader, independent of the crown and sometimes acting in opposition to the crown's interests (Yoffee 1977). Local community organizations, however, such as the port-authority, the assembly, and the elders, who appear as the authorities who decide cases in the Old Babylonian period, have a long history in Mesopotamia. In one of the classic articles on early Mesopotamian history, Jacobsen (1943, see also 1957, 1978–9) argued that secular kingship arose not from sacral auspices but from community assemblies. He contended that the incessant warfare among city-states in the early third millennium BC resulted in the election or appointment of a war leader. His major source was the poem "Gilgamesh and Akka" (Katz 1993), which refers to a "council of city-elders" and a "council of guruš (male citizens)." Gilgamesh, king of Uruk, who wants to go to war against the king of Kish, is rejected by the council of elders, but with the assent of the council of guruš is able to proceed. Some commentators have questioned Jacobsen's use of this text, since it was written much later than the time it purports to describe, and his references are to even later texts that refer to divine assemblies which Jacobsen thought were allusions to early Mesopotamian assemblies. Mario Liverani (1993:61, n. 72) thought that references in literary texts that were written in the Old Babylonian period but referred to earlier times were specifically intended as commentaries on the presence of Old Babylonian assemblies and their relations to the power of kings. Since councils of elders are attested in the third millennium (Westenholz 1984; Wilcke 1970, 1973, 1974) but there is nowhere a council of guruš, Dina Katz thinks that the second council in "Gilgamesh and Akka" is a literary parallelism, not part of the historical substance of the times. In light of later evidence of "councils of great and small" in Old Assyrian texts of the early second millennium BC (Larsen 1976; Veenhof 1995), in which only the great meet for certain issues and of "councils of old and young" in the Neo-Babylonian period of the mid-first millennium BC (Dandamaev 1982), the reference in "Gilgamesh and Akka" seems less likely to be merely a literary invention.

Igor M. Diakonoff (1969, 1982), Ignace J. Gelb (1969, 1979), and Gelb, Steinkeller, and Whiting (1991) have pointed to the pre-Akkadian and Akkadian period land-sale documents as implying the existence of assemblies. In some of these documents, leaders of extended family groups sold their land to elites. These lands were corporately owned, as argued by Diakonoff, since members of the selling lineage witnessed the document and received gifts from the purchaser, usually clothes and other goods, but silver as well. We infer that the sellers never actually moved from their land but became clients of the powerful and wealthy land purchaser. For Diakonoff, the leaders of these corporate groups were the "elders" of the assemblies in the third millennium.

The best evidence for assemblies in the third millennium comes from the Syrian site of Ebla (Durand 1989), in which a lexical item, KA UNKEN, is equated with *tātamum*, a rare word that later, in the early second millennium BC at Mari, is a synonym for the normal Akkadian word for assembly (*puhrum*).

From the Old Assyrian texts at Kanesh in the early second millennium BC, Mogens Trolle Larsen (1976) inferred not only the existence, but more importantly, the functions of the assembly at Assur and in its merchant colonies in Anatolia. Its foremost duties were to serve as a court of law and especially to settle claims made by merchants who were traveling among the various posts in the long-distance trading system that was centered in Assur (see also Veenhof 1995). The "house of the eponymy,"[2] sometimes called (or part of) the "city-hall," was responsible for choosing from the assembly of "great and small" the nobleman who held the eponym by which designation the year was named. In Larsen's view the assembly and eponymy consisted of the leaders of wealthy merchant families and the landed elite. Although royal power certainly existed in the Old Assyrian period, the nobility shared political power with the king.

This brief survey of assemblies in Mesopotamia and especially their legal roles reminds us of the many ethnological accounts of councils and assemblies as venues for dispute-resolution (Hoebel 1954; Gluckman 1973; Abel 1973; Moore 1978;

---

[2] The eponym (limmum) was the name of an important citizen that was used as the year-name in the Assyrian dating system.

Roberts 1979; see also for classical Athens, D. Cohen 1995). Arenas exist in all societies for disputes to be played out. In them, conflict can be pursued and the hierarchy of social power (Black 1976) can be affirmed or negotiated. Dispute-settlement arenas can also serve as instruments of social change. It would take a truly corrosive skepticism to believe that pre-literate Mesopotamian societies did not have elders who convened assemblies and dealt with trouble-cases.

Law codes in Mesopotamia did not supplant assemblies. Rather, they served a political purpose, because states were always attempting to reduce the competing power of the local authorities, especially the traditional legal powers of these social groups. This process of "simplification" did not work. Strongly centralized regimes (such as those in the Third Dynasty of Ur) did seek to monopolize decision-making, just as they sought to disembed and redistribute resources from local groups. Nevertheless, councils, assemblies, and groups of elders were consistent features of Mesopotamian life and cannot be reduced to first steps in a legal process that culminated in formal court proceedings of the state or decisions by the king himself (as some commentators have argued). Furthermore, local councils and assemblies did not disappear over time in Mesopotamia. Indeed, under Achaemenid rulers (539–331 BC) we read of "councils of Egyptians" (Dandamaev 1982) and "elders of Jews" (Zadok 1979) living in Babylonia, each corporate group apparently empowered to decide cases pertaining to its members.

Whereas Mesopotamia has been sometimes labeled an example of "oriental despotism," there were constant tensions among local groups and their leaders and the alternately rising and waning power of centralized states that tried to simplify these complex spheres of interaction. In considering principles of justice and of legal rationality, no straightforward evolutionist scenario of a progression from prehistoric assemblies and their traditional leaders as decision-makers to the rule of law through written law codes can be defended. Law codes were not the foundations of order in Mesopotamian society but were, among other things, instruments used to proclaim a simplicity that did not exist. If there were norms and rules of behavior in Mesopotamia, which there certainly were, Mesopotamians strove constantly to subvert them, as I show in the next chapter.

Leaders of the earliest states tried to make their societies simpler for their own advantage, but this only made life more complex for citizens.

5

IDENTITY AND AGENCY IN
EARLY STATES: CASE STUDIES

> Feminists can no longer assume substantial commonalities in the power held,
> exercised, or suffered by women *as women*; their own critical and empirical
> explorations make it clear that, even within a single society, the extent and kinds of
> power women exercise varies dramatically across class, race, and ethnic divisions,
> and also through the life cycles of individual women.
>
> (ALISON WYLIE 1992:59)

The term "agency" is much in vogue in the archaeology of the early third millennium
AD (Dobres and Robb 2000), but archaeologists have not agreed on its meaning.
It has been, for example, the subject of a recent essay in which an archaeologist
discusses how great men achieved status and transformed traditional societies by
getting access to guns or iron axes (Flannery 1999). This is held to explain how the
old order succumbed to the forces of European progress. "Agents," however, are not
just powerful men, but can be anyone. They are people who belong to several kinds
of social groups simultaneously and who must negotiate their economic and social
status and even their identity in certain historical moments. Modern archaeologists
want to study how individuals experience material conditions and how new beliefs
and meanings are inscribed in individual lives, especially in times of social change
(Meskell 2003). Archaeologists who infer beliefs from material culture subscribe to
the motto of William Carlos Williams, "no ideas but in things," and historians have
always been able to study the lives and actions of individuals as depicted in texts.
Historical archaeologists are doubly armed.

Archaeologists have reacted to neo-evolutionist preoccupations with whole systems and systems theory that had flattened out or even effaced questions of the

quality and complexity of lives. In reaction, archaeologists now focus social evolutionary studies on understanding the development of new social roles and new
identities and the degrees to which they are embedded in, and/or free-floating with
respect to, emerging relations of power. In cities and states, individuals who were
members of various organizations often had to make choices among the options
open to them. The cumulative amount and the direction of such choices in prehistory allow us to explain the evolution of the earliest states (e.g. in Chapter 9) and, as
we shall see (in Chapter 6), their collapses.

Matters of agency and identity are obviously not restricted to cities and states.
A good example in the anthropological literature of how individuals make critical
choices in their lives is the famous case of the social "split" and eventual abandonment
of the Hopi town of Oraibi (or Orayvi) in the early years of the twentieth century.
One commentator has described this case as "social stratification in an 'egalitarian'
society" (Levy 1992);[1] I summarize it briefly here before turning to examples of
identity and agency in early states. Oraibi was founded probably in the 1200s and
was the only town on the Hopi Third Mesa until the twentieth century. In 1906, the
town was "split" between two factions, "Friendlies," those amenable to Anglo ways, or
at least wishing to use Anglos and their ways for their own purposes, and "Hostiles,"
who opposed such accommodation. Hostiles were driven from Oraibi and eventually
founded new villages on Third Mesa. Eventually, Oraibi was abandoned.

The social divisions and identities at Oraibi were complex, since individual Hopis
were members of clans, sodalities, and family units. They were participants in ritual
life within and beyond the village, and they were farmers dealing with the realities of
year-to-year changes in climate conditions that in the best of times were harsh. Mis-
sionaries had come to Oraibi by 1870, and tourism had reached Hopi and increased
in the 1880s. The leading clans at Oraibi had separate and different responsibili-
ties and privileges in the all-important ritual sphere and in land-tenure. Individuals
belonged to clans from the maternal line, but maintained affinal ties to their fathers'
clans also. Kiva societies and religious societies provided further measures of identity,
in particular with new "godparents." After the visit of a Hopi chief and leader of one
clan to Washington, DC, and his meeting with the president, his faction of Friendlies
gained the upper hand in their contest with Hostiles. These factions crosscut the
other kin-based, ritual, and work group identities at Oraibi.

Community and personal values and historical events, not least concerning the
intrusion in Oraibi of various competing religions and economic ventures from the

---

[1] Elizabeth Bridges and Severin Fowles, experts in Southwest archaeology, have recently studied this case and
provided me the information that I briefly recapitulate here.

outside world, which increasingly impinged on the village, combined to force choices in Oraibi of *which* identity needed to be assumed as a priority for action. In the end, the village was abandoned, a new one was founded, and there were demographic movements throughout Third Mesa for decades to come. Only by asking who benefited from which decisions and who did not, and how Hopis perceived benefits, do we allow ourselves to understand the processes of social change and abandonment (which are still being debated). I cite this case, which is of multiple identities and forced choices in a non-state society, as an introduction to examples of identity in the earliest states.

In the last chapter I discussed attempts by states to "simplify" multiple and overlapping social roles in their societies and also their lack of success in doing so. Early states and their governments, far from being monolithic and totalitarian, were not simply unstable, which they often were, but often were uninterested in organizing the activities of members of community groups. Examples of agency such as I now present from the Old Babylonian period in Mesopotamia show that such choices as could be and were made by Mesopotamians did not necessarily challenge the ideologies of governance and especially the accepted dependence of citizens on the gods and their earthly representatives, kings. I portray in the next chapter, by way of contrast, actions that resulted in the shedding of identities, which involved both implicit and explicit ideological challenges, and this resulted eventually in the collapse of Mesopotamian civilization. The examples I have chosen in this chapter concern women's roles, the structures in which they were embedded, and how these structures could be malleable, in one case, to the advantage of female actors.

As in languages (Greenberg 1966; Waugh 1982), the feminine is often the marked gender in historical documentation, because in early documents (from Mesopotamia and elsewhere) references to women are relatively rare and tend to connote extraordinariness. In terms of Carlo Ginzburg's investigations, called "microhistory," in which "a close reading of a relatively small amount of exceptional data, related to a possibly circumscribed belief, can be more rewarding than the massive accumulation of repeated evidence" (Ginzburg 1989:164; see Muir 1991), women's records have reason to be privileged. To paraphrase Giovanni Levi (1992): microhistory is not simply a smaller-scale focus, but the employment of different combinations of scales through which one may get to the unapparent historical importance of atypical social institutions. By using this microhistorical focus, I explore the contradictions of normative systems, the overlapping networks of social and economic power, how political institutions shaped and were shaped by social institutions, and the meaning of belief systems in the lives of ancient Mesopotamian women.

In two contrasting examples from Old Babylonian Mesopotamia (ca. 2000–1600 BC), I evaluate how women played out their social identities according to the conflicts and solidarities of everyday life. In the first example I discuss *nadītu*-women, high-status women who were attached to convent-like establishments but whose activities extended far beyond a religious and contemplative life. I present a single court-case from the period, in which the disposition of the estate of a naditu was litigated, to highlight the salient elements and choices available in this peculiar institution.

In the second example, I discuss *kezertu*-women, decidedly lower-class women whose lives were in the main under the control of others, including elite women as well as men of various statuses. The documents relating to kezertus unexpectedly require us to explore the successful resistance in the southernmost part of Mesopotamia to conquerors from the city of Babylon. I also consider the rural opposition to urban policies in southern Mesopotamian cities at this time.

A PECULIAR INSTITUTION IN OLD BABYLONIAN MESOPOTAMIA

The Old Babylonian period followed that of the Third Dynasty of Ur (ca. 2100–2000 BC), one of the most centralized states in Mesopotamian history. After the collapse of this hyper-bureaucratic state, rival princes constructed and dissolved alliances, seized control of palaces, and proclaimed themselves legitimate successors to older royal houses. In the myriad new contests for independence and dominion, social and economic life became transformed in unprecedented ways, as we may trace in one archive from the minor town of Dilbat (Koshurnikov 1984a,b; Yoffee 1988).

A stranger rides into town – a little Clint Eastwood music here, please – probably from neighboring Marad. Perhaps not an arresting incident, but it is unusual to be able to infer such movements in our texts. The stranger bought a house, actually only a room or two, judging from the size of the real estate, jointly with a local Dilbatian. This may have been necessary since the stranger had no kin in Dilbat and thus was unable to secure property, which was inalienable to outsiders. From this modest beginning, he bought adjoining structures, consolidating his holdings. He bought and sold real estate, once being sued for part of a field he mismeasured. When the stranger died, his property was divided among his sons under Babylonian norms of partible inheritance (his daughters having received their inheritance as dowries). The cleverest of the inheritors succeeded in buying property from his brothers, and he eventually accumulated an enormous landholding in Dilbat, far more extensive than his father's. One sure indication of the status of this "son of the stranger" – my suggested movie title for this story – is that his daughter was assigned to be a naditu in the temple of Shamash in the town of Sippar, about 50 km to the northeast (see Figure 9.1).

Naditus (see the extraordinary and pioneering work of Rivkah Harris 1964, 1975; also Renger 1967) were for the most part elite women, daughters of kings, merchants, and community leaders. As females, they received their inheritance in the form of dowries. They did not marry, but were assigned to the *gagûm* precinct of the temple of Shamash in Sippar[2] at an early age, receiving a distinctive name and dedicating their lives to Shamash and his divine consort Aya. Their dowries consisted of two parts, immovable and movable property (Dalley 1980). The immovable property was real estate, basically houses and fields; a naditu could not sell this, since it belonged to her brothers and passed at her death to those brothers or their heirs. Naditus, however, did enjoy usufruct rights on the fields.

With their movable property, often described as "ring-money," naditus bought, sold, and leased land. Gains from these transactions they could bequeath to whom they chose – mainly other, younger naditus and/or their personal women servants, who were then freed upon taking care of the old woman and performing the funerary rites.

The institution of naditus was established in the early part of the Old Babylonian period and did not outlast that time. It was created precisely in the conditions of political and economic uncertainty that followed the collapse of the Ur III state, a time in which new properties were being accumulated and new problems were arising of how to keep them together over generations. One partial solution was found by assigning female inheritors to a temple, forbidding them to marry and thus to alienate family property.

Since naditus of Shamash in Sippar did not marry, it had long been supposed that they had no children (nor any sexual activity). Several documents, however, show this not to have been the case. In one text, when a naditu bore a child, the baby was adopted, as the text says, "fresh from the womb" by her brother (Finkelstein 1976). The text then stipulates that the brother must pay the wet-nursing fee for three years, perhaps so his sister could see her son grow to childhood. No father is mentioned in the text for the very good reason that this child will be acknowledged only in the family of the naditu and that his mother's property would pass to him through his uncle's (and adopted father's) estate. Legal recognition of children of naditus was

[2] The situation of naditus (Akkadian plural is *nadiātu*) differs in other cities, e.g. Nippur; see Stone 1982 and Renger 1967.

prohibited, because a father and his kin could be claimants on the naditu's family's property.

A particularly interesting court case, but by no means an atypical one, shows the complications in the estate of a naditu and the legal wrangling that often occurred after her death. The legal case at hand (Harris 1969; Charpin 1986, 2000; Yoffee 2000) leads to more questions than I can elucidate here.

The document begins with the declaration that the naditu Belessunu, daughter of Manium, bequeathed her estate to another naditu, Amat-Mamu. The estate consisted of about 15 hectares of agricultural land, a house in the gagum, undeveloped house property in Sippar, two slaves, and two copper kettles. This property was distinct from Belessunu's own inheritance share, which she could not bequeath as she chose, since it would pass to her brothers upon her death. It was rather the product of Belessunu's business transactions using her ring-money.

The reason for such a bequest to a younger naditu instead of to a family member was because the naditu's brothers often failed to supply the required support for their sister and because naditus often outlived their brothers (and perhaps were estranged from their heirs). Naditus also developed fond attachments to other naditus. In this instance the inheritance document was drawn up in Belessunu's golden years, and Amat-Mamu agreed, in exchange for the right to manage the aged naditu's property, to support Belessunu as long as she would live. The support consisted of specified amounts of grain, wool, and oil and special offerings at the time of six religious festivals. Amat-Mamu also paid off all outstanding obligations incurred by Belessunu, and Belessunu was declared incompetent. Anyone who would loan Belessunu money or anything else should not expect a return on his claim.

It was clearly to the advantage of Amat-Mamu to support Belessunu even though Amat-Mamu came from a rich family. Her great-grandfather was a well-known purchaser of land, his children were titled officials of the realm, and some of his sisters and daughters were naditus or were in other religious service.

The reason for the existence of this document, however, was not simply the statement of the extent of Belessunu's inheritance and its rights given to Amat-Mamu. In fact, after Amat-Mamu had supported Belessunu in her last two years of life, the daughters of the brothers of Belessunu, who were also naditus, sued to claim that they were legally entitled to the agricultural property of Belessunu. They did not claim Belessunu's house in the gagum, which, as her personal property, could not be construed to be part of their family's property, but only for the items that were part of the dowry that had been given to Belessunu in trust for the heirs of their fathers (the brothers of Belessunu).

The text goes on to state that this case had already been tried at the gate of Shamash temple in Sippar before the "headman" (rabianum) and the port-authority (karum) of Sippar. These local authorities examined the relevant documents: the tablets specifying the property that the father of Belessunu had given her and other tablets documenting gifts that had been given to Belessunu, and also documents produced by the claimants. The authorities then threw the case out of court and warned the claimants not to raise further claims. All the relevant documents, including the record of the legal decision, were then deposited in the house of the brother of the father of Amat-Mamu.

At this point in the document, its purpose becomes clear. All of the tablets that had been deposited in the house of the uncle of Amat-Mamu "went missing." It seems likely (but is nowhere stated) that it was the brothers of Amat-Mamu who had stolen the documents. They did this (or might have done this) in order that they (or their heirs) could later establish their own claims to the property that Amat-Mamu had been bequeathed from Belessunu, and which Amat-Mamu could herself bequeath to whomever she chose, not necessarily a member of her own family.

The headman and port-authority, however, drew up a new document – the one we are discussing – as a summary of all the other transactions we have reported. They further stipulated that if any other tablets turn up, they are the property of Amat-Mamu. They state clearly that neither the kin of Amat-Mamu nor that of Belessunu have any claim to the property of Belessunu, which she had lawfully bequeathed to Amat-Mamu. All parties swore by Shamash and Marduk, the chief gods of Sippar and Babylon, by King Samsu-iluna. The witnesses to this text are then listed, including the headman and members of the port-authority, and the text is dated January 10 (as it were), 1735 BC. To summarize, we can see from this text, to which could be added numerous, similar, if less complicated examples, that the unusual division of property of naditus, intended to keep the estates of wealthy citizens together, gave ample opportunity for litigation.

What can we infer about the quality of the lives of naditus? In their letters, naditus express heartfelt devotion to the gods of the temples in which they lived. They also lived a long time, mostly freed from the rigors of childbirth of normal Mesopotamian women – unless an accident happened – co-residing with about fifty other naditus in their gagum in Sippar. All of them had been initiated with ceremonial feasts, were given special names that indicated their religious affiliation, and were then ushered into the august presence of the gods.

In case anyone has missed the point, let me draw the analogy explicitly to medieval nuns, convents, and especially to the fascinating religious organizations called beguinages. This analogy of medieval nuns to naditus has been offered before but criticized as an anachronism, mainly as failing to account for the wealth of Old Babylonian naditus. In medieval English cloisters, however, there lived daughters of high-born men, especially well-educated daughters of the newly rich merchant class, who brought dowries with them, in spite of the church's injunction against the exaction of dowries. In practice, few girls' families could afford to send their daughters to a convent. In the later Middle Ages, it was not uncommon for some nuns to have private incomes, private rooms with maids, and individual disposal of money and goods. Although the celibate ideal was fundamental and the nuns were called to do the work of the Lord, there was widespread evidence of human frailty (according to the remarkable study of Eileen Power [1922]). While the majority kept their vows, the image in fiction of the priest's mistress being a nun had a basis in reality. Since the church condemned apostasy more than unchastity, however, there was more dishonor in casting aside the veil than in bearing a child (Power 1922).[3] In medieval Europe, specifically in the Low Countries, single women could retreat from the world into beguinages (Simons 2001) – institutions of chaste women (some from the best families), but outside monastic orders. These were religious movements of the laity, and some of the beguines were low wage earners in the textile industry, whereas others were teachers.

Perhaps Old Babylonian naditus, freed from the authority of fathers and husbands, enjoyed productive and interesting careers, interlacing their religious devotions with their business practices. Indeed, their lives might have been more interesting than other Mesopotamian women's, if I may hazard such a judgment. Such a view is similar to (and inspired by) the opinion of Eileen Power in her comparison of the lives of medieval English nuns to other medieval women. In Jo Ann McNamara's book

[3] This analogy to medieval nuns may shed light on Caroline Janssen's discussion (1991) of "hungry naditums" during the reign of Samsu-iluna, son of Hammurabi. The text she cites is one of a number of school copies, some dating to more than a century after the date of its composition. The text contains two directives from the king (Samsu-iluna) to a variety of people, including the port-authority of Sippar, the judges of the part of Sippar called Sippar Amnanum, sanga priests, the overseer of the naditus, and the doorkeepers of the gagum. The first directive relates that the people of Sippar had encloistered their daughters but then didn't give them sufficient food. The king orders that the fathers and brothers of naditus must guarantee in writing that they will support their naditu relatives. The second directive orders that if a man has a debt, the creditor will not be able to seize the property of a naditu relative of the debtor. Whereas Janssen meditates on the possible reasons for the impoverishment of naditus during the reign of Samsu-iluna, Power showed that it was quite normal for many medieval nuns to suffer want in the cloister. "In the history of the medieval nunneries of England there is nothing more striking than the constant financial straits to which they were reduced" (Power 1922:161). Janssen considers that the institution of naditus was coming asunder in the period of Samsu-iluna and that the reference to the hungry naditus being given food from the stores of "our lord" refers to Samsu-iluna himself. "Our lord," however, probably refers to Shamash, patron deity of the temple in which the gagum is located, which storage house must bail out naditus whose families were not providing them with required support. If there was a crisis in the gagum at this time, it may have been due to failure of the "empire" of Hammurabi in the time of Samsu-iluna (which I discuss below).

on medieval nuns (1996), the retreat from the world clearly opened up opportunities for women.[4] The most interesting facet of the comparison, in any case, is that medieval English nuns, beguines of the Low Countries, and Old Babylonian naditus were often high-born and wealthy women, products of ages in which new wealth and status were being created, and in which new social and economic dislocations were mediated by the most venerable symbols and deeply felt emotions.

IMAGINING SEX IN AN EARLY STATE

The woman was dressed in purple and scarlet and glittered with gold and pearls, and she was holding a gold winecup filled with the disgusting filth of her prostitution; on her head was written a name, a cryptic name: "Babylon the Great, the mother of prostitutes and all the filthy practices of the earth."   (REVELATIONS 17:4–5)

Through the ages Mesopotamia has served as an "other" for its neighbors, who constructed a prototypically bizarre culture, the opposite of their own civilized one, especially in regard to sex and particularly to prostitution. Of course, such cultural constructions often tell more about the commentator than about the ancient situation. This is as true of modern times as of the near contemporaries of Babylon. Pride of place goes to Herodotus (1954:121–2), who reported famously about women's sexual duties in Mesopotamia:

There is one custom amongst these people which is wholly shameful: every woman who is native of the country [Babylonia] must once in her life go and sit in the temple of Aphrodite and there give herself to a strange man. Many of the rich women, who are too proud to mix with the rest, drive to the temple in covered carriages with a whole host of servants following behind, and there wait; most, however, sit in the precinct of the temple with a band of plaited string round their heads – and a great crowd they are, what with some sitting there, others arriving, others going away – and through them all gangways are marked off running in every direction for the men to pass along and make their choice. Once a woman has taken her seat she is not allowed to go home until a man has thrown a silver coin into her lap and taken her outside to lie with her. As he throws the coin, the man has to say, 'In the name of the goddess Mylitta' – that being the Assyrian name for Aphrodite. The value of the coin is of no consequence; once thrown it becomes sacred, and the law forbids that it should ever be refused. The woman has no privilege of choice – she must go with the first man who throws

---

[4] McNamara argues that stories of salacious nuns are constructions by others, not the nuns themselves. Nuns speak convincingly in defense of chastity, and chastity is in fact empowering, allowing scholarly and artistic freedom, but its creative intensity could also make convents into emotionally risky places where hysteria and flagellations were not uncommon.

her money. When she has lain with him, her duty to the goddess is discharged and she may go home, after which it will be impossible to seduce her by any offer, however large. Tall, handsome women soon manage to get home again, but the ugly ones stay a long time before they can fulfill the condition which the law demands, some of them, indeed, as much as three or four years.

In his novel, *Creation*, Gore Vidal (1981:94–5) has reworked the story, not without interest to us, as I shall show:

Like every visitor to Babylon, we went straight to the temple of Ishtar, where the women prostitute themselves. According to the ancient law of the land, each Babylonian woman is required to go, once in a lifetime, to the temple of Ishtar and wait in the courtyard until a man offers her silver to make love to him. The first to offer her the money gets her. In other temples to the goddess, young men and boys act as prostitutes, and the man who goes with a temple catamite is thought to have earned himself the special blessing of the goddess. Luckily for the Babylonian male, he is *not* required once in a lifetime to be a temple prostitute. Only the ladies are so honored.

Strangely enough, Babylonian men seldom visit the temple. I suppose that they are used to it. Also, they must experience a certain embarrassment at the sight of their wives or sisters or daughters serving the goddess. Fortunately, a sufficient number of strangers come from every part of the world to help the ladies achieve Ishtar's blessing.

According to custom, you make your choice by dropping silver into a woman's lap. She then rises, takes your arm and leads you into the temple, where hundreds of wooden partitions have been set up to create a series of doorless cells. If you can find an empty cell, you couple quickly on the floor. Although spectators are not encouraged by the eunuchs, good-looking women or men often attract a considerable audience – briefly. The circumstances are such that precipitous speed tends to be the rule in Ishtar's service. For one thing, to disguise the all-pervading odor of sexuality, so much incense is burned in braziers that not only is the stifling air an opaque blue, but if one stays too long in celebration of the goddess, one is apt to turn blue oneself.

Ever since the discovery and translation of the Old Babylonian documents referring to naditus, Mesopotamian scholars have rejected the story told by Herodotus. Naditus were themselves in service to a goddess, Aya, the divine spouse of Shamash in Sippar, but the very term naditu was derived from a word meaning "fallow," not likely in the semantic territory of prostitution – rather the opposite. Naditus did not marry but were the real estate ladies of the Old Babylonian period. There is no Mesopotamian evidence of "ritual prostitution," according to many commentators. However, new texts concerning naditus show that some of them did have children. Although we have no idea how or under what circumstances this happened, at least one distinguished commentator described naditus as prostitutes (in passing as he discussed other Mesopotamian terms for prostitution).[5] There are, however, new data in the Old Babylonian period that we can examine and which impinge on the delicate issue of ritual prostitution.

The primary sources for this investigation come mainly from a single, small administrative archive from the Old Babylonian city of Kish. Using this limited corpus to explore larger topics requires some justification, in light of Marvin Powell's admonition (1978) that one can rarely reconstruct social context from the circumscribed nature of such small administrative archives. I do so by referring again to the school of "microhistory" which holds that small points of entry that begin with atypical data can often inform about large social structures that are more massively documented.

The archive in question (Yoffee 1998) comes from the latter part of the Old Babylonian period. This is the time after the centralized regime of Hammurabi (1792–1750), who conquered all of middle and southern Mesopotamia, had collapsed. It had lasted all of fifteen years before the first large-scale revolts had broken out, and in the south, the territory that had been conquered by Hammurabi was then ruled not by the leaders of individual city-states but by "kings of the Sealand," that is, the marshy land bordering the Gulf. Having lost its southern conquests, Babylon was still capital of a territorial state that included the nearby city of Kish, and it remained powerful in central Mesopotamia until the end of the dynasty of Hammurabi in 1595 BC.

Texts in our archive that refer to kezertus[6] at Kish became known only in 1963 (Szlechter 1963). On the basis of these few documents and some scattered other

---

[5] W. G. Lambert (1992) considers naditus to have been prostitutes, the normal term for which is *harimtu* (which Julia Assante [1998, 2002] translates unconvincingly as "single woman"). Certain lexical lists equate various categories of women with harimtu, especially kezertu (see above in this chapter) and *ugbabtu*. In a roundabout way in lexical texts, as discussed by Lambert, the term *šamuhtu* is equated with harimtu and also with naditu. Lambert asserts that naditus existed after the Old Babylonian period, citing a solitary, unpublished text (in his note 18) to a "late Babylonian ritual for Esagil in Babylon for the month of Kislimu ([sal]na-di-tum)." Although Lambert thinks that Old Babylonian naditus were "investment bankers," he does cite Finkelstein's discovery that a naditu could have a child and implies (curiously) that these investment bankers were also prostitutes dedicated to temples.

Klaas Veenhof (1994) translates the term *šilip rēmim* ("fresh out of the womb") as a "child which had lost its mother prematurely, either in consequence of her death or because she was forced to give it away, to dispose of it since it was unwanted or illegal." In Finkelstein's celebrated text and in some of the new texts discussed by Veenhof, it is clear that the newly born child of a naditu is adopted by her brother. Finkelstein had argued that it was not sexual congress that was prohibited to naditus, but that legal children were, since they (or their fathers and other paternal kin) could then claim the naditu's family property. In one of Veenhof's texts, it is a man who sells the newly born child into adoption. This occurred presumably because the naditu mother had died in giving birth, and thus the sale of his son confirmed the father's formal renunciation of any claim to the naditu's family's estate. It is difficult, but perhaps not impossible, to believe that the father of a prostitute's child (or, a woman having sexual congress as part of a ritual; see above in this chapter) could claim a share in her estate.

[6] The Akkadian singular is *kezertu*, plural *kezrētu(m)*.

references from various time periods, the *Akkadisches Handwörterbuch* in 1965 and the *Chicago Assyrian Dictionary* in 1971 inferred the meaning of the term. Since kezertu is derived from the verb *kezēru,* which means "to curl the hair," kezertu is "a woman with curled hair (a characteristic of a certain status)." Since lexical texts (mostly from later periods) conjoin kezertu with harimtu, the normal Akkadian word for "prostitute," the dictionaries also gloss kezertu as "prostitute."

The amount of material on kezertus increased substantially with J. J. Finkelstein's publication (1972) of twenty-four more texts now housed at the Yale Babylonian Collection. These texts were from the same archive published earlier, and while it could be shown from internal criteria that they all came from Kish, they were bought from dealers and did not come from the formal excavations at Kish (Moorey 1978). Indeed, the texts from the late Old Babylonian period that come from Kish and dated to the last three kings of the Old Babylonian period were purchased by museums (Donbaz and Yoffee 1986; Dalley and Yoffee 1991). Although discussions of kezertus, and especially whether they were really prostitutes, has not lagged (Finkelstein 1972; Arnaud 1973; Wilcke 1976–80; Charpin 1986; Sallaberger 1988; Goodnick Westenholz 1989; Spaey 1990; Wilhelm 1990; Lambert 1992; Tanret and Van Lerberghe 1993; Henshaw 1994), the relevant texts have not been studied exhaustively.

Most of the texts record debts, the remainder of an amount of silver that was owed from the kezertu account and that came from expenditures for a "rite" or "benefice" (Akkadian *parṣu*). The money was owed by a (named) woman, wife of a (named) man, to the "supervisor of the kezertus." The debt is declared not to be the responsibility of the woman or her husband but must be repaid by another man. The texts are witnessed and dated.

The "supervisor of kezertus" also managed a number of economic activities, collecting silver and gold, loaning sesame and barley, and receiving shipments of bread. He also commissioned rites/benefices that took place outside the city, along a canal, and he recorded the men who sponsored the ceremonies and who had to pay taxes to the palace.

But who were the kezertus, and what did they do in the rites whose costs were being documented by the "supervisor of the kezertus"? A unique text in the archive, a document without a single verb, provides us with our first clue. The document is simply a list of eight women, all un-named, who were of elite status, since they were glossed as daughters, brides, or wives of named officials, some of them from villages near Kish. Each of these women was assigned a kezertu, one kezertu being assigned to three women, and the text concludes laconically: "Total: eight kezertus." The kezertus, un-named, were apparently of low status and at the service of un-named women who were clearly identified as elite.

In the Old Babylonian period, the time of the Kish archive, there are only a few other references to kezertus. From the city of Mari two texts list kezertus among the women of the harem, of low status and in association with "concubines" (Bottéro 1957; Durand 1990: 291, n. 52). In a letter from Mari (Dossin 1967: no. 140), the king Zimri-Lim writes to a woman, perhaps the wife of a local potentate, about establishing good relations. He promises to send a "high-quality kezertu" to her when he can obtain one in a future campaign. In a letter from Hammurabi to his administrator in the conquered south, the king asks for kezertus to be sent to Babylon (Frankena 1966: no. 34). Another letter (Finkelstein 1968a: no. 28) records the purchase of a kazertu (as it is spelled in this text).

Post Old-Babylonian references, most famously in the Gilgamesh Epic and the Erra Epic, connect kezertus to the cult of Ishtar in Uruk and to prostitutes (Henshaw 1994: 197 ff.; Arnaud 1987: no. 602:345 is a new lexical text with a reference to kezertu). In the Gilgamesh Epic, Ishtar gathered kezertus along with other prostitutes, and Uruk is described as the city of prostitutes. The women have distinctive hair-dos, sing songs, and dance in cultic performances (Postgate 1979:92; Alster 1992:200; Roth 1983; Menzel 1981:29–32 discusses male and female "whores of Ishtar"). In a Sumerian literary text (Roth 1983:275, 278; Güterbock 1983:159), a female slave is "expelled from the escorts, rejected by the troops, and shunned by the people." The daughter of her owner, a godless man, becomes a kezertu.

Maureen Gallery (1980) has suggested that the rite and ceremony connected with kezertus can be explained by comparison to several contemporary texts from Sippar. In these texts, parsus (rites or benefices) were organized by certain women in celebration of the goddess, and foodstuffs that were provided in the ceremonies were disbursed to members of the temple community, the recording of which was the purpose of the text. The rites in these texts are explicit: "companionship," "escortship," and "prostitution."[7]

In her learned explication of the objects recorded with the women and the rites, Gallery defined the objects as "combs" and "combing/scraping tools." She connected these objects to kezertus since (as already noted) the verb kezēru means "to curl the hair." Another text connects rites with "prostitution" (Finkelstein 1968a: no. 45) and the "lamentation priest" of the goddess Annunitum.

As it happens, the house of a lamentation priest of Annunitum (in Sippar) has recently been excavated, and texts found in it contribute significantly to the understanding of the relations between rites, the temple's priests and bureaucracy, the role of the palace (which collected taxes on rites), and the officials who are mentioned

---

[7] Ru'ūtum, rēdûtum, harimūtum.

in the kezertu archive from late Old Babylonian Kish (Van Lerberghe and Voet 1991: texts 64–6; Tanret and Van Lerberghe 1993). The lamentation priest sang dirges at funerary rites and various other ceremonies (Cohen 1981:40 ff.; 1988:13 ff., 31; Dossin 1938) that included fire-eaters, jugglers, and wrestlers (Blocher 1992). He also administered a section of the temple economy, including assigning rites and collecting the profits therefrom.

The economic records of this lamentation priest (whose name is Ur-Utu) in Sippar show that he assigned a rite, through the intermediary of a "commissioner,"[8] to a woman and her husband, who then arranged for a "guarantor" who actually funded the ceremony. He had to repay the official from the bureaucracy of the lamentation priest who had loaned the money to him. The rite/ceremony was explicitly called "prostitution"[9] and the performers (and the guarantor) of the ceremony, males as well as females,[10] had to make an initial payment to the lamentation priest in order to pay for the food, drink, and other expenses of the ceremony.

We can interpret the kezertu archive from Kish by analogy with the documents from the lamentation priest's house at Sippar, since both are economic records of ceremonies. The (remainder of an) amount of money that was owed by a woman (and her husband) had to be repaid by the "guarantor" to the supervisor of kezertus, the official who commissioned the rite, and he also paid a tax to the local palace of the city which must have officially sanctioned the ceremony. The ceremony took place in the countryside, along a stretch of water. The performers in the ceremony were kezertus, low-status women in service of the goddess Ishtar, who were assigned to the elite woman – often a woman from a nearby village – who had the honor of conducting (or otherwise providing the occasion for) the ceremony. The ceremony involved sexual acts in celebration of the goddess.

The simple translation of "prostitute" to describe the performances of kezertus is, of course, an anachronism that misleads (Goodnick Westenholz 1989, 1995), for their purpose is not that of a wage earner in sexual professions. The performances of kezertus also have nothing in common with the story of Herodotus about the average woman's sexual duties in service to Ishtar. It seems that Herodotus, writing in the fifth century BC, the author of the Book of Revelations in the first century AD, and modern commentators alike have poorly understood (or willfully misunderstood) the practices of people whose cultures were much different from their own. One can open the imagination, perhaps, by considering a range of ethnographic and historical documentation that allows such customs, such as kezertu performances,

---

[8] I follow the translations and terminology of Tanret and Van Lerberghe (1993).
[9] *Harimūtu* and *rēdûtu*.   [10] Gore Vidal's fiction turns out not to be fantasy.

to be explained as other than barbarous. One such ethnographic analogy concerns the practices of devadasis in pre-modern India (Margalin 1985; Kersenboom-Story 1987; Prasad 1991). Apparently first attested in the twelfth century AD, these women were consecrated to the worship of certain gods, were highly literate and skilled entertainers, and also engaged in sexual unions with kings, priests, and the faithful of all castes. Neither devadasis nor kezertus can be considered "prostitutes," since their sexual roles were part of a religious system, not an economic one. Decontextualizing the performances of these women as "ritual prostitutes" can only lead to stigmatizing them and the belief systems in which they lived.

Artifacts from Kish, mostly unprovenienced (Moorey 1975, 1978), include many terracotta plaques of naked women, sexual scenes, and depictions of the goddess Ishtar herself (Opificius 1961; Blocher 1987). Elizabeth Carter (1997) has shown that in Susa in the Old Babylonian period such plaques are associated with those of musicians and empty beds. She notes that the excavators have considered that the area in the temple where more than 200 of these plaques were found was a "beer hall and brothel associated with the cult."

Although we can only dimly perceive the roles played by kezertus in the cult, since our archive, it must be stressed, concerns economic records of a bureaucracy, not an anthropological description of religious practices, we know a lot more about how kezertus came to be present in Kish in the late Old Babylonian period than what exactly they did in Kish. Other tablets from Kish document that the fact kezertus had moved from Uruk along with the entire cult of Ishtar, including lesser divinities and the retinue of priests and attendants. These include the purification priest of the divine Ishtar, the lamentation priest, the temple manager, the "barber," and other minor officials, along with the goddesses Nanaya and Kanisurra (Reiner 1974; Wilcke 1976–80; Edzard 1980).

Reconnaissance surveys of the city of Uruk by members of the Deutsches Archäologisches Institut show that in the late Old Babylonian period the city was abandoned (van Ess 1991:91). Other cities in the south were similarly abandoned in this period (Stone 1977), perhaps because of natural shifts in the bed of the Euphrates river, military action by Hammurabi and his son Samsu-iluna (Renger 1970), who fought to control the south, or both. Tactics of local resistance in the south against domination by the city of Babylon and its realm may also have played a role.

The local kings who fought against Babylon were called "kings of the Sealand," since the marshy region of southern Iraq afforded the possibility of guerilla warfare against the Babylonian army. The kings of the Sealand also exploited their position in conflict against the leaders of southern cities who had been co-opted by the initially victorious Babylonian kings. They were puppets of the Babylonian crown, urban officials administering local palaces and temple-estates. Although there were presumably disaffected urban dwellers in the southern cities, most of the organized resistance came from the countryside. This scenario of factionalism in the south, with pro- and anti-northern elements in Uruk and other southern cities, is reminiscent of the politics in the mid-first millennium BC. At that time, Chaldean kings in the southern countryside used the marshy southlands as their base to evade northern armies and to gather support against urban, largely pro-northern forces (Brinkman 1964). The kings of the Sealand seem to have forced the urban population out of the cities and into the countryside that they controlled.

Since Uruk was being progressively abandoned, the temple establishment of "Ishtar of Uruk" had to move. Kish, which was also a venerable center of Ishtar worship (Sallaberger 1988), was a logical choice for the new home of Ishtar of Uruk, the attendant divinities associated with her, priests, officials, and various functionaries. Furthermore, the ruling families of Babylon, only 15 km from Kish, had long been allied with kinsmen from Uruk, considering themselves of "one house" (Falkenstein 1963). Women were exchanged in marriage between the kings of Babylon and Uruk in the early Old Babylonian period, and a southern ruler asked the Babylonian king, his relative, for help against his local southern enemies. When circumstances made the occupation of Uruk impossible, the religious establishment of the temple of Ishtar of Uruk, the goddess of love and sex, moved into Babylonian territory, and Kish became the new home of kezertus.

CONCLUSION: ENCOUNTERS WITH WOMEN IN EARLY STATES

Because women are not usually the subjects of ancient texts, and they are usually not the subjects of archaeological analysis, except for the reconstructions of households, it is a fortunate happenstance to be able to observe the activities and motivations of women in early states. The two case-studies I have presented in this chapter, on elite women and some decidedly un-elite ones, bring us tantalizingly close to the certain daily activities of transactions, disputes, and rituals that took place in Old Babylonian cities. It is this sort of behavior that is not normally characterized in the grand histories of Mesopotamia, which tend to portray kings and their accomplishments and accounts of ethnic and social struggle. Of course, there is much that we do not know and may never know about the nature of the rites that kezertus performed along stretches of water in the countryside, or how naditus got illegal children.

Nevertheless, these studies of Old Babylonian women remind us that in ancient Mesopotamian cities much of the economic transactions and legal cases we read in texts almost four thousand years old cannot be understood apart from the cultural context that gave meaning to these activities. Although Mesopotamian cities were the prime arenas in which individuals and networks of social groups interacted with one another and with the "great institutions" of temple and palace (Van De Mieroop 1997), the larger belief system that overarched cities was as important as the political victories of kings that occasionally drew them together in regional political systems. This microhistorical investigation of kezertus and naditus in the Old Babylonian period of Mesopotamia depicts aspects of women's lives that were atypical to be sure, but it is the very quality of exceptionality that makes these case-studies pertinent to the understanding of identity and agency in early states. The lives of these women were remote from state intervention, and this is relevant to a social theory that is concerned with what states do not do, and how individuals construct their lives, to the extent and under the circumstances they can (see Meskell 2003 for ancient Egyptian examples).

Naditus were products of a time when there was a sudden absence of central control in cities as rival princes were competing for independence and dominion just after 2000 BC (and the fall of the Third Dynasty of Ur). New fortunes were being made and new ways were invented to keep these estates intact over generations. Naditus, while a distinctive phenomenon of the Old Babylonian period, skillfully managed their new social arrangements within traditional Mesopotamian forms. Although the economic raison d'être of the peculiar institution is clear, there was no thought to challenge Mesopotamian ideology and certainly no questioning of the legitimate roles of temples, which were enriched by the activities of naditus and kings alike. The wealth of naditus and their ability to construct their own lives must be seen as the fulfillment, not the reversal, of tradition. When central governments in city-states became stronger, and then Hammurabi of Babylon conquered all of Babylonia (central and southern Mesopotamia/Iraq), restrictions were placed on the accumulation of wealth. The family from Dilbat that I discussed earlier, which had become rich through the negotiations of its founder and his clever son, who had eventually sent his daughter to be a naditu in Sippar, became absorbed into the realm of the newly centralized Babylonian state. Family members became royal officers, instead of local real-estate entrepreneurs. As I have noted – and shall elaborate in the next chapter – the state of Hammurabi lasted less than two decades.

The appearance of kezertus in Kish was a consequence of the political activities of the time after Hammurabi, resistance in the south to rule from Babylon, and the abandonment of Uruk which necessitated the migration of the entire court of the goddess Ishtar of Uruk to Kish. Elite women hired kezertus to perform in ceremonies,[11] but since our texts are only the economic records of their payments, they do not inform us about the nature of the ceremonies or the role of elite women in sponsoring them.

These two case-studies may be seen as a contribution to feminist history – at least I hope they are – but in the frame of this book I mean to stress how they correct an image of ancient states that was (and is) evident in the neo-evolutionist literature, namely that states were totalitarian political systems that corporately did things. There were many things that the early state governments did not do, distant as they were from the daily lives of men and, as I have shown in this chapter, of women.

In the next chapter I present cases in which individuals in the earliest states exercised options among their real and potential identities, and were able to shed one identity in preference for another. Indeed, the collapse of Mesopotamian civilization can best be understood in the concatenation of actions of individuals who no longer wished to be Mesopotamian.

---

[11] Although the palace did not organize these ceremonies, several texts (see above) do mention a "tax" that was paid to the palace. In the Old Assyrian period (see next chapter), family-firms organized long-distance trade, entered into trading agreements with other firms, and also paid a tax to the palace. The palace was naturally not a disinterested observer in the privately run long-distance trade, since it could make a profit from the trade.

6

THE COLLAPSE OF ANCIENT STATES AND CIVILIZATIONS

There's a lot of ruin in a nation.

ADAM SMITH

1988 was a banner year for the archaeological study of the "collapse" of ancient states and civilizations: two books on the subject appeared in that year, *The Collapse of Complex Societies* by Joseph Tainter (1988) and *The Collapse of Ancient States and Civilizations*, edited by George Cowgill and myself (Yoffee and Cowgill 1988). These books marked exceptions in social evolutionary theory, which was mainly concerned with the origin, development, and growth of particular states. Although I have criticized such studies as failing to explain the changes over time in social roles and the relations of domination, the proliferation of new, multiple, and overlapping identities in early urban communities, and the development of new ideologies of centralization, it is equally clear that discussion of the collapse of ancient states and civilizations, with the notable exceptions of the Maya and Roman cases, was, before 1988, conspicuous by its absence from the literature on social evolution.

The concern with rise, to the near exclusion of collapse, in social evolutionary studies, had important theoretical ramifications: social change was perceived as a process of mutually supportive interactions that produced an irreversible succession of levels of holistic sociocultural integration (Adams 1988). Studying collapse requires that levels be broken down into institutional groupings of partly overlapping and partly opposing fields of action that lend the possibility of instability, as well as stability, to overarching societal institutions. Flux and the possibility of reversibility of the forces of social integration that were hardly captured in studies of the rise of states were central issues in new studies of collapse. Collapse studies are important, therefore, not only because they deal with significant but often poorly understood sociocultural phenomena, but also because they provide excellent points of entry into the social configuration of the societies that were doing the collapsing. Collapse studies also yield fresh perspectives with which we may evaluate conditions of rise.

Students of collapse have challenged views that assumed that human sociocultural systems inherently tend to persist or expand. They have argued that early states were not in harmonious adjustment and that collapse cannot be explained as due to extraneous disturbances or deviations in a dominant process of development that brought down societies that otherwise were in reasonably good shape. The earliest states did not function without a good deal of bungling and by generating considerable conflict. They were at best half-understood by the various people who made them, maintained them, coped with them, and struggled against them (Cowgill 1988; Kaufman 1988).

Archaeologists must, of course, be wary of taking inexorable decline for granted. Obviously, anything that does not last forever has a beginning and an end, and ancient states did (somehow) come into being and (somehow) went out of being. Social evolutionary studies, including both rise and collapse, have to ask why certain things happened at certain times, and also why something else did not happen instead (which is the subject of the next chapter).

THEORIZING COLLAPSE

The subject of "collapse" has been a focus in the writings of historians and philosophers for at least two millenniums. Scholars and the public alike share concerns over the future of their own societies and look to the past for lessons about decline and collapse. Collapse studies in archaeology are important, therefore, if for no other reason than to show that the suppositions and "common knowledge beliefs" that many people have had about collapse in the past are extremely questionable.

The notion of the ancient Greeks that civilizations are organisms and go through cycles of birth, growth, decay, and death is probably the best known of all ideas of how civilizations decline and fall (although the idea of progress in antiquity was also pervasive [Nisbet 1980; Bock 1978]). This organismic view, resumed in the early twentieth century by Oswald Spengler in his *Decline of the West* (1918–22) and Arnold Toynbee in *A Study of History* (1933–54, first ten volumes), found an interested and admiring public. Both Toynbee and Spengler were world historians, in the sense that the entire history of humanity came into their purview. Indeed, for them history was without a central point of reference. In principle, this perspective was not unlike that of the anthropological evolutionists, who held that any culture could be typed as representing a stage of human social development.

Spengler's "comparative morphology of cultures" identified spiritual principles in which all avenues of human expression, from art and literature to governmental organization, were organically connected. Each of Spengler's nine or ten cultures produced its own "civilization," by which Spengler meant the late, declining phase of a culture, the rigidified form of life that followed the expanding, ripe, mature phase. However, Spengler's poetry and immense canvas have been criticized for their lack of objective content. Also, the whole speculative superstructure rests on the flimsiest of empirical foundations. Spengler provides neither reasons for the origin of his cultures nor any explanation for culture change, and the biological imagery in Spengler is meant to obviate such questions. Cultures exist with the aimlessness of flowers in the field; Aztec culture perished through Spanish assault "like a sunflower whose head is struck off by one passing" (Biddess 1980). Spengler was less interested in providing a "falsifiable" model for the rise and fall of civilizations than he was in noting that "Faustian" (i.e. Western European) civilization exhibited in the early twentieth century the same symptoms as other historic, declining cultures.

Toynbee was concerned with formulating explicit and causal statements to account for the origin and collapse of civilizations. Best known of these formulations is his challenge-and-response hypothesis of growth and development. Among diverse cultures, growth is selected for when certain environmental obstacles are presented that humans have to overcome. The stony land of Athens, for example, is contrasted with the fat land of Thebes as an explanation for the development of the "Hellenic model" of historical process. Challenges must not be too daunting, however, for civilizations can never arise in the bleak tundra or the exuberant rainforest. Given the proper obstacles to overcome, however, an ineffable manifestation of the spirit is gradually set in motion: initial political disunity is transformed into a state that is the expression of underlying cultural unity.

The collapse of civilizations for Toynbee is symmetrically accounted for by a breakdown of creative spirit and the estrangement of the intellectual elite from the masses. This breakdown is not regular, as in Spengler's biological rhythms, but collapse is just as surely the destiny of civilizations. Its course depends on how the civilization responds to its challenges, and it is internal processes (not simply barbarians or advanced invaders) that deal the final blow to civilizations.

What I wish to emphasize in this brief discussion of the views of Spengler and Toynbee is their conception of collapse. That is, collapse for both meant a collapse of the spirit that animates a civilization. Furthermore, they viewed a "civilization" as a set of cultural values, beliefs about politics, and that several political systems could share the ideology of statedom. These insights were dismissed by materialist neo-evolutionists, who in the end produced studies as reductionist as Toynbee's and Spengler's.

Neo-evolutionism and collapse

In Elman Service's "Law of Evolutionary Potential" (1960), initial social development leads to a "radiating expanding movement" but then settles into the "eventual stasis of success" (1975:313). The more specialized and adapted a form in a given evolutionary stage, the smaller the potential for passing to the next stage (1960:97). For Service, although development was attributable to the "solution of problems posed by the outside environment by means created inside itself – i.e. inside its bureaucracy" (1975:321), collapse is due to the backlash of diffusion and adaptation. Social organizations are initially successful (if they are successful) because they adapt well to their environmental niches. Eventually, however, they become statically specialized and overadapted, less viable than more generally adapted competitors who vanquish them. Rise is seen as a continuous, organized build-up, whereas collapse is an abrupt and usually chaotic breakdown.

As I have already noted, in the neo-evolutionist paradigm societies passed through a series of stages or levels, each stage representing a package of interlinked institutions of government, economy, and social organization. Changes had to proceed "holistically," since all institutions were closely interconnected and so moved in the same direction and at the same pace from stage to stage. Although I have already argued that this model was inadequate to explain the rise of ancient states, for which purpose it was formulated, its deficiencies are even more glaring when it is applied to situations of collapse. Most apparent in scenarios of collapse is that whereas some institutions fail, others do not. Indeed, in no example of the collapse of ancient states does collapse represent a total institutional breakdown. Collapse does mean a drastic restructuring of social institutions, usually in the absence of a political center, but it is what happens after the collapse of the center that is of most interest to us.

Kent Flannery (1972) wrote the key neo-evolutionist paper on collapse, although it focused on rise. Using the perspective and lexicon of general systems and information theory, Flannery asserted that complexity could be measured according to the amounts of "segregation" (that is, social differentiation) and "centralization" (or social integration) in a society. Change in this scheme proceeds according to the evolutionary mechanisms of "promotion," in which a special-purpose system takes on general system characteristics, and "linearization," in which centralized authority bypasses local authorities to create new possibilities within a society. These mechanisms for growth, however, can easily become "pathologies" by which central authorities "meddle" in stable, lower-order systems and by which a special-purpose system "usurps" the role of the general-purpose system (as in "what's good for General Motors is good for the USA"). The resulting "hypercoherence" from these pathologies threatens systemic variability by imperiling the flexibility of institutions to deal with stress selectively. Failure in one part of the system affects all the other parts in a domino theory of disaster.

Although Flannery's evolutionary model usefully identified some institutional properties in ancient states and the fragility of interdependent linkages of social grouping, it was criticized for its inability to isolate any specific dimensions of causality in social change (Athens 1977; Salmon 1982a).[1] Part of the problem was that Flannery, writing in the early 1970s as an orthodox neo-evolutionist, saw the evolutionary mechanisms and pathologies as existing in bundles of homeostatic adaptations, in discrete stages and levels. Collapse, thus, could be explained neatly by "hypercoherence": when social institutions become so integrally connected that failure in one important subsystem affects all others, the whole hierarchy comes crashing down like a house of cards. (Flannery's image was that of a string of Christmas tree lights that short-circuits when one bulb sparks.) Collapses of ancient states in the real world, however, were seldom wholly catastrophic, but rather must be investigated institution by institution.

Roy Rappaport's article on "maladaptation" (1977) was a commentary on collapse as systems failure, but in a blacker mood than Flannery's essay. In Rappaport's view, adaptation denotes a systemic homeostasis in which a range of variability is activated in response to various perturbations, especially environmental ones. If adaptation is functional, it is also evolutionary, since once a homeostatic boundary is exceeded, a new adaptive range forms. For Rappaport, social evolution appears as a series of stages, each measured, in part, according to the increase in special-purpose systems that are co-ordinated by progressively centralized organizations. In the more complex, differentiated societies certain principles of hierarchical organization inhere. Lower-order subsystems must have degrees of autonomy built in, since too much detailed information can overload the capacities of higher-order regulators (which are more concerned with setting system-wide goals and values than with the daily operations of lower-order subsystems).

Such complex systems are profoundly maladaptive in Rappaport's view since, instead of maintaining flexible responses to stress, the interconnections in these

---

[1] For a more comprehensive critique of "systems-thinking," see Brumfiel 1992.

hierarchical systems mean that change in one component is likely to cause change in others (as it was in Flannery's essay). Additionally, the distance between higher-order and lower-order decision-making institutions results in delays in the transmission of information or a loss of information altogether. Such complex, hierarchical systems are maladaptive because diversity and flexibility progressively diminish in them, and the network of overspecialized interconnected systems is ill-equipped to deal with stress on lines of communication and production. When resources become exhausted or cannot be efficiently distributed, collapse or revolution ensues. Civilization, for Rappaport, is only an unsuccessful experiment and collapse inevitable, a conclusion that is nothing if not Spenglerian and Toynbeean.

An especially parsimonious version of neo-evolutionist and systems-theory approaches to the collapse of ancient states was the adaptation of catastrophe theory, a specialized branch of mathematical topology, by Colin Renfrew (1978). Catastrophe theory models abrupt changes in the behavior of systems that are the result of internal systemic properties, not external factors. "Civilization . . . can be expressed in terms of a single variable or several variables" (Renfrew 1978:212). For example, in the case of the Maya collapse, "investment in charismatic authority" is balanced by "net rural marginality." The time is reached when the rural countryside cannot deliver the needed food to support the ceremonies of the state, and collapse results.

Mayanists are, of course, interested in how cities, the centers of ritual and pomp, extracted resources from the countryside. David Webster (2002), in the latest study of the Maya collapse, notes that collapse was neither sudden nor uniform across the Maya region. In the southern lowlands, classic period city-states were gradually abandoned (in the ninth and tenth centuries AD) but, in the north, Maya cities did not collapse. According to Webster, the failure to reoccupy Maya cities in the lowlands implies not only the failure of the subsistence system but also the belief system of the classic Maya. In the north, where cities were not abandoned, roles of rulers and the relations of citizens to rulers changed considerably, and city-states persisted.

Although not formally part of the archaeological or anthropological neo-evolutionist approach to the collapse of ancient states, the economist Herbert Simon's (1965) concept of "near-decomposability," which he used to explain the breakdown of complex social organizations (among other types of complex systems), is perhaps the most interesting of the systems-theory approaches to the subject. For Simon, all complex systems are hierarchically composed of many stable lower-level and intermediate units that are strongly interconnected horizontally but less strongly coupled vertically. Furthermore, the strength of the vertical linkages diminishes according to their height in the hierarchical scale. Although lower-level controls manage short-term and local affairs, higher-level controls exist precisely to provide system-wide decision-making capability. In this analysis, the process of collapse, but not its cause, is roughly predictable because the survivors of systemic failure are not randomly formed associations (or social groups), but precisely those intermediate and lower-level units that existed before the formation of higher-level ones. Furthermore, the reversibility of collapse is a clear possibility, since the products of decomposition may become the building blocks for subsequent hierarchical arrangement.

It is this last proposition that is most attractive, because the most frequent result of the collapse of ancient states was the eventual rise of new states that were often consciously modeled on the state that had done the collapsing. One may also see in ancient states the presence and power of local controls, for example in the community assemblies I discussed in Mesopotamia, which existed alongside the king and state. As we can see in Mesopotamia, however, bureaucrats of the crown were also members of the community or of entrepreneurial families and organizations, and on the level of individuals there are many identities and social roles that cannot be neatly separated into *either* the community *or* the state, since people can be members of both.

In the process of state formation the countryside was comprehensively restructured, villages were abandoned, and people moved into new cities. Subsequently, new villages were founded, and agricultural systems and land tenure were transformed in relation to the presence of cities. It is therefore impossible to posit, as Simon did, stable or unchanging lower-order systems of communities or rural life, since the countryside, like cities, has its own complex history of development. States were not composed of timeless villages and customs on top of which were built urban environments. In times of disintegrating political systems, the countryside not only absorbed people fleeing from cities but attracted new people who came to take advantage of the weakness of urban rulers.

George Cowgill (1988) noted that terms such as "promotion," "linearization," and "near-decomposability" may not be "wrong" – and may well serve as starters for organizing hard thinking about ideas and data. Nevertheless, the language of systems theory, as used by archaeologists and other social scientists, tends to invite increasingly elaborate abstractions of intertwined institutions and has impeded our ability to break down complex data and social arrangements and prevent the examination of social institutions that are normally not well integrated. Our task in investigating collapse is to delineate the patterns of social roles and identities that were created, manipulated, reproduced, and reconfigured in ancient states and to understand the circumstances in which identities were altered and even relinquished.

Collapse as the drastic restructuring of social institutions

De-mythologizing the collapse of ancient states and civilizations entails, first, per-ceiving the structural tensions inherent in ancient states. These tensions were not "pathologies" but institutional cleavage planes that can be seen in the evolution of the earliest states. The founding fathers of social analysis – Marx, Durkheim, and Weber – are still the touchstones of modern inquiries of this structural analysis. It is unnecessary (and impossible) here even to review the main elements of their thoughts, since the collapse of pre-modern states was not a major focus in their work. The collapse of ancient states and civilizations was considered, as much as it was considered at all, mainly as a prelude to the analysis of the appearance and distinctive character of post-medieval Western civilization. Marx, as is well known, argued that contradictions within a social order – especially between the forces and relations of production – cause a society's breakdown and create the conditions for new levels of sociocultural integration. Weber developed a multidimensional model of inequality and political struggle, and stressed the persistent nature of some social corporations, even in the face of rapid transformation of other social corporations. Shmuel Eisenstadt (1964, 1969, 1988) has explored Weber's insight with reference to early historical states, and his work is worth recapitulating here.

Eisenstadt argued that early historic states were centrally organized with differ-entiated roles and activities existing in executive, military, and religious hierarchies. Political goals emanate from the executive center but in establishing them the center also provides arenas of political struggle within itself. Tension between the center and periphery also exists, since the center is concerned with detaching the means for political action from the periphery, and groups on the periphery are reluctant to surrender their local political autonomies. Eisenstadt's periphery consists of tra-ditional aristocracies, kin-based units, peasants, and specialized economic groups, such as craftspeople and merchants. Recruitment to the center rests on either politi-cal or economic motives, both of which are detached from the ascriptive qualities of individuals. Indeed, the fundamental organizing principle of early states is precisely that which counteracts the traditionally ascribed ties that characterize much of the periphery. In order to support itself, the center must be able to garner "free-floating resources." That is, it must disembed from the periphery those goods and services not irrevocably bound within the subsistence and socially prescribed activities of those groups. In order to channel these resources to itself, the center must address con-cerns of the periphery through the establishment of juridical activities, by defending the society or expanding the society's boundaries, and by upholding the dominant cultural symbols of the entire collectivity. Thus, the center attempts to legitimize the process whereby it withdraws goods and services (e.g. taxes and corvée labor) from the periphery.

Stability in historic states and civilizations is maintained when those in the periphery consider that the resources they provide the center also return benefits to them. These benefits may be material – the circulation of goods and services and the settlement of disputes – but also lie in the creation of values and symbols that supply both this- and other-worldly well-being. The locally organized institutional structures of the periphery, however, were never monopolized by the state, neither in the bases of organization or in the internal management of productive resources. Although the political center, for its own goals, may seek to control the extraction, production, and/or distribution of certain key materials, the goods and services required by the state for its continued stability must be acquired from the traditionally organized groups that provide them in return for real and perceived benefits.

By its very nature the set of balances that determines the flow of resources, the establishment of political goals, and the allocation of power between the center and the periphery and within the center itself is fragile. Critical for Eisenstadt is the management of those free-floating resources. Problems can occur when the center refuses to incorporate the needs and orientations of local leadership in the formulation of political goals, in some cases attempting to replace the beliefs and values of peripheral groups with the beliefs and values of the central ruling elite. Significant stress can also occur within the center when one interest group is able to reduce or eliminate access to the arena of political struggle by other groups.

Collapse, in general, tends to ensue when the center is no longer able to secure resources from the periphery, usually having lost the legitimacy through which it could disembed goods and services of traditionally organized groups. The process of collapse entails the dissolution of those centralized institutions that had facilitated the transmission of resources and information, the settlement of intergroup disputes, and the legitimate expression of differentiated organizational components. The maintenance of those institutions demands a flexibility, a resilience of responses to stresses that are continually produced, often contradictorally, by the various competing groups on the periphery and those within the center itself, as well as by external threats or expansionist policies. A maximizing strategy, in which the political center tends to channel resources and services for its own, rather than for societal, ends, and in which support and legitimation from the periphery are therefore eroded, can lead to collapse. Economic disaster, political overthrow, and social disintegration are the likely products of collapse.

It may further be observed that successful methods of gaining political ascendancy do not necessarily ensure success in maintaining the political system. Political maintenance is achieved by broadening the means of support for the state by meeting the needs and demands of old-line elites and by creating institutions that effectively and legitimately restructure the production and distribution of resources. Especially critical for the stability of a state is the transformation of a loyal and personally ascribed cadre of supporters into a bureaucratic hierarchy in which organizational self-perpetuation is subservient to the establishment of political goals.

Eisenstadt has also discussed the development of what Karl Jaspers called the "Axial Age" civilizations (Eisenstadt 1986). Such civilizations are characterized by the development of new kinds of ideologies and new "carriers" of them. Peter Machinist (1986:183, whom I have already quoted on this point) has characterized these ideologies as striving:

to present a comprehensive view of the world, not merely of any particular group, and argue that the main task is to remake present reality, corrupt and imperfect as it is, in accordance with the dictates of higher moral order. Socially Axial Age civilizations come to be pervaded by new kinds of groups, labeled by Eisenstadt "autonomous elites," because their existence, recruitment, and legitimacy do not depend finally on the political establishment, nor on traditional kinship ties, but on individual qualifications, especially intellectual ability. It is the *raison d'être* of these groups, in turn, to create, promulgate, and refine the new ideologies.

The regeneration of the state depends on the continued existence of the ideology of statecraft and of its carriers. Indeed, in most instances it appears that the earliest states often and repeatedly broke apart politically without incurring the particularly severe social troubles that precluded their active restructuring. I illustrate this by means of an extended example from Mesopotamia.

THE COLLAPSE OF ANCIENT MESOPOTAMIAN STATES AND CIVILIZATION

Although Mesopotamianists have argued about the exact date of the birth of the state in Mesopotamia, few have ventured to specify a date for the origin of Mesopotamian civilization. These questions, of course, are antiquarian, endless, and say little about the nature of states in Mesopotamia, what they do and do not do, or how the lives and identities of ancient Mesopotamians were altered in the process of social and political change. Nevertheless, the distinction between the terms "state" and "civilization" is not just semantic, nor does it lie in the appearance of certain "indicators" (Service 1975:178) or of a certain "style" (Chang 1980:365). By Mesopotamian civilization I mean that specific and reproducible set of cultural boundaries that encompassed a variety of peoples and greater and smaller political systems. The difference between Mesopotamian civilization and the Mesopotamian state is real and easily apparent. Indeed, in the political sense of the state, historians and archaeologists are well aware that the term "Mesopotamia" is by no means easy to define and even has the disconcerting ability to dematerialize entirely. Mesopotamia existed predominantly as a cellular pattern of city-states that rarely acted in political concert.

In contrast to questions of origin, both the collapse of the Mesopotamian state and the collapse of Mesopotamian civilization have been discussed and their dates ascertained. Thus, no one could argue, after the conquest of Babylonia by Cyrus the Great of Persia in 539 BC, that a Mesopotamian political system was ever again autonomous and dominant in the land, that the rulers of Mesopotamia thought of themselves as Mesopotamian, or that Mesopotamia existed in any way apart from a larger and non-Mesopotamian institutional order in which it was firmly embedded.

On the other hand, no one would imply by this determination of the end of the Mesopotamian state that the trappings of Mesopotamian civilization – literature, customs, languages, religion, including mechanisms of the divine legitimation of kingship – came to an abrupt and final conclusion. It is clear, however, that Mesopotamian civilization itself did end. We might assign this terminus to AD 75, as a shorthand, since this was the year of the last dated tablet, an astronomical almanac (Sachs 1976). This assignment is arbitrary, since there are a few clay tablets on which fragmentary cuneiform inscriptions are written on one side and Greek letters, transliterations of the Mesopotamian Akkadian, are found on the other. These seem to date until the third century AD and show that ancient languages were still learned, and that Mesopotamian temples, where the inscriptions were found, were still active until at least that date (Geller 1997).

Before the final collapse of the last Mesopotamian state there were many other extraordinary failures of centralized Mesopotamian political systems, and I shall review the most important of these in this section. None of these collapses, however, precluded the possibility that new, characteristic Mesopotamian polities would emerge from the decomposition of their predecessors. These collapses have been ascribed to a variety of causes in both contemporary and modern analytical writings: non-indigenous peoples, bureaucratic mismanagement, disruption of trade routes, environmental degradation, divine behavior especially in reaction to human sin, and others. Such reasons for collapse have often been selected according to the biases of the writer, ancient as well as modern, and according to the nature of the data – from temple or palace archives or from trade colonies – which represent those oddments of the past that were recorded, have managed to survive the ages, and have been fortuitously recovered (and published) in the present. By surveying several political collapses I intend to filter, as it were, the biases inherent in particular geographical and temporal sources and to discern what patterns of political behavior, if any, are basic within Mesopotamia, as well as to consider what may be specific to any phase of its political history.

The Old Akkadian state (ca. 2350–2200 BC)

From the mosaic of competing city-states that characterized the Early Dynastic periods of Mesopotamia in the early third millennium BC, Sargon forged the first pan-Mesopotamian state (as I discussed in Chapter 3). Sargon, however, departed from the practice of all his predecessors by attempting to legitimize his deeds as a king of all Mesopotamia, not just as a king of a dominant city-state. Having begun his ascent to power from the venerable city of Kish (which he had conquered), he built a new capital at Akkade (Weiss 1975). The new capital symbolized a change in the political tradition in Mesopotamia, ending, at least for a time, the internecine rivalries and transcending the local political traditions in the city-states to a higher conception of a single Mesopotamian political system.

In order to stabilize his rule, Sargon significantly changed the ideology of domination. In addition to building his new capital, he installed his daughter, Enheduana, as priestess of the moon-god at Ur and established the principle that only the ruler of the entire land (minimally, the ruler of Ur) held the prerogative of such an appointment. To administer the new territorial state, Sargon appointed royal officials who served alongside the local rulers of the conquered city-states (Foster 1982). These new officials were charged with breaking down the boundaries between city-states and furnishing material support (mainly foodstuffs) to the army. A single delivery of 60,000 dried fish was recorded in Lagash and distributed in the form of rations. To high retainers of Sargon, land was allocated.

Many changes in material culture (though not in ceramics) occurred under the Akkadian dynasty in seal designs (Boehmer 1965; Nissen 1993) and in plastic art, in which royal power was depicted (Amiet 1976; Winter 1996). Under Naram-Sin, the grandson of Sargon, the ideology for territorial rulership was enlarged in a number of ways. For example, the king's name was written with the semantic classifer "divinity," implying that he exercised the right to rule because he was more than human (Farber 1983).

In spite of such ideological and administrative changes, the territorial state of the Akkadians collapsed quickly after the death of Naram-Sin, who was followed only by shadowy epigones. Indeed, the signs of instability in the state were present from the outset. In every transition from one king to his successor, rebellions erupted in the land, led by rulers of the formerly independent city-states. The tensions of territorial rule were considerable and can be classified into two groups. First, the uneasy sharing of power between royal appointees from Akkade and local city-state rulers occurred especially in the redistribution of land to royal officials and the requisitioning of labor and resources by them. Second, the imperial ambitions of the Akkadian kings led them to military campaigns in northern Mesopotamia (including northern Iraq, Syria, and Anatolia), in the east, and in the south (Michalowski 1993a). In his classic study on the fall of the Akkadian regime, Speiser (1952) noted that it was the very success of the Akkadian army in these distant regions that galvanized local populations into forming alliances and conducting effective guerilla operations against the Akkadian kings.

These two groups of tensions, one internal, the other external, can be interrelated as reasons for the collapse of the House of Akkade (Cleuziou 1994; Glassner 1994a, 1994b). Labor for the army and support for the troops heightened the pressure on the new administrative institutions to fund the imperial campaigns and the projects set by bureaucrats in the capital. On the one hand, the state of Akkade promoted unprecedented amounts of social and economic mobility in the land. No longer was the city-state the basic arena in which wealth and status could be created. On the other hand, stretching the resources of the city-states resulted in resistance on the part of the local rulers and traditional elite, who, in the end, were able to resist the demands of the central administration and so bring it down.[2]

The collapse of the Akkadian state can therefore be ascribed to the failure of Sargon and his descendants to integrate the traditional leadership of the city-states into the new venture of the territorial state and its imperial ambitions. Perhaps this experiment into Mesopotamian political unity would have been more successful had the Akkadian kings not been so preoccupied with foreign expeditions. The resulting lack of attention to internal problems of centralization, combined with the increased demands to fund these campaigns, eventually increased the traditional centripetal tendencies among the city-states and also made the state vulnerable along its flanks. Victim to these economic and political dislocations, and unable to marshal support from the city-states that were determined to re-establish their local autonomies, the Akkadian dynasty collapsed, and Akkade itself became a rural village (Brinkman

---

[2] Weiss and Courty (1993, 1994) have claimed that volcanic disturbances and/or a climatic episode of decade-long aridity at Leilan in Syria caused the depletion of resources and eventually population displacements that drove Syrians into Mesopotamia and precipitated the collapse of Akkade. The evidence for this remains elusive (Zettler 2003) and some cities, like Lagash, persisted throughout the collapse period and into the next eras of political centralization in Mesopotamia.

1968:145, n. 874), remembered only vaguely in later legend. The irony, of course, is that the prime causes for the collapse of the dynasty of Sargon were just those deeds – extensive military conquests and the foundation of a new territorial capital – that have captured the minds of both Mesopotamian and modern observers of this period. The idea of political unification in Mesopotamia may have lain in the logic of evolutionary development that long preceded Sargon, but it was that king who transformed the logic into a palpable, historical paradigm. The deeds of Sargon and his dynasty became part of the "textual community," "defined by and through a corpus of shared texts which provided it with a moral and spiritual unity" (Cooper 1993), as scribes copied and celebrated the exploits of the Akkadian dynasty to the end of Mesopotamian civilization.

The Third Dynasty of Ur (ca. 2100–2000 BC)

According to the "Sumerian King List," no city-state could even claim pre-eminence in the land after the fall of Akkade: "Who was king, who was not king?" reads the text, which, from its point of view that only one city could and should be the rightful successor to Akkade, means there was anarchy in the land. In fact, during the reign of the last Akkadian kings, southern city-states had achieved their own traditional autonomy, whereas in central Mesopotamia, Guti rulers, hostiles from the Zagros mountain region, controlled some cities and countryside (Hallo 1971). After Utuhegal, king of Uruk, defeated the Guti and took control over Ur, a new dynasty there – the third dynasty of Ur to be mentioned in the "Sumerian King List" – under Ur-Namma (2112–2095 BC), son or brother of Utuhegal, began to consolidate power.

The son of Ur-Namma, Shulgi, who reigned nearly fifty years, transformed polit-ical administration in Mesopotamia, affecting major aspects of social and economic life. Beginning in his twentieth regnal year, he deified himself, created a standing army, reorganized temple households, established a new system of weights and mea-sures, began a series of campaigns near and far, and created a bureaucratic system that managed regular systems of taxation from the Mesopotamian core and a separate series of imposts from the periphery (Steinkeller 1987a). In the thirty-ninth year of his reign, he founded a depot, ancient Puzrish-Dagan (Arabic site name, Drehem), near the religious center of Nippur, mainly for the collection and distribution of animals (Sigrist 1992).

From Drehem (and texts from other sites), we read the details of receipts of animals classified according to species, origin, the sort of fodder consumed, color, the officials who brought them in, in which pens they were kept, and their eventual destinations (for example, to temple kitchens). In the texts (about 30,000 of which have been published [Civil 1987; Sallaberger 1999]), we note festivals, river ordeals, and votive offerings, among other things. On large tablets, clerks added the daily receipts into six-monthly or yearly accounts. The tablets were stored in baskets that were tagged (Jones and Snyder 1961), and a system of double-entry bookkeeping was invented (Hallo and Curtis 1959; Snell 1982). From other sites, notably Umma and Lagash, texts record the Ur III system of weaving (Jacobsen 1953a; Waetzoldt 1972), metalwork (Bjorkman 1968; Limet 1960; Loding 1974), leather-working (Stol 1983), pottery manufacture (Waetzoldt 1971; Steinkeller 1996), and woodworking and other craft work (e.g. Neumann 1987; Van De Mieroop 1987). Many studies have examined the recruitment of labor, which is meticulously recorded (Englund 1990; Maekawa 1987; Powell 1987; Waetzoldt 1987). Local rulers of cities like Lagash celebrated festivals in cities and villages in their provinces, collecting revenues and monitoring laborers (Beld 2002).

The traditional picture of the Ur III state is of an enormous bureaucratic pyramid controlling communal and private action. However, most of our documents come from royal archives or from temple archives that were under the control of the palace. There is evidence of private sales, mainly of humans as slaves and of animals, but also of house property and orchards (Steinkeller 1989). Hallo (1972) and Zettler (1987, 1992) have shown that temple offices were inherited and so controlled within elite families, and Maekawa (1996) has argued that some officials attempted to embezzle property and were punished for this by the state. One infers from Steinkeller's studies of "foresters from Umma" (1987b) and of pottery manufacturers (1996) that extended families were charged with providing goods to the state in return for land allotments.

The dynasty fell precipitously. The two immediate successors of Shulgi ruled nine years each and were occupied with defending outer provinces (Michalowski 1976; Wilcke 1970) and taxing the local economies to fund these ventures. During the twenty-four year reign of the last king, Ibbi-Sin, the fabric of the administration rapidly unraveled (Jacobsen 1953b). Local city-states began to assert their independence from Ur, and a provincial governor, Ishbi-Erra, from distant Mari up the Euphrates, seized power in the southern city of Isin. Within twenty-five years after the founding of Drehem, provinces and cities were able to break away from Ur's control and to resume their normal autonomy and neighborly struggles for hegemony. With supplies of food denied the capital, famine resulted, and the essentially unproductive and bloated bureaucracy fell asunder. Enemies of Ur on the margins of Mesopotamia conducted sorties into the heartland, eventually raiding Ur itself and dragging the dynasty's last king into captivity. Ishbi-Erra attempted to reorganize a rump state on the model of Ur's imperial system, but the scribal formularies of the Ur III administration were only hollow techniques in the absence of real dominion.

The collapse of the Third Dynasty of Ur has been ascribed in some Mesopotamian and modern accounts to activities of tribal groups, in particular Amorites. In the "Myth of Martu," for example, Amorites are described as uncivilized, for they "know not grain . . . eat uncooked meat" and do not bury their dead (Buccellati 1966:92–3, 330–31). Furthermore, a wall (really a series of fortresses) was erected to the northeast (from Ur) to protect the realm against groups of Amorites (Wilcke 1969; Michalowski 1976). Since kings with Amorite names led rival dynasties in newly independent city-states after the fall of Ur, these references have been interpreted to imply a process of conquest and assimilation of Amorites into Mesopotamian society. Amorite behavior is more complex than the data from literary compositions and royal inscriptions might suggest. Before and during the Ur III period, Amorites held royal commissions, appeared in military service to the crown, and were litigants in lawsuits. Amorites were interpreters, mayors, farmers, and weavers. Although some documents suggest that Amorites were rude, agricultural folk, others show them peacefully integrated within Mesopotamian society. Rather than apply a model of intrusion, conquest, and assimilation of Amorite foreigners into Mesopotamian society, a different scenario of social and political change has emerged to explain the collapse of the Ur III state.[3]

If all Amorites were not collectively ranged in hordes against the Ur III state, being Amorite was not yet beyond usefulness, especially in the political arena. Leaders of named sub-groupings of Amorites contested with all-comers after the fall of Ur, especially with other Amorite leaders, for control of rival city-states. Alliances and calls for ethnic solidarity were established between Amorite princes. Amnanum Amorites in Babylon and Uruk pledged mutual support, as the king of Uruk writes, in order to mobilize people from both city-states, since the leaders were "of one house" (Falkenstein 1963) – presumably of one lineage. The ethnic denotation of Amorites is justified, since being Amorite has little to do with any common subsistence pattern (pastoralists vs. agriculturalists), or a common residential pattern (nomads vs. city dwellers), or any common economic status. The term "tribe" or "tribal organization" does not seem appropriate to describe Amorite behavior, since tribe usually denotes a social organization without strong hierarchical authority and in which surplus production and storage are limited (Fried 1975; Sahlins 1968). The term "ethnic group," however, which allows for the existence of more than one type of social and economic organization within the same bounded unit, characterizes the range of activities of Amorites.

Genealogies uniting many groups of Amorites and also incorporating others were constructed by the most successful of Amorite leaders in Babylonia and Assyria after

---

[3] Salinization, once thought a contributing factor to the instability of the ruling house, now seems of little consequence (Powell 1985) in the story of the collapse of the Ur III state.

the fall of Ur (Kamp and Yoffee 1980). These genealogies, the "Assyrian King List" and the "Genealogy of Hammurabi," served to legitimize claims to regional power over many social groupings. Amorites came to power not as crude foreigners taking over power from effete urbanites, but as well-organized forces whose leaders, like Ishbi-Erra (the name is pure Amorite), were urban. They took advantage of the tottering Ur III state by using traditional bonds of kinship precisely because these bonds extended beyond the borders of particular city-states and so gave them a political advantage.

The Ur III dynasty typifies the apogee of centralization among early Mesopotamian states and is likewise the supreme example of an unsuccessful and short-lived attempt at pan-Mesopotamian political unity. To the brief time-span from about the last third of Sulgi's reign to the first third of Ibbi-Sin's ill-fated years, about forty years in all, we owe tens of thousands of economic documents now found in museum collections or in private hands all over the world. Similarly, the Ur III royal court commissioned magnificent hymns to its kings that were faithfully copied in the scribal academies of subsequent periods as classics of Sumerian literature (Hallo 1962, 1963). The quantity and quality of these sources from the royal house of Ur motivate scholarship today in roughly inverse proportion to the stability and normative character of the Ur III state.

The Old Babylonian and Old Assyrian states (ca. 2000–1600 BC)

Emerging from the period of political rivalries among city-states following the collapse of Ur (Goddeeris 2002; Van De Mieroop 2004), new coalitions began to form in Babylonia (southern Mesopotamia), eventually resulting in a northern core led by kings of Babylon, the sixth in this line being Hammurabi, and a southern core headed by Rim-Sin of Larsa. Hammurabi's defeat of territories to the west and east of Babylon culminated, in his thirty-first year, in a decisive victory over Rim-Sin and in the consequent unification of Babylonia from the Gulf roughly to today's Baghdad. Although many administrative documents, letters, and legal records attest to the vigor of his administration in Babylon, Hammurabi's empire, formed during the last years of his reign, was beset by a serious rebellion in the south during the ninth year of his son and successor and, in fact, did not outlive that son's reign. The northern core around the city of Babylon remained intact for another four generations of rulers, and the dynasty was finally removed in a raid by a Hittite king from Anatolia. Power was transferred to a "non-Mesopotamian" group of Kassites, probably originally from the Zagros mountain area. Some Kassites were in control of territory along the Middle Euphrates, others were residents of some Mesopotamian cities (Charpin 1977).

Evidence of economic and administrative documents written in the time of the last kings of the dynasty (Richardson 2002; Yoffee 1977) refutes the view that the royal house fell as if struck by "a bolt from the blue" (Postgate 1977:100, echoed by Oates 1979:84), namely by the Hittite raid. Indeed, the regional state imposed by Hammurabi on conquered territories was resisted from the outset. In spite of the proclamations in Hammurabi's so-called law code that all subject cities would prosper under his just rule, the provincial administration systematically bypassed local authorities and sought mainly to enrich the distant capital in Babylon (see Chapter 4).

In the initial success of the state, Hammurabi and his successor Samsu-iluna engineered great feats of canal irrigation, both to open up agricultural land and to enable easier transport of goods. They glorified the capital in Babylon by erecting temples and richly furnishing them. The loss of revenue accompanying the rebellion of the conquered territories in the south (for which see Chapter 5), however, did not bring with it a change in these royal activities. Building and waterworks projects were still undertaken and large pools of manpower had to be mobilized and military expeditions funded.

In order to support these operations the crown had to manage its diminished resources more intensively. Instead of maintaining squads of laborers year-round, the crown now had to hire manpower seasonally. Local headmen witnessed contracts of hire or even acted as middlemen by supplying harvest laborers. In the late Old Babylonian period, new officials were created by the crown precisely to negotiate these transactions with local authorities. Furthermore, the crown became a credit institution, loaning its supplies of wool and grain on a short-term basis, perhaps in order to pay these laborers and new officials for whom its own estates were unable to provide sufficiently. In these loan contracts sometimes a clause was inserted to the effect that the crown could call for repayment at any point it chose. If, however, it exercised this option before the term of the loan, it lost whatever interest would have accrued. Military officers in the provinces turned their territories into fiefdoms and withheld goods from the capital (Richardson 2002).

The archaeological surveys of Robert Adams (1981) have shown a progressive tendency during the late Old Babylonian period for once-nucleated settlement patterns to become dispersed into smaller communities that are more evenly spaced along watercourses. This settlement configuration was a predictable result of increased crown reliance on traditional local authorities and military leaders in the countryside who were able to resist the demands of the centralized state. Also, at the end of the Old Babylonian period, many loans were issued by temples (Harris 1960), a situation that contrasts markedly with that of Hammurabi's time (Charpin 1982). In times of obvious fiscal and political uncertainty, the temple seems to have provided a refuge for unfortunate citizens of Babylonia – and managed as well to make a profit from the pious debtors.

Carlo Cipolla (1970:7, 11) has asserted that:

in the early phase of a decline . . . the problem does not seem to be so much that of increasing visible inputs – capital or labour – as that of changing ways of doing things and increasing productivity. The survival of the political system demands such basic change. But it is typical of mature empires to give a negative response to this challenge . . . since change hurts vested interests.

Indeed, the Old Babylonian political system could have changed to meet the new conditions of the loss of Hammurabi's conquests, but it did not do so. The result was the disintegration of political authority into traditionally organized local units with their elites and the new elites of autonomous military garrisons. The character of the succeeding Kassite power structure has been called "tribal" (Brinkman 1980:464), because it was not highly centralized and land was owned by kinship groups. In sum, the collapse of the Old Babylonian dynasty of Hammurabi occurred not primarily as a result of externally applied pressures, but rather from the failure of central policies and the inability to establish a territorial state that was seen as legitimate in the eyes of conquered citizens of formerly autonomous city-states. This condition was easily exploited by local power blocks, ambitious military captains, foreign raiders, and leaders of ethnic groups whose members lived both in several cities and in the countryside.

Meanwhile, in north Mesopotamia (that is, Assyria), several Assyrian states rose and fell while Babylon was achieving power in the south. Situated in a dry-farming region and thus not completely dependent on irrigation for agricultural productivity, Assyria was a land of few cities, although cities in this region appeared as early as did those in the south (Emberling 2003). In the formative period of the Old Assyrian state in the twentieth century BC, Ilushuma, prince of the city of Assur, claimed he led an Assyrian force to Babylonia in order to "free" the citizens of several Babylonian cities. As plausibly interepreted by Mogens Trolle Larsen (1976), this campaign probably refers to Ilushuma's aim to open trade routes in the south to Assyrian merchants. There is no evidence of Assyrian domination of Babylonian cities in this period. Indeed, most of the sources for the Old Assyrian period are concerned with Assyrian mercantile activities (Veenhof 1997, 1999, 2001; Dercksen 1999, 2000; Michel 2001, 2003). Overwhelmingly, these sources come not from Assyria itself but from an Assyrian trading colony, Kanesh, located in the heart of Anatolia, about 470 miles northwest of Assur (Larsen 1974, 1976, 1977; Veenhof 1972, 1999; Dercksen 1999, 2000).

Mesopotamians in both the north and the south had been familiar with Anatolian resources – obsidian, copper (Derckser 1996), precious metals – for millenniums. Sargon of Akkade himself undertook a military campaign on behalf of merchants in Anatolia, as is reported in a literary text (Goodnick Westenholz 1997), and the monument of an Akkadian king has been found in southern Turkey (Lloyd 1978:138). During the Old Assyrian period (mainly in the nineteenth century BC), this trade was not based on Assyrian political control of any strategic resources or territory. Rather, the trade attested in thousands of economic documents and letters was clearly entrepreneurial. Assyrian family firms moved textiles, some obtained in Babylonia, and tin (whose origin is still obscure [Yener 2000]) from Assur to Anatolia by means of donkey caravans. There the Assyrian merchants exchanged these goods for silver and gold, which they shipped to Assur.

Profit was made solely on organizational ability, Assyrians moving goods from where they were plentiful to where they were scarce. For example, in Assur, where silver was scarce, the silver to tin ratio was about 1:15, whereas in Anatolia, where silver was comparatively plentiful, the ratio was about 1:7 (Veenhof 1972). If fifteen units of tin could be economically transported from Assur to Anatolia, two units of silver could be obtained. These two units of silver could then be brought to Assur and turned into thirty units of tin. Assuming a constant demand, the knowledge of where and how to get tin, and the technology of how to move the tin to Anatolia, great profit could be and was made by Assyrian merchants. Long-term business contracts were negotiated whereby joint capital could be accumulated and continuity in business relationships assured for decades (Larsen 1977). In one such document, an Assyrian state official sanctions the proceedings, thus attesting to the interest the Assyrian government had in trade. Indeed, the leading merchant families of Assur held high government ranks, and the early Old Assyrian state was administered by councils of "great and small," at a city-hall, which co-existed along with the king and royal court. It is in this light that Ilushuma seems to have campaigned to open and/or to keep open markets so that this system of international venture trade could function in one of its important nodes. Assyrian kings also established treaties (Eidem 1991; Derckser 2000; Veenhof 2003b) with potentates so that Assyrian traders could ply their wares.

Why did this profitable mercantile system that supported the activities of the Assyrian state collapse? Although the Old Assyrian trading system continued through the conquest of Assyria by Shamshi-Adad, an Amorite prince from the middle Euphrates area near Mari in the early eighteenth century BC, dislocations in the activities of merchants and especially their access to governmental councils were severely affected (in ways not yet fully studied). This Old Assyrian state, which saw itself as the continuation of native dynasties (Larsen 1976), collapsed after the short-lived rule of the sons of Shamshi-Adad, and indeed Assyria disappears from historical records for about four hundred years. It is significant that Old Assyrian trade flourished during the period in which there was no single political power in Babylonia, namely in the time before Hammurabi. Similarly, in Assyria itself the power of the king was circumscribed by councils of elites, including the heads of merchant families, although merchants were obliged to obey laws, remit taxes to the palace, and caused the state to prosper through their activities. By the early eighteenth century BC, however, the regional political situation had changed. Babylonia was united by Hammurabi, and Anatolia, previously a land of many princes, was coming under the power of the emergent Hittite state. Old Assyrian trade, for all its immense prosperity, was extremely fragile. The Assyrian merchant colonies and the Assyrian political system that flourished on the profits of the trade were dependent on the relatively unrestricted passage of traders and goods over long distances. When constraints were imposed on this passage by the rise of strong centralized governments that attempted to control production and exchange, foreign trade and the political system that was built upon it were jeopardized. After Shamshi-Adad's imperial ambitions in Assyria came to nought, the Old Assyrian political and economic system seems to have been reduced to the essentially rural countryside that was its original base. Only as a response to military pressures five hundred years later did a new centralized state rise in Assyria.

THE END OF THE CYCLE?

By the middle of the second millennium BC, the former Mesopotamian political and economic centrality in Western Asian affairs had broken down considerably. New states appeared in Iran, Syria, and Anatolia that were as strong as those in Assyria and Babylonia. Although the scribes in these states wrote mostly in the cuneiform script that was developed to represent Sumerian and Akkadian, they adapted it to write their own languages and literatures. In the fourteenth century BC, Assyria experienced a political renascence, substantially in response to new states on its borders that were threatening it. By creating an effective military regime to combat these enemies, which included the Kassite state of Babylonia to the south of them, Assyrian kings began to centralize their power at the expense of the traditional Assyrian nobility that had shared power in the Old Assyrian state. The constant fighting resulted in a tough and large Assyrian army, which expansionist kings led throughout Western Asia. The climax of this expansion came in the seventh century, with Assyrian hegemony over

Egypt, the Levant, and southern Mesopotamia. This climax, however, was followed rapidly by the loss of these territories. The Assyrian army was defeated in 614 BC by Medes from Iran and soon thereafter by a coalition of Medes and Babylonians. Except for a few outposts (Postgate 1994) and some individuals named in Babylonian documents (Zadok 1984), Assyrian political and social institutions ceased to exist in Assyria.

Why did the Assyrian state fall, and why did it not rise again? The reforms of the Assyrian king Tiglath-Pileser III in the eighth century BC marked the high point of the increasingly centralized royal administration of Assyria. At this time, the policies of governing vast expanses of territory included mass deportations (as a last resort against recalcitrant provinces) to Assyria or elsewhere in the empire (Oded 1979). These deportees provided important labor in the foundation of lavish new royal capitals that several kings built to mark administrative and dynastic changes and as military personnel.

One of the more interesting facets of Assyrian policy concerned its "Babylonian problem." This "cultural struggle," already detectable in the second millennium BC (Machinist 1976), preoccupied Assyrian affairs in its latter years. For Assyrians, Babylonia was the heartland of Mesopotamian culture, although, in Assyrian eyes, it was also politically chaotic and even decadent. When an increasingly anti-Assyrian Babylonia was defeated by Sennacherib in 689 BC and Babylon itself was pillaged, the carnage was considered an impiety in Assyria itself and, after the assassination of Sennacherib, his successor Esarhaddon rebuilt Babylon and restored its prosperity. Then, an Assyrian prince, Shamash-shum-ukin, was installed as king of Babylonia, although subject to his younger, but abler, brother Asshurbanipal, who took the throne in Assyria. In short order, Shamash-shum-ukin led a revolt against Assyria that lasted four years and ended with a total Assyrian victory. The ruinous civil war severely diverted manpower and wealth from Assyria's other pressing foreign-policy needs. The loss of taxes and tribute from the West could hardly be overcome, and the opportunity for subject territories to consolidate their forces and resolution was not missed. The Mesopotamian civil war was very much a Pyrrhic victory for the Assyrians.

It is relatively easy to understand why, with the defeat of the Assyrian army in 614, the Assyrian state fell. It is less easy and much more important to explain why it did not regenerate, as many defeated states in Mesopotamia had done. Obviously, the loss of revenues to support the enormous military and bureaucratic establishments meant the certain failure of Assyrian urban life. However, it is also clear that the agricultural basis for the Assyrian economy had also been undermined by having to provide for the army's expeditionary ventures and the new capitals of imperial administration. The old rural estates, now worked by substantial numbers of unfree and non-Assyrian labor, had been increasingly granted to generals and bureaucrats for their services to the realm. Since the Assyrian state rested on the success of its military machine, when enemies struck a mortal blow at a weakened Assyria, not only did the empire and state dissolve, but the Assyrian heartland itself was reduced to its very basis of agricultural subsistence. The population of Assyria, which included a large number of deported people, was no longer predominantly Assyrian, and the traditional nobility had long been systematically removed as a hindrance to royal centralization and military efficiency.

No reformulation from such a collapse was possible. Most of the people in the countryside and in what remained of Assyrian cities were non-Assyrians who had been incorporated within the empire, many forcibly imported. These people did not think of themselves or of their culture as Mesopotamian, as is indicated by the increased use in Assyria of the Aramaic language alongside Assyrian, which it eventually outweighed. One reason for the overt displays of "Mesopotamian-ness" by the Assyrian warrior kings – for example, by gathering classics of Mesopotamian literature in vast libraries – may well have been the attempt to stress traditional ties with a past they themselves no longer shared with many of the inhabitants of Assyria. Such displays may also have played roles in the internecine power struggles within the Assyrian ruling elite.

As Assyrian fortunes waned, those of Babylonia waxed ephemerally bright. Powerful kings from the Chaldean tribes, which had consolidated their power in Babylonia (partly in response to Assyrian intervention there in the seventh century BC), ruled the south in the aftermath of the Assyrian collapse. One of these, Nebuchadnezzar II, mimicked the Assyrian strategy of campaigning abroad and deporting large segments of rebellious populations to his homeland. The end of Babylonia, too, followed closely its greatest imperial success. The reign of the last king of Babylonia, Nabonidus, who spent his final decade at the oasis of Tayma in western Arabia (Michalowski 2003), was brought to an end by Cyrus the Great of Persia, perhaps to the relief of important elements of the Babylonian population. Once the hub of the Western Asian universe, Mesopotamia had become now merely a province, albeit an important one, in a completely new form of imperial system.

Collapse as the mutation of social identity and suffocation of cultural memory

Although political systems in Mesopotamia had passed from Mesopotamian hands to foreigners, Mesopotamian civilization did not undergo a similar collapse.

Mesopotamian culture persisted in belief systems, languages and traditional learning, material objects and buildings, and local assemblies. Non-native rulers honored venerable rituals and sponsored the composition of royal inscriptions that proclaimed their control of Mesopotamia. Of course, social and cultural change did occur, and by the time the last cuneiform document was written, the once-vital civilization had been reduced to a recondite and dying art. Finally, even the memory of Mesopotamia was barely kept alive, less by the peoples who lived in Mesopotamia than by those whom Mesopotamians had once conquered.

If the rise of Mesopotamian civilization is not simply or most significantly about when the state appeared but concerns the creation of new ideologies about who has power and how it is got, and how social identities are transformed in the process, we can ask a new kind of question about the collapse of Mesopotamian civilization: why was it reasonably important for people to be "Mesopotamian" in the fourth century BC, and why was it of little or no practical use to be "Mesopotamian" in the first century AD?

Discussing the nature of "Mesopotamian" identity leads to an irony. Over time, the amount of ethnic and linguistic diversity in Mesopotamia increased. However, the expected increase in cultural heterogeneity, which might have challenged "Mesopotamian-ness," is often extremely difficult to detect other than in the personal names of people, including royal personages. Although attempts have been made to match this or that bit of material culture or literary expression or legal institution or religious practice with one or another of the ethnic groups, this task has not been successful. To date, although the presence of Amorites and Kassites in Mesopotamian history is important and undeniable, not one text in the Amorite or Kassite language has been found.[4]

In the record of more than three thousand years, Mesopotamian culture was not sealed and static, of course, but had to be learned and transmitted and to be of social importance to its members. Indeed, Mesopotamian culture was preserved for three millenniums, in some cases almost in ossified form,[5] over diverse social orientations and city-state and regional spheres of political independence. The appearance of new ethnic groups and new cultural systems does not explain why Mesopotamian culture was no longer transmitted. Leaders of ethnic groups which were not bounded within particular city-states or regions had a clear interest in maintaining and reproducing Mesopotamian cultural institutions, not fractionalizing Mesopotamian culture. Rather, by adopting venerable institutions and conservatively preserving them, they

---

[4] Grammars of both of these languages have been written exclusively from analyses of personal names, which contain a certain amount of linguistic features (Gelb 1980; Balkan 1954).

[5] The last Mesopotamian texts were written partly in Sumerian, a language that had not been spoken in the land for more than two thousand years before these late texts were written (Cooper 1999).

could legitimize their governance. It is not so much that these ethnic groups were assimilated into Mesopotamian society as that they actually became the *carriers* and guardians of Mesopotamian cultural tradition. Ethnic group leaders ruled the land as Mesopotamians.

The position of ethnic groups as insiders in Mesopotamia, however, changed over time. In the first millennium BC, neo-Assyrian and neo-Babylonian policies of forced incorporation of foreigners[6] were obviously different from the processes of social interaction in the third and second millenniums BC. With the conquest of Babylonia by Cyrus the Great, the many local social orientations in Mesopotamia (and in his other subject territories) seem to have been equally and explicitly recognized by the new rulers as long as they did not come into conflict with imperial Persian ideology. Although Cyrus modeled his inscriptions on Assyro-Babylonian antecedents, and documents dated to Achaemenid Persian kings look much like neo-Babylonian examples, rulers of this period did not attempt to promote their "Mesopotamianness," and a return to a Mesopotamian ideology of rule was impossible.

Alexander the Great conquered the Achaemenid Persian dynasty in 333 BC, and Hellenistic rule, under the Seleucid dynasty, lasted until 143 BC; in that time the identities of the inhabitants of Mesopotamia underwent decisive change.[7] Although these changes may seem inevitable, scholarly opinion on the impact of foreign rule in Mesopotamia has been divided. Views of the impact of the Greeks themselves have changed in recent years and have affected the way we might explain collapse. Traditionally, Hellenistic studies could be characterized as investigating the conscious and purposeful diffusion of Greek language and culture throughout the Hellenistic world. Greeks were driven by a civilizing mission to infuse superior Greek culture into the despotic and superstitious kingdoms of Egypt and Western Asia (Bury 1925; Green 1990). In modern interpretations, however, politically correct Greek scholars find Greek culture was quite isolated from native life and its impact limited (Walbank 1993; Sherwin-White and Kuhrt 1993). Once proud of the Greek civilizing influence on the East, Classicists now seem pleased to portray the gentle or practically small impact of Westerners on the historic ways of Mesopotamia. Seleucids helpfully rebuilt Mesopotamian temples, used Mesopotamian literary forms, inherited functioning political organizations, and hardly dented the social and cultural systems of the land. In the view of some, it was the Greeks who got "orientalized" rather than the other way around (Potts 1997).

---

[6] The first deportations by the renascent Middle Assyrian kings occurred towards the end of the second millennium BC.

[7] Jane Rempel has provided much of the research and analysis of Hellenistic Mesopotamia (see Rempel and Yoffee 1999).

But what did change? Is the present view a reflection of new, self-effacing trends in Classical scholarship, signs of more sensitive, anti-colonialist and respectful Classicists, who are determined to banish the specter of Hellenism, and her bed-mate, Orientalism, from Hellenistic Mesopotamia?

Much hangs on whether and how ethnic incorporation in Mesopotamia had changed in this period, whether people resisted attempts to dissolve their identity when incorporated within a larger society, and how they perceived social, economic, and/or political advantage. In considering civilizational collapse as a mutation of social identity, the main concern is whether and, if so, why Mesopotamians minimized their differences with Greeks, including differences in their material culture. Although many archaeologists have found many aspects of continuity in certain classes of material culture, one needs to evaluate the meaning of this continuity.

According to Classical conventions, the most notable aspect of the material record of Hellenistic Mesopotamia is the appearance of traditionally Greek installations. The Seleucids founded a series of new cities throughout their kingdom, the most notable being Seleucia-on-the-Tigris (Downey 1988; Invernizzi 1993). The straight layout of streets and the presence of an agora and a theater conform to the canon of newly founded cities throughout the Hellenistic world. Additionally, a clear Seleucid presence can be confirmed in existing Mesopotamian cities. In Babylon itself there was a Hellenistic Greek occupation concentrated in the *homera* mound of the city. In this area there are the remains of a Greek theater, Greek pottery, figures, and seals all dating from the third century BC. Other Greek fixtures in Babylon, such as a gymnasium used for the mental and physical education of Greeks, have been attested through inscriptions.

These clear Hellenistic Greek imprints on the archaeological record of Seleucid Mesopotamia exist in concert with equally clear instances of continuities in the functioning of Mesopotamian society. The textual record, for example, indicates the continuation of traditional methods of recording historical events, such as the persistence of Babylonian chronicles and astronomical diaries. In addition, archives of clay tablets provide evidence for continuities in legal and administrative practices, that temple estates were still in existence, and that heads of these estates were notables in their respective cities. This picture of certain continuities in Mesopotamian culture existing alongside examples of a Seleucid Greek imprint on the landscape is particularly agreeable to the current "isolationist" interpretations of a Greeks–Mesopotamians divide in this period.

However, the continued functioning of a traditional Babylonian temple administration occurred with the acceptance and support of the Seleucid administration, and this fundamentally altered the nature and boundary of authority of the temple and its community. Seleucid support was anything but tacit, since traditional sanctuaries were rebuilt, enlarged, and refurbished, for example, in Uruk (Potts 1997:291; Downey 1988; Sherwin-White 1987), the oldest Mesopotamian city of all, where there was a resurgence of the temple of Anu. Whereas documents attest that the rebuilding of these temples in Uruk was undertaken by an old, established Urukian family, whose leading members were Anu-uballiṭ Nicharchos and Anu-uballiṭ Kephalon, funding was supplied and sanctioned by Seleucid kings. Seleucid kings themselves renovated sanctuaries in Babylon and Borsippa. In addition to these physical rebuildings, Seleucid rulers participated in rituals in the temples. Seleucids offered land grants and tax exemptions to Babylonian elites, and the Babylonian elite in turn made sure that Seleucids were viewed as a favorable stage in Mesopotamian history (Sherwin-White 1987).

Clearly the Seleucids had an active policy of patronage of the traditional structures of Mesopotamian life. Whether their motivation was purely political or whether they were responsive to Mesopotamian traditions on a more personal level, this patronage resulted in the sponsorship and promotion of Mesopotamian institutions and organizations, especially religious ones. However, these institutions functioned within the realm of Seleucid political power. By supporting certain Mesopotamian features, the Seleucids disempowered traditions, rendered organizations benign, and delimited their character and denuded them of political impact.

That a new avenue to political power had been introduced can be seen from Seleucid support of non-traditional, i.e. Hellenistic Greek, identities among the Mesopotamian elite. For example, the first Urukian mentioned above, Anu-uballiṭ Nicharchos, received his second name, which is Greek, as a gift from the Seleucid king Antiochus II, and Anu-uballiṭ recorded this fact prominently on the foundation deposit of his reconstruction of the Bīt Rēš sanctuary – the act of a pious and traditional Mesopotamian. Berossus, a Mesopotamian cleric, wrote a history of Babylonia in Greek, using Seleucid dates and Greek philosophical concepts, for a Seleucid audience, not one of his fellow Babylonians. Seleucids interacted with Mesopotamians and supported Mesopotamian institutions, but they did so on their Hellenistic Greek terms, using Hellenistic Greek conventions. The result was a proliferation of identities, not simply "Greek" and/or "Mesopotamian" ones (Hall 1997, 2002; Malkin, ed. 2001).[8]

A brief look at the material culture of the age underscores the point. In Hellenistic Babylonia, seals were used by Seleucid officers, municipal officials, and private individuals. They were used to seal Greek or Aramaic texts written on parchment

---

[8] I thank Daniel Shoup and Seth Button for drawing these references to my attention.

and to validate cuneiform texts written on clay tablets. Not surprisingly, the Seleucid seals carried the name of the officer or office in Greek and were decorated with Hellenistic Greek imagery, often similar to that found on Seleucid coins (Wallenfels 1996). There are also private seals on cuneiform texts, many decorated with traditional Mesopotamian motifs (Invernizzi 1984). There are, however, private Babylonian seals with Greek iconography, and personal choice appears to have determined this use. For example, one prominent Mesopotamian family, with many high-level religious and civic administrators among its ranks, chose to depict Seleucid-style motifs in seals of its members. At the same time, another Urukian family chose to revive specific Neo-Babylonian seal motifs that had not been employed for several centuries. Not only can this be seen as a personal choice, it is a choice that must have carried considerable weight and import. The use of an older, traditional social currency or, alternatively, a purposeful association with a new one was a decision that must have been made in full awareness of the existence of the other option.

The pottery of Seleucid Mesopotamia similarly reflects a mélange of continuities and changes (Hannestad 1988; Valtz 1991). Whereas the bulk of the ceramic evidence points to a considerable continuity in pottery production, the marked introduction of new forms shows that continuities in ware or form were chosen or continued to exist in an environment where other options were available, and even more desirable in some circumstances.

This overview of some of the perceived continuities and changes in the material culture of Hellenistic Mesopotamia illustrates that the labeling dichotomy of "continuity" or "change" is not particularly helpful in understanding the impact of Hellenism on Mesopotamians. One does not see a picture of holistic change, but even clear continuities do not function in an unchanged world and, because of this, they may be questioned as continuities. That is, material continuity was not simply an act of following unquestioned cultural forms but was a kind of subversion, since a choice of displaying "Mesopotamian-ness" was significant in a world in which being Mesopotamian was not free of consequences. A facile quantitative assessment of overall artifactual continuity masks the social tensions that can be observed in finer-grained analyses of material culture.

It is interesting that the overt patronage of Mesopotamian religion, as well as many major Greek constructions, can be dated to the reigns of the earlier Seleucid kings, or roughly the third century BC. Throughout the Seleucid period, however, the cuneiform archives were progressively limited towards more restricted, religious contexts, as the Seleucid administration increasingly demanded that documentation be recorded on Greek (or Aramaic) parchment (Doty 1977). Also, by the second century BC, Mesopotamians commonly bore Greek second names and occasionally had pure Greek names.

Some traditional literary and socioeconomic forms can no longer be attested among the cuneiform texts of the period, and some new texts were composed. For example, the "late Babylonian list of scholars" (Klotchkoff 1982), whose date in the Seleucid system corresponds to 165 BC, records the names of ancient Mesopotamian sages and the kings they advised. The text is not a copy of an ancient tablet, strictly speaking, but an original attempt to portray Mesopotamian history and some of its most famous figures. It draws on the venerable tradition of the seven sages (Reiner 1961) and Mesopotamian king lists. The learned author of the text makes many mistakes – at least by modern scholarly standards – in several of his historical references, and the text was "written by a nostalgic Babylonian erudite in order to save from oblivion the knowledge about the glorious Babylonian past" (Klotchkoff 1982:154). Mesopotamian culture lived on, but only (or mainly) in temple estates, and the many texts from this late period are records of the temples' economic as well as their ritual activities. The vestiges of this community continued to produce cuneiform texts for another three hundred years, the last, wistful texts containing barely decipherable wedges on one side and hopeful transliterations on the other.

The collapse of Mesopotamian civilization and its regeneration

After the conquest by Cyrus, the role of Mesopotamian culture in legitimizing statecraft and incorporating the participation of the multiplicity of social orientations in Mesopotamia became progressively reduced. Mesopotamian culture was only one of several available options, and one that was useful only in increasingly restricted contexts. Eventually, Mesopotamian documents dealt only with the atrophied temples and their landholdings.

Although Mesopotamian civilization did not collapse in pace with the fall of the state in Mesopotamia, the demise of the Mesopotamian political system did mean that subscription to Mesopotamian cultural norms no longer provided any advantage in the spheres of official life or in economic activities now in the hands of Achaemenid Persian, Seleucid, and eventually Parthian administrations. Mesopotamian culture had been demoted, in effect, to one among many social orientations. Progressively, under Seleucid and later administrations, traditional Mesopotamian identities became only dim reflections of an antique past, especially for members of the various and newly incorporated ethnic groups who had little reason to identify with, much less actively preserve and transmit, the heritage of Mesopotamia.

However, a conclusion that Mesopotamian identity, shed for good reasons and then moribund for about two millenniums, had irrevocably perished is erroneous. One result of the excavations in Iraq and decipherments of the ancient scripts by Europeans in the mid-nineteenth century has been a revivification of Mesopotamian identity. People who today identify themselves as Chaldeans and whose sacred texts are in Aramaic trace their ancestry to the Chaldeans of southern Iraq who ruled southern Mesopotamia in the seventh and sixth centuries BC.[9] Modern Assyrians, from northern Iraq and nearby lands, whose liturgy is also in Aramaic, identify themselves as heirs to the ancient kings and people of Assyria. Although modern Chaldeans and Assyrians assert strongly their connection with the most ancient historical past of pre-Islamic Iraq, more Chaldeans and Assyrians now live in the USA, especially in the Detroit and Chicago areas, than in Iraq itself.

In 1990, in the midst of the first Gulf War, when the ruler of Iraq had invaded Kuwait, I was watching an American newscast of events on one of the major channels. The anchorman reported over pictures of Saddam Hussein, whom he described as dressed in the costume of Nebuchadnezzar II, king of Babylon, who sacked Jerusalem and deported tens of thousands of Jews to Iraq. The implication was clear that Saddam Hussein, just like his honored ancestor, intended the destruction of the Jewish state. However, there on the screen, as anyone who had studied Mesopotamian history and archaeology could see, was Saddam Hussein dressed as Hammurabi, the "lawgiver" of Babylon. Was this sloppy journalism or was it disinformation fed to the TV network by the US State Department? Of course, it is a considerable irony that Hammurabi was no lawgiver but in fact a ruthless conqueror of his own land and a consummate propagandist who cloaked his conquests in the rhetoric of justice and equity.

The scribes who wrote the Gilgamesh Epic had their hero proclaim, among other things, that heroic deeds are meaningful only when they are suitably published and find their way into the school curriculum. The rediscovery of ancient Mesopotamia in the nineteenth century AD proves Gilgamesh correct, because modern students began to learn anew about Mesopotamia and its most famous hero. Ancient Mesopotamia is again important for those concerned about the background of the Bible, for modern Mesopotamians who study their own history, and for those who seek to control the destiny of the Mesopotamian past.

9 Chaldean kings include Merodach-Baladan, Nebuchadnezzar II, and Belshazzar.

7

SOCIAL EVOLUTIONARY
TRAJECTORIES

The worst thing one can do with words is to surrender to them.

GEORGE ORWELL

Although recent investigations into the collapse of states have opened new avenues to the exploration of social change that does not lead to "higher" levels of social integration, archaeologists are only beginning to consider the evolutionary distinctiveness of prehistoric societies that few would label a state. These societies have their own histories and cannot be relegated as stages in overall global trajectories towards states. For example, Susan McIntosh and colleagues (McIntosh 1999) have discarded the old neo-evolutionist band-tribe-chiefdom-state taxonomy in order to characterize "alternate" forms of leadership in prehistoric African societies. In his *Society Against the State*, the anthropologist Pierre Clastres (1989) argued that some societies not only were not on a putative, normative pathway to statehood but also resisted such a social trajectory.

To the extent that archaeologists have sought to explain different evolutionary pathways, they have, not unnaturally, focused on environmental conditions. In prehistoric Australian hunter-gatherer societies, one observes no great inequalities in economic power, no privileged access to symbols of community legitimacy that integrate forms of social heterogeneity, and no specialized political roles apart from those determined within the web of kinship (Mulvaney and Kamminga 1999; Murray 1998). Although significant changes in technology and economy occurred in Australian prehistory, they did not lead to village farming communities, much less states. Archaeologists have evaluated possible reasons for this, including the lack of suitable plants and animals to domesticate, adaptations to extreme aridity, frequent droughts and raging fires, and long-term, successful patterns of nomadic lifeways that offered little incentive to increase the yield of localized plants and to produce storable surpluses (Flood 1990). That is, the clear and important economic changes in Australian hunting and gathering were not transformative, and large-scale changes in social and political organization did not attend them. Indeed, there were instances in which a trajectory towards social and economic differentiation and stratification was involuted. Rhys Jones (1978) studied a situation in which prehistoric Tasmanians stopped eating fish after many hundreds of years in which fish were an important part of their diet. Whereas this decision makes no sense to some archaeologists, it shows for others that choices made by hunter-gatherers cannot be reduced to optimal strategies for exploiting the environment. Jones (1977) also considered that the separation of Tasmania from the mainland, which occurred after the rise in ocean levels after the Pleistocene, limited contacts with the mainland and restricted the flow of ideas into Tasmania. The result was an "impoverishment" in the variety of tools in comparison with the mainland. The history of Aboriginal Australia is rich and complex, and it can by no means be consigned to a stage in the evolution of states.

EVOLUTIONARY HISTORY OF THE CHACO "RITUALITY"

The argument about environmental instability and especially of prolonged drought as a "constraint" on the evolution of societies can be examined in light of archaeological research in Chaco Canyon, New Mexico.[1] Chaco Canyon, part of the San Juan Basin in northwestern New Mexico (see Figures 7.1, 7.2), was the center of the Anasazi/ancestral pueblo world from about AD 900 to 1150 (or a little later). In 850 Chaco was much like everywhere else in the northern Southwest[2] and, on

---

[1] A number of new studies on Chaco have resulted from a series of conferences sponsored by the National Park Service, and I draw considerably on the result of these new essays (Cordell, Judge, and Piper 2001; Kantner and Mahoney 2000; Cameron and Toll 2001). See also the overviews in Cordell 1997, Plog 1997, Mills 2002, Kantner 2003, and Noble 2004, and detailed analyses in Lekson 1999, Vivian 1990, Sebastian 1992, and Doyel 1992. (This is by no means an exhaustive list of the recent publications on Chaco. A "capstone" volume synthesizing the separate volumes and papers from the National Park Service conferences will be edited by Steve Lekson – see Lekson 2005.) This chapter on Chaco is only an outsider's appreciation of the archaeological work on Chaco that continues, fortunately, unabated.

[2] Shabik'eschee village in Chaco in AD 500, however, was one of the largest pithouses villages in the region and significantly had a great kiva. Richard Wilshusen, Mark Varien, and their colleagues working in southwestern Colorado have suggested there was a migration from substantial but not multistoried villages in the Pueblo I period into the San Juan Basin at the end of the 800s (Joan Mathien, personal communication).

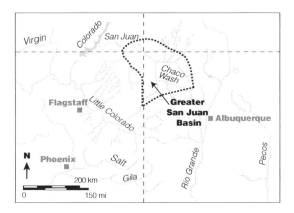

Figure 7.1 Northern Southwest (after Adler 1996:2)

environmental grounds, does not seem the foremost candidate for the spectacular social transformations that ensued. Summers were short and hot, winters long
and bitterly cold, edible plants and animals were few, and there was little wood for
fires and for building. There was not much land to cultivate, and water for irrigation was available only periodically but often in large quantities (Lekson 1994). In
contrast to the even harsher environment of the San Juan basin, which surrounded
Chaco Canyon, however, Chaco was something of an oasis (Vivian 2003; Judge 2003).
Chacoans constructed gridded gardens, canal systems, dams, and exploited a small
natural lake. Although Chaco was environmentally a good place to live in the San
Juan Basin, it offered less water, worse soils, and fewer trees and other resources than
neighboring regions on the edge of the basin that were well known to Chacoans.

In 1050 there was a "big bang"[3] at Chaco, which became distinguished by its "great
houses," the largest of which is Pueblo Bonito (see Figures 7.3, 7.4, 7.5), a four- or five-
story structure built of sandstone masonry and holding about 650 rooms. Although
the great houses had distinctive shapes (Figure 7.4), they were all multistoried blocks
of rooms around a central plaza. Most of the rooms were not residential, since they
lacked the signatures of domestic life, such as hearths. There were, however, large
cooking pits in the plazas of some great houses. Entering the canyon, the sight of
Chacoan grandeur must have been awe-inspiring. An Anasazi who had seldom or
never seen a structure larger than a few "unit-pueblos," which consisted of a dozen
(or fewer) rooms and a kiva (or circular structure used for ceremonies) and housed

---

[3] Or, a second big bang, following the initial burst of development at Chaco, 850–900. Chaco researchers now
often use the term "big bang," which was adopted by Tim Pauketat to explain the rapid development of
Cahokia (see below).

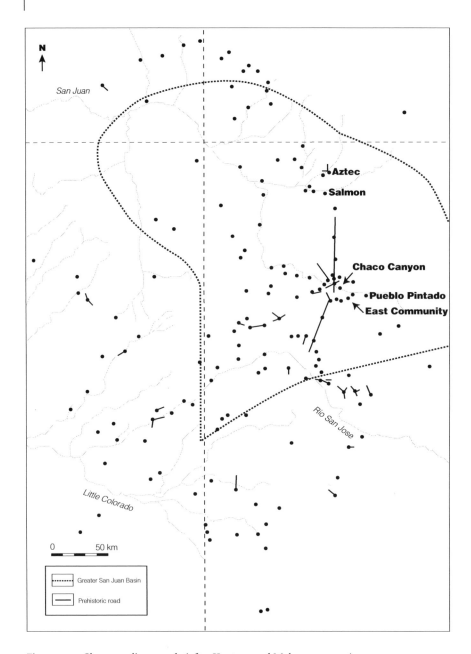

Figure 7.2   Chaco, outliers, roads (after Kantner and Mahoney 2000:2)

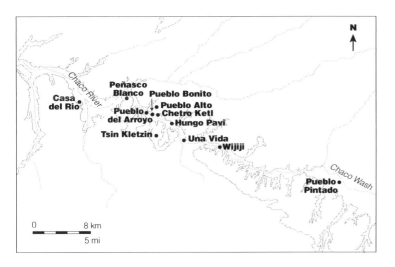

Figure 7.3 Great house sites of Chaco Canyon (after Doyel 1992:76)

a nuclear or extended family, rarely grouped into modest villages, was confronted by a cleft in the earth that was filled with a dozen, comparatively huge structures that were without precedent in the Anasazi world.

The great houses were clustered on the north side of the canyon, "confronting and balancing the earth shapes" (after Scully, quoted in Stein and Lekson 1994:52), whereas "small houses" (single-story structures with kivas incorporated in the roomblocks) were situated on the other side of the canyon. There were also "communities" of smaller structures associated with many of the great houses. Trash mounds near the great houses were themselves monumental constructions, and excavations at some (especially Pueblo Alto) have shown that the trash was stratified. After episodes of feasting and deposition, trash weathered until the next episode.[4] There were formal paths (or roads) between the mounds and great houses that created routes and lines of sight to other monumental structures. Great kivas, shrines, observation and signaling posts, and ramps were integrated into the landscape.

Since few of the rooms in the great houses in Chaco were permanently occupied, the population of the entire canyon was modest, in the neighborhood of about three thousand people (Kantner and Mahoney 2000; see Cordell and Judge [2001:8], who estimate the population of the "Chaco *region*" at less than three thousand; see also Bernardini 1999, Neitzel 2003). Lekson (1999) estimates the population of the

---

[4] Wirt Wills's (2001) argument that the *construction* of trash mounds was not for a ritual purpose is critically considered by Catherine Cameron (2002).

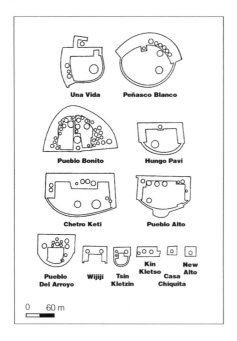

Figure 7.4   Shapes of great houses (after Lekson 1987:3)

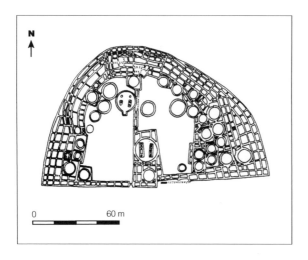

Figure 7.5   Pueblo Bonito (after Cordell 1984:251)

San Juan Basin (about 40,000 km²) in the low tens of thousands and that of the entire "northern Southwest" (about 600,000 km²) at about one hundred thousand.

Indications of status, prestige, and wealth at Chaco are notable. Macaws, parrots and copper bells from Mexico, shells from the Pacific coast, and turquoise from other regions of the Southwest stand out in assemblages and contexts of household production. Chacoans clearly knew about Mesoamerica, and the status of elites was presumably increased by the acquisition of exotic items, but these few indications of contact show the relatively minor degree of Mesoamerican influence rather than its pervasive and determinative presence at Chaco.

There are two elaborate burials in the earlier stages of Pueblo Bonito (Pepper 1920; Akins 2003), one with his head smashed and showing chop and cut marks suggesting a violent death. These burials were accompanied by thousands of beads and pendants and pieces of turquoise, along with dozens of ceremonial sticks and hundreds of vessels. Above the two bodies sixteen burials were placed on a wood floor, and they were also accompanied by precious objects. In 1909 G. R. Pepper thought the main burials represented members of the priesthood, and Nancy Akins (2003) finds no reason to disagree with this assessment. Pepper thought some of the items resembled "badges of office carried by Hopi and Zuni priests" during cere-monies (Akins 2003:96). Ritual caches were found in another great house, Chetro Ketl (Vivian, Dodgen, and Hartmann 1978). Residents of great houses were better nour-ished (that is, they were larger) than those in small houses, and the pathologies in the elite bodies are not the same as in non-elite individuals. Joan Mathien (2003) concludes that the large amounts of turquoise (56,000 pieces) recovered in the two burials at Pueblo Bonito (and in the less impressive burials of about a hundred other individuals) were ritual items, but the total volume of all the pieces would fit in a single grocery bag (Mathien, personal communication, 2003). Although some archaeolo-gists have inferred social stratification at Chaco from the impressive architecture, Mary Metcalf (2003:78) considers that "all of Pueblo Bonito's eleventh-century con-struction could have been completed by 30 people working 40 hours per week for 10 years."

Pottery was imported into Chaco and found typically in the communities around great houses. The connections of Chaco to its region are described as the "Chaco system" or the "Chaco phenomenon." A system of roads connected an area of "out-liers" – pueblos strongly resembling great houses – of about 100,000 km² (38,000 mi²) and also great houses within the canyon (Figure 7.2 above). These "roads," often only short segments approaching pueblos, were up to 10 m wide in the canyon. Leading to one prominent outlier, Salmon Ruin, the "Great North Road" split into four parallel segments. The roads were not simply transportation routes, since they were finely built, "over-engineered," and too broad in parts to have been designed to transport crops, goods (including cooking pots), and logs (which were brought from up to 80 km from Chaco). The Chaco outliers consisted of about 200 (or more) sites, large and small, which evince the same architectural characteristics of the Chaco great houses. "For more than 200 years, Chaco Canyon was the locus of the most elaborate manifestation of these structures" (Kantner and Mahoney 2000:7).

Although some archaeologists have described Chaco as a tribute-gathering state (Wilcox 1993), most Chaco experts have been impressed with the arguments of Toll (1984, 1985) and Judge (1989) that Chaco was a ritually based pilgrimage center (see Renfrew 2001). The major dissenter from this trend is Stephen Lekson (1999, 2000), who considers that Chaco was an elaborately planned ceremonial city, Pueblo Bonito was a palace (as were other great houses), and an elite community in Chaco Canyon ruled a large region.

Robert Drennan coined the term "rituality," which I have adopted (Yoffee, Fish, and Milner 1999; Yoffee 2001), because it is apparent that Chacoan "complexity" cannot be reduced to one or another of the canonical neo-evolutionist stages, and also that political and economic explanations cannot account for major aspects of Chaco society. By emphasizing ceremonialism and rituals at Chaco, however, I do not imply that production of food and the elaborate canals and field systems that were crucial to it were unimportant. On the contrary, people lived in Chaco Canyon, and those entering the canyon had to be fed. There would have been no Chaco rituality without the elaborate agricultural systems that made even a modest aggregation of people possible.

Three factors have led Lekson (and other archaeologists) to campaign for Chacoan "complexity." First, and probably most important, Chaco is larger, contains more parts, and is structurally more heterogeneous than earlier societies in the area. It is thus complex when compared with the simpler architecture and less densely occupied sites that preceded it.

Second, archaeologists increasingly employ an array of scientific research technologies derived from chemical, physical, geological, botanical, cartographic and other analytical principles, all involving computerized storage and data manipulation. The complexity of recovery and analysis has become for some archaeologists a short-hand for the complexity of the ancient society being studied. That is, it is easy for archaeologists to conflate the complex practice of research with the subject of study. Patricia Gilman, the excavator of a pithouse village (consisting of about a dozen subterranean rooms) in remote southeastern Arizona, has described the site as "incredibly complex," which is a fair reflection of the difficulties involved in excavating it properly. The problems of "excavating Chaco" – that is, investigating a dozen or more great houses, many dozens of smaller sites, analyzing artifacts of all kinds, and understanding Chaco society – are certainly highly complex.

A third factor influencing some archaeologists to describe prehistoric societies as "complex" is the work of the Santa Fe Institute (SFI) on "complex adaptive systems" (CAS; see, for example, Kohler and Gumerman 2000). Research on CAS at the SFI encompasses turbulence in hydrodynamic systems, pre-biotic chemical evolution, central nervous systems, vertebrate immune systems, political systems, and the global economy. It is the SFI's goal to bring together specialists in these (and many other) domains to learn whether there is in complex adaptability some logic common to all of them. I digress on the subject of CAS for two reasons. First, a number of Southwest archaeologists have worked at the SFI and try to model social change in the prehistoric Southwest using complex adaptive system methods, and so discuss "complexity." Second, I shall adapt CAS perspectives to a study of the evolution of Mesopotamian states in Chapter 9 and want to provide a background for that discussion.

A complex adaptive system is a network of interacting parts that exhibits a dynamic, aggregate behavior. This system behavior cannot be reduced to the "sum of its parts" because the action of some parts is always affecting the action of other parts, so that equilibrium of the entire system is never reached or maintained for very long. There is no optimum state of system performance, and the system can always surprise, as when a small initial perturbation can result in a large outcome. Per Bak's principles of avalanches of sand piles, Christopher Langton's "phase transitions," and Stuart Kauffman's "order on the edge of chaos" (all discussed in Kauffman 1993) account for instances of rapid change that is the disproportional output from small inputs. The system can always perform better or can unravel into new parts that were not the constituents of the old system.

Such complex systems cannot be calculated or predicted through standard mathematical descriptions because their operations are not fixed within a few variables and controlled by some central process or mechanism. Rather, aggregate – or emergent – behavior derives from interactions, which themselves continuously change internally, and because many systems are in contact with one another and so affect the landscape of all of them. Indeed, it is often difficult to specify the boundaries of a system. The environment that embeds systems is hardly external, providing a standard through which performance of systems can be measured. The natural property of complex adaptive systems is that of "self-organization" (or "self-organized criticality"), and it is the internal dynamics of such systems, not only their response to something external, that can occasion rapid and profound change.

Complex adaptive systems have the capacity to learn from interactions with other systems and the environment. They tend to anticipate the future by seeking new interactive ways while also applying old ways of interaction that have already "worked." Thus, CAS are often (or maybe always) inefficient, sacrificing efficiency for the ability to remain flexible.

I mean to show by this lengthy excursus on CAS and the SFI that not only are ancient states and civilizations complex systems in the terms of the SFI, but so are all human societies playgrounds for social negotiation and for the empowerment of the few, and their parts remain far from some equilibrium with each other and their environment. Of course, then, Chaco is complex, but, by saying it is complex, we know very little more than we did before we applied this label. As Ben Nelson (1995) puts it, the task is not to ask *whether* a society is complex but *how* it is complex.

The term "rituality" is useful particularly because it is a neologism and owes nothing to neo-evolutionist theory. The term also must be unpacked, and the unique cluster of Chaco Canyon great houses and other structures must be explained in their own historical context, and not necessarily as a type of city or town in the nomenclature of Western urban geography.

Rituality, of course, suggests that the fundamental component of the existence of Chaco and of the Chacoan network was its elaborate ceremonial apparatus. Although there may be a consensus that Chaco was a pilgrimage center, this is not to suggest that there were not important aspects of political leadership and social struggle at Chaco. There were certainly leaders, architects, and planners, and there is evidence of conflict and warfare within the Chaco system (Le Blanc 1999), just as there is evidence of leadership and status. By using the term "rituality," I do not mean to imply there was (or was not) a "pax Chacoana" (Lekson 2002), an absence of competition and violence among people of the same or similar beliefs. Various groups and social identities seem to have co-existed in Chaco within the context of the relations that called them into being. Although these relations were irreducibly ceremonial, as it seems to many, the term "rituality" is not intended to substitute a mode of cultural integration in place of what others have seen as a political integration. Whatever coherence the Chaco rituality might have had was the product of many local and regional decisions, and such stability as Chaco may have achieved (for a century or less after the Big Bang of 1050) covered over the multiple cleavage plains that made Chaco, and indeed much of the prehistoric Southwest, a classic example of organizational flexibility in a harsh and unpredictable environment.

I use the term Chaco rituality to emphasize that the ritual nature of Chaco cannot be regarded as an epiphenomenon to economic and/or political institutions. Chaco was unique in the history of the Southwest, central in time and space to Indians in the northern Southwest, the fulcrum of ceremonies that created and enabled social and political interactions among the Anasazi. The Chaco phenomenon was short-lived. Signs of trouble after 1100 were followed by a half-century-long drought from 1135–80, after which the canyon was nearly abandoned.[5] No such aggregation of ritual architecture ever again appeared, and native histories seem to warn of the ultimate perils of that previously splendid, but dangerously hubristic, world. The severe drought not only exacerbated the problems of producing food in the canyon and the flow of supplies into Chaco but also doubtless presented a theological problem for a belief system that guaranteed the harmony of the universe and the prosperity of congregants.

As in other "collapses," of course, all aspects of Chaco culture did not end, and collapse is really a species of cultural transformation. Lekson (1999) has argued persuasively that the site of Aztec to the north became the new center of what might be called the "Chaco old order," and he has provocatively claimed that Chaco beliefs, and some Chacoans who carried them, led to the rise of Paquime in Chihuahua. Eventually, however, the old order at Chaco did fail – or was drastically transformed – and new orders, such as the Katsina belief system (Adams 1991) and the symbols and beliefs underlying the Salado interaction sphere (Crown 1994), replaced it. Lekson writes that the memory of a "White House" (1999:145) in modern Puebloan societies refers to a past world in which katsinas taught dances and ceremonies, but which was ultimately violent and unsuccessful. Lekson suggests that "White House" was Chaco and that its lessons became incorporated in Puebloan histories.

NON-NORMATIVE THINKING IN SOCIAL EVOLUTIONARY THEORY

Linda Cordell and Fred Plog (1979) attempted to escape the "confines of normative thought" in Southwestern prehistory by rejecting aspects of the direct historical approach. That is, they held that models of social organization generated from studies of modern pueblo societies should not be simply imposed on ancient Anasazi pueblos or the Chaco phenomenon. Specifically, they suspected that prehistoric societies were more stratified and politically more centralized than modern pueblo societies. If, however, direct historical analogies from modern pueblos should not be used to

---

[5] After about 1100, there are already signs of trouble at Chaco in the McElmo phase, when new construction techniques and new pottery appear (Cordell 1997; Van Dyke 2004).

interpret ancient social organizations, one might ask which other analogies would be more useful to archaeologists (Levy 1994).

John Ware (2001) slants the issue slightly by arguing that most of the analogies that have been used for interpreting Anasazi organization have come from studies of Western Pueblos. There, matri-clans and principal lineages of these clans controlled rituals. Eastern Pueblos, however, developed ritual sodalities that functioned independently and alongside kinship hierarchies, providing ceremonial and political direction to these pueblos. Ware considers the possibility that there were such ritual sodalities at Chaco, and these became increasingly differentiated socially and economically through internal competition (among great houses) over exclusive knowledge and access to the accouterments of ritual performance. This kind of power had distinct limits. At Chaco there were no centralized workshops, and most imported goods (especially the large amount of imported pottery) were utilitarian objects that were certainly not limited to an elite segment of society.

For decades Southwest archaeologists have considered that the intensive archaeological research in the area and especially the fine chronological control provided by tree-ring dating, along with the ethnographic and ethnohistoric research on the successors of prehistoric populations, have made the region a laboratory for the methods by which ancient social organizations *in general* can be inferred. Linda Cordell, however, has reminded us that the exceptional Southwestern data and analyses might be typical only within their own "boundary conditions." This means (but not to put words into Cordell's mouth) that Chaco (and by extension the Southwestern history in which Chaco is a part) must be understood within its own history and experiences. Modern pueblos are fundamentally different from prehistoric ones because, among other things, warfare was outlawed by the Spanish, belief systems and ceremonies were condemned, and a new "traditionalism" emerged as part of the construction of a new identity in the face of assimilationist pressures (Fowles 2004).

Chacoan great houses were planned, artful, and built to last, most taking decades to complete (Metcalf 2003).[6] They required "persistence rather than technique . . . an exercise of patience" (Lekson 1994:24). Given the extent of the system and the diverse nature of the ceremonial structures, it is possible that some great houses were constructed by people living in different outlying areas. It was the overarching ceremonial system that held diversity together in a ritual system, and this system is what made

---

[6] The masonry at Chaco, highly visible in the stabilized great houses today and greatly admired by visitors, was plastered over and not visible in the past (Cameron 2002). Perhaps the artfulness of Chacoan construction was admired in the past by the gods themselves. In Mesopotamia, inscriptions were carved into cliff-faces, parts of inscribed statues were placed in walls, and paving stones contained inscriptions. These could not have been read by human beings, but the messages were not intended for humans.

Chaco unique. However, bequeathed a legacy of neo-evolutionism, archaeologists aren't used to finding uniqueness, and it makes them uncomfortable.

The Chaco rituality may not be exactly like the past anywhere else. Many archaeologists now are properly skeptical of a comparative method that simply "drops a deductive scheme from above down on the evidence" (Rudolph 1987:742). Although it seems to many that the interpretation of Chaco as a ceremonial realm is clear enough, we hesitate to celebrate our hard-won knowledge because it is so hard for us Western folk to "take seriously . . . the ceremonial and symbolic as anything but the instrument of the efficient" (Rudolph 1987:742). We have lost the capacity, by and large, to estimate the power and reality of ceremony, and it is hard even to find the proper language to appreciate the purpose of ritual. Whereas Kertzer (1988) writes that ritual constitutes power and communicates power relations, power need not be embodied solely in the sphere of kings, rulers, and political administrators. If it is agreed that the Chaco rituality was not organized by kings, we may still envision a species of contradiction and struggle between those elites invested in the performance of ritual at Chaco and other elites of the local social organizations that comprised the greater Chaco network. Competition among various kinds of leaders that was brought to a new intensity in the time of climatic disasters in the 1100s might well account for, or at least have been an important factor in, the collapse and subsequent abandonment of Chaco. That is, it was not simply the social and economic network that shattered, but also the core beliefs that made the phenomenon possible.

Severin Fowles (2004) considers that ritual in prehistoric pueblos *is* a species of politics. That is, Western models, especially neo-evolutionist ones, misconstrue the meaning of religion in societies in which there is no division between religion and politics, and classify societies, like Chaco, as "pre-political." The "embeddedness" of politics and major aspects of the economy in ritual cannot be explained in neo-evolutionist thought, which is, finally, a surrender of the non-Western past to untenable theory and its unsuitable lexicon.

SOUTHWEST AND SOUTHEAST

The foregoing capsule of evolutionary history of Chaco depicts a prehistoric society that was not part of a trajectory towards statehood, not a "stage" in someone else's history. Chaco is also an example of the power of ritual and ceremonial specialists, great leaders at the center of a far-flung confederacy of believers. It will not have escaped readers, however, that I have also argued that "ideological power" was a fundamental aspect of the evolution of the earliest states. In ancient states, no less than in Chaco, ritual and ceremonial specialists held considerable power over people and resources. Ceremonies of social incorporation are found in all ancient states, and edifices where those ceremonies took place are the most visible monuments in them.

If "ideological power" is integral in the evolutionary trajectory of ancient states and civilizations, what then is the difference in such trajectories and the ritual power at Chaco? The question may be illuminated (and also complicated) by a glance at the evolution of Mississippian polities ("chiefdoms") in southeastern North America from about AD 1000–1400 (Figure 7.6). The Mississippian is distinguished according to various criteria, including distinctive artifacts, the "Southeastern ceremonial complex," and especially by large, multi-mound sites in this period, such as Cahokia (Figure 7.7), Moundville, Etowah, and others, which were ceremonial centers. Central mounds were the locations of "temples," in which the veneration of ancestors of the leaders of societies took place.[7]

The Mississippian culture enfolded many ethnic and linguistic groups, elite networks of exchange, factions, cadet lineages, town councils, wars, long-distance trade, and migration of many groups across the countryside. The Mississippian world embodied a network of ideas that provided space for individuals and groups to assume new identities, especially in ritual spheres. The highly visible earthen mounds with "temples" at the top, which were charnel houses, represented rules about death and pollution and leadership. The formation of these large mounds created "Mississippian-ness" and characterized polities big and small, centers and peripheries. The Mississippian landscape also entailed the cultural forgetting of other symbols, other kinds of monuments, other rules of performance and practice.

Calling the Mississippian societies "chiefdoms" means for Mississippianists only that the polities were not quite states and very far from bands or tribes. Although I do not object to the term in this usage, it obviously doesn't tell us much about how such societies developed, how they worked, and how and why they collapsed.

Mississippian societies, as I discussed briefly in Chapter 2, cycled from more to less complex forms because of structural contradictions in their social organization. They did not develop economically stratified societies, cities and urban offices, and (as far as can be ascertained) an ideology of "statecraft." Major sites like Cahokia collapsed and were abandoned soon after the apogee of their construction, which was also the case at Chaco. However, Mississippian societies are unlike Chaco in many respects,

---

[7] For literature, see Cobb 2003; Milner 1998; Muller 1997. Having discussed the archaeology of the Chaco phenomenon, and now in moving on to Mississippian archaeology, the prospect of being left to steam and molder in the compost heap of archaeologists who wandered too far from their putative expertise looms all too vividly. I shall be brief.

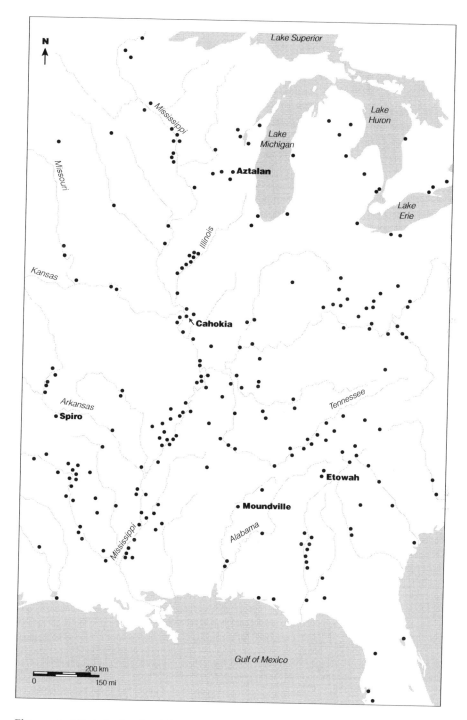

Figure 7.6   Mississippian sites (after Coe, Snow and Benson 1986:54)

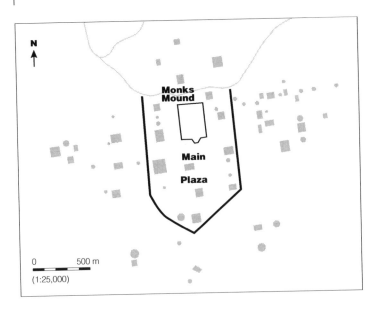

Figure 7.7   Cahokia (after Coe, Snow and Benson 1986:75)

the most obvious of which is that Chaco was a unique phenomenon in the Southwest, a singularity in time and space, whereas there were many major Mississippian multi-mound centers in the Southeast. Although some archaeologists have classified both Chaco and Cahokia as "chiefdoms," their histories were remarkably different. What is most comparable in them is that few archaeologists call Chaco and Cahokia states.

Many archaeologists, however, call Chaco and Cahokia "complex societies." That is, although neo-evolutionists denied that there were major similarities between chiefdoms and states, because stages had to be holistically separate, one finds in the Mississippian local councils, elite networks, and overarching ideology – institutions that are also characteristic in the earliest states. What are the differences, then, between Chaco and Cahokia on the one hand and Uruk and Teotihuacan on the other?

In Chaco and Cahokia political leadership was apparently embedded in ritual networks that discouraged forms of economic inequality other than between ritual leaders and followers, and the social roles of individuals in Chaco and Cahokia were strongly ascribed in social and ritual units. Trends towards urbanism, which are evident at Cahokia and seem quite similar in their rapidity to those that led to the earliest cities, were short-circuited as new forms of governance did not accompany the substantial demographic and economic changes that created new urban-like settings.[8] Instead of developing new principles of leadership, new ideologies of domination and new offices to be contested in cities, along with new social identities of citizens, who were also members of various social and economic groups, Cahokia – as rapidly as it emerged – collapsed.

TOWARDS A HISTORY OF SOCIAL EVOLUTIONARY TRAJECTORIES

In Figure 7.8 I aim to depict two social evolutionary principles. First, the Chaco rituality and the Mississippian chiefdoms must be understood on their own terms, not as variability among so-called chiefdoms and not as representatives of stages in the trajectory towards states. Similarly, Australian aboriginal societies have distinct histories that do not simply underlie the evolutionary history of other societies. From a common base of "bandishness" – that is, the long-term and varied conditions of societies dependent on hunting, fishing, and gathering – different roots and pathways to different kinds of inequality and power developed. This is not a Whiggish view of social evolution, however, since prehistoric and historic migrations and contacts could (and did) transform trajectories.

Second, in the development of the earliest states, in which degrees of economic, social, and political differentiation and stratification all co-occurred, one can study and weight the various nascent domains of power so as to explain the considerable variability among the earliest states.

One exercise in the weighting of power has been proposed by Richard Blanton, Gary Feinman, Steven Kowalewski, and Peter Peregrine (1996) in their "dual-processual model." As Mesoamericanists, they devised this model to explain the differences between the Maya states, in which there were kings and writing, and Teotihuacan, in which kings were not depicted and there was no Teotihuacan native writing. In their "model," there are two strategies to political power, "corporate" strategy, in which power is shared in a council of leaders, and "network" strategy, in which individual rulers exercise power. Although the authors declare that the two strategies could co-exist in the same society, one of them was normally dominant. However, the restraints on using the strategies as just another typology quickly fell, as the authors and many colleagues began to sort societies into either corporate or

---

[8] I compare the pace of changes at Cahokia further and in comparison to the trajectory of changes in Mesopotamia (and in other states) in the conclusion to Chapter 9.

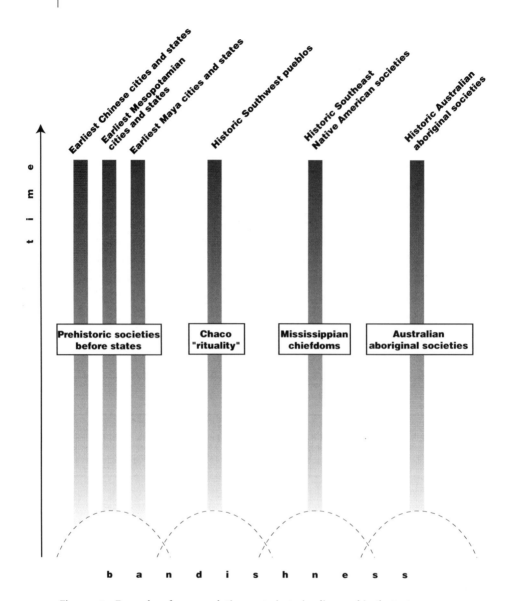

Figure 7.8 Examples of some evolutionary trajectories discussed in the text

network types. Often, earlier phases were corporate – that is, without strong leaders – and later phases were network.

Lacking in the exposition of the corporate–network model is an explanation of why one strategy became dominant, or what the mechanisms were for change from one strategy to the other one. In the earliest states, as I have stressed, it is unproductive to reduce the many kinds of social groups and the numerous leaders and sorts of leaders, each with a different way to attract followers, all of which co-exist, into leadership strategies. And why should one wish to characterize all of a state (or a non-state, for that matter) solely by its form of leadership?

The term "heterarchy" (Crumley 1987, 1995; Ehrenreich, Crumley, and Levy 1995; Crumley 2003), which I have already discussed in Chapter 2 in passing, has also been proposed to account for variability in societies. Heterarchy simply refers to the existence of many hierarchies in the same society and thus aims to explore arenas of social co-operation and conflict. It calls attention especially to how some aspects of social and economic organization cannot be reduced to political hierarchies.

Heterarchy isn't a theory at all, but a way to organize thoughts on social structure. It requires an unarchaeological conceit: one doesn't seek to find a heterarchy. One attempts to identify the kinds of social groups in a society, the locations of various social groups, and the interactions among the various hierarchical structures of these groups. By studying the kinds of hierarchies in various societies and in ascertaining which hierarchies do not exist in some societies, one can begin to differentiate between the trajectories that lead to states from other histories, histories that are just as complex but different. Indeed, one could argue that the nature of complexity and heterarchy at Chaco and Cahokia are greater than in the periods that preceded the formation of the earliest states (as I emphasize in Chapter 9).

In the next chapter I explore how archaeologists attempt to determine – within the structure of archaeological theory – just what is analogical and comparable in social evolutionary trajectories.

8

NEW RULES OF THE GAME

Blessed be the Lord, our God, who introduces variety amongst His creatures.

OLD HEBREW PRAYER TO BE UTTERED WHEN SEEING
A MONSTER, ACCORDING TO ISAIAH BERLIN

The old rules of social evolutionary theory that were used to explain the rise of the earliest states haven't worked – as I have argued in the preceding chapters. Indeed, the neo-evolutionist model developed by social anthropologists in the 1950s and 1960s and then operationalized and employed by archaeologists in subsequent decades now hinders research or, more often, is simply ignored by contemporary archaeologists. The old neo-evolutionist game was played on the central assumption that modern "traditional" societies represent stages in the development of the earliest states. These old rules were developed within American departments of anthropology as archaeologists, seeking respect from their social anthropological colleagues (as well as jobs, promotions, grants, and status), attempted to model prehistoric societies via analogies to cases described by ethnographers.

These archaeologists, who thus claimed to be genuine anthropologists, were surprised when their colleagues insisted that "traditional" societies had histories of their own and could not be inserted as "models" into a prehistoric, neo-evolutionary trajectory. In the 1980s and 1990s the whole edifice of social evolutionary theory was abandoned by non-American archaeologists, who were never part of an academic anthropological establishment. The remaining neo-evolutionists were disquieted further when many archaeologists turned to evidence provided by ancient historical sources, from Mesopotamian cuneiform tablets to New World *relaciones* and *visitas*, new decipherments of Maya glyphs and Chinese oracle bones, and art historical evidence from Egypt to Teotihuacan, evidence of particulars that confounded facile analogies. Mirroring trends within social anthropology, modern archaeologists now traverse the boundaries of the social sciences and the humanities, prehistory and history, as they investigate and compare trajectories of social change.

In previous chapters I have traced the evolution of spatially large and densely populated cities from small, special-purpose sites and modest villages and discussed how highly stratified and differentiated societies emerged from societies with little division of labor other than specified by kinship rules. New rules of social evolutionary theory are analytical constructs, not classificatory dogmas, and focus on how social roles were altered and/or abandoned and new ones adopted or created in the development of the earliest cities, states, and civilizations. The new rules of social evolutionary theory must also address how and why the earliest states varied enormously, why the earliest states "collapsed" and did or did not regenerate, and why some societies did not become states. In this chapter I consider how archaeologists must generate new rules to compare and contrast evolutionary trajectories and to incorporate appropriate analogies in archaeological investigations. No one, not even archaeologists, is a *tabula rasa*, and no archaeological inferences are structured apart from comparisons, contrasts, and analogies.

THE GAME OF ARCHAEOLOGICAL NEOLOGISMS

Self-conscious statements about comparisons, analogies, and the process of inference in archaeological theory do not have a long history. In the 1960s and 1970s, archaeologists (worldwide), flushed with an explosion of empirical data and armed with new methods of regional surveys, establishment of temporal controls, and the employment of machine-assisted analytical techniques, began the first halting steps – triumphantly broadcasting that they were explaining the past rather than simply describing it – to construct appropriate social theory within archaeology. Their enthusiasm for "building archaeological theory" led to the invention of a fun, new indoor pastime: "The Game of Archaeological Neologisms."

The basic rule of the game was to proceed down the alphabet adjectivizing the common noun "archaeology." Thus, there was "analytical archaeology" (Clarke 1968), "behavioral archaeology" (Schiffer 1976), "cognitive archaeology" (Renfrew 1993), "demographic archaeology" (Hassan 1981), "economic archaeology" (Dennell 1979), etc., the most dramatic entry being "post-processual archaeology" (Hodder 1985). Having found a suitable modifier to "archaeology," the idea was to write a book on the neologism, hold a conference on it, or at the very least to contribute an article to a journal with the neologism as its title. Although the highest marks were awarded to those whose neologism implied a full-fledged "Kuhnian paradigm shift," most of the neologisms were quickly recognized as advertisements for the radical insight of their creators.

It was clear, of course, that much of this "archaeological" grand theory was borrowed from other fields, social anthropology and ecology at first, but under post-processual critiques greatly opening to embrace psychology, phenomenology, feminism, literary criticism, and much else. Indeed, just as processual archaeology became everyone's archaeology, with its central concerns on research design and quantitative analysis now standard operating procedures (and its positivist and nomothetic rhetoric jettisoned by most workers), so post-processual archaeology has impelled important and new investigations into matters of ideology, symbols, identity, and landscape (while most archaeologists have abandoned claims of extreme relativism).

The engineering of archaeological theory: mining and bridging

Although post-processual archaeologists have insisted on studying "agency" (how people negotiated, within constraints, their own existences), there have been few post-processual studies of social change. This is perhaps because the post-processual faithful, having rejected social evolutionism, did not recognize that social evolutionary theory (when freed of neo-evolutionist dogma) was precisely about changes in the content of people's roles, the appearance of new roles, and the disappearance or subordination of old roles (Runciman 1989:8). Over time, some sorts of behavior were rendered possible while other behaviors became less possible or impossible (Wolf 1990). From societies in which roles were differentiated largely according to sex and age there emerged socially and economically riven societies with a specialized division of labor and centralized governments.

Since neo-evolutionism, as I have argued, was borrowed by archaeologists from social anthropological theory, archaeological theory became largely a mining-and-bridging exercise. That is, archaeological theoreticians have been deferential to theory from other fields (Chippendale 1993) because they consider their footing to be exceedingly insecure. Trained in skills of excavation and analysis of material culture, archaeologists looked for models and analogies that gave them confidence that a reconstruction of social organization from the fragmentary residues of the past was not utterly unlikely. Since for many archaeologists *real* theory exists in sociocultural anthropology (or sociology, biology, geography, economics, etc.), the archaeologist's task is to "mine" these fields for a putatively appropriate theory, then to modify or "bridge" it so as to understand past societies and instances of social change.

Although banner-raising and proselytizing for an archaeological theory or school of archaeology has now little interest for modern archaeologists and especially for their students, there are still papers purporting to be about archaeological theory, but in which lugubrious philosophical generalizations say little or nothing about archaeological particulars. Such papers have produced an unfortunate effect on many working archaeologists, who conclude that social theory in archaeology consists of worthless abstractions and recondite language and is utterly unconnected to the recovery and interpretation of artifacts, features, and settlement patterns. However, a popular reaction among professional archaeologists, who have been well instructed that all archaeological interpretation is theory-laden, and who thus seek not to be stigmatized as atheoretical (let alone anti-theoretical), is to claim that they are doing "middle-range theory."

HOW ARCHAEOLOGISTS LOST THEIR INNOCENCE

Archaeological theory achieved a measure of self-conscious respectability in 1973 in David Clarke's tour de force article, "Archaeology: The Loss of Innocence," which showed that theory permeated every level of archaeological activity (Clarke 1973). Not only was there analytical and interpretive theory, there was also retrieval theory and post-depositional theory, among other forms of archaeological theory. Agreement that archaeologists had theory, however, did not lead to unanimity among archaeologists as to what archaeological theory was or where it came from. The diversity of opinion on what constituted archaeological theory can be reckoned from the following quotations that I have culled (or perhaps better, filleted and partially refleshed) from major essays of the time:

What archaeologists need is an evolutionary theory, a theory that can be borrowed in unadulterated form, namely modern biological theory, because biology is . . . struggling with similar problems in a similar context as archaeology. (DUNNELL 1982:19, 20)

I don't believe there's any such thing as archaeological theory. For me there's only anthropological theory. Archaeologists have their own methodology and ethnologists have theirs; but when it comes to theory, we all ought to sound like anthropologists.

(The Old Timer, cited by FLANNERY 1982:269–70; this position is refuted by Flannery in FLANNERY AND MARCUS 1983:361–2)

If archaeologists can gain a healthy skepticism regarding received conceptualizations of nature and seek to place themselves in positions relative to nature and experience where the adequacy and/or ambiguity of the received comments may be evaluated, then they can hope to gain some objectivity relative to the utility of their concepts. Once archaeologists learn to look at systems from the realistic perspective of an observer in a well, they will see many new things which can aid in the organizational diagnoses of past systems.

(BINFORD AND SABLOFF 1982:150, 151)

Archaeology is a mediated relation between what happened and its representation. Material culture is a constructed network of significations, irreducibly polysemous, a contextualized matrix of associative and syntagmatic relations involving parallelism, opposition, linearity, equivalence, and inversion between its elements.

(SHANKS AND TILLEY 1987:103, 114, 115, 134)

In the 1970s British archaeologists who were concerned that theory should be integral to the discipline of archaeology founded the Theoretical Archaeology Group (TAG), a new learned society, which seemed to be dedicated to the proposition that archaeological papers should be delivered with the auditorium lights on.[1] In the 1980s, however, appeals to the ideas of thinkers such as Foucault, Giddens, and Heidegger as critical to the formation of grand social theory made many archaeologists uncomfortable about the role of archaeologists as theory-builders (Watson 1992; Yoffee and Sherratt 1993).

Many archaeological practitioners, therefore, nervous about their ability to operationalize (or even understand) grand theory, claimed they were constructing archaeological theories of the "middle-range," namely theories that could be developed to help explain limited aspects of the archaeological record. For example, at the 1985 meeting of the Australian Archaeological Association (AAA) in Tallebudgera, Queensland, a variety of volunteered papers, all of which reported on new field research, were gathered on the last morning of the meeting in a panel labeled "middle-range theory." In the afternoon session, another set of papers on field research was called "the captain's platter." Although there was no discernible distinction in theoretical orientation between the two panels' papers, the morning session's participants had seized the moral high ground as theoreticians.

Although "middle-range theory" has served as a respectable middle ground between, say, the nomological "processualists" of the 1970s and recursively phenomenological "post-processualists" of the 1980s and 1990s, there is a specific and valuable meaning to the term "middle-range theory." Examination of the term leads us to review how most archaeologists would like to regard theory: a systematic set of assumptions and procedural statements that allows one to investigate observed phenomena.

---

[1] TAG papers are now often accompanied by slides and refer to archaeological data.

LEVELS OF ARCHAEOLOGICAL THEORY

Thanks to an excellent article by Mark Raab and Albert Goodyear (1984), we know that the term "middle-range theory" was first used in archaeology by Lewis Binford in the introduction to his collection of articles called *For Theory Building* (1977), then in his book *Bones* (1981) and in his contribution (1982) to a Southampton conference on theory in archaeology.[2] What Binford meant by the term "middle" is a bridge connecting the "behavioral dynamics that produced phenomena" (translation: the constantly changing human behavior of a past society) and "the static phenomena of the archaeological record" (translation: the unchanging residues of those human behaviors).

"Middle" is also central in importance in archaeological theory because once one knows how the archaeological record was formed, one is on the right path to understand the behavior of the people who produced it. Michael Schiffer's "behavioral archaeology" added concern with the changing nature of the archaeological record and pleaded attention, thereby, to "site formation processes." As Raab and Goodyear pointed out, however, both views could be described as archaeological methodology rather than social theory. Indeed, Binford's call for "good instruments for measuring specified properties of the past" and Schiffer's emphasis on taphonomy and experimental archaeology make this concern with methods clear. Furthermore, in Raab and Goodyear's view, use of the term "middle" requires specification of what "high" and "low" levels of theory are. Binford wrote sparingly about high-level theory, which he called "general theory" and which vaguely referred to "cultural organizations and change." Schiffer (1988) divided theory into three domains, each of which has low, middle, and high aspects. The organization of social systems, about which Schiffer expressed little interest, was only one of the domains (but see now Schiffer and Lamotta 2001).

In Gordon Willey and Jeremy Sabloff's (1980) review of the concept of middle-range theory, the authors echoed Binford's view: middle-range theory concerns the process by which living behavior entered the archaeological record. By low-level theory they followed Schiffer's concern with cultural and natural transformations of materials from systemic to archaeological context. High-level theory meant "explanations of behavior of whole cultural systems," for example the rise of states. None of these scholars, however, spilled much ink on how one gets from level to level, and they didn't discuss what might be the utility in demarcating levels of theory.

---

[2] Other discussions of "middle-range theory" may be found in Trigger (1995) and Kosso (1991).

Although Raab and Goodyear identified the prior use of the term middle-range theory in Robert Merton's (1949) debate with fellow sociologist Talcott Parsons, more use can be made of Merton's views than they consider. For Merton, the middle-level of theory is middle because it "rests between the working theories that guide daily activity and all-inclusive, unified, ideal theories of behavior, organization, and change." For Raab and Goodyear, having reclassified Binford's "middle" to "lower" level theory, because it involves mainly methodological procedures, their new middle followed Merton in that it refers to any set of "causal or potentially causal statements about aspects of cultural systems that can be tested empirically." They envisioned that these aspects might eventually be amalgamated into more inclusive theories, presumably those on the high-level of theory.

Levels of archaeological theory exist, if indeed they exist at all as discrete levels, as a hierarchy of propositions that afford linkage between matters of data collection (and the primary analysis of data) and the process of inference within which patterns of data are held to represent social phenomena. The levels of theory I demarcate are hierarchical *only* in degrees of abstraction, not in chronology of employment (or even in importance, which can be debated).

Following Merton, the first level is the "level of working theories that guide daily activity." In archaeology, these activities pertain to the recovery, identification, and classification of archaeological materials. The activities include the study of formation-processes, use-wear, sampling, stratigraphy, dating, botany, zoology, ceramics, decipherment, and ethnohistoric and art-historical analyses among others. These activities are what most archaeologists do most of the time. I shall not attend further to them here in part because they have been the subject of mainline, successful archaeological research for the past century (and the excellent studies of Binford and Schiffer can be cited here as examples). Many of these activities could be called "methodology," but in order not to bruise the sensibilities of some archaeologists, I call this level not "low-level theory," as Raab and Goodyear have done, but "basic-level theory" or BLT. The ingredients of BLTs provide sustenance to archaeologists. Indeed, this level of theory is quintessentially archaeological. This is not because BLTs do not employ sophisticated theories drawn from physics, chemistry, biology, geology, linguistics, and art history, but because in sum and in intention the combination of BLTs necessary to interpret the archaeological record cannot be encompassed by any other single discipline.

Middle-level theories (MLT) are concerned with contextually appropriate explanatory frameworks. By this I mean that certain theories may be appropriate for the understanding of hunter-gatherers whereas others may be appropriate for investigating the nature and growth of ancient cities. Middle-level theories are also

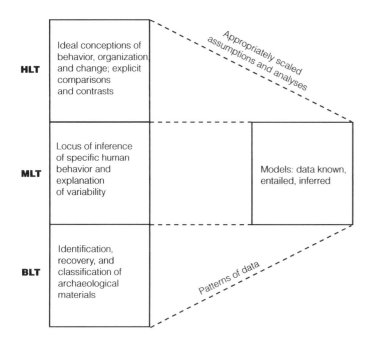

Figure 8.1 Structure of archaeological theory

middle because they are the locus of inference between the methodological oper-ations on the basic level and the assumptions, analogies, and comparisons that every investigator uses in problem-selection, hypothesis-formation, and analysis. Outcomes of middle-level applications of theory are models that include known data and data from analogies and comparisons drawn from high-level theory (see Figure 8.1).

High-level theories (HLT), following Merton, are "those all-inclusive, unified, ideal theories of behavior, organization, and change." The high-level theory that is most familiar to archaeologists is formalist economics theory, the theory that the cost of a good is proportional to the distance the good is moved; that economic goals are optimized; and that there are regularities of supply and demand. Archaeologists use this high-level theory because they regularly recover economic data, and they try to relate such data to social and political organization and change. Also, archaeologists can easily "scale" formalist economics into the middle-level, creating appropriate explanations for the organization of various kinds of societies. High-level theory must be scalable. For example, formalist economics can be used to develop both "optimal foraging strategy" (or "site-catchment analysis"), which might be appropriate in studying hunter-gatherer societies, and also "central-place theory," which might be appropriate for understanding market behavior and the location of settlements in early states.[3]

Archaeologists have seldom, if ever, formulated high-level theories, although the high-level theory of neo-evolutionism might seem to be one such example. In fact, not only was this theory derived from social anthropologists, but the conception of neo-evolutionist stages also depended significantly on the type of economics called substantivism. Substantivist economics, in opposition to formalist economics, holds that the principles of economic exchange were not universal but were embedded in a characteristic social organization. The dominant economic mode of certain stages (bands, tribes) was reciprocity, whereas chiefdoms were typified by redistribution, and states (at least later ones) by markets. Having rejected the putative high-level theory of neo-evolutionism, however, we need to ask how and whether modern archaeologists should conceive levels of theory. Most importantly, we must ask whether a consideration of the structure of archaeological theory will be useful in considering the rival claims of knowledge that are based on the same data.

SOURCES OF ANALOGY IN ARCHAEOLOGICAL THEORY

Inference using high-level theory is a matter of setting out the systematic set of assumptions and procedural statements that allow one to investigate observed phenomena and to model human behavior. The process, ideally, includes making explicit which analogies and comparisons an investigator chooses to structure the process of model-building. Analogies are inevitable (Wylie 1982, 1985, 2002) and the use of analogies, or "prior probabilities" (Salmon 1982b), which come from ethnography, history, or abstract logic, give confidence to the archaeological investigator that his or her reconstruction of fragmentary data is not unique and hence unlikely. Analogies are posited because they yield data and patterns of data in one example that are considered reliable and that in whole, or more often in part, are held to resemble data and patterns of data in the case being investigated. The danger in the use of "prior probabilities" in archaeological theory, however, is that the past can be condemned to resemble some form of the historical present, that nothing new about the past can be discovered, and that theory itself cannot be "ampliative", that is, allow us to find novelty and even singularity in ancient societies and processes of change.

---

[3] I do not argue that "optimal foraging strategy" or "central-place theory" are correct, but only that they are drawn from the same high-level-theory assumptions.

The choice of analogy and comparison in archaeological theory is critical within the levels of archaeological theory in the following manner. On the basic level archaeologists must publish all relevant data and how they were recovered and classified, since replicability of fundamental analytical procedures is the foundation of arguments of plausibility. Modeling on the middle level is then a process of linking patterns of data classification to the posited analogies drawn from the high level of theory. These models of social organization and change must not only account for all the relevant data that impinge on a problem: they must also state what data do not exist but are entailed by the analogies, assumptions, and comparative cases used by the investigator.

Extant data, thus, do not simply prove or disprove models, but find meaning within models. Choices between rival claims of knowledge can be considered by showing that some models incorporate more data or account for data more parsimoniously (that is, more simply and logically) than other models. Furthermore, new data can be produced (through fieldwork) or old data can be re-examined to determine whether data fit or do not fit the predicted entailments in the competing models. Research programs can be structured to improve both databases and logical inadequacies in the models.

Let me offer a brief example of how the process works. About twenty years ago there raged (briefly) a debate about the nature of Monte Albán in Oaxaca, Mexico, which was explained as a "disembedded capital" by Richard Blanton (1976, 1980, 1983). This was rejected by Robert Santley (1980) and Gordon Willey (1979) but defended by Kent Flannery (1983) and Blanton and his colleagues (most recently 1999). Blanton's argument is that the city was founded in a politically neutral area (in fact on a hilltop) that was previously unoccupied and in the center of a valley consisting of three branches (Figure 8.2). Good agricultural land near the city was lacking, and water had to be brought up the hill in the dry season. No central marketing facility or network of roads to possible markets was found in the 6.2 km² site (Figure 8.3), populated in AD 100–200 by 15,000 or more inhabitants (and at its height in AD 500–800 by 25,000–30,000). The site consisted of temples, palaces, and various residences, and Monte Albán was the locus of regional decision-making and ritual. Employing the analogy of Washington, DC, Brasilia, and Canberra, Blanton termed Monte Albán a "disembedded capital," meaning that it was established and maintained not because it was in a favorable environmental location or indeed for any reasons of economic felicity. Rather, these capitals were politically neutral and were chosen so as not to favor one of two or more rival places. Monte Albán was founded as a center for a confederacy of autonomous Oaxacan districts that bonded together as a defensive strategy (possibly against groups from Veracruz or Puebla, and later

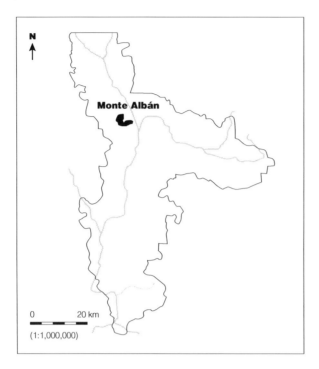

Figure 8.2   Valley of Oaxaca

against the huge and expansionist power of Teotihuacan to the north [Winter 2001])
or possibly as an offensive tactic against nearer neighbors.

Some Mesoamericanists criticized this interpretation because they were reluctant
to believe that prehistoric cities could have no real economic basis for their existence.
Robert Santley looked for suitable agricultural land at the base of Monte Albán and
argued that it was the center of a locally oriented system of exchange of goods and
services. Marcus Winter (1984) also argued that Monte Albán had a clear economic
base with good land to the east and that as a market center it was well positioned to
co-ordinate economic activities within the region.

This brief example represents typical situations in archaeology, in which interpretation depends as much on the assumptions and analogies that scholars bring to
the investigation as it does on the specific analysis of data. In this case we can examine the comparisons and analogies of both positions and aim the critique towards
new research. First, Blanton's analogy with modern "disembedded capitals" is flawed,
since these capitals are the products of already highly stratified states, whereas Monte
Albán was founded in the formative period of regional growth and of social differentiation. Santley's faith that beneficent economic circumstances accounted for the

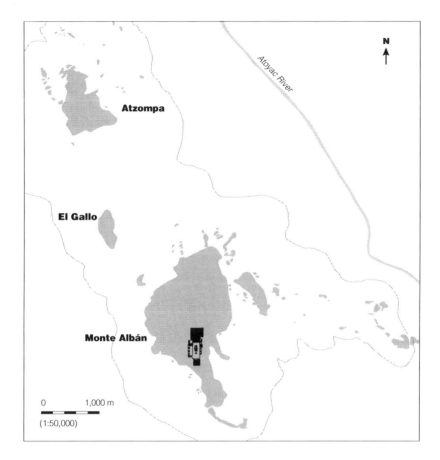

Figure 8.3   Monte Albán (drawn by Juan Cruz Pascual)

rise of Monte Albán seems a residue of adaptationist, if not environmental determinist, assumptions characteristic of the 1960s, and his opponents have dismissed this theoretical position. Nevertheless, it seems to me that Santley's argument of the economic and political embedment of Monte Albán bears consideration and even fits aspects of Blanton's reasoning, once the inappropriate analogies are jettisoned.

First, we may suggest comparisons and analogies to the founding of Monte Albán from the record of other ancient states. In ancient Western Asia, for example, Jerusalem[4] was founded or selected by King David precisely because it was a neutral place between two main competing regions and political systems (Joffe 1998). Jerusalem became the center of a centralized administrative system of the new United Kingdom of Israel. The new capital was founded both to defend Israel against its

[4] Jerusalem is discussed in Blanton et al. (1999:66).

enemies and to weaken the power of rival groups, especially a rural clericy that was distrustful of earthly kings, even their own. Similarly, when Assyrian kings in the late second millennium BC and in the early first millennium were centralizing their own power at the expense of local nobility, they founded new capitals, brought new people to settle the capitals, and established new bureaucrats to manage the inflow of resources that military successes were providing. These capitals, like Monte Albán, were far from being "disembedded." It is impossible to understand their formation unless the degree of social and political embeddedness in their region is calculated. One might consider that Monte Albán was founded by a confederacy of Oaxacan districts (Blanton's position) precisely to embed it in a new political and economic polity (which is Santley's position).

Although it is beyond the scope of this chapter to speculate further about the growth and decline of Monte Albán,[5] it can be noted that the examples of Jerusalem and of the Neo-Assyrian capitals concern the rise of "secondary states": that is, the rise of secondary states is not separable from regional trends and the impingement of prior states. Monte Albán has a history, and this history requires that political and economic activity there be placed in a larger context than just the valley of Oaxaca. When Teotihuacan collapsed (ca. AD 600), for example, it seems that Oaxacan villages grew in size, population, and in the amount of social stratification and became independent of Monte Albán, although it remained an important city until AD 800. While archaeological research must perforce be focused on sites and in local regions, explanations for social and political change must often seek larger historical contexts, as comparisons with other ancient states suggest.

ANALOGY AND THE COMPARATIVE METHOD

Whereas archaeologists have always relied on analogies and always will (Wylie 1982, 1985, 2002; Gould and Watson 1982; Murray 1988, 1992; Bernbeck 1997, 2000; Stahl 1993; Verhoeven nd), little attention has been devoted to the *source* of analogies, which sorts of analogies seem to work, and which others are less likely to be useful. The "tyranny" of ethnographic studies of hunter-gatherers as useful analogies for understanding prehistoric hunter-gatherers was critiqued already by Martin Wobst about

---

[5] There have, of course, been many studies of the founding of Monte Alban since this debate of about 20 years ago (Sanders and Nichols 1988; Marcus 1990; Blanton et al. 1982; Kowalewski et al. 1989; Balkansky 1998; Spencer and Redmond 2001, 2003; Elson 2003). Arguments concern internal conflict within Oaxaca and/or how an Oaxacan confederacy might have been formed as part of (and in reaction to) a larger set of interregional interactions.

a quarter-century ago (1978). The subdiscipline of ethnoarchaeology (see David and Kramer 2001; Verhoeven nd) is founded on analogical principles. It holds that archaeologists should study modern material culture in "traditional" societies that can then be used as analogies or guideposts for interpreting the material residues of the past. Ethnoarchaeologists, for example, have observed in modern "traditional" villages how wealth and/or family size can be correlated with house size. It is recognized, however, that such analogies are often imperfect when transposed to the past. For example, Kathryn Keith (1999) was puzzled that houses in Old Babylonian cities exhibited few differences in wealth, status, or size, which tended to be modest. However, from the texts found in the houses she determined that many heads of households were rich and had estates in the countryside and even in other cities.

Analogies drawn from ethnographic investigations and then used to interpret the past are appropriate, indeed essential, on the basic level of theory, that is, in the analysis of specific technologies, the construction of artifacts, and their life-histories. Analogies require a structure in which two entities that share some similarities are assumed to share many others, that there are underlying principles of connection between the source-side and the side that is the subject of the investigation. By learning how pots or tools are made in traditional ways in the present, archaeologists gain better understanding of how similar artifacts may have been made and used in the past.

Many analogies on the higher and middle levels of archaeological theory that have to do with social organization and especially social change, however, have been and must be unsuccessful. First, claims that modern villages (for example, in rural areas of the Middle East) may be analogies with ancient villages (for example, in ancient Mesopotamia) must ignore the history of village life in both past and present. For the same reasons, analogies with social change in recent history have been used inappropriately to model social change in the evolution of ancient states (or in the prehistoric Southwest, as I noted in the last chapter). Finally, arguments stating that prehistoric societies from one region may be used as analogies with societies in other regions, even though the evolutionary histories of these societies is completely different – for example, that Cahokia or Chaco might be a stage in the development of some ancient state – are easily criticized. This is so even if aspects of Chaco and/or Cahokia social organization are not wholly dissimilar to institutions in the earliest states.

Although I criticize the use of analogy in middle and higher levels of social evolutionary theory, I do not reject the comparative method in archaeological theory. Comparison, as opposed to analogy, entails the examination of two or more entities with the view of discovering resemblances and differences between them. Comparisons in social evolutionary theory must be located within contextually appropriate histories. For example, it is now well within archaeologists' abilities to compare ancient states with one another (Trigger 2003; Baines and Yoffee 1998), both in their organizational forms and in their developmental sequences. The comparative method enables archaeologists to discern, for example, that Mesopotamian and Maya city-state patterns are broadly comparable but are different from Teotihuacan, which was a single city-state. City-states are also different from the territorial state of ancient Egypt. Nevertheless, the depiction and veneration of ancient kings in Egypt seems quite similar to that in the Maya city-states. In Mesopotamian city-states, assemblies and councils co-existed with kings and royalty, which might be comparable to organization in the Maya city-states, where council houses have been found (Fash 1991). However, the Maya council houses are viewed by some as late developments and perhaps not typical of Maya political organization. In the Indus Valley city-states and in Teotihuacan it has been suggested that a largely faceless leadership structure existed. Comparisons among these earliest states allow research to be structured: are inferred institutions unique or common? If institutions in one early state are different from those in others, why should this be so?

Comparisons may also be drawn among evolutionary trajectories. I have noted that the evolution of the earliest states is marked by explosive, supernova-like development of extremely large cities. The evolution of the earliest states is also marked by the emergence of domains of power and aspects of differentiation and specialization within these domains. In cities new leadership structures and new ideologies emerged. By investigating the specific nature of the domains of power, the importance of such domains of power in each society, research may be structured to explain similarities and differences among the earliest states and also the nature of societies that did not become states.

These new rules of the game, however, are not recipes for analysis. I began this book by declaring that the greatest myth of the earliest states was that there was only one type of archaic state. The search for appropriate comparisons among the earliest states is a relatively new enterprise in social evolutionary theory, and it is important that the project's goals include not only explanations of why things happened as they did, but also why they didn't happen some other way.

Two centuries ago humans knew very little about their past, and history began in biblical times, in the Classical world of Greece and Rome, in the Chinese dynastic cycle, in the epic poetry of the Vedas, and in the oral histories of many peoples. We flatter ourselves now that, on the basis of much successful research, we are able to conceive the past on its own terms, having rejected facile analogies and simplistic theories that were current only a few decades ago.

Notwithstanding these gains in knowledge, archaeologists have been and are now both admired and criticized by the public for their reconstructions of the past. On the positive side, archaeologists are magicians, able to bring a hidden past amazingly back to life. On the negative side, the public is baffled by archaeologists who often offer contradictory versions of that past. Within archaeology itself, multiple interpretations of the past have been encouraged by some post-processual archaeologists who disdain any method that might allow a choice among rival claims to knowledge. If there is such a thing as archaeological anomie, it is on this point.

In this chapter I have attempted to resolve some of these issues by advocating that archaeologists justify their choice of comparisons and link these explicitly to the analysis of data within a structure of archaeological theory. Although I agree with post-processualists that neo-evolutionists erroneously restricted comparisons to finding representative of stages of organizations (e.g. of chiefdoms), I do not follow their arguments that comparisons are in themselves unhistorical (or even antihistorical). History is not a hyper-particularist collection of oddments of the past – what historians call antiquarianism – but is a method of explaining causes and effects. The version of world history that I have been calling social evolutionary theory in fact requires a revivified comparative method that importantly includes comparisons of developmental sequences. Such investigations must include appraisals of what social changes occurred in the past as well as those that did not occur. The goal of these new rules of the game is to understand the past on its own terms, insofar as this can be imagined. I do not say that the game is easy; I do think we've made a good start.

9

ALTERED STATES: THE
EVOLUTION OF HISTORY

What is called collective memory is not a remembering but a stipulating; that
this is important, and this is the story about how it happened, with the pictures that
lock the story in our minds. Ideologies create substantiating archives of images,
representative images, which encapsulate common ideas of significance and trigger
predictable thoughts, feelings.

SUSAN SONTAG (2003:86)

I began this book by delineating the myths that archaeologists created about "the
archaic state": the earliest states were very similar to one another (and so represent the
evolution of "the archaic state"); they were large, territorial creatures, evolved from
"chiefdoms" and from earlier stages that could be known through ethnographic
analogies; they were dominated by ineffably and irresistibly powerful rulers, who
controlled, or even monopolized, all means of production and the distribution of
goods and services, and monitored the flow of information in them, and instituted
true law.

These myths of the earliest states and their evolution are products of archaeological theory, the attempt to understand a process whose outcome is observed but
whose dynamics and details are imperfectly known from the observation. Although
it is hardly necessary to repeat the social science mantra that "all observation is
theory-laden," it is surprising that the myths created by leading archaeological theoreticians have had such little influence on how research was conducted and data
analyzed. Although some archaeologists did set out to find (or identify) states or chiefdoms or some other type in the archaeological record, other archaeologists never
stopped finding counter-indications to the myths: complex veins of stratification and

196

differentiation, many kinds of hierarchies, the large sizes and political independence of the earliest cities, the limits on absolute power of rulers, and endemic struggle for power in the earliest states.

Archaeologists now utilize such information by asking new questions that were mostly ignored in old social evolutionary theory. The central concerns – in addition to understanding economic and demographic patterns and environmental change that are germane and indispensable to all archaeological research – are to explain how the content of social roles changed as actors exploited the ambiguities of inherited forms, evaluated their options, borrowed ideas and materials from other groups, and created new forms to answer to changing circumstances (after Wolf 1990). In the evolutionary trajectories towards the earliest states, new socioeconomic and governmental roles were invented in cities as powerful leaders competed to control not only resources and labor, but also the symbolic capital that had to be marshaled in order to recombine differentiated social units into new and viable political systems. Ideologies of the state were created to provide explicit systems of meaning about social, political, and economic relations and especially how leadership should be exercised and on what basis it could be contested. States were not simply enclosures of power but guardians of ideas about themselves.

Evolutionary trajectories towards states occurred all over the world after the Pleistocene and were based on varying means of gaining power and access to goods and labor. Ideologies that there should be a central ruling system were created in new seats of government and state ceremony, into which states' resources needed to flow. Interactions in these urban places created and provided new social and political landscapes for the inhabitants of states. New and dense urban interactions resulted in behavioral maps in which residence, movement, and identity were stipulated and restricted. Monuments in cities glorified the present and testified that the past led inevitably to cities. The so-called "Sumerian King List" of Mesopotamia put it succinctly: kingship descended from heaven to cities. The countryside was remade (or, better, made for the first time) in response to the power and privilege located in cities, and it was defined by and against those in cities. The countryside provided, in turn, a refuge for those fleeing from cities and power bases for rural leaders who resisted or tried to resist the demands of urban elites.

States collapsed and were often re-made according to ideological templates that were created in their formation. Societies on the peripheries of states were stimulated to become states, or they were assigned as peripheral organizations by states. And, as I have argued, some societies turned away from a trajectory in which accumulations of power might have led to cities and states. I repeat my earlier claim: social evolutionary theory is world history.

AN ESSAY ON THE EVOLUTION OF MESOPOTAMIAN STATES AND CIVILIZATION

In this final chapter, I trace the process of how new social roles and identities were created and abandoned, how social and economic inequalities were established, and how new arenas of power emerged in Mesopotamian states and civilization, the area I know best. I discuss economic, demographic, and technological changes, how customs and practices were altered and re-constituted in cities, and how rulers came to rule. However, I do not pretend to offer a whistle-stop tour of Mesopotamian prehistory.[1]

My goal is, rather, to explore by means of an extended example the paradoxes of social evolutionary theory to which I have referred: trends towards the earliest states included simplicity as well as complexity; politically independent cities flourished within civilizational umbrellas that overarched them; and strong central governments, mighty rulers, and ideologies of central power co-existed with systemic fragility, endemic competition for power, and normative collapse.

After a period of about five thousand years from the appearance of the first agricultural villages in ancient Iraq there appeared Mesopotamian cities, city-states, and Mesopotamian civilization. (Table 9.1 and Figure 9.1 orient the reader to the named time-periods and sites discussed in this chapter.) There was no early Mesopotamian state, if one means by the term a long-lasting, regional political system whose rulers in their capital city governed many other cities and their associated countrysides. Instead, early Mesopotamia was a land of city-states. There was, however, an enduring cultural boundary that spanned these city-states so that each of them recognized the others as members of a cultural system, sharing among other things the same beliefs and (broadly similar) material culture, ways of writing, and an ideal that only one city should rule all the others even though this was seldom achieved in reality. This civilizational boundary incorporated distinct regions, Assyria in the north and Babylonia in the south, and many different ethnic groups, most with their own languages and histories, who participated in and contributed to the web of Mesopotamian culture.

My evolutionary history enfolds a necessary methodological conundrum or question: can one reconstruct a prehistory that avoids the sense of inexorability that it must lead to the city-states and civilization of historic Mesopotamia? Mesopotamian

---

[1] See the most recent synthetic accounts, e.g. Roger Matthews (2000, 2003), Jean-Daniel Forest (1999, 1996), Susan Pollock (1999), Mitchell Rothman (2001), Peter Akkermans and Glenn Schwartz (2003), Robert Englund (1998), Reinhard Bernbeck (1994, 1995), David Wengrow (1998, 2001), Stuart Campbell (2000).

Table 9.1 Chronological table of selected periods in Mesopotamia
(Calibrated dates of prehistoric periods are taken from Hours, Aurenche,
Cauvin, Cauvin, Copeland, and Sanlaville 1994; Evin 1995; Porada,
Hansen, Dunham, and Babcock 1992)

Periods	Approximate years BC
Early Holocene and Neolithic	10,000–6,000
Hassuna	7,100–6,600
Samarra	7,000–6,300
Halaf	6,400–5,500
Ubaid	6,500–4,000
Uruk	4,000–3,100
Early Dynastic	2,800–2,350
Old Akkadian/Akkade	2,350–2,200
Ur III	2,100–2,000
Old Babylonian	2,000–1,600
Old Assyrian	1,950–1,750
Middle Babylonian/Kassite	1,600–1,150
Middle Assyrian	1,400–1,000
Neo-Babylonian	1,000–539
Neo-Assyrian	1,000–610
Late Babylonian	
Achaemenid Persian	539–333
Hellenistic/Seleucid	333–190
Parthian and Sasanian dynasties	190 BC–AD 642
Islamic conquest	AD 642

historians often view Mesopotamian prehistory as a long, largely incomprehensible and dreary backdrop to the events documented in cuneiform writing. Indeed, Mesopotamian histories often have the urgency of a von Däniken script: after a long period in which little of consequence occurred, vast building schemes and imperial adventures were undertaken by great men who transformed their world. The Mesopotamian historian's myopia is, of course, matched by the prehistorian's tendency to fold his or her tent and steal away at the dawn of history (after Kohl 1978:475), as if knowledge of Mesopotamian history was quite irrelevant to the understanding of the prehistoric institutions that underlay, and in a real sense caused, the economies and societies of the historic periods. This evolutionary history has no stages and several surprises. I borrow some concepts and terminology from research on "complex adaptive systems" (see Chapter 7) as metaphors for social instabilities in times of little change, unexpected consequences of minor perturbations in social organizations, and occasional, extremely rapid evolutionary change.

Initial conditions and emergent properties

The earliest states appeared both in the Old and New World approximately four to five thousand years after the appearance of the first settled villages that depended on agriculture (domesticated wheat, barley, millet, maize, rice, and/or potatoes). Agricultural villages were the necessary but not sufficient conditions that set the stage for the evolution of the earliest states. Towards the end of the Pleistocene period, which was very cold and dry, until about twelve thousand years ago in Western Asia, Upper Paleolithic hunters and gatherers had invented new technologies that allowed them to expand their subsistence strategies and to establish camp sites. In the cycles of amelioration of the harsh climatic conditions at the beginning of the Holocene in Mesopotamia, following 10,000 BC,[2] natural resources for people (especially those including the cereal grasses, wheat and barley) flourished, and bands of people, probably extended families, founded longer-lasting settlements, including permanent ones. These settlements subsisted on the extensive stands of grasses and other local resources (such as land snails and vetches), and engaged in forms of animal husbandry as well as hunting.

Some of these earliest village sites (Figure 9.2) in the 9000s and 8000s BC, like Abu Hureyra 1 (the early occupation) in Syria and Hallan Çemi in Anatolia, which were pre-agricultural villages, were by no means small (Abu Hureyra was about 10 hectares in size). At Hallan Çemi considerable feasting and ceremony occurred – celebrations of residence, as it were (Rosenberg and Redding 2000). Nemrik, Qermez Dere (both in northern Iraq), and Abu Hureyra 2 and Mureybit (both in Syria), in the later 8000s and 7000s, were villages in which plants and animals were domesticated after the sites were founded. Domestication occurred not to relieve hunger but as a process whereby humans increasingly selected, as part of collection, processing, and reseeding activities, certain genetically recessive traits in the grasses, such as hardiness of plant stems and seeds, at the expense of dominant traits that allowed stands of grains to reproduce effectively without human intervention (Watson and Kennedy 1991). The seeds from recessive phenotype plants were easily collected, then

---

[2] The "Younger Dryas" was a severe cold spell that interrupted the progressive amelioration of climate in the ninth millennium BC. Its effects are debated. See Moore, Hillman, and Legge 2000; H. E. Wright 1993; McCorriston and Hole 1991; Belfer-Cohen and Bar-Yosef 2000.

stored and subsequently planted; fields had to be weeded to keep out the dominant forms. People also selected animals that were smaller and gentler, had more wool, or possessed other traits that made them useful to sedentary people, who protected them from wild competitors. Some early villages were impressive features in the landscape. At the site of Göbekli Tepe, megaliths and pillars were erected, some weighing about 50 tons, indicating the labor of many people, more than could have existed in any one village. Furthermore, there seems to be no domestic quarters at Göbekli Tepe, and the entire site "served a mainly ritual function" (Schmidt 2000:46) for those in its region, settled people, and mobile ones alike.

In the 7000s and early 6000s people founded villages in new niches, both in the natural habitat zone of wild plants and animals and increasingly to the south along the Mesopotamian plain and away from the region that was the scene of the first villages. In these permanent villages, such as Maghzaliya, which were not large, an impressive variety of groundstone implements was used for grinding seeds, and storage facilities, both pits and structures, sturdy houses, and defensive structures were built.

It is not my intention to review the process of settled village life and the development of agricultural practices site by site, and I have already conflated specific finds in different regions, although I have maintained the broad contemporaneity of sites and finds. What is important in this narrative is the "emergent properties" of certain phenomena in these earliest villages. By emergent properties I mean those qualities that arise out of initial conditions of climate change and also changes in the relations among animals, plants, and humans. The ensuing consequences for culture are not reducible to those conditions or predictable from them. New social interactions and new forms of behavior do not develop in a stage-like procession, and the consequences of emergent properties are expected only in hindsight.

Although the domestication of plants and animals is defined as a process in which certain naturally occurring recessive traits are increased and reproduced by humans so that these plants and animals are dependent on the activity of people, people also become dependent on domesticants. In settled agricultural villages fewer species were exploited than earlier. The tasks of harvesting plants and tending to animals in villages exerted a "pseudo-pressure" (Bronson 1975) such that labor needs for harvesting, weeding, storage, tending animals, and distribution of surplus products restricted the movement of a certain number of individuals in a village, whereas others were progressively occupied in tasks, such as manufacturing crafts and exchange, that had little to do with the production of that surplus.

Population in early villages grew as lengthening the spacing between births, normal in mobile societies, became less of a concern, and children became a valuable source of labor in agriculture and animal husbandry. More sites were founded, and there was an expansion of villages into new niches. The new villages, however, were probably not only a result of population growth. Rather, the earliest villages were subject to the vagaries of drought and other climatic changes, the onset of disease, which was easily communicated in villages, and crop failures. In sum, there was a change in the amount or proportions of natural risk and the reproduction of a labor force, which people could calculate, and which led to a new strategy of mobility in early agricultural societies. Villagers forced to move took with them domesticated plants and animals, and these could prosper in new zones in which natural competitors were absent. Mobile populations in these zones also began to adopt domesticated products brought to these areas.

Because early villagers, who had become increasingly specialized in the exploitation of local resources, knew a great deal about near and more distant places and the resources in those areas, village life led also to increased exchange with distant villages, although much exchange was probably "down-the-line," from village to village, rather than direct, long-distance travel (Renfrew 1975). Some of the resources gained through this exchange, such as obsidian, were practical for daily life. Others, such as semi-precious stones, symbolized the status of certain individuals who acquired them. Exchange had social ramifications, since it could also create status. Whereas tasks of production and distribution in early villages could be negotiated within the kinship and social system, exchange required individuals to establish ties to people who were not relatives.

The existence of village life also provided opportunities for those who could exploit areas that were marginal for agriculture. Some people (often, presumably, kinsmen of villagers) could convert calories from less fertile land by tending animals and moving them seasonally to better pastures. These specialized herders could only flourish, however, by exchanging animal products for agricultural goods and craft products produced by villagers. Consequently, new divisions of labor arose in villages, in which women occupied with larger numbers of childen and food preparation also produced textiles and craft items, which could be exchanged with other villages and with the pastoral nomads. Partial crania of animals, figurines, wall paintings, and feathers (of raptors, whose bones are found) were employed in dances and ceremonies in early villages, which were also the scenes of social and economic interactions between settled and mobile people.

If these early settlements were scenes of new economic activities and social rules, village life also affected the local environment in unprecedented ways. Both the new socioeconomic behaviors and environmental degradation can be discussed with reference to the early agricultural village in Jordan, 'Ain Ghazal, which flourished in the late 7000s–early 6000s. The excavators (see Banning and Byrd 1987; Byrd 2000) have investigated the planning of houses, construction of stone walls, roofing material, plastered floors and walls, and, surprisingly, extensive remodeling in the houses. The alterations in these structures produced smaller units, re-routed circulation paths in the houses, and in general resulted in subdivisions of the structures. The excavators were perplexed by the nature of these re-buildings: why should people in a newly set-tled village expend a great deal of energy and expertise in planning and maintaining houses and then repeatedly re-model them? Why should these re-buildings result in cell-like subdivisions of the original structures?

In historic periods in Mesopotamia, about five thousand years after the aban-donment of 'Ain Ghazal, there are plenty of recorded instances when houses were remodeled on the death of the male owner. At this time we know that property was partible and all children inherited sections of paternal (really bilateral) estates. It was common for one of the adult heirs to buy the property of his brothers and sisters and so reassemble the dispersed estate.

It may be possible that such re-modelings of houses in the early village of 'Ain Ghazal were the result of the changing nature of property ownership and inheri-tance rules. Indeed, it seems logical that, precisely in early sedentary communities, rules of intergenerational transfer of immovable property were developed and sig-nificantly affected the nature of the newly settled families themselves. Kent Flannery once argued (1972) that social changes were reflected in domestic architecture in the transition from round houses, typical of most early villages, to rectilinear forms, which encompassed extended family units and kept discrete certain activity areas. Although this interpretation now seems excessively mechanistic (see Byrd 2000 and below), the process of social change in early villages might have led to the cell-like forms such as those in 'Ain Ghazal. Indeed, the repeated plasterings that accompa-nied such subdivisions at 'Ain Ghazal, and which required the burning of enormous quantities of trees to make the lime plaster (Kingery, Vandiver, and Prickett 1988), seems to have led to the deforestation of the region and so the abandonment of the site.

Naturally, processes of social change must be considered in appropriate tempo-rally, spatially, and developmentally specific sequences, and I do not mean to imply that social organization at late-Neolithic (PPNB) 'Ain Ghazal is any way similar to early-second-millennium Babylonia. Nevertheless, the re-modeling of houses at 'Ain Ghazal may reflect the earliest example of how inheritance practices of subdividing house property are worked out in many cultures, in historic Mesopotamia as well as other places in other times – for example, in Ptolemaic Egypt (Bowman 1986). Unlike domestication, which was part of a post-Pleistocene growth trajectory that was irreversible, sedentism is a social process that is often begun and never quite finished.

Emergent properties of villages dependent on agriculture in northern Mesopotamia led to the formation of new rules of social behavior, the appearance of new rituals, ceremonies, and beliefs, the co-ordination of labor to schedule tasks and promote exchange, the alteration of the natural and cultural landscape, the beginnings of new statuses and social relationships, and expansion into new regions. These changes were largely encompassed within individual villages that were relatively modestly differentiated socially and economically, moderately stable for several thousands of years, and without notable aspects of powerful leadership structures. The emergent properties of the earliest villages, however, also led to the formation of "interaction spheres" in which the identities of villagers were significantly altered, and new social and political relationships emerged.

Interaction and identity

The term "interaction sphere" entered the archaeological literature in 1964 with Joseph Caldwell's description of the Hopewell interaction sphere of eastern North America. For Caldwell, the specific problem was how to explain nominally distinct Middle Woodlands assemblages (ca. 250 BC–AD 250) that possessed significant similarities in the material residues of mortuary practices. He invented the term interaction sphere to denote that there were social, ideological, and trade connections among populations that shared thereby a restricted corpus of material culture – in the Hopewell case, of pipes, figurines, copper axes – namely those objects associated with the interment of honored dead. Struever and Houart (1972) observed that such characteristic Hopewell items not only reflected membership in a "burial cult," but also denoted the location of "transaction centers" through which the goods moved interregionally.

The interaction sphere concept, as formulated by Caldwell, describes the condition in which those otherwise politically autonomous societies were culturally connected on a regional basis. That is, the boundaries of local social systems could be identified by distinctive settlement patterns in specific ecological or geographic circumstances, the practice of appropriate subsistence techniques, and the maintenance and reproduction of historically determined cultural ways and associated material expressions. Nevertheless, the circulation of certain goods bounded these local systems within a large, regional or supra-regional area. In order to ensure the flow of these goods, a common code of values and beliefs, manifested in a shared corpus of symbols, was invented to facilitate the social interaction needed to exchange the goods. This common code, if it was not conceived by elites, soon became controlled by them. Thus for Caldwell the formation of an interaction sphere through the material means of communication had evolutionary implications: it connected distinct peoples above the local ties of kinship; it promoted the adoption of innovations and ideas among different people; and it increased the status of local elites and so formed the foundation from which more stratified societies could emerge (Schortman and Urban 1987).

The problem of inferring the existence of interaction spheres that connect local societies into regional associations was also addressed by David Clarke (1978:61, 369), who asserted that "cultures" in prehistory should not be confused with "anthropological cultures," by which he meant local ethnolinguistic groups:

The anthropologist looks at aspects of the social system of cultures [whereas] archaeologists . . . look at the material system of the same cultures [and find that] . . . the systems are not the same yet neither are they unconnected. Serious dangers await those who transfer observations about the one class of system to the other and yet it is important that the coupling between the different systems and their attributes should be . . . made explicit . . . The archaeological entities reflect realities as important as those recognized by . . . other disciplines. . . . [They] are equally real . . . and simply different.

Interaction sphere is a useful term in prehistory since it implies that certain material features found over a large area reflect a set of cultural or other relations that transcend localized nets of institutions and distinct peoples embedded in them.

In the Hassuna, Samarra, and Halaf periods of Mesopotamia (Table 9.1, Figures 9.3, 9.8), sometimes called the "later Neolithic" (roughly in the 6000s and 5000s BC), sites are scarcely larger than those of the earlier Neolithic villages (but see below for possible exceptions). New sites in the Hassuna are in the northern plains of Mesopotamia, but Samarra sites cluster farther south in the central alluvial valley. The Hassuna and Samarra were interaction spheres.

The Hassuna, Samarra, and Halaf cultures were first known as decorated ceramic assemblages. At the type site of Hassuna and other sites as well, the stratigraphic sequence of ceramic types indicates the following stylistic overlaps: Hassuna wares are the earliest, but are partly contemporary with Samarra wares, which are in turn earlier than, but partly contemporary with, Halaf wares. At Yarim Tepe I (Figure 9.4), probably the most important Hassuna site in terms of its architectural elaboration, the characteristic Hassuna ceramics (Figure 9.5) of the early levels are mixed with Samarra wares (Figure 9.6) in the upper ones. The Halaf village of Yarim Tepe II was founded on a small Hassuna village, and the cemetery of Yarim Tepe II was placed on top of the abandoned village of Yarim Tepe I. The architecture of Yarim Tepe I, consisting of both rectangular and circular structures, forms a rough oval with the center of the site unoccupied, which was presumably the scene of dances and ceremonies as well as other communal activities.

Samarra wares are found mainly in sites in central Mesopotamia, the most important of which are Tell es-Sawwan and Choga Mami. At the former there are notably large houses of similar T-shapes (Figure 9.7), about 160 m², one apparently in part an infant necropolis with 200 burials beneath its floor, of which 75 percent of those with skeletal material are infant and child burials. At Choga Mami there were irrigation constructions, necessary for agriculture in an area well outside the dry-farming regions of the north.

Joan Oates (1973) has written that the Samarra culture was an adaptation to the needs of irrigation agriculture in central Mesopotamia, whereas Hassuna reflects an adaptation to the northern dry-farming zone. However, the decorated pots, which were – among other things – expressions of cultural identity, and which form the basis for these cultural distinctions, were not ecologically adaptive. Rather, people living in each zone interacted more intensively with their neighbors than they did with those living in other zones.

The distribution of Halaf ceramics (Figure 9.8), which overlap in time with Samarra wares but continue later than Samarran examples, barely reaches the Mesopotamian alluvial plain. Rather, decorated (as opposed to the standard undecorated) Halaf pottery (Figure 9.9), often described as the finest prehistoric ware in Mesopotamia, is found from Lake Van in the north (and perhaps as far as Transcaucasia [Adam Smith, personal communication]) to the Mediterranean in the west and into Iran on the east. Remarkably, over this wide expanse the pottery shows significant similarity in construction and in designs (although there are also important variations in space and time in designs as well as in the proportions of the pots that were decorated [Reinhard Bernbeck and Geoff Emberling, personal communications]). At the site of Sabi Abyad in Syria there is a transition from local assemblages to Halaf (Akkermans and Schwartz 2003); other Halaf sites seem to be new foundations. Two large Halaf sites, Domuztepe and Kazane, in Anatolia, which are currently being investigated, are 20 hectares or more in extent; the amount of the Halaf occupation of these sites is, however, unknown.

One characteristic feature of Halaf sites is the so-called tholoi, circular buildings, which co-exist with rectilinear ones in Halaf sites. In sites like Yarim Tepe III and Sabi Abyad, finds in and/or near the circular structures include pots, beads, figurines, spindle whorls, pestles, loom weights, bone awls, and clay "sling balls." David Wengrow (2001) suggests that these circular structures were women's workrooms used in food-processing and weaving. Rectilinear buildings, such as those at Sabi Abyad, were used to store grain and may have been locations where accounts were calculated, since clay sealings were found in them.

The single most discussed structure in a Halaf site is the so-called "potter's workshop" in level TT6 at Arpachiya (Figure 9.10), a rectilinear building of about 20 m × 10 m that was deliberately burned (according to Stuart Campbell 2000). The structure was so named by the original excavator (Max Mallowan) because of the amount and quality of Halaf ceramics that were stacked in two rooms and the presence of several kilns near the house. In association with the polychrome plates and bichrome jars were found palettes, red ochre lumps, lithics including cores and debitage, spindle whorls, bone implements, stone vessels, beads, jewelry, marine shells, seals and sealings, and stone axes with no use-wear. Mallowan thought the house represented a specialized activity location for the production of high-quality ceramics for the city of Nineveh nearby (from which a sounding indicated Halaf occupation). Stuart Campbell argues the house was ritually destroyed, which would account for the absence of looting or recovery of materials in the house. In his opinion, the presence of the sealings and lithic manufacture point to the regulation of goods by the inhabitant(s) or owner(s) of the structure. The central location of the "house" along with the high-quality dinnerware and jewelry do not lead one to suppose that the resident was a simple craftsman.

Neutron-activation studies of Halaf pottery[3] (Davidson and McKerrell 1976, 1980; Frankel 1979; Watkins and Campbell 1987) have suggested that high-quality Halaf ceramics were produced by artisans attached to the estates of elite persons in a limited number of centers and were circulated to other regions. The stylistic similarity of the design motifs over the large territory recognized as Halaf is thus the more remarkable. It seems that the production and distribution of Halaf ceramics and other material too were controlled by emerging elites who maintained regular networks of communication and who became bound by particular sets of interests. The circulation of Anatolian obsidian and copper, turquoise, marine shell, and other exotics was facilitated by a system of symbols that provided a shared cultural bond.

In older literature the Halaf was interpreted as a migration of people from the north who were acquainted with the sources of obsidian. They founded settlements as ethnic newcomers into the northern Mesopotamian plain as well as adjacent areas,

---

[3] According to Gil Stein (personal communication reporting on studies by James Blackman), these neutron-activation studies, which were conducted decades ago, are not statistically significant.

displacing Hassunans. Certainly there was a northern component to the Halaf, and new settlements were founded by those using Halaf ceramics. However, Halaf assemblages appear in the later stages of some settlements, and knowledge of obsidian and its sources goes back to the earliest villages in West Asia.

The Halaf is certainly not an adaptation to a specific environment since it covers many environments in West Asia (although does not reach the south). It also dubiously reflects a single ethnolinguistic group over the large extent of territory reflected in the Halaf assemblages. The Halaf decorated ceramics are only a part of the ceramic assemblage in most sites, and the ornate plates, jars, and bowls were presumably used in the serving and consumption of food. Materials used in the consumption of food and drink are also "a way of seeing and knowing the world" (Wengrow 2001:177), in which individual expression resided within collective norms. Food preparation was at least partly the product of women's work groups, and special food was served at feasts in which rules of hospitality were observed. Halafian motifs using cattle imagery, and the finding of cattle bones in Halaf sites, further indicate the use of ornately decorated Halaf ceramics in feasts.

The Halaf represents something quite different from the preceding, but overlapping, Hassuna and Samarra spheres of interaction. Each of those seems to have been a geographically localized bundle of interactions that "united" their regions. These interactions, which included exchanges of goods and (presumably) marital partners (Bernbeck 1994), are discerned in the shared corpus of pottery motifs in each region. It is inferred that these regionally distinctive ceramic repertories represent shared values of and for elite specialists and the creation of a shared history. When a Samarra site is found in Syria (e.g. Baghouz) or Samarra ware is found in northern Mesopotamia, the appropriate conclusion is not that irrigation (as identified in sites in the Samarran core in central Mesopotamia) was imported to those regions, but that central Mesopotamians were trading and passing along ideas in these areas. In any case, central Mesopotamia is not a sharply defined geographical zone, and movement of peoples is not only to be expected but a crucial part of the emergent properties exhibited by these early interaction spheres. Overlaps in the ceramic stratigraphy between Hassuna and Samarra indicate communication between the two regions.

The Halaf, by way of contrast, was an interregional sphere of interaction. The great similarity of Halaf motifs, coupled with the circulation of pottery from specialized centers and the amount of inferred feasting, shows new divisions of labor and the attempt to control the production of pots and also the important symbols – the metalinguistic code – that enabled the exchange of goods over long distances and across many ethnic boundaries.

The formation of Mesopotamian civilization and Mesopotamian city-states

To the identities of villagers in Mesopotamia in the Hassuna, Samarra, and Halaf periods as members of family and kin groups were added new identities as participants in regional and/or interregional interaction spheres. In the succeeding Ubaid period of Mesopotamian prehistory, the shape of interaction spheres changes, as does the meaning of interaction in Mesopotamia.

The size of Ubaid sites does not increase notably over those in previous periods, and there are no prominent Ubaid sites that control other, lesser Ubaid sites (Henrickson and Thuesen 1989). The Ubaid, which precedes the period of state formation in Mesopotamia, has been called a "chiefdom" (Stein 1994), but it does not look anything like, for example, the classic chiefdoms of the American Southeast, and sites in Mississippian chiefdoms are much larger and more complex than any known Ubaid sites. It is in the Ubaid that region-wide belief systems were formalized in Mesopotamia, certain sites became temple centers, and symbols of cultural commonality were both locally restricted within sites and geographically widespread. If the roots of Mesopotamian civilization were formed in the Ubaid period, it is in the emergent properties of the Ubaid, not the gradual step-upward in site sizes and social complexity, that the phase transition to Mesopotamian cities can be explained.

Both in the northern region of Mesopotamia and for the first time in the south, similar ceramic types and, significantly, temple architecture at the major sites of Eridu (Figure 9.11) in the south and Gawra in the north (Figure 9.12) seem to reflect a cultural unity (see also Stein and Özbal 2001). The Ubaid is found not only in Mesopotamia but also extends to Syria, Anatolia, and Iran, although some "Ubaid" characteristics might be a reflection of technological change – the use of the slow wheel in pottery manufacture. In a number of sites on the eastern Arabian coast, Ubaid ceramics are found, but these were transported by Ubaid traders from southern Mesopotamia. Evidence of pre-Ubaid sites in southern Mesopotamia and the connection of the earliest Ubaid wares (or pre-Ubaid wares [Ubaid 0]) to "transitional" forms, such as at Choga Mami ("Choga Mami transitional" wares), shows that the Ubaid was an indigenous development in southern Mesopotamia, nearly as early as the end of Hassuna in the north (see Table 9.1). The direction of cultural impact during the Ubaid was south to north, since Ubaid 1 ceramics are not found in the north, and the characteristic temple architecture of the Ubaid period appears early at Eridu in the south but only at the end of the Ubaid at Gawra in the north (Breniquet 1996). The cultural unity of the Ubaid in Mesopotamia also included an originally northern component, as domesticated plants (and animals) had been moved from the north to an environmental niche in which they did not naturally occur in the south. The south provided fertile ground and easy access to water, and so people could ultimately produce much larger surpluses than in the north. Furthermore, in the south there was relatively easy access to seasonal pasture lands in the uplands (in the Zagros foothills and upland valleys), which set in motion the interaction between nomads and settled villagers that persists, to a recognizable extent, to this day.

Houses in Ubaid villages and Ubaid villages themselves were only in a few instances larger than those in earlier periods (Figures 9.13, 9.14).[4] The temples themselves at Eridu and Gawra look like domestic houses, and Jean-Daniel Forest (1996) has argued that they are in fact houses of leaders. However, the arrangement of temples at the Gawra acropolis and the long developmental history of temple architecture at Eridu point in another direction, that belief systems ritualized domestic relations, eventually on a monumental scale. In literate Mesopotamia, the word for temple is the same as the word for house, and a temple is simply the "house of a god." Of course, the gods needed to be fed and clothed (Oppenheim 1977), which required that the temples own agricultural lands and herds, and temples needed to have craftsmen to fashion the rich raiment and ornament of the god. Meals were presented to the god, who ate and drank as much as he (or she) wished, after which the left-overs passed to the priests and retainers of the divine house. The temples at Eridu and Gawra were central places of worship (possibly pilgrimage sites) for Ubaid villagers, who donated food and other items for the well-being of the deity and the priests.

According to Stein and Özbal (2001), Ubaid villagers possessed "hybrid identities," those from their local village and kin-groups, etc., but now also as "Mesopotamians" (to use an anachronistic but geographically evocative term). The material common-alities of everyday life, as seen in Ubaid ceramics, and the architectural reflections of belief systems, as seen in the temple plans, implied connections between the south and north of Mesopotamia, although there were distinctive aspects of material culture in each region. It is hard not to think of the Ubaid as the cultural precursor of historic Mesopotamian civilization, in which the northern region of Assyria and the southern one of Babylonia were equally Mesopotamian. They shared the same broad contours of belief, literature, education, and material culture, but also main-tained their separate political systems as well as particular customs, divinities, and ceremonies.

The evolution of city-states is a phenomenon of the late 3000s and early 2000s BC, and it happened rapidly: at around 4000 BC, the beginning of the Uruk period, there

---

[4] Little is known of the domestic occupation of Eridu. Both there and in Susa large cemeteries were found. The sites were locations of temples and/or other ceremonial precincts (Pollock 1999:195, 200; Potts 1999:45–69).

were few villages of more than about 10 hectares and with more than a few hundreds of people. By 3300 BC, the city of Uruk encompassed about 250 hectares (2.5 km^2) and is thought to have had a population of about 20,000 people (see Figure 3.31). One can see in Figure 9.14 that a large Ubaid village drawn at the scale of Uruk (Figure 3.31) appears as a mere dot on the map. Other cities – Kish, Nippur, Girsu, and Ur in the south, and Brak in the north – also had developed through the middle 3000s and early 2000s (Figures 3.28, 3.32, 9.21). Although this evolution represented a "phase transition" (an extremely rapid evolution), as important as the actual pace of change is its unexpectedness and unprecedented result.

The Uruk period (ca. 4000–3100 BC) begins with a change in the nature of decorated ceramics, or more precisely the progressive absence of decorated pottery, and it ends in history, the first written texts. Although trends in pottery manufacture serve as chronological markers of the change from Ubaid to Uruk (since there is no architecture known from the early Uruk period), they are also witnesses of massive social change. By the late Uruk period, sites are littered with "beveled-rim bowls," crude hand-formed and completely undecorated pots that were used as bread molds and/or as ration containers (Figure 9.17). Daily consumption had become simplified and regulated for large numbers of dependants, such that everyday activities were subject to mass production and routinization by the new state and its officers.

The Eanna temple precinct at Uruk, which was not the only temple center there (see the "White Temple," Figure 9.16), was itself larger than all but the largest villages of earlier periods (Figure 9.15). It included several temples (which have the same basic layout as Ubaid temples, only massively larger), a sunken courtyard, a pillared terrace, a possible palace, and other buildings in which were found rich artifacts. There were also craft production areas in Eanna. The Uruk vase (Winter 1983) shows figures of authority, symbols of deities, and processions of slaves and tribute-bearers. Mesopotamian cities were densely populated sites of written records of various sorts.

Although Mesopotamian writing had precursors in the various forms of sealings and tokens (Figures 4.2, 9.18), it was invented, probably in Uruk itself, as a new semiotic system, a complete transformation of earlier systems of communication and record-keeping. The new system, which seems to have been designed by one person (because, according to Piotr Michalowski, how could a committee have done it?), included pictographic signs, abstract depictions, rebus combinations, semantic classifiers, and columnar syntax. It subsequently underwent processes of phoneticization and grammatical precision, and syntactic order. Most of the earliest texts concern commodities and the officials responsible for them. Some of the earliest texts, however, were used in the education of scribes. Such texts include lists of officials and professions, names of cities, and other "encyclopedias" of knowledge (Figure 9.19).

The proliferation of officials connected with temples and palaces and also the listings of community leaders leads to the impression that in the density of inter-actions in early cities the state created itself. In the late 3000s and early 2000s BC, thousands of people gathered from the countryside into cities (Figures 3.29, 3.30). Cities were nodal points for military protection from neighbors and distribution points for agricultural laborers (who as members of temple or palace estates traveled to a patchwork of fields) and for water distribution systems to those fields. Emerging cities were also the locations of important shrines, evolving from pilgrimage sites of earlier periods. In cities, structures of administration were invented to account for workers, to feed dependent laborers, and to simplify the complexities of social life.

The implosive transformations in the division of labor in Mesopotamian cities in the middle and late Uruk periods had explosive repercussions well beyond Mesopotamia. Recent research along the middle Euphrates in Syria and southern Anatolia and also in Iran (Rothman 2001) has disclosed sites with characteristic Uruk architecture (including the size of bricks), ceramics (especially beveled-rim bowls), seals and sealings, numerical tablets, and decorative arts. Some of these set-tlements were fortified and seem to have been southern Mesopotamian enclaves in the midst of local cultures. Guillermo Algaze (2001) has employed a modified world-systems model in which competitive Uruk city-states established colonies up the Euphrates in order to control important trade routes over which commodities flowed to the comparatively resource-poor cities in the alluvium. This mercantile model was first proposed to account for the Mesopotamian presence on the Iranian plateau (by Harvey Weiss and Cuyler Young [1975]) at the site of Godin Tepe, where Mesopotamians were considered coresidents with local folk.

The extent of such settlements of the "Uruk expansion" (Figure 9.20) has shown the complexity of the situation. Gil Stein's analysis (1999) of the site of Hacinebi in southern Anatolia shows that Anatolians were by no means overwhelmed by southern Mesopotamians, and that Mesopotamians and Anatolians lived peacefully at the site, if in different neighborhoods. Stein has proposed a "distance-decay" model, in which Mesopotamians became less dominant the further they were from southern Mesopotamia. Algaze believes that the Mesopotamian settlements (in Anatolia) may have "budded off" from Syrian colonies. Algaze also believes that various "Uruk" colonies were founded by individual Mesopotamian city-states, since there was no regional state in southern Mesopotamia in the Uruk period. Although our knowledge of competing Mesopotamian city-states is only inferred (from the surveys of Robert Adams [see Pollock 2001] and from evidence of the early third millennium), Holly Pittman (personal communication), on the basis of stylistic similarities in cylinder seal designs, sees connections with the city of Susa; the other large sites could have been sources of Uruk expansion.

Whereas the world-system model employed by Algaze has been criticized for marginalizing the periphery, denying creative response to a dominant core, and for reducing the clear Mesopotamian presence outside Mesopotamia to that of economic exploitation, the connection of expansionist policies in the social and political life in Uruk city-states in the mid- and late Uruk period seems cogent. The large-scale change in the division of labor that accompanied the formation of temples and temple estates in the south made feasible Mesopotamian expeditionary activities into distant, but scarcely unknown, lands.

The Uruk city-states, however, were hardly problem-solvers (as functionalist neo-evolutionary accounts have read), and the newly restructured countryside provided means for resistance to the rulers and officialdoms in the cities. There were collapses in both Uruk itself and in the far peripheries of the Uruk expansion at the end of the Uruk period. In the distant ends of the Uruk expansion, local populations resumed control of their cities and villages, although the effects of southern Mesopotamian presence as cultural hegemony remained (in the form of Mesopotamian gods and beliefs, literature, and education, which persisted for the next two-and-a-half millenniums). In the south, Mesopotamian city-states like Uruk collapsed and were reformulated on the patterns set in the late fourth millennium. Through vicissitudes of political and social change, Uruk remained a Mesopotamian city until the last days of Mesopotamian civilization.

Newly founded Mesopotamian cities of the late Uruk period and early third millennium BC, through massive structures and monuments, residential quarters and streets, and city walls (best known in Uruk itself and dating to about 2800 BC), presented a sharp differentiation between themselves and their hinterlands. In cities standardizations of administration through writing performed by a scribal class and a uniform numerical system (both of which took centuries to develop in the 2000s) were the more impressive for their uniformity over city-states that were politically independent, alternately at war, or allied in various confederations. These alliances were built not only for purposes of defense and expansion but because a Mesopotamian belief system connected cities, and offerings and pilgrimages to particularly sacred temples and gods in various cities were stipulated. The memories of the past were not so much created as they were creatively forgotten. In the "Sumerian King List" (composed at the end of the third millennium but referring to earlier history) kingship descended first to Eridu, which was the earliest site of southern Mesopotamian temple construction. Cities were eternal, and so was the ideology that there was only one Mesopotamia, a concept that was hypothetically invented in the Ubaid period, although it was seldom achieved in early Mesopotamian political history. The rules of political behavior, of what kings owed the populace and what people owed the king, and the natural order of officials who served the king, were established in the first cities.

If the ideology of the state was an invention in the late Uruk period, however, it did not dissolve the many other, older forms of power in Mesopotamian society. Leaders of "ethnic groups," whose means of social identification were created or reconfigured in the interactions with many other groups in the new states, were powerful figures in Mesopotamia (Emberling and Yoffee 1999; Kamp and Yoffee 1980). Indeed, the number of such groups and the amount of their effective control of land and people did not diminish over time in a Mesopotamia in which political leadership was focused in cities. Such leaders could mobilize followers who lived both in cities and in the countryside, and so had effective means of seizing political power in times of the weakness of urban rulers and their followers. Mesopotamians had many identities, as citizens of cities and members of ethnic groups, of temple communities, and of occupational groups (especially visible in merchant associations). These identities were to a certain extent malleable, as Mesopotamians could privilege one aspect of their identities over others as circumstances dictated.

Finally, in Mesopotamia in the crystallization of city-states in the Uruk period, temples were transformed from modest sites of ritual and ceremony into enormous land-holding units with their own ranks of priests and bureaucrats, craftspeople, and farmers. Some of the clients were votives, that is, poor people, blind people, and handicapped people who were dedicated to service in the temples (Gelb 1972). Kings enriched temples since they depended on the goodwill of the gods for their rule, and kings performed righteous activities as part of their duties and beliefs. Nevertheless, there was a certain tension throughout Mesopotamian history between on the one hand the temples as estates that were distinct from royal estates, and religious leaders who had much power, and on the other the kings who led ceremonies, required religious legitimacy, rebuilt temples, and often seized the property of temples.

The evolutionary trajectory to Mesopotamian city-states, ideologies, landscapes, and memories, as I have depicted, included periods of important social changes that were hardly reflected in the size and character of village life. Subsequently, cities appeared almost as supernovas, and societies changed utterly. Even these changes, however, did not eliminate power bases of kin-group leaders. Rather, it was the rules of incorporation of social groups, the means by which power could be got, that were altered. As the countryside was rebuilt in the evolution of cities, in a process of urbanization and ruralization, the power of leaders in the countryside increased, and vulnerable cities were their foremost targets. Although some archaeologists and historians seem to have believed the propaganda of the rulers of earliest cities and states that they were all-powerful, it is all too clear that they were not.

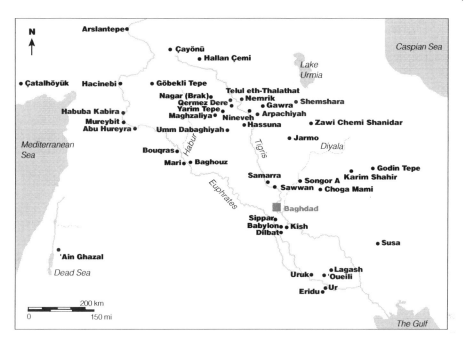

Figure 9.1   Selected Mesopotamian sites from various periods

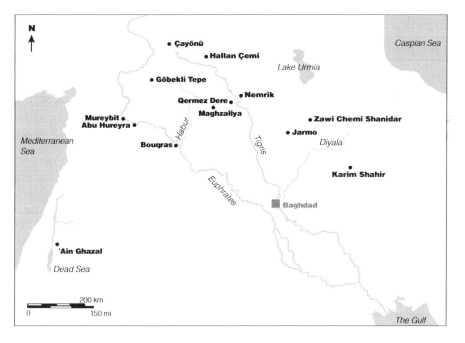

Figure 9.2   Selected early Holocene and Neolithic sites

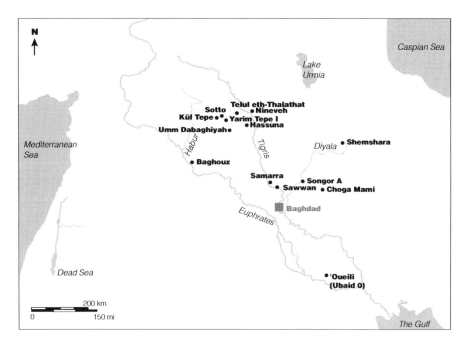

Figure 9.3   Selected Hassuna and Samarra sites

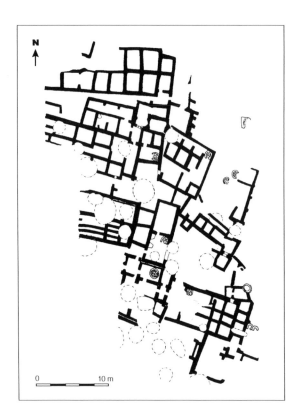

Figure 9.4   Yarim Tepe I (after Merpert and Munchaev 1993, Figure 6.3)

Figure 9.5 Hassuna ceramics (after Matthews 2000:38–9)

Figure 9.6 Samarra ceramics (scale 1:2) (after Tulane in Braidwood 1944 and Yasin 1970, Figure 5)

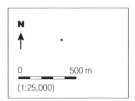

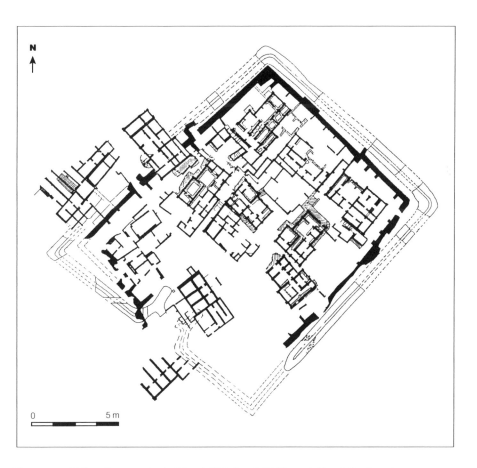

Figure 9.7 Tell es-Sawwan, levels III and IV (after el-Wailly and Abu al-Soof 1965)

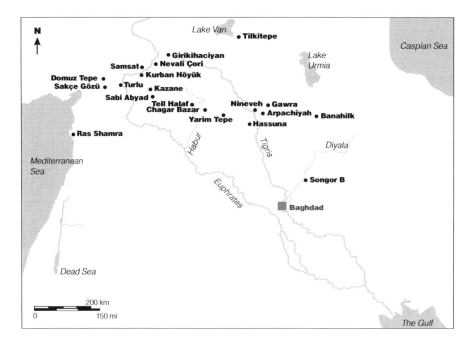

Figure 9.8   Selected Halaf sites

Figure 9.9   Halaf ceramics (after Nissen 1983:49)

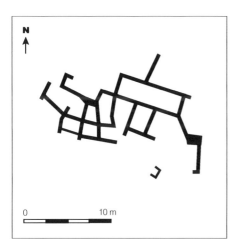

Figure 9.10 Tell Arpachiyah burnt house (after Campbell 2000:7)

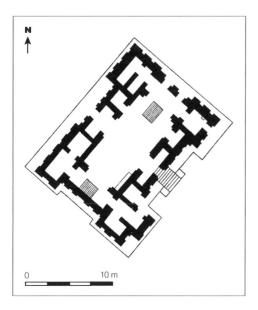

Figure 9.11 Eridu, temple VII (after Safar et al. 1981:88)

Figure 9.12   Tepe Gawra, acropolis, level XIII (after Tobler 1950, pl. XI)

Figure 9.13   Tell Madhhur house (after Roaf 1989, Figure 15)

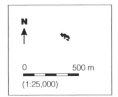

Figure 9.14 Tell Abada village (after Forest 1996:60)

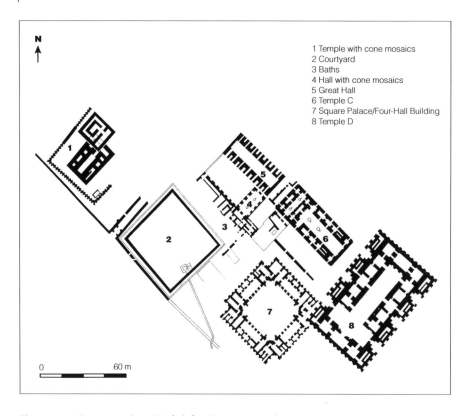

1 Temple with cone mosaics
2 Courtyard
3 Baths
4 Hall with cone mosaics
5 Great Hall
6 Temple C
7 Square Palace/Four-Hall Building
8 Temple D

Figure 9.15   Eanna precinct, Uruk (after Forest 1996:131)

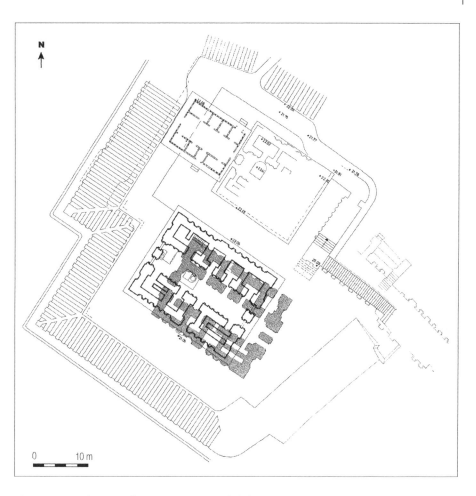

Figure 9.16 White temple, Anu ziggurat, Uruk (after Forest 1996:134)

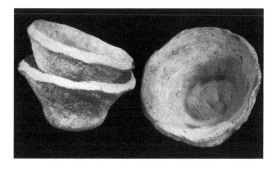

Figure 9.17 Beveled-rim bowls

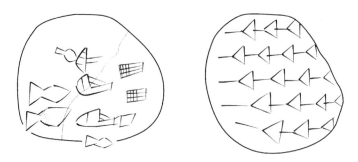

Figure 9.18   Archaic tablet scribal exercises (after Nissen, Damerow and Englund 1990:147, 148)

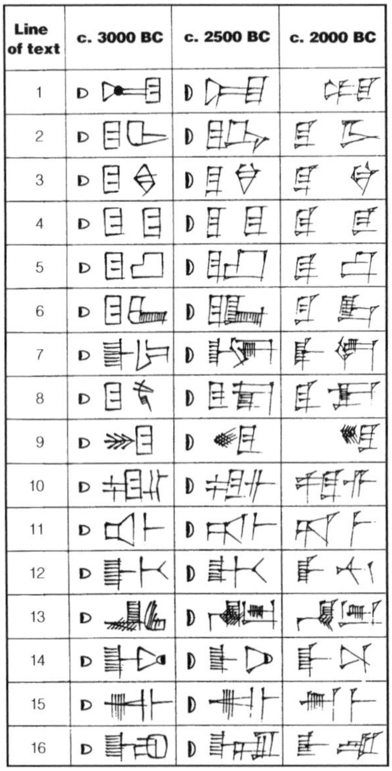

Line of text	c. 3000 BC	c. 2500 BC	c. 2000 BC
1			
2			
3			
4			
5			
6			
7			
8			
9			
10			
11			
12			
13			
14			
15			
16			

Figure 9.19   Archaic tablet list of professions with later copies (after Postgate 1992:55)

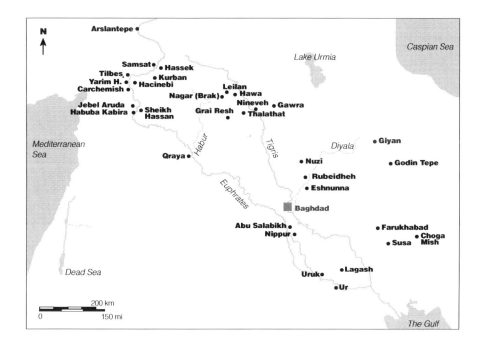

Figure 9.20 Uruk expansion sites

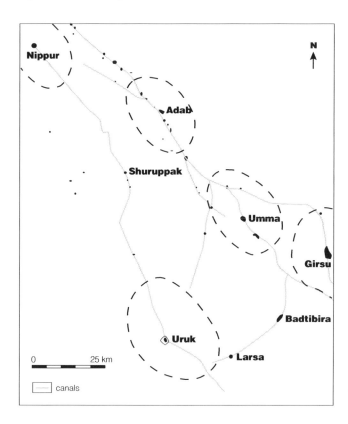

Figure 9.21 Some southern Mesopotamian city-states in the early third millennium BC
(after Nissen 1988:133)

EVOLUTIONARY HISTORIES OF THE EARLIEST CITIES, STATES, AND CIVILIZATIONS

In what way is the evolution of the earliest cities, states, and civilizations in Mesopotamia representative of the evolution of other early states? How does the evolution of the earliest states and civilizations differ from other evolutionary trajectories that do not lead to states? How is research on these questions to be structured?

The central myth about the study of the earliest states, as I have reiterated, is that there was something that could be called *the* archaic state, and that all of the earliest states were simply variations on this model. I claim to have refuted this and other myths of the archaic state and also have argued that there are useful ways of comparing and contrasting evolutionary histories. I conclude this book by considering a few more ways of how a new social evolutionary theory can do just that and also discuss one last myth that must be rebutted.

Gregory Possehl, one of the most knowledgeable archaeologists of the Indus Valley societies, at the outset of his recent and excellent book (2002:5–6), writes that "the Indus Valley civilization is an example of archaic sociocultural complexity, but without the state." He says this because although "there is no real consensus among archaeologists on the definition of the archaic *state*," archaeologists do insist on finding kings, and kings are hard to find in the Indus Valley cities; nor are there palaces, bureaucracies, or "other trappings of 'stateness'" (Possehl 2002:6). Possehl then goes on to describe Indus Valley cities, social and economic differentiation, large public ceremonial areas with very large buildings and monuments, record-keeping of various sorts, and the restructuring of the countryside around politically independent cities that shared a common ideology.

Possehl also provides illustrations of noble-looking individuals, houses that are considerably larger than other houses, and argues that public ceremonies had to be led by a figure of considerable authority, such as the "priest-king" (who graces the cover of his book and 2002:114). Here a comparison with Mesopotamian states is useful, especially because Possehl rightly rejects Mesopotamia as *the* model for the archaic state. In Mesopotamia, it is notoriously hard to find palaces: the "palace" in the late Uruk period is so termed because it is large and has a different plan (as a "Vierhallenbau") than temples (see Figure 9.15, building 7). In Early Dynastic Kish "palaces" are also so designated because their shapes are not temple-like. In the Third Dynasty of Ur at the end of the third millennium BC, there are magnificent temples and ziggurats, and we have a list of kings, but where is the palace? In the great city of Teotihuacan there was a "ciudadela" for public ceremonies, but there are only arguments, no certainties, about the existence of a royal residence (Cowgill 1983). In Mesopotamia, archaeologists find temples because temples are built and re-built on sacred land and in prominent locations. Palaces, on the other hand, are personal residences and administrative seats of rulers who build them in places distant from the palaces of former kings or from historic venues of state ceremony (as at Teotihuacan). Certainly, Indus Valley city-states look different from Mesopotamian city-states. They were ruled differently and seem to have had different rules about how power was to be exhibited in them and, presumably, about how power was to be contested. Their development and collapse were also different from what they were in Mesopotamia, as Possehl shows.

No state evolved without the potential for the production of large and regular surpluses that could be stored, for years if need be (see Colson 1979). Base camps of hunter-gatherers were transformed into relatively long-lasting villages that subsisted on the emerging plenty and eventually on domesticated plants and animals. Village agriculture narrowed the choices of resources exploited by people and led to population growth within villages and demographic expansion into new regions. Bennet Bronson (1975) described these post-Pleistocene changes within a "growth model," which I think explains V. G. Childe's dramatic phrase, the "Neolithic revolution." Bronson meant that given the specific biological changes in humans that prevailed towards the end of the Pleistocene, long-term knowledge of the characteristics of flora and fauna, and the crucial climate change at the end of the Pleistocene, there was a tendency towards "growth," both in a demographic and social sense of the term, that was irreversible. The processes of growth were not characterized by stable systems whose limitations had to be overcome, but rather by constant change in unstable post-Pleistocene societies.

I have elaborated this growth model in this chapter by noting that the earliest villages in Mesopotamia, and I believe elsewhere, persisted as modest villages for thousands of years, while social roles and identities changed in significant ways. From the environment of village life, the circulation of goods and marital partners led to institutionalized interconnections among unrelated people and to the formation of interaction spheres. Codes of communication and symbols of shared beliefs allowed and expressed new aspects of cultural identity among villagers. Certain individuals, nascent elites, began to restrict access to the technology of symbol manufacture and also the means of communication and the venues of communication such as feasts and ceremonies. Control over these symbols and esoteric knowledge became a domain of power in these early villages.

Many archaeologists have commented on the development and nature of regional and interregional interaction in the evolution of the earliest civilizations. Gordon Willey (1992), discussing "horizontal integration" in Mesoamerica and South America, stressed that such horizonal styles of the Olmec and Chavín were not reflections of political domination but of cultural interconnection. Ritual elites occupied central places in these interaction spheres that were composed of villages and monumental ceremonial structures. K.-C. Chang (1986:234–45, 409–11) called the Longshan period in China (roughly mid- to late third millennium BC) an interaction sphere, in that it spanned several local cultures. In Mesopotamia, the formation of larger spheres of interaction over time and the growth of a belief system that connected both northern and southern Mesopotamia resulted not only in regularized exchanges of goods but also reasons to shift production goals from local consumption to production for exchange.

Within interaction spheres, cities crystallized, at some point, rapidly (in the language of complex adaptive systems) as phase transitions. By this term is meant the sharp transition from one state of being to another. For example, when one boils water, molecules become excited, and at 100 degrees Celsius, not 99 degrees, water turns to steam; one grain of sand added to an otherwise stable pile can cause an avalanche. In Mesopotamia, villages that were centers of production and exchange, that were located on trade routes and/or rivers, that lay near great agricultural land, seats of temples and regional worship, and that were defensible locations from attacks by neighbors – for hundreds or thousands of years – suddenly became cities, as people from the countryside increasingly moved into them (see Figures 3.10, 3.23, 3.29, 3.30).

Why did other settlements that were centers of worship, exchange, and favorable locations within interaction spheres – such as Chaco or Cahokia – not become cities? One possible reason is that the evolutionary history of agricultural villages in the American Southwest and Southeast was different from that in trajectories towards states. Chaco and Cahokia became reliant on maize a few hundred years before their "big bangs" that perhaps not coincidentally took place in the eleventh century AD. There was a rapid transition to these sites, which were many times larger and more complex than those of previous periods, but these sites were organized, it seems, by traditional leaders whose authority was not the product of thousands of years of cumulative social change that were ultimately dependent on the production and management of agricultural surpluses. From the first agricultural villages to the earliest states, the process took thousands of years. Could Chaco and/or Cahokia have become states given enough time? I see no reason that they could not have done, but history is not fiction, and what happened happened. Both Chaco and Cahokia were larger than the villages from which the earliest cities emerged. Their very complexity made them unstable, and they collapsed. A collective memory that there had always been rulers, that social and economic inequality was natural, and that political leadership must be different from hieratic principles did not evolve or was only weakly evolved in them, and local decisions and eventually European contact set social change in other directions.

It is our last myth, then, that cities, states, and civilizations are rare and precious entities in the evolution of human societies and so require special explanations for their development. This myth seems based on two quantitative fallacies. First, there is a fallacy of time. Because most of human (pre)history consists of hunter-gatherer societies, states – which rest on agricultural surpluses – have been reckoned atypical. Second, most anthropological archaeologists study societies that are not highly stratified and so see states as the products of exceptional kinds of change. Our growth model, however, holds that states are the expected products of post-Pleistocene circumstances, and the histories of societies that do not become states require as much explanation as do the various kinds of the earliest states that did evolve.

Although this book is about the evolution of the earliest cities, states, and civilizations, it would be indeed a myth to claim that social evolution has only to do with these kinds of sites and social institutions. Neo-evolutionism sought to package all social systems within a comprehensive model of development, which I have described as an illusion of history, a series of myths, although so abstract as to contain few heroes or villains. Indeed, as one neo-evolutionist had the temerity to put it, archaeologists should not ultimately be interested in the artifact or the Indian behind the artifact, but the system behind the Indian. Humanists have always been suspicious of elegant theories that leave people out of history. Although I have traced broad evolutionary schemes in this book, produced social-science-like generaliza-tions and even one "law," and have asserted that calculating numbers of people and the size of settlements are indispensable goals in social research (even if the num-bers are often little more than educated guesses), and have sometimes even written (I fear) in socialscientese, I have tried to resist the reductionist and dehuman-izing tendencies inherent in much social evolutionary research. There are many speculations in this book and considerable uncertainty about how societies and their developmental histories can be compared and contrasted, and my "new rules of social evolutionary theory" are not meant as substitutes for creative thinking about how people understood their lives. I do not apologize for all this distressing openendedness. Indeed, unburdening archaeological research from some of its central myths (which are masquerades of systematically organized knowledge), including some that may have been created by this book, can lead to what archaeologists do best: tenaciously discovering, precisely dissecting, and pleasurably confronting the living, surprising past.

ACKNOWLEDGMENTS

Since I have been thinking and writing about the topics in this book for about a quarter-century, I have many people, universities, and institutions to thank for their support, which has made this book possible. Although my list of indebtedness is long, I don't have the courage to try to name all the individuals who have listened to me attempting to sort through various aspects of what have become chapters in this book.

I have tried out almost every idea in this book, in one form or another, not only in many invited lectures but also in the classes I have taught at the University of Arizona, Dept. of Anthropology (1972–93) and at the University of Michigan, Depts. of Near Eastern Studies and Anthropology (1993–to date). The Dept. of Anthropology in Tucson, and Raymond H. Thompson, its long-time Head, created room for a text-based Mesopotamianist to teach within the most congenial and, I think, best department of anthropology that has ever existed. I owe Ray, my former colleagues, and generations of talented students especial thanks. My students in archaeology seminars at Michigan, which consist of anthropologists, Near Easterners, and classical archaeologists, continue to provide me (in equal measure) the needed skepticism about and the confidence in the ideas they must perforce endure. There will be few archaeologists/ancient historians who enjoy the rare interdisciplinary atmosphere in such seminars.

My oldest friends, John Baines, Richard Eaton, Peter Machinist, and Piotr Michalowski, will recognize that many of my ideas and choicest terminology in this book were generated from our discussions over the years. Many of my best thoughts are derivations from their wise and informed advice. Other great friends,

Carla Sinopoli and Steve Lekson, have provided particularly felicitous observations; I credit Steve with inventing the term "bandishness," although he is not responsible for the way that I have used it.

Two institutions provided the financial wherewithal at crucial points in my writing. The School of American Research in Santa Fe in 1991–92 awarded me a residential fellowship (with NEH funds), which enabled me to weave the first strands in the narrative that has become this book. I thank Douglas W. Schwartz, then president of the SAR, and everyone at SAR for a wonderful year. Subsequently, Joan O'Donnell, then editor of the SAR Press, invited me to spend part of the summer of 2000 at SAR, and this was critical for my re-conceptualization of the book. Thanks, Joan, and again SAR for pushing the project forward. I gratefully acknowledge the grant from the Salus Mundi Foundation that allowed me to spend another year in Santa Fe, 2002–03, when I wrote the first draft of the book. I salute its learned, amiable, and generous director, Richard Diebold.

What control I may claim on the data from the far-flung cities, states, and civilizations I discuss in this book is due to many friends who have answered questions and sent learned papers. I needed a lot of help in the construction of Table 3.1 and thank all those who are listed there for allowing me to cite them. Some scholars whom I knew only from their reputations responded graciously and unselfishly to my queries. I am indebted to the following list of colleagues (and apologize to those whom I may have inadvertently omitted from the list): Brian Byrd, John Clark, Linda Cordell, Suzanne Fish, Renee Friedman, McGuire Gibson, John Janusek, David Jeffreys, Jing Zhichun, Mark Kenoyer, Stephen Lekson, Liu Li, Bruce Mannheim, Joan Mathien, Lynn Meskell, Tim Murray, Katharina Schreiber, Jason Sherman, Joseph Tainter, Nicholas Tripcevich, Alexei Vranich, David Webster, David Wengrow, and Marcus Winter. I want to thank Liu Li especially not only for sending me many unpublished manuscripts and illustrations, but also for answering numerous questions, and trying to rein in my enthusiasm for interpreting Chinese data that increasingly intrigued me.

Several friends read many chapters of the manuscript, Severin Fowles, John Baines, Lars Fogelin, Steve Houston, and Stephen Shennan. Thank you. Other friends read the entire manuscript in its first draft: Reinhard Bernbeck, Susan Pollock, Robert Powers, Adam Smith, and (skilled editor) Jane Kepp. Because of you the present book, thankfully, resembles the draft you read only slightly. Steve Houston then read the updated manuscript and provided further helpful comments. I also want to thank the friends who have co-authored papers with me, Kathryn Kamp, George Cowgill, Geoff Emberling, John Baines, Jane Rempel, Suzanne Fish, and George Milner. Your wisdom and many of your words have inevitably been incorporated in this book.

I had great good fortune in working with talented individuals who prepared the illustrations for this book. Nicholas Tripcevich, graduate student at University of California, Santa Barbara, began the process of drawing sites to a 1:25,000 scale. Elisabeth Paymal in Ann Arbor redrew the few maps that Nico had prepared before he went to the field in the Fall of 2003, and she prepared all the other illustrations in the book. She lent me not only her skills in illustration but her valuable advice on what to illustrate and how best to do it. I suspect there will be many archaeologists who will use Elisabeth's illustrations more than the text of this book.

Geoff Emberling agreed early on to read the entire manuscript, prepare the basic bibliography, and restrain my furthest reaches into speculation. His intelligence and archaeological sensibilities have improved every part of this book.

Finally, I thank Barbara Weber Yoffee, who has meant the most in the writing of this book and who means the most to me. Dein ist mein ganzes Herz.

References

Abel, R. 1973, The Comparative Study of Dispute Institutions in Society. *Law and Society Review* 8:217–347.

Adams, E. Charles 1991, *The Origin and Development of the Pueblo Katsina Cult.* Austin: University of Texas Press.

Adams, R. McC. 1966, *The Evolution of Urban Society: Early Mesopotamia and Prehispanic Mexico.* Chicago: Aldine.

1981, *Heartland of Cities: Surveys of Ancient Settlement and Land Use on the Central Floodplain of the Euphrates.* Chicago: University of Chicago Press.

1988, Contexts of Civilizational Collapse: A Mesopotamian View. In *The Collapse of Ancient States and Civilizations*, ed. N. Yoffee and G. Cowgill, pp. 20–43. Tucson: University of Arizona Press.

Akins, N. 2003, The Burials of Pueblo Bonito. In *Pueblo Bonito: Center of the Chacoan World*, ed. J. Neitzel, pp. 94–106. Washington: Smithsonian Institution Press.

Akkermans, P. and G. Schwartz 2003, *The Archaeology of Syria.* Cambridge: Cambridge University Press.

Algaze, G. 2001, Initial Social Complexity in Southwestern Asia: The Mesopotamian Advantage. *Current Anthropology* 42:199–233.

Alster, B. 1992, Two Sumerian Short Tales Reconsidered. *Zeitschrift für Assyriologie* 82:186–201.

Amiet, P. 1976, *L'Art d'Agadé au Musée du Louvre.* Paris: Editions des Musées Nationaux.

Anderson, B. 1983, *Imagined Communities: Reflections on the Origin and Spread of Nationalism.* London: Verso.

Anderson, D. 1990, Political Change in Chiefdom Societies: Cycling in the Late Prehistoric Southeastern United States. Doctoral dissertation, Museum of Anthropology, University of Michigan.

1994, *The Savannah River Chiefdoms: Political Change in the Late Prehistoric Southeast.* Tuscaloosa: University of Alabama Press.

Arnaud, D. 1973, La prostitution sacrée en Mésopotamie: un mythe historique. *Revue de l'histoire des religions* 183:111–115.

1987, *Recherches au pays d'Aštata: Emar* IV.4. Paris: Editions Recherche sur les Civilisations.

Assante, J. 1998, The kar.kid/*harimtu*, Prostitute or Single Woman? A Reconsideration of the Evidence. *Ugarit-Forschungen* 30:5–96.

2002, Sex, Magic and the Liminal Body in the Erotic Art and Texts of the Old Babylonian Period. In *Sex and Gender in the Ancient Near East*, ed. S. Parpola and R. Whiting, pp. 27–52. Helsinki: The Neo-Assyrian Text Corpus Project.

Athens, S. 1977, Theory Building and the Study of Evolutionary Process in Complex Societies. In *For Theory Building in Archaeology*, ed. L. Binford, pp. 353–384. New York: Academic.

Bagley, R. 1999, Shang Archaeology. In *The Cambridge History of Ancient China: From the Origins of Civilization to 221 B.C.*, ed. M. Loewe and E. Shaughnessy, pp. 124–231. Cambridge: Cambridge University Press.

Baines, J. and C. Eyre 1983, Four Notes on Literacy. *Göttinger Miszellen* 61:65–96.

Baines, J. and J. Málek 2000, *Cultural Atlas of Ancient Egypt*, revised ed. New York: Checkmark.

Baines, J. and N. Yoffee 1998, Order, Legitimacy, and Wealth in Ancient Egypt and Mesopotamia. In *Archaic States*, ed. G. Feinman and J. Marcus, pp. 199–260. Santa Fe: SAR Press.

2000, Order, Legitimacy, and Wealth: Setting the Terms. In *Order, Legitimacy, and Wealth in Ancient States*, ed. J. Richards and M. Van Buren, pp. 13–17. Cambridge: Cambridge University Press.

Balkan, K. 1954, *Kassitenstudien.* New Haven: American Oriental Society.

Balkansky, A. 1998, Origin and Collapse of Complex Societies in Oaxaca (Mexico): Evaluating the Era from 1965 to the Present. *Journal of World Prehistory* 12:451–493.

Banning, E. and B. Byrd 1987, Houses and the Changing Residential Unit: Domestic Architecture at PPNB 'Ain Ghazal, Jordan. *Proceedings of the Prehistoric Society* 53:309–325.

Barnes, H. E. 1960, Foreword to *Essays in the Science of Culture*, ed. G. Dole and R. Carneiro, pp. xi–xlix. New York: Crowell.

Bawden, G. 1989, The Andean State as a State of Mind. *Journal of Anthropological Research* 45:327–332.

Beld, S. 2002, The Queen of Lagash: Ritual Economy in a Sumerian State. Doctoral dissertation, Department of Near Eastern Studies, University of Michigan.

Belfer-Cohen, A. and O. Bar-Yosef 2000, Early Sedentism in the Near East: A Bumpy Ride to Village Life. In *Life in Neolithic Farming Communities: Social Organization, Identity, and Differentiation*, ed. I. Kuijt, pp. 19–37. New York: Kluwer Academic/Plenum Publishers.

Bellah, R. 1964, Religious Evolution. *American Sociological Review* 29:358–374.

Bernbeck, R. 1994, *Die Auflösung der häuslichen Produktionsweise. Das Beispiel Mesopotamiens.* Berliner Beiträge zum Vorderen Orient 14. Berlin: Dietrich Reimer.

1995, Lasting Alliances and Emerging Competition: Economic Developments in Early Mesopotamia. *Journal of Anthropological Archaeology* 14:1–25.

1997, *Theorien in der Archaeologie.* Tuebingen and Basel: A. Francke Verlag.

2000, Towards a Gendered Past: The Heuristic Value of Analogies. In *Vergleichen als archaeologische Methode: Analogien in den Archaeologien*, ed. Alexander Gramsch, pp. 143–150. Oxford: British Archaeological Reports, International Series 825.

Bernardini, W. 1999, Reassessing the Scale of Social Action at Pueblo Bonito, Chaco Canyon, New Mexico. *Kiva* 64:447–470.

Biddess, M. 1980, Purveyor of Harsh Prophecies and Poetic Truths. *The Times Higher Education Supplement*, August 1, p. 9 (London).

Billman, B. 1996, *The Evolution of Prehistoric Political Organization in the Moche Valley, Peru*. Doctoral dissertation, University of California, Santa Barbara.

2003, Review of *Archaic States* (ed. G. Feinman and J. Marcus). *American Anthropologist* 105:868–869.

Binford, L. 1977, *For Theory Building in Archaeology: Essays on Faunal Remains, Aquatic Resources, Spatial Analysis, and Systemic Modeling*. New York: Academic Press.

1981, *Bones: Ancient Men and Modern Myths*. New York: Academic Press.

1982, Objectivity – Explanation – Archaeology 1981. In *Theory and Explanation in Archaeology*, ed. C. Renfrew, M. Rowlands, and B. A. Segraves, pp. 125–138. New York: Academic Press.

Binford, L. and J. Sabloff 1982, Paradigms, Systematics, and Archaeology. *Journal of Anthropological Research* 38(2):137–153.

Bjorkman, J. 1968, A Sketch of Metals and Metalworkers in the Ancient Near East. MA thesis, University of Pennsylvania.

Black, D. 1976, *The Behavior of Law*. New York: Academic Press.

Blanton, R. 1976, Anthropological Studies of Cities. *Annual Review of Anthropology* 5:249–264.

1980, Cultural Ecology Reconsidered. *American Antiquity* 45:145–151.

1983, The Founding of Monte Albán. In *The Cloud People*, ed. K. Flannery and J. Marcus, pp. 83–87; see also editors' notes, pp. 79–83. New York: Academic Press.

Blanton, R., G. Feinman, S. Kowalewski, and L. Nicholas 1999, *Ancient Oaxaca: The Monte Albán State*. Cambridge: Cambridge University Press.

Blanton, R., G. Feinman, S. Kowalewski, and P. Peregrine 1996, A Dual-Processual Theory for the Evolution of Mesoamerican Civilization. *Current Anthropology* 37:1–14.

Blanton, R., L. Finsten, and E. Fisch 1982, *Monte Alban's Hinterland*. Ann Arbor: University of Michigan Museum of Anthropology Memoir 15.

Blocher, F. 1987, *Untersuchungen zum Motiv der nackten Frau in der altbabylonischen Zeit*. Münchener Vorderasiatische Studien 4. Münich: Profil.

1992, Gaukler im Alten Orient. In *Außenseiter und Randgruppen. Beiträge zu einer Sozialgeschichte des Alten Orients*, ed. V. Haas, pp. 79–111. Xenia 32. Constance: Universitätsverlag.

Bock, K. 1978, Theories of Progress, Development, Evolution. In *A History of Sociological Analysis*, ed. T. Bottomore and R. Nisbet, pp. 39–79. New York: Basic Books.

Boehmer, R. 1965, *Die Entwicklung der Glyptik während der Akkad-Zeit*. Berlin: Walter de Gruyter.

Boltz, W. 1986, Early Chinese Writing. *World Archaeology* 17(3):420–436.

1999, Language and Writing. In *The Cambridge History of Ancient China: From the Origins of Civilization to 221 B.C.*, ed. M. Loewe and E. Shaughnessy, pp. 74–123. Cambridge: Cambridge University Press.

Bottéro, J. 1957, *Textes économiques et administratifs*. Archives Royales de Mari 7. Paris: Imprimérie Nationale.

Bowman, A. 1986, *Egypt After the Pharaohs*. Berkeley: University of California Press.

Braidwood, R., L. Braidwood, E. Tulane, and A. Perkins 1944, New Chalcolithic Material of Samarran Type and Its Implications. *Journal of Near Eastern Studies* 3:47–72.

Breniquet, C. 1996, *La disparition de la culture de Halaf. Les origines de la culture d'Obeid dans le Nord de la Mésopotamie*. Paris: Editions Recherche sur les Civilisations.

Brinkman, J. 1964, Merodach-Baladan II. In *Studies Presented to A. Leo Oppenheim*, ed. R. Biggs and J. Brinkman, pp. 6–53. Chicago: University of Chicago Press.

  1968, *A Political History of Post-Kassite Babylonia (1158–722 B.C.)*. Analecta Orientalia 43. Rome: Pontificium Institutum Biblicum.

  1980, Kassiten. *Reallexikon der Assyriologie* 5(5/6):464–473.

Bronson, B. 1975, The Earliest Farming: Demography and Cause and Consequence. In *Population, Ecology, and Social Evolution*, ed. S. Polgar, pp. 53–78. Mouton: The Hague.

Brumfiel, E. 1992, Breaking and Entering the Ecosystem – Gender, Class, and Faction Steal the Show. *American Anthropologist* 94:551–567.

Buccellati, G. 1966, *The Amorites of the Ur III Period*. Naples: Istituto Orientale di Napoli.

Bury, J. 1925, The Hellenistic Age and the History of Civilization. In *The Hellenistic Age*, ed. J. Bury, pp. 1–30. Cambridge: Cambridge University Press.

Byrd, B. 2000, Households in Transition: Neolithic Social Organization within Southwest Asia. In *Life in Neolithic Village Farming Communities: Social Organization, Identity, and Differentiation*, ed. I. Kuijt, pp. 63–98. New York: Kluwer Academic/Plenum Publishers.

Caldwell, J. 1964, Interaction Spheres in Prehistory. In *Hopewellian Studies*, ed. J. Caldwell and R. Hall, pp. 133–143. Illinois State Museum Scientific Papers 12(6). Springfield: Illinois State Museum.

Cameron, C. 2002, Sacred Earthen Architecture in the Northern Southwest: The Bluff Great House Berm. *American Antiquity* 67(4):677–695.

Cameron, C. and W. Toll 2001, Deciphering the Organization of Production in Chaco Canyon. *American Antiquity* 66:5–13.

Campbell, S. 2000, The Burnt House at Arpachiyah: A Reexamination. *Bulletin of the American Schools of Oriental Research* 318:1–40.

Carneiro, R. 1968, Ascertaining, Testing, and Interpreting Sequences of Cultural Development. *Southwestern Journal of Anthropology* 24:354–374.

  1970, A Theory of the Origin of the State. *Science* 169:733–738.

  1981, The Chiefdom: Precursor of the State. In *The Transition to Statehood in the New World*, ed. G. Jones and R. Kautz, pp. 37–79. Cambridge: Cambridge University Press.

Carter, E. 1997, Review of A. Spycket, *Ville royale de Suse VI: Les figurines de Suse. Journal of the American Oriental Society* 117:359–361.

Chakrabarti, D. 1995, *The Archaeology of Ancient Indian Cities*. New Delhi: Oxford University Press.

  1999, *India, an Archaeological History: Palaeolithic Beginnings to Early Historic Foundations*. New Delhi: Oxford University Press.

Chang, K. C. 1980, *Shang Civilization*. New Haven: Yale University Press.

1983, *Art, Myth, and Ritual: The Path to Political Authority in Ancient China*. Cambridge: Harvard University Press.

1984, Ancient China and Its Anthropological Significance. *Symbols* (Spring/Fall): 2–22. Now reprinted in *The Breakout: The Origins of Civilization*, ed. M. Lamberg-Karlovsky, pp. 1–11. Peabody Museum Monographs 9. Cambridge, MA: Harvard University (2000).

1986, *The Archaeology of Ancient China*, fourth ed. New Haven: Yale University Press.

1999, China on the Eve of the Historical Period. In *The Cambridge History of Ancient China: From the Origins of Civilization to 221 B.C.*, ed. M. Loewe and E. Shaughnessy, pp. 37–73. Cambridge: Cambridge University Press.

Chapdelaine, C. 2000, Struggling for Survival: The Urban Class of the Moche Site, North Coast of Peru. In *Environmental Disaster and the Archaeology of Human Response*, ed. G. Bawden and M. Reycraft, pp. 121–142. Maxwell Museum of Anthropology, Anthropological Papers No. 7. Albuquerque: Maxwell Museum of Anthropology.

Charpin, D. 1977, L'onomastique hurrite à Dilbat et ses implications historiques. In *Problèmes concernant les hurrites*, ed. M.-T. Barrelet, pp. 51–70. Paris: Centre Nationale de la Recherche Scientifique.

1982, Marchands du palais et marchands du temple à la 1ère dynastie de Babylone. *Journal Asiatique* 270:25–65.

1986, Transmission des titres de propriété et constitution des archives privées en Babylonie ancienne. In *Cuneiform Archives and Libraries*, ed. K. Veenhof, pp. 121–140. Uitgaven van het Nederlands Historisch-Archaeologisch Instituut te Istanbul 57. Leiden: Nederlands Historisch-Archaeologisch Instituut te Istanbul.

2000, Lettres et procès paléo-babyloniennes. In *Rendre la justice en Mésopotamie: archives judiciaires du Proche-Orient ancien, 111e–Ier millénaires avant J.-C.*, ed. F. Joannès, pp. 69–111. Paris: Presses Universitaires de Vincennes.

Childe, V. G. 1950, The Urban Revolution. *Town Planning Review* 21:3–17.

Chippendale, C. 1993, Ambition, Deference, Discrepancy, Consumption: The Intellectual Background to a Post-Processual Archaeology. In *Archaeological Theory: Who Sets the Agenda?* ed. N. Yoffee and A. Sherratt, pp. 27–36. Cambridge: Cambridge University Press.

Chowning, A. 1979, Leadership in Melanesia. *Journal of Pacific History* 14:66–84.

Cipolla, C. 1970, *The Economic Decline of Empires*. London: Methuen.

Civil, M. 1969 ed., *The Series lú=ša and Related Texts*. Materials for the Sumerian Lexicon 12. Rome: Pontificium Institutum Biblicum.

1987, Ur III Bureaucracy: Quantitative Aspects. In *The Organization of Power: Aspects of Bureaucracy in the Ancient Near East*, ed. M. Gibson and R. Biggs, pp. 43–53. Studies in Ancient Oriental Civilization 46. Chicago: The Oriental Institute.

1995, Ancient Mesopotamian Lexicography. In *Civilizations of the Ancient Near East*, ed. J. Sasson, vol. IV, pp. 2305–2314. New York: Charles Scribner's Sons.

Clarke, D. 1968, *Analytical Archaeology*. London: Methuen.

1973, Archaeology: The Loss of Innocence. *Antiquity* 47:6–18.

1978, *Analytical Archaeology*, second ed. rev. R. Chapman. London: Methuen.

Clastres, P. 1989, *Society Against the State: Essays in Political Anthropology*, trans. R. Hurley. New York: Zone Books.

Cleuziou, S. 1994, La chute de l'empire d'Akkadé: Hommes et milieux au Moyen-Orient. *Les nouvelles de l'archéologie* 56:45–48.

Cobb, C. 2003, Mississippian Chiefdoms: How Complex? *Annual Review of Anthropology* 32:63–84.

Cohen, D. 1995, *Law, Violence, and Community in Classical Athens*. Cambridge: Cambridge University Press.

Cohen, M. 1981, *Sumerian Hymnology, the Eršemma*. Hebrew Union College Annual Supplement 2. Cincinnati: Hebrew Union College.

1988, *The Canonical Lamentations of Ancient Mesopotamia*. Bethesda: CDL Publications.

Colson, E. 1979, In Good Years and in Bad: Food Strategies of Self-Reliant Societies. *Journal of Anthropological Research* 35:18–29.

Cooper, J. 1980, Apodotic Death and the Historicity of "Historical" Omens. In *Death in Mesopotamia: Papers Read at the XXVIe Rencontre Assyriologique Internationale*, ed. B. Alster, pp. 99–105. Copenhagen: Akademisk.

1983, *Reconstructing History from Ancient Inscriptions: The Lagash-Umma Border Conflict*. Sources from the Ancient Near East 2(1). Malibu: Undena.

1986, *Presargonic Inscriptions. Sumerian and Akkadian Royal Inscriptions 1*. New Haven: American Oriental Society.

1993, Paradigm and Propaganda: The Dynasty of Akkade in the 21st Century. In *Akkad: The First World Empire. Structure, Ideology, Traditions*, ed. M. Liverani, pp. 11–23. History of the Ancient Near East/Studies 5. Padua: Sargon srl.

1999, Sumer. *Supplément au Dictionnaire de la Bible* 72:78–93.

Cordell, L. 1997, *Archaeology of the Southwest*, second ed. San Diego: Academic Press.

Cordell, L. and W. J. Judge 2001, Perspectives of Chaco Society and Polity. In *Chaco Society and Polity: Papers from the 1999 Conference*, ed. L. Cordell, W. J. Judge, and J. Piper, pp. 1–12. Albuquerque: New Mexico Archaeological Council.

Cordell, L., W. J. Judge, and J. Piper 2001 eds., *Chaco Society and Polity: Papers from the 1999 Conference*. New Mexico Archaeological Council Special Publication 4. Albuquerque 2001.

Cordell, L. and F. Plog 1979, Escaping the Confines of Normative Thought: A Reevaluation of Puebloan Prehistory. *American Antiquity* 44:405–429.

Cowgill, G. 1983, Rulership and the Ciudadela: Political Inferences from Teotihuacan Architecture. In *Civilization in the Ancient Americas: Essays in Honor of Gordon R. Willey*, ed. R. Leventhal and A. Kolata, pp. 313–343. Santa Fe: University of New Mexico Press.

1988, Onward and Upwards with Collapse. In *The Collapse of Ancient States and Civilizations*, ed. N. Yoffee and G. Cowgill, pp. 244–276. Tucson: University of Arizona Press.

1997, State and Society at Teotihuacan, Mexico. *Annual Review of Anthropology* 26:129–161.

Creamer, W. and J. Haas 1985, Tribe Versus Chiefdom in Lower Central America. *American Antiquity* 50:738–754.

Crown, Patricia L. 1994, *Ceramics and Ideology: Salado Polychrome Pottery*. Albuquerque: University of New Mexico Press.

Crumley, C. 1987, A Dialectical Critique of Hierarchy. In *Power Relations and State Formation*, ed. T. Patterson and C. Gailey, pp. 115–159. Washington, D.C.: Archeology Section/American Anthropological Association.

1995, Heterarchy and the Analysis of Complex Societies. In *Heterarchy and the Analysis of Complex Societies*, ed. R. Ehrenreich, C. Crumley, and J. Levy, pp. 1–6. Archeological Papers of the American Anthropological Association 6. Washington, DC: American Anthropological Association.

2003, Alternative Forms of Social Order. In *Heterarchy, Political Economy, and the Ancient Maya: The Three Rivers Region of the East-Central Yucatan Peninsula*, ed. V. Scarborough, F. Valdez, Jr., and N. Dunning, pp. 136–145. Tucson: University of Arizona Press.

Dahlin, B. 1984, A Colossus in Guatemala: The Preclassic Maya City of El Mirador. *Archaeology* 37:18–25.

Dalley, S. 1980, Old Babylonian Dowries. *Iraq* 42:53–74.

Dalley, S. and N. Yoffee 1991, *Old Babylonian Texts from Kish in the Ashmolean Museum: Texts from Kish and Elsewhere*. Oxford Editions of Cuneiform Texts 13. Oxford: Oxford University Press.

Dandamaev, M. 1982, The Neo-Babylonian Elders. In *Societies and Languages of the Ancient Near East: Studies in Honour of I. M. Diakonoff*, ed. M. Dandamaev, I. Gershevitch, H. Klengel, G. Komoróczy, M. T. Larsen, and J. N. Postgate, pp. 38–41. Warminster: Aris and Phillips.

David, N. and C. Kramer 2001, *Ethnoarchaeology in Action*. Cambridge: Cambridge University Press.

Davidson, T. and H. McKerrell 1976, Pottery Analysis and Halaf Period Trade in the Khabur Headwaters Region. *Iraq* 38:45–56.

1980, The Neutron Activation Analysis of Halaf and 'Ubaid Pottery from Tell Arpachiyah and Tepe Gawra. *Iraq* 42:155–167.

Dawdy, S. 2003, La Ville Sauvage: 'Enlightened' Colonialism and Creole Improvisation in New Orleans, 1699–1769. Doctoral dissertation, Ann Arbor, University of Michigan.

de Maaijer, R. 1998, Land Tenure in Ur III Lagaš. In *Landless and Hungry: Access to Land in Early and Traditional Societies*, ed. B. Haring and R. de Maaijer, pp. 50–73. Leiden: Research School CNWS.

Dennell, R. 1979, Economic Archaeology. In *The Cambridge Encyclopedia of Archaeology*, ed. A. Sherratt, pp. 38–42. London: Trewin Copplestone.

Dercksen, J. G. 1996, *The Old Assyrian Copper Trade in Anatolia*. Uitgaven van het Nederlands Historisch-Archaeologisch Instituut te Istanbul 75. Leiden: Nederlands Historisch-Archaeologisch Instituut te Istanbul.

1999, On the Financing of Old Assyrian Merchants. In *Trade and Finance in Ancient Mesopotamia*, ed. J. G. Dercksen, pp. 85–99. Uitgaven van het Nederlands Historisch-Archaeologisch Instituut te Istanbul 84. Leiden: Nederlands Historisch-Archaeologisch Instituut te Istanbul.

2000, Institutional and Private in the Old Assyrian Period. In *Interdependency of Institutions and Private Entrepreneurs*, ed. A. Bongenaar, pp. 135–152. Uitgaven van het Nederlands Historisch-Archaeologisch Instituut te Istanbul 87. Leiden: Nederlands Historisch-Archaeologisch Instituut te Istanbul.

Diakonoff, I. 1969, The Rise of the Despotic State in Ancient Mesopotamia. In *Ancient Mesopotamia: Socio-Economic History – A Collection of Studies by Soviet Scholars*, ed. M. Diakonoff, pp. 173–203. Moscow: Nauka.

1982, The Structure of Near Eastern Society before the Middle of the 2nd Millennium B.C. *Oikumene* 3:7–100.

Dobres, M.-A. and J. Robb 2000, *Agency in Archaeology*. New York: Routledge.

Dombradi, E. 1996, *Die Darstellung des Rechtsaustrags in den altbabylonischen Prozessurkunden*. Freiburger Altorientalische Studien 20. Stuttgart: Franz Steiner.

Donbaz, V. and N. Yoffee 1986, *Old Babylonian Texts from Kish Conserved in the Istanbul Archaeological Museums*. Bibliotheca Mesopotamica 17. Malibu: Undena.

Dossin, G. 1938, Un ritual du culte d'Ištar. *Revue d'Assyriologie* 35:1–13.

1967, *La correspondance feminine*. Archives Royales de Mari 10. Paris: Geuthner.

Doty, L. 1977, Cuneiform Archives from Hellenistic Uruk. Doctoral dissertation, Yale University.

Douglas, B. 1979, Rank, Power, Authority: A Reassessment of Traditional Leadership in South Pacific Societies. *Journal of Pacific History* 14:2–27.

Downey, S. 1988, *Mesopotamian Religious Architecture: Alexander through the Parthians*. Princeton: Princeton University Press.

Doyel, D. 1979, The Prehistoric Hohokam of the Arizona Desert. *American Scientist* 67(5):544–554.

1992 ed., *Anasazi Regional Organization and the Chaco System*. Maxwell Museum of Anthropology Anthropological Papers 5. Albuquerque: University of New Mexico Press.

Drennan, R. and C. Uribe 1987 eds., *Chiefdoms in the Americas*. Boston: University Presses of America.

Driver, G. and J. Miles 1952, *The Babylonian Laws*, vol. I: *Legal Commentary*. Oxford: Clarendon Press.

Dunnell, R. 1982, Science, Social Science, and Common Sense: The Agonizing Dilemma of Modern Archaeology. *Journal of Anthropological Research* 38:1–25.

Durand, J.-M. 1989, L'assemblée en Syrie à l'époque pré-amorite. In *Miscellanea Eblaitica*, ed. P. Fronzaroli, vol. II pp. 27–44. Quaderni di Semitistica 16. Florence: Università di Firenze, Dipartimento di Linguistica.

1990, Documents pour l'histoire du Royaume de Haute-Mésopotamie II. *Mari Annales de Recherche Interdisciplinaires* 6:277–301.

Earle, T. 1977, A Reappraisal of Redistribution: Complex Hawaiian Chiefdoms. In *Exchange Systems in Prehistory*, ed. T. Earle and J. Ericson, pp. 213–229. New York: Academic Press.

1987, Chiefdoms in Archaeological and Ethnohistorical Perspective. *Annual Review of Anthropology* 16:279–308.

1997, *How Chiefs Come to Power: The Political Economy in Prehistory*. Stanford: Stanford University Press.

Earle, T. 1991 ed., *Chiefdoms: Power, Economy, and Ideology*. A School of American Research Book. Cambridge: Cambridge University Press.

Edzard, D. O. 1980, Kanisurra. *Reallexikon der Assyriologie* 5:389.

Ehrenreich, R., C. Crumley, and J. Levy 1995 eds., *Heterarchy and the Analysis of Complex Societies*. Archeological Papers of the American Anthropological Association 6. Arlington, VA: American Anthropological Association.

Eidem, J. 1991, An Old Assyrian Treaty from Tell Leilan. In *Marchands, diplomates et empereurs: Etudes sur les civilisations mésopotamiennes offertes à Paul Garelli*, ed. D. Charpin and F. Joannès, pp. 185–207. Paris: Editions Recherches sur les Civilisations.

Eilers, W. 1932, Die Gesetzesstela Chammurabis. *Der Alte Orient* 13:1.

Eisenstadt, S. 1964, Social Change, Differentiation, and Evolution. *American Sociological Review* 29:375–386.

1969, *The Political Systems of Empires: The Rise and Fall of the Historical Bureaucratic Societies.* Reprint, with a new introduction, of 1963 edition. New York: Free Press.

1986 ed., *The Origins and Diversity of Axial Age Civilizations.* Albany: State University of New York Press.

1988, Beyond Collapse. In *The Collapse of Ancient States and Civilizations*, ed. N. Yoffee and G. Cowgill, pp. 236–243. Tucson: University of Arizona Press.

Eisenstadt, S. (with M. Curelaru) 1976, *The Form of Sociology – Paradigms and Crises.* New York: Wiley.

Elson, C. 2003, Elites at Cerro Tilcajete. Doctoral dissertation, Ann Arbor, University of Michigan.

El-Wailly, F. and B. Abu al-Soof 1965, The Excavations at Tell es-Sawwan: First Preliminary Report (1964). *Sumer* 21:17–32.

Emberling, G. 1997, Ethnicity in Complex Societies: Archaeological Perspectives. *Journal of Archaeological Research* 5:295–344.

2003, Urban Social Transformations and the Problem of the "First City": New Research from Mesopotamia. In *The Social Construction of Ancient Cities*, ed. M. Smith, pp. 254–268. Washington, DC: Smithsonian Books.

Emberling, G., J. Cheng, T. Larsen, H. Pittman, T. Skuldboel, J. Weber, and H. T. Wright 1999, Excavations at Tell Brak 1998: Preliminary Report. *Iraq* 61:1–41.

Emberling, G. and H. McDonald 2001, Excavations at Tell Brak 2000: Preliminary Report. *Iraq* 63: 21–54.

2003, Excavations at Tell Brak 2001–2002: Preliminary Report. *Iraq* 65:1–75.

Emberling, G. and N. Yoffee 1999, Thinking About Ethnicity in Mesopotamian Archaeology and History. In *Fluchtpunkt Uruk. Archäologische Einheit aus Methodischer Vielfalt. Schriften für Hans Nissen*, ed. H. Kühne, R. Bernbeck, and K. Bartl, pp. 272–281. Rahden: Marie Leidorf.

Englund, R. 1990, *Organisation und Verwaltung der Ur III-Fischerei.* Berliner Beiträge zum Vorderen Orient 10. Berlin: Dietrich Reimer Verlag.

1998, Texts from the Late Uruk Period. In *Mesopotamien. Späturuk-Zeit und Frühdynastische Zeit*, ed. P. Attinger and M. Wäfler, pp. 15–233. Orbis Biblicus et Orientalis 160/1. Freiburg, Switzerland: Universitätsverlag.

Evin, J. 1995, Possibilité et necessité de la calibration des datations C-14 de l'archéologie du Proche-Orient. *Paléorient* 21:5–16.

Fairservis, W. 1989, An Epigenetic View of the Harappan Culture. In *Archaeological Thought in America*, ed. C. C. Lamberg-Karlovsky, pp. 205–217. Cambridge: Cambridge University Press.

Falkenstein, A. 1963, Zu den Inschriftfunden der Grabung in Uruk-Warka 1960–1961. *Baghdader Mitteilungen* 2:1–82.

Farber, W. 1983, Die Vergöttlichung Narām-Sîns. *Orientalia* N.S. 52:67–72.

Fash, W. 1991, *Scribes, Warriors and Kings: The City of Copán and the Ancient Maya*. London: Thames and Hudson.

Feinman, G. and J. Marcus 1998 eds., *Archaic States*. Santa Fe: SAR Press.

Feinman, G. and J. Neitzel 1984, Too Many Types: An Overview of Sedentary Prestate Societies in the Americas. *Advances in Archaeological Method and Theory* 7:39–102.

Finkelstein, J. 1968a, *Cuneiform Texts . . . in the British Museum* 48. London: British Museum.

   1968b, Law in the Ancient Near East (Ha-Mishpat ba-Mizrah ha-qadmon). *Encyclopedia Miqra'it* 5:588–614.

   1972, *Old Babylonian Documents*. Yale Oriental Series 13. New Haven: Yale University Press.

   1976, *šilip rēmim* and Related Matters. In *Kramer Anniversary Volume*, ed. B. Eichler, pp. 187–194. Alter Orient und Altes Testament 25. Kevelaer: Butzon and Bercker.

Flannery, K. 1972, The Cultural Evolution of Civilizations. *Annual Review of Ecology and Systematics* 3:399–426.

   1982, The Golden Marshalltown: A Parable for the Archaeology of the 1980s. *American Anthropologist* 84:265–278.

   1983, Archaeology and Ethnology in the Context of Divergent Evolution. In *The Cloud People: Divergent Evolution of the Zapotec and Mixtec Civilizations*, ed. K. Flannery and J. Marcus, pp. 361–362. New York: Academic Press.

   1999, Process and Agency in Early State Formation. *Cambridge Archaeological Journal* 9:3–21.

Flannery, K. and J. Marcus 1983 eds., *The Cloud People: Divergent Evolution of the Zapotec and Mixtec Civilizations*. New York: Academic Press.

Flood, J. 1990, *Archaeology of the Dreamtime*. Sydney: Collins.

Forest, J.-D. 1996, *Mésopotamie. L'Apparition de l'état (VIIe-IIIe millénaires)*. Paris: Méditerranée.

   1999, *Les premiers temples de Mésopotamie (4e et 3e millénaires)*. British Archaeological Reports, International Series 765. Oxford: Archaeopress.

Fortner, J. 1996, Adjudicating Entities and Levels of Legal Authority in Lawsuit Records of the Old Babylonian Era. Doctoral dissertation, Cincinnati, Hebrew Union College.

Foster, B. 1982, *Umma in the Sargonic Period*. Memoirs of the Connecticut Academy of Arts and Sciences 20. Hamden: Connecticut Academy of Arts and Sciences.

Fowles, S. 2004, The Making of Made People. The Prehistoric Evolution of Hierocracy among the Northern Tiwa of New Mexico. Doctoral dissertation, Ann Arbor, University of Michigan.

Frankel, D. 1979, *Archaeologists at Work: Studies on Halaf Pottery*. London: British Museum.

Frankena, R. 1966, *Briefe aus dem British Museum (LIH und CT 2–33)*. Altbabylonische Briefe 2. Leiden: Brill.

Fried, M. 1960, On the Evolution of Social Stratification and the State. In *Culture in History: Essays in Honor of Paul Radin*, ed. S. Diamond, pp. 713–731. New York: Columbia University Press.

   1967, *The Evolution of Political Society: An Essay in Political Anthropology*. New York: Random House.

   1975, *The Notion of Tribe*. Menlo Park, CA: Cummings.

Friedman, J. 1974, Marxism, Structuralism and Vulgar Materialism. *Man* N.S. 9:444–469.

Friedman, J. and M. Rowlands 1977, Notes Towards an Epigenetic Model of the Evolution of "Civilisation". In *The Evolution of Social Systems*, ed. J. Friedman and M. Rowlands, pp. 201–276. London: Duckworth.

Fry, R. 2003, The Peripheries of Tikal. In *Tikal: Dynasties, Foreigners, and Affairs of State*, ed. J. Sabloff, pp. 143–170. Santa Fe: School of American Research.

Gallery, M. 1980, Service Obligations of the Kezertu-women. *Orientalia* 49:333–340.

Geertz, C. 1980, *Negara: The Theatre State in Nineteenth-Century Bali*. Princeton: Princeton University Press.

Gelb, I. J. 1968, An Old Babylonian List of Amorites. *Journal of the American Oriental Society* 88:39–46.

1969, On the Alleged Temple and State Economies in Ancient Mesopotamia. In *Studi in Onore di Edoardo Volterra*, pp. 137–154. Milan: A. Giuffr'è.

1972, The Arua Institution. *Revue d'Assyriologie* 66:1–32.

1979, Definition and Discussion of Slavery and Serfdom. *Ugarit Forschungen* 11:283–297.

1980, *Computer-Aided Analysis of Amorite*. Assyriological Studies 21. Chicago: Oriental Institute.

Gelb, I. J., P. Steinkeller and R. Whiting 1991, *Earliest Land Tenure Systems in the Near East: Ancient Kudurrus*. Oriental Institute Publications 104. Chicago: Oriental Institute.

Geller, M. 1997, The Last Wedge. *Zeitschrift für Assyriologie* 87:43–95.

Gibson, M. 1972, *The City and Area of Kish*. Coconut Grove, FL: Field Research Projects.

Ginzburg, C. 1989, *Clues, Myths, and the Historical Method*, trans. John and Anne Tedeschi. Baltimore: Johns Hopkins University Press.

Glassner, J.-J. 1994a, La chute de l'empire d'Akkadé, les volcans d'Anatolie et la désertification de la vallée du Habur. *Les nouvelles de l'archéologie* 56:49–51.

1994b, La chute de l'empire d'Akkadé ... (suite): Entre Droit épigraphique et Gauche archéologique, y-a-t-il une place pour la science? *Les nouvelles de l'archéologie* 57:33–41.

Gluckman, M. 1973, Limitations of the Case-method in the Study of Tribal Law. *Law and Society Review* 7:643–666.

Goddeeris, A. 2002, *Economy and Society in Northern Babylonia in the Early Old Babylonian Period (ca. 2000–1800 BC)*. Orientalia Lovaniensia Analecta 109. Leuven: Peeters.

Godelier, M. 1977, *Perspectives in Marxist Anthropology*, trans. R. Brain. Cambridge: Cambridge University Press.

1986, *The Mental and the Material: Thought, Economy and Society*, trans. M. Thom. London: Verso.

Goodnick Westenholz, J. 1989, Tamar, qēdēša, qadištu, and Sacred Prostitution in Mesopotamia. *Harvard Theological Review* 82(3):245–265.

1995, Heilige Hochzeit und kultische Prostitution im alten Mesopotamien: sexuelle Vereinbarung im sakralen Raum? *Wort und Dienst* (Jahrbuch der Kirchlichen Hochschule Bethel, ed. H.-P. Staehli) 23:43–62.

1997, *Legends of the Kings of Akkade: The Texts*. Mesopotamian Civilizations 7. Winona Lake, IN: Eisenbrauns.

Gould, R. and P. J. Watson 1982, A Dialogue on the Meaning and Use of Analogy in Ethnoarchaeological Reasoning. *Journal of Anthropological Archaeology* 1:355–381.

Green, P. 1990, *From Alexander to Actium*. Berkeley: University of California Press.

Greenberg, J. 1966, *Language Universals.* The Hague: Mouton.

Griffeth, R. and C. Thomas 1981 eds., *The City-State in Five Cultures.* Santa Barbara: ABC-Clio.

Grube, N. 2000, The City-States of the Maya. In *A Comparative Study of Thirty City-State Cultures,* ed. M. Hansen, pp. 547–565. Det Kongelige Danske Videnskabernes Selskab Historisk-filosofiske Skrifter 21. Copenhagen: C. A. Reitzels.

Güterbock, H. 1983, A Hurro-Hittite Hymn to Ishtar. *Journal of the American Oriental Society* 103:155–164.

Haas, J. 2001 ed., *From Leaders to Rulers.* New York: Plenum.

Hall, J. 1997, *Ethnic Identity in Greek Antiquity.* Cambridge: Cambridge University Press.

   2002, *Hellenicity: Between Ethnicity and Culture.* Chicago: University of Chicago Press.

Hallo, W. 1962, The Royal Inscriptions of Ur: A Typology. *Hebrew Union College Annual* 33:1–43.

   1963, Royal Hymns and Mesopotamian Unity. *Journal of Cuneiform Studies* 17:113–118.

   1971, Gutium. *Reallexikon der Assyriologie* 3:708–720.

   1972, The House of Ur-Meme. *Journal of Near Eastern Studies* 31:87–95.

Hallo, W. and J. Curtis 1959, Money and Merchants in Ur III. *Hebrew Union College Annual* 30:103–139.

Hallpike, C. 1986, *The Principles of Social Evolution.* Oxford: Clarendon Press.

Hannestad, L. 1988, Change and Conservatism: Hellenistic Pottery in Mesopotamia and Iran. *Akten des XIII. Internationalen Kongresses für klassische Archäologie,* pp. 179–186. Mainz am Rhein: Philipp von Zabern.

Hansen, M. 2000 ed., *A Comparative Study of Thirty City-State Cultures.* Det Kongelige Danske Videnskabernes Selskab Historisk-filosofiske Skrifter 21. Copenhagen: C. A. Reitzels.

   2002, *A Comparative Study of Six City-State Cultures.* Det Kongelige Danske Videnskabernes Selskab Historisk-filosofiske Skrifter 27. Copenhagen: C. A. Reitzels.

Harris, M. 1968, *The Rise of Anthropological Theory.* New York: Crowell.

Harris, R. 1960, Old Babylonian Temple Loans. *Journal of Cuneiform Studies* 14:126–132.

   1961, On the Process of Secularization under Hammurabi. *Journal of Cuneiform Studies* 14:126–132.

   1964, The naditu Woman. In *Studies Presented to A. Leo Oppenheim,* ed. R. Biggs and J. Brinkman, pp. 106–135. Chicago: University of Chicago Press.

   1969, Notes on the Babylonian Cloister and Hearth: A Review Article. *Orientalia* N.S. 38:133–145.

   1975, *Ancient Sippar: A Demographic Study of an Old-Babylonian City (1894–1595 B.C.).* Uitgaven van het Nederlands Historisch-Archaeologisch Instituut te Istanbul 36. Leiden: Nederlands Historisch-Archaeologisch Instituut te Istanbul.

Hassan, F. 1981, *Demographic Archaeology.* New York: Academic Press.

   1993, Towns and Villages in ancient Egypt: Ecology, Society, and Urbanism. In *The Archaeology of Africa,* ed. T. Shaw, P. Sinclair, B. Andah, and A. Okpoko, pp. 551–569. London: Routledge.

Hegmon, M. 2003, Setting Theoretical Egos Aside: Issues and Theory in North American Archaeology. *American Antiquity* 68:213–243.

Henrickson, E. and I. Thuesen, 1989 eds., *Upon This Foundation: The 'Ubaid Reconsidered.* Copenhagen: Museum Tusculanum Press.

Henry, D. 1989, *From Foraging to Agriculture: The Levant at the End of the Ice Age.* Philadelphia: University of Pennsylvania Press.

Henshaw, R. 1994, *Female and Male. The Cultic Personnel. The Bible and the Research of the Ancient Near East.* Princeton Theological Monograph Series 31. Allison Park, PA: Pickwick.

Herodotus, 1954, *The Histories.* Trans. A. de Sélincourt. Harmondsworth: Penguin.

Hodder, I. 1985, Postprocessual Archaeology. *Advances in Archaeological Method and Theory* 8:1–26.

Hoebel, E. 1954, *The Law of Primitive Man.* New York: Atheneum.

Hours, F., O. Aurenche, J. Cauvin, M.-C. Cauvin, L. Copeland, and P. Sanlaville 1974, *Atlas des Sites du Proche-Orient (14000–5700 BP).* Travaux de la Maison de l'Orient méditerranéen 24. Lyons: De Boccard.

Hsu, C.-Y. 1986, Historical Conditions of the Emergence and Crystallization of the Confucian System. In *The Origins and Diversity of Axial Age Civilizations,* ed. S. N. Eisenstadt, pp. 306–324. Albany: SUNY Press.

1988, The Roles of the Literati and of Regionalism in the Fall of the Han Dynasty. In *The Collapse of Ancient States and Civilizations,* ed. N. Yoffee and G. Cowgill, pp. 176–195. Tucson: University of Arizona Press.

1999, The Spring and Autumn Period. In *The Cambridge History of Ancient China: From the Origins of Civilization to 221 B.C.,* ed. M. Loewe and E. Shaughnessy, pp. 545–586. Cambridge: Cambridge University Press.

Invernizzi, A. 1984, Note on the Art of Seleucid Mesopotamia. In *Arabie orientale, Mésopotamie et Iran méridional de l'Age du Fer au début de la période islamique,* ed. R. Boucharlat and J.-F. Salles, pp. 27–31. Paris: Editions Recherche sur les Civilisations.

1993, Seleucia on the Tigris: Centre and Periphery in Seleucid Asia. In *Centre and Periphery in the Hellenistic World,* ed. P. Bilde, T. Engberg-Pedersen, L. Hannestad, J. Sahle, and K. Randsborg, pp. 230–250. Aarhus: Aarhus University Press.

Isbell, W. and G. McEwan, 1991 eds., *Huari Administrative Structure: Prehistoric Monumental Architecture and State Government.* Washington, DC: Dumbarton Oaks.

Jacobsen, T. 1943, Primitive Democracy in Ancient Mesopotamia. *Journal of Near Eastern Studies* 2:159–172.

1953a, On the Textile Industry at Ur under Ibbī-Sîn. In *Studia Orientalia Ioanni Pedersen,* pp. 172–187. Munksgaard: Hauniae.

1953b, The Reign of Ibbī-Suen. *Journal of Cuneiform Studies* 7:36–47.

1957, Early Political Development in Mesopotamia. *Zeitschrift für Assyriologie* 52:91–140.

1978–9, Iphur-Kīshi and His Times. *Archiv für Orientforschung* 26:1–14.

Janssen, C. 1991, Samsu-Iluna and the Hungry *naditums. Mesopotamia History and Environment,* Series I. Northern Akkad Project Reports 5:3–39.

Janssen, J. 1983, El-Amarna as a Residential City. *Bibliotheca Orientalis* 40:273–288.

Janusek, J. 2002, Out of Many, One: Style and Social Boundaries in Tiwanaku. *Latin American Antiquity* 13:35–61.

Janusek, J. and D. Blom 2004, Identifying Tiwanaku Urban Populations: Style, Identity, and Ceremony in Andean Cities. In *Population and Preindustrial Cities: Cross-Cultural Perspectives,* ed. G. Storey (in press).

Joffe, A. 1998, Disembedded Capitals in Western Asian Perspective. *Comparative Studies in Society and History* 40:549–580.

Johnson, A. and T. Earle 1987, *The Evolution of Human Societies: From Foraging Group to Agrarian State*. Stanford: Stanford University Press.

Jones, R. 1977, The Tasmanian Paradox: In *Stone Tools as Cultural Markers: Change, Evolution, Complexity*, ed. R. Wright, pp. 189–204. Canberra: Australian Institute of Aboriginal Studies.

1978, Why Did the Tasmanians Stop Eating Fish? In *Explorations in Ethnoarchaeology*, ed. R. Gould, pp. 11–47. Albuquerque: University of New Mexico Press.

Jones, T. and J. Snyder 1961, *Sumerian Economic Texts from the Third Ur Dynasty*. Minneapolis: University of Minnesota Press.

Judge, W. J. 1989, Chaco Canyon-San Juan Basin. In *Dynamics of Southwestern Prehistory*, ed. L. Cordell and G. Gumerman, pp. 209–262. Washington, DC: Smithsonian Institution.

2003, A Trial Timeline Model for Chacoan Society and Polity. Unpublished paper.

Kamp, K. and N. Yoffee 1980, Ethnicity in Ancient Western Asia during the Early Second Millennium B.C.: Archaeological Assessments and Ethnoarchaeological Prospectives. *Bulletin of the American Schools of Oriental Research* 237:85–104.

Kantner, J. 2003, *Ancient Pueblo Southwest*. Cambridge: Cambridge University Press.

Kantner, J. and N. Mahoney 2000 eds., *Great House Communities across the Chacoan Landscape*. Anthropological Papers of the University of Arizona 64. Tucson: University of Arizona Press.

Kantorowicz, E. 1957, *The King's Two Bodies: A Study in Medieval Political Theology*. Princeton: Princeton University Press.

Kaplan, D. and R. Manners 1972, *Culture Theory*. Englewood Cliffs, NJ: Prentice-Hall.

Katz, D. 1993, *Gilgamesh and Akka*. Groningen: Styx.

Kauffman, S. 1993, *The Origins of Order*. Oxford: Oxford University Press.

Kaufman, H. 1988, The Collapse of Ancient States and Civilizations as an Organizational Problem. In *The Collapse of Ancient States and Civilizations*, ed. N. Yoffee and G. Cowgill, pp. 219–235. Tucson: University of Arizona Press.

Keightley, D. 1979–80, The Shang State as Seen in the Oracle-Bone Inscriptions. *Early China* 5:25–34.

1983, The Late Shang State: When, Where, and What? In *The Origins of Chinese Civilization*, ed. D. Keightley, pp. 523–564. Berkeley: University of California Press.

1999, The Shang: China's First Historical Dynasty. In *The Cambridge History of Ancient China: From the Origins of Civilization to 221 B.C.*, ed. M. Loewe and E. Shaughnessy, pp. 232–291. Cambridge: Cambridge University Press.

Keith, K. 1999, Cities, Neighborhoods, and Houses: Urban Spatial Organization in Old Babylonian Mesopotamia. Doctoral dissertation, Ann Arbor, University of Michigan.

2003, The Spatial Patterns of Everyday Life in Old Babylonian Neighborhoods. In *The Social Construction of Ancient Cities*, ed. M. Smith, pp. 56–80. Washington, DC: Smithsonian Books.

Kemp, B. 1989, *Ancient Egypt: Anatomy of a Civilization*. London: Routledge.

Kemp, B. and S. Garfi 1993, *A Survey of the Ancient City of El-'Amarna*. London: Egypt Exploration Society Occasional Publication 9.

Kenoyer, J. M. 1997, Early City-States in South Asia: Comparing the Harappan Phase and Early Historic Period. In *The Archaeology of City-States: Cross-Cultural Approaches*, ed. D. Nichols and T. Charlton, pp. 51–70. Washington, DC: Smithsonian Institution Press.

1998, *Ancient Cities of the Indus Valley Civilization*. Karachi: Oxford University Press.

Kersenboom-Story, S. 1987, *Nityasumangali: Devadasi Tradition in South India.* Delhi: Motilal Banarsidass.

Kertzer, David 1988, *Ritual, Politics, and Power.* New Haven: Yale University Press.

Kingery, W. D., P. Vandiver, and M. Prickett 1988, The Beginnings of Pyrotechnology, Part II: Production and Use of Lime and Gypsum Plaster in the Pre-Pottery Neolithic Near East. *Journal of Field Archaeology* 15:219–244.

Kirch, P. 1984, *The Evolution of Polynesian Chiefdoms.* Cambridge: Cambridge University Press.

Kirch, P. and R. Green 2001, *Hawaiki, Ancestral Polynesia: An Essay in Historical Anthropology.* Cambridge: Cambridge University Press.

Klotchkoff, I. 1982, The Late Babylonian List of Scholars. In *Schriften zur Geschichte und Kultur des Alten Orients* vol. XV, ed. H. Klengel, pp. 143–148. Berlin: Akademie-Verlag.

Knight, V. Jr. 1990, Social Organization and the Evolution of Hierarchy in Southeastern Chiefdoms. *Journal of Anthropological Research* 46:1–23.

Kohl, P. 1978, The Balance of Trade in Southwestern Asia in the Mid-Third Millennium B.C. *Current Anthropology* 19:463–492.

Kohler, T. and G. Gumerman 2000 eds., *Dynamics in Human and Primate Societies: Agent-Based Modeling of Social and Spatial Processes.* Santa Fe Institute Studies in the Sciences of Complexity. New York: Oxford University Press.

Kolata, A. 1997, Of Kings and Capitals: Principles of Authority and the Nature of Cities in the Native Andean State. In *The Archaeology of City-States: Cross-Cultural Approaches*, ed. D. Nichols and T. Charlton, pp. 245–254. Washington, DC: Smithsonian Institution Press.

2003, *Tiwanaku and Its Hinterland: Archaeology and Paleoecology of an Andean Civilization* vol. II. Washington: Smithsonian Institution Press.

Koschaker, P. 1917, *Rechtsvergleichende Studien zur Gesetzgebung Hammurapis.* Leipzig: Verlag von Veit & Comp.

Koshurnikov, S. 1984a, Life in Old Babylonian Dilbat. Paper presented at the 31st Rencontre Assyriologique Internationale in Leningrad, July, 1984.

1984b, Semejnyj Arxiv Starovavilonsogo Vremeni iz Goroda Dil'bata (An Old Babylonian Family Archive from the City of Dilbat). *Vestnik Drevnej Istorii* 2:123–141.

Kosso, P. 1991, Method in Archaeology: Middle Range Theory as Hermeneutics. *American Antiquity* 56:621–627.

Kowalewski, S., G. Feinman, L. Finsten, R. Blanton, and L. Nicholas 1989, *The Prehispanic Settlement Patterns in Tlacolula, Etla, and Ocotlan, the Valley of Oaxaca*, Mexico. Ann Arbor: University of Michigan Museum of Anthropology Memoir 23.

Kraus, F. 1960, Ein zentrales Problem des altmesopotamischen Rechtes: Was ist der Codex Hammurabi? *Genava* 8:283–296.

1984, *Königliche Verfügungen in altbabylonischer Zeit.* Leiden: E. J. Brill.

Læssøe, J. 1950, On the Fragments of the Hammurabi Code. *Journal of Cuneiform Studies* 4:173–187.

Lambert, W. 1992, Prostitution. In *Außenseiter und Randgruppen. Beiträge zu einer Sozialgeschichte des Alten Orients*, ed. V. Haas, pp. 127–157. Xenia 32. Constance: Universitätsverlag.

Landsberger, B. 1939, Die babylonischen Termini für Gesetz und Recht. In *Symbolae ad Iura Orientis Antiqui Pertinentes Paulo Koschaker Dedicatae*, ed. J. Friedrich, J. G. Lautner and J. Miles, pp. 219–234. Leiden: E. J. Brill.

Larsen, M. T. 1974, The Old Assyrian Colonies in Anatolia. *Journal of the American Oriental Society* 94:468–475.

1976, *The Old Assyrian City-State and its Colonies*. Mesopotamia 4. Copenhagen: Akademisk.

1977, Partnerships in the Old Assyrian Trade. In *Trade in the Ancient Near East*, ed. J. Hawkins, pp. 119–145. London: British School of Archaeology in Iraq.

2003, *The Aššur-nādā Archives*. Leiden: Nederlands Instituut voor het Nabije Oosten.

Laufer, B. 1918, Review of R. Lowie, *Culture and Ethnology*. *American Anthropologist* 20:90.

Le Blanc, S. 1999, *Prehistoric Warfare in the American Southwest*. Salt Lake City: University of Utah Press.

Lekson, S. 1994, Thinking about Chaco. In *Chaco Canyon: A Center and Its World*, photographs by Mary Peck with essays by S. Lekson, J. Stein, and S. Ortiz, pp. 11–44. Santa Fe: Museum of New Mexico Press.

1999, *The Chaco Meridian: Centers of Political Power in the Ancient Southwest*. Walnut Creek, CA: Altamira Press.

2000, Great! In *Great House Communities across the Chacoan Landscape*, ed. J. Kantner and N. Mahoney, pp. 157–163. Anthropological Papers of the University of Arizona 64. Tucson: University of Arizona Press.

2002, War in the Southwest, War in the World. *American Antiquity* 67:607–624.

2005 ed., *The Archaeology of Chaco Canyon: An Eleventh-Century Pueblo Regional Center*. Santa Fe: School of American Research Press.

Lesser, A. 1952, Evolution in Social Anthropology. *Southwestern Journal of Anthropology* 8:134–146.

Levi, G. 1992, On Microhistory. In *New Perspectives on Historical Writing*, ed. P. Burke, pp. 93–113. University Park: Pennsylvania State University Press.

Levy, J. 1992, *Orayvi Revisited: Social Stratification in an "Egalitarian" Society*. Santa Fe: School of American Research Press.

1994, Ethnographic Analogs: Strategies for Reconstructing Archaeological Cultures. In *Understanding Complexity in the Prehistoric Southwest*, ed. G. Gumerman and M. Gell-Mann, pp. 223–244. Santa Fe Institute Studies in the Sciences of Complexity Proceedings 16. Reading, MA: Addison-Wesley.

Lilley, I. 1985, Chiefs Without Chiefdoms. *Archaeology in Oceania* 20:6–65.

Limet, H. 1960, *Le travail du métal au pays de Sumer au temps de la IIIe dynastie d'Ur*. Bibliothèque de la Faculté de Philosophie et Lettres de l'Université de Liège 155. Paris: Société d'Edition "Les Belles Lettres."

Liu, Li. 1996a, Mortuary Ritual and Social Hierarchy in the Longshan Culture. *Early China* 21:1–46.

1996b, Settlement Patterns, Chiefdom Variability, and the Development of Early States in North China. *Journal of Anthropological Archaeology* 15:237–288.

2000, The Development and Decline of Social Complexity in China: Some Environmental and Social Factors. *Indo-Pacific Prehistory: The Melaka Papers. Bulletin of the Indo-Pacific Prehistory Association* 20(4):14–33.

2003, "The Products of Minds as well as of Hands": Production of Prestige Goods in the Neolithic and Early State Periods of China. *Asian Perspectives* 42(1):1–40.

Liu, Li and Xingcan Chen 2003, *State Formation in Early China*. London: Duckworth.

Liverani, M. 1990, *Prestige and Interest: International Relations in the Near East ca. 1600–1100 B.C.* History of the Ancient Near East/Studies 1. Padua: Sargon srl.

     1993, Model and Actualization. The Kings of Akkad in the Historical Tradition. In *Akkad: The First World Empire. Structure, Ideology, Traditions*, ed. M. Liverani, pp. 41–67. History of the Ancient Near East/Studies 5. Padua: Sargon srl.

Lloyd, S. 1978, *The Archaeology of Mesopotamia.* London: Thames and Hudson.

Loding, D. 1974, A Craft Archive from Ur. Doctoral dissertation, University of Pennsylvania.

Lovejoy, A. O. and G. Boas 1965 [1935], *Primitivism and Related Ideas in Antiquity.* Baltimore: Johns Hopkins Press.

Machinist, P. 1976, Literature as Politics: The Tukulti-Ninurta Epic and the Bible. *Catholic Biblical Quarterly* 38:455–482.

     1986, On Self-Consciousness in Mesopotamia. In *The Origins and Diversity of Axial Age Civilizations*, ed. S. Eisenstadt, pp. 183–202. Albany: State University of New York Press.

Maekawa, K. 1987, Collective Labor Service in Girsu-Lagash: The Pre-Sargonic and Ur III Periods. In *Labor in the Ancient Near East*, ed. M. Powell, pp. 49–71. American Oriental Series 68. New Haven: American Oriental Society.

     1996, Confiscation of Private Properties in the Ur III Period: A Study of é-dul-la and níg-GA. *Acta Sumerologica* 18:103–168.

Mailer, N. 1973, *Marilyn, a Biography. Pictures by the World's Foremost Photographers.* New York: Grosset & Dunlap.

Maine, H. 1861, *Ancient Law.* London: Oxford University Press.

Maisels, C. 1993, *The Near East: Archaeology in the "Cradle of Civilization."* London: Routledge.

Malkin, I. 2001 ed., *Ancient Perceptions of Greek Ethnicity.* Washington, DC: Center for Hellenic Studies.

Mann, M. 1986, *The Sources of Social Power.* Cambridge: Cambridge University Press.

Marcus, J. 1990 ed., *Debating Oaxacan Archaeology.* Ann Arbor: University of Michigan Museum of Anthropology Paper 84.

Margalin, F. 1985, *Wives of the God-King: Rituals of the Devadasis of Puri.* Oxford: Oxford University Press.

Martin, S. and N. Grube 2000, *Chronicle of the Maya Kings and Queens.* New York: Thames and Hudson.

Mathien, F. J. 2003, Artifacts from Pueblo Bonito: One Hundred Years of Interpretation. In *Pueblo Bonito: The Center of the Chacoan World*, ed. J. Neitzel, pp. 127–142. Washington: Smithsonian Institution Press.

Matthews, R. 1993, *Cities, Seals and Writing: Archaic Seal Impressions from Jemdet Nasr and Ur.* Materialien zu den frühen Schriftzeugnissen des Vorderen Orients 2. Berlin: Gebr. Mann.

     1997, Girsu and Lagash. *The Oxford Encyclopedia of Archaeology in the Near East* v. 2, ed. E. Meyers, pp. 406–409. New York: Oxford University Press.

     2000, *The Early Prehistory of Mesopotamia 500,000 to 4,500 bc.* Subartu V. Turnhout: Brepols.

     2003, *The Archaeology of Mesopotamia: Theories and Approaches.* New York: Routledge.

McCorriston, J. and F. Hole 1991, The Ecology of Seasonal Stress and the Origins of Agriculture in the Near East. *American Anthropologist* 93:46–69.

McGuire, R. 1983, Breaking Down Cultural Complexity: Inequality and Heterogeneity. *Advances in Archaeological Method and Theory* 6:91–142.

McIntosh, S. 1999 ed., *Beyond Chiefdoms: Pathways to Complexity in Africa.* Cambridge: Cambridge University Press.

McNamara, J. 1996, *Sisters in Arms: Catholic Nuns through Two Millennia.* Cambridge: Harvard University Press.

Meek, R. 1976, *Social Science and the Ignoble Savage.* Cambridge: Cambridge University Press.

Menzel, B. 1981, *Assyrische Tempel.* Rome: Biblical Institute.

Merpert, N. and R. Munchaer 1993, Yarim Tepe I. In *Early Stages in the Evolution of Mesopotamian Civilization,* ed. N. Yoffee and J. Clark, pp. 73–114. Tucson: University of Arizona Press.

Merton, R. 1949, *Social Theory and Social Structure.* Glencoe, IL: Free Press.

Meskell, L. 2002, *Private Life in New Kingdom Egypt.* Princeton: Princeton University Press.

2003, *Material Biographies: Object Worlds from Ancient Egypt and Beyond.* London: Berg.

Metcalf, M. 2003, Construction Labor at Pueblo Bonito. In *Pueblo Bonito: Center of the Chacoan World,* ed. J. Neitzel, pp. 72–79. Washington: Smithsonian Institution Press.

Michalowski, P. 1976, The Royal Correspondence of Ur. Doctoral dissertation, Yale University.

1983, History as Charter: Some Observations on the Sumerian King List. *Journal of the American Oriental Society* 103:237–248.

1990, Early Mesopotamian Communicative Systems: Art, Literature, and Writing. In *Investigating Artistic Environments in the Ancient Near East*, ed. A. Gunter, pp. 53–69. Washington, DC: Smithsonian Institution Press.

1993a, Memory and Deed: The Historiography of the Political Expansion of the Akkad State. In *Akkad: The First World Empire. Structure, Ideology, Traditions*, ed. M. Liverani, pp. 69–90. History of the Ancient Near East/Studies 5. Padua: Sargon srl.

1993b, On the Early Toponymy of Sumer: A Contribution to the Study of Early Mesopotamian Writing. In *Kinattūtu ša dārâti: Raphael Kutscher Memorial Volume*, ed. A. Rainey, pp. 119–133. Tel Aviv: Institute of Archaeology of Tel Aviv University.

1993c, Tokenism. *American Anthropologist* 95:996–999.

1994, Writing and Literacy in Early States: A Mesopotamianist Perspective. In *Literacy: Interdisciplinary Conversations*, ed. D. Keller-Cohen, pp. 49–70. Cresskill, NJ: Hampton.

2003, The Doors of the Past. In *Festschrift für Hayim and Miriam Tadmor*, ed. A. Ben-Tor, I. Eph'al, and P. Machinist, pp. 136–152. Eretz Israel 27. Jerusalem: Israel Exploration Society.

2004, The Life and Death of the Sumerian Language in Comparative Perspective. *Acta Sumerologica* (Japan) 22 (forthcoming).

Michel, C. 2001, *Correspondance des marchands de Kaniš au début du IIe millénaire avant J.-C.* Paris: Editions du Cerf.

2003, *Old Assyrian Bibliography.* Leiden: Nederlands Instituut voor het Nabije Oosten.

Michels, J. 1979, *The Kaminaljuyu Chiefdom.* College Park: Pennsylvania State University Press.

Millon, R. 1973, *Urbanization at Teotihuacán, Mexico,* vol. 1, *The Teotihuacán Map,* part 1, *Text.* Austin: University of Texas Press.

1988, The Last Years of Teotihuacan Dominance. In *The Collapse of Ancient States and Civilizations,* ed. N. Yoffee and G. Cowgill, pp. 102–164. Tucson: University of Arizona Press.

Mills, B. 2002, Recent Research on Chaco: Changing Views on Economy, Ritual, and Society. *Journal of Archaeological Research* 10(1):65–117.

Milner, G. 1998, *The Cahokia Chiefdom: The Archaeology of a Mississippian Society*. Washington, DC: Smithsonian Institution Press.

Moore, A., G. Hillman, and A. Legge 2000, *Village on the Euphrates: From Foraging to Farming at Abu Hureyra*. Oxford: Oxford University Press.

Moore, S. 1978, *Law as Process: An Anthropological Approach*. London: Routledge & Kegan Paul.

Moorey, P. R. S. 1975, The Terracotta Plaques from Kish and Hursagkalama, c.1850 to 1650 B.C. *Iraq* 37:79–99.

    1978, *Kish Excavations 1923–1933*. Oxford: Clarendon Press.

Morgan, L. H. 1889, *Ancient Society* (reprinted edition, 1964; edited by and with an introduction by L. White). Cambridge, MA: Harvard University Press.

Muir, E. 1991, Introduction: Observing Trifles. In *Microhistory and the Lost Peoples of Europe*, ed. E. Muir and G. Ruggiero, pp. vii–xxvii. Baltimore: Johns Hopkins University Press.

Muller, J. 1997, *Mississippian Political Economy*. New York: Plenum.

Mulvaney, D. and J. Kamminga 1999, *Prehistory of Australia*. Washington, DC: Smithsonian Institution Press.

Murowchick, R. 1994 ed., *China: Ancient Culture, Modern Land*. Cradles of Civilization 2. Norman: University of Oklahoma Press.

Murray, T. 1988, Ethnoarchaeology or Palaeoethnology? In *Archaeology with Ethnography: An Australian Perspective*, ed. B. Meehan and R. Jones, pp. 1–16. Canberra: Research School of Pacific Studies, Australian National University.

    1992, Tasmania and the Construction of the Dawn of Humanity. *Antiquity* 66:730–743.

    1998, The Archaeology of Complex Societies. *National Library Australian Essay Australian Book Review* No. 199: 32–34.

Neitzel, J. 2003 ed., *Pueblo Bonito: Center of the Chacoan World*. Washington, DC: Smithsonian Institution Press.

Nelson, B. 1995, Complexity, Hierarchy, and Scale: A Controlled Comparison Between Chaco Canyon, New Mexico, and La Quemada, Zacatecas. *American Antiquity* 60:597–618.

Netting, R. 1972, Sacred Power and Centralization: Aspects of Political Adaptation in Africa. In *Population Growth: Anthropological Implications*, ed. B. Spooner, pp. 219–244. Cambridge, MA: MIT Press.

    1993, *Smallholders, Householders: Farm Families and the Ecology of Intensive, Sustainable Agriculture*. Stanford: Stanford University Press.

Neumann, H. 1987, *Handwerk in Mesopotamien*. Schriften zur Geschichte und Kultur des alten Orients 19. Berlin: Akademie-Verlag.

Nichols, D. and T. Charlton 1997 eds., *The Archaeology of City-States: Cross-Cultural Approaches*. Washington, DC: Smithsonian Institution Press.

Nisbet, R. 1980, *History of the Idea of Progress*. New York: Basic Books.

Nissen, H. 1977, Aspects of the Development of Early Cylinder Seals. In *Seals and Sealing in the Ancient Near East*, ed. M. Gibson and R. Biggs, pp. 15–23. Bibliotheca Mesopotamica 6. Malibu: Undena.

1983, *Grundzüge einer Geschichte der Frühzeit des Vorderen Orients*. Darmstadt: Wissenschaftliche Bibliothek.

1986, The Archaic Texts from Uruk. *World Archaeology* 17(3):317–334.

1988, *The Early History of the Ancient Near East*. Chicago: University of Chicago Press.

1993, Settlement Patterns and Material Culture of the Akkadian Period: Continuity and Discontinuity. In *Akkad: The First World Empire. Structure, Ideology, Traditions*, ed. M. Liverani, pp. 91–106. History of the Ancient Near East/Studies 5. Padua: Sargon srl.

2001, Cultural and Political Networks in the Ancient Near East in the Fourth and Third Millennia BC. In *Uruk Mesopotamia and its Neighbours: Cross-cultural Interaction in the Era of State Formation*, ed. M. Rothman. Santa Fe: School of American Research Press.

Nissen, H., P. Damerow, and R. Englund 1990, *Frühe Schrift und Techniken der Wirtschaftsverwaltung im alten Vorderen Orient. Informationsspeicherung und -verarbeitung vor 5000 Jahren.* Bad Salzdetfurth: Franzbecker. Translated in 1993, with fewer color photos, as *Archaic Bookkeeping: Early Writing Techniques of Economic Administration in the Ancient Near East.* Chicago: University of Chicago Press.

Noble, D. 2004 ed., *In Search of Chaco: New Approaches to an Enduring Enigma*. Santa Fe: School of American Research.

Oates, J. 1973, The Background and Development of Early Farming Communities in Mesopotamia and the Zagros. *Proceedings of the Prehistoric Society* 39:147–181.

1979, *Babylon*. London: Thames and Hudson.

Oded, B. 1979, *Mass Deportations and Deportees in the Neo-Assyrian Empire*. Wiesbaden: Dr. Ludwig Reichert Verlag.

Opificius, R. 1961, *Das altbabylonische Terrakottarelief.* Untersuchungen zur Assyriologie und Vorderasiatischen Archäologie 5. Berlin: Walter de Gruyter.

Oppenheim, A. L. 1977, *Ancient Mesopotamia: Portrait of a Dead Civilization*. Chicago: University of Chicago Press.

Parsons, T. 1964, Evolutionary Universals in Society. *American Sociological Review* 29:339–357.

1966, *Societies: Evolutionary and Comparative Perspectives*. Englewood Cliffs, NJ: Prentice-Hall.

Patterson, T. C. 1997, *Inventing Western Civilization*. New York: Monthly Review Press.

2003, *Marx's Ghost: Conversations with Archaeologists*. Oxford: Berg.

Paynter, R. 1989, The Archaeology of Equality and Inequality. *Annual Review of Anthropology* 18:369–399.

Peebles, C. and S. Kus 1977, Some Archaeological Correlates of Ranked Societies. *American Antiquity* 42:421–428.

Pepper, G. 1920, *Pueblo Bonito*. Anthropological Papers of the American Museum of Natural History 27. New York: American Museum of Natural History.

Plog, F. 1974, *The Study of Prehistoric Change*. New York: Academic Press.

Plog, S. 1997, *Ancient Peoples of the American Southwest*. London: Thames and Hudson.

Polanyi, K. 1957, The Economy as Instituted Process. In *Trade and Market in the Early Empires*, ed. K. Polanyi, C. Arensberg, and H. Pearson, pp. 243–269. Glencoe, IL: The Free Press.

Pollock, S. 1999, *Ancient Mesopotamia: The Eden that Never Was*. Cambridge: Cambridge University Press.

2001, The Uruk Period in Southern Mesopotamia. In *Uruk Mesopotamia and Its Neighbors: Cross-Cultural Interactions in the Era of State Formation*, ed. M. Rothman, pp. 181–231. Santa Fe: School of American Research Press.

Porada, E., D. Hansen, S. Dunham, and S. Babcock 1992. The Chronology of Mesopotamia. In *Chronologies in Old World Archaeology*, 3rd edn, ed. R. Ehrlich, pp. 77–121. Chicago: University of Chicago Press.

Pospisil, L. 1973, E. Adamson Hoebel and the Anthropology of Law. *Law and Society Review* 7:539–559.

Possehl, G. 1997, The Transformation of the Indus Civilization. *Journal of World Prehistory* 11:425–472.

2002, *The Indus Civilization: A Contemporary Perspective*. Walnut Creek, CA: Altamira.

Postgate, J. N. 1977, *The First Empires*. Oxford: Elsevier.

1979, On Some Assyrian Ladies. *Iraq* 41:89–103.

1992, *Early Mesopotamia: Economy and Society at the Dawn of History*. London: Routledge.

1994, The Four "Neo-Assyrian" Tablets from Šēḫ Ḥamad. *State Archives of Assyria* 7:109–124.

2002 ed., *Artefacts of Complexity: Tracking the Uruk in the Near East*. Iraq Archaeological Reports 5. Warminster: Aris & Phillips.

Postgate, J. N. and M. Powell 1988 eds., *Bulletin of Sumerian Agriculture* 4: Irrigation and Cultivation in Mesopotamia, part 1.

1990, *Bulletin of Sumerian Agriculture* 5: Irrigation and Cultivation in Mesopotamia, part 2.

Potts, D. 1997, *Mesopotamian Civilization: The Material Foundations*. Ithaca: Cornell University Press.

1999, *The Archaeology of Elam: Formation and Transformation of an Ancient Iranian State*. Cambridge: Cambridge University Press.

Powell, M. 1978, Texts from the Time of Lugalzagesi: Problems and Perspectives in their Interpretation. *Hebrew Union College Annual* 49:1–58.

1985, Salt, Seed, and Yields in Sumerian Agriculture: A Critique of the Theory of Progressive Salinization. *Zeitschrift für Assyriologie* 75:7–38.

1987 ed., *Labor in the Ancient Near East*. American Oriental Series 68. New Haven: American Oriental Society.

1989–90, Maße und Gewichte. *Reallexikon der Assyriologie* 7:457–530.

Power, E. 1922, *Medieval English Nunneries c. 1275 to 1535*. Cambridge (UK): The University Press.

Prasad, A. 1991, *Devadasi System in Ancient India*. Delhi: H. C. Publishers.

Raab, M. and A. Goodyear 1984, Middle-Range Theory in Archaeology: A Critical Review of Origins and Applications. *American Antiquity* 49:255–268.

Rappaport, R. 1977, Maladaptation in Social Systems. In *The Evolution of Social Systems*, ed. J. Friedman and M. Rowlands, pp. 49–73. London: Duckworth.

Ratnagar, S. 2000, *The End of the Great Harappan Tradition*. New Delhi: Manohar.

Reiner, E. 1961, The Etiological Myth of the Seven Sages. *Orientalia* 30:1–11.

1974, The Sumero-Akkadian Hymn of Nanâ. *Journal of Near Eastern Studies* 33:221–236.

Reiner, E. and M. Civil 1969 eds., *A Reconstruction of Sumerian and Akkadian Lexical Lists*. Materials for the Sumerian Lexicon vol. 12. Rome: Pontificium Institutum Biblicum.

Rempel, J. and N. Yoffee 1999, The End of the Cycle? Assessing the Impact of Hellenization on Mesopotamian Civilization. In *Munuscula Mesopotamica: Festschrift für Johannes Renger*, ed. B. Böck, E. Cancik-Kirschbaum, and T. Richter, pp. 385–398. Münster: Ugarit-Verlag.

Renfrew, C. 1973, *Before Civilization*. London: Jonathan Cape.

1975, Trade as Action at a Distance: Questions of Integration and Communication. In *Ancient Civilization and Trade*, ed. J. Sabloff and C. C. Lamberg-Karlovsky, pp. 3–59. A School of American Research Book. Albuquerque: University of New Mexico Press.

1978, Trajectory Discontinuity and Morphogenesis: The Implications of Catastrophe Theory for Archaeology. *American Antiquity* 43:203–222.

1986, Introduction. In *Peer-Polity Interaction and Socio-Political Change*, ed. C. Renfrew and J. Cherry, pp. 1–18. Cambridge: Cambridge University Press.

1993, Cognitive Archaeology: Some Thoughts on the Archaeology of Thought. *Cambridge Archaeological Journal* 3:248–250.

2001, Production and Consumption in a Sacred Economy: The Material Correlates of High Devotional Expression at Chaco Canyon. *American Antiquity* 66(1):14–25.

Renger, J. 1967, Untersuchungen zum Priestertum der altbabylonischen Zeit. *Zeitschrift für Assyriologie* 58:110–188.

1970, Zur Lokalisierung von Karkar. *Archiv für Orientforschung* 23:73–78.

Richardson, S. 2002, The Collapse of a Complex State: A Reappraisal of the End of the First Dynasty of Babylon, 1683–1597 BC Doctoral dissertation, Columbia University.

Roaf, M. 1989, Ubaid Social Organization and Social Activities as Seen from Tell Maddhur. In *Upon This Foundation: The Ubaid Reconsidered*, ed. E. Henrikson and I. Thuesen, pp. 91–146. Copenhagen: Museum Tusculanum Press.

Roberts, S. 1979, *Order and Dispute*. Harmondsworth: Penguin Books.

Rosenberg, M. and R. Redding 2000, Hallan Çemi and Early Village Organization in Eastern Anatolia. In *Life in Neolithic Farming Communities: Social Organization, Identity, and Differentiation*, ed. I. Kuijt, pp. 39–61. New York: Kluwer Academic/Plenum.

Roth, M. 1983, The Slave and the Scoundrel: CNS 10467, A Sumerian Morality Tale. *Journal of the American Oriental Society* 103:275–282.

1995, *Law Collections from Mesopotamia and Asia Minor*. Writings from the Ancient World 6. Atlanta: Scholars Press.

Rothman, M. 2001 ed., *Uruk Mesopotamia and Its Neighbors: Cross-Cultural Interactions and their Consequences in the Era of State Formation*. Santa Fe: School of American Research Press.

Rudolph, S. 1987, Presidential Address: State Formation in Asia – Prolegomenon to a Comparative Study. *Journal of Asian Studies* 46:731–746.

Runciman, W. 1982, Origins of States: The Case of Archaic Greece. *Comparative Studies in Society and History* 24:351–377.

1989, *A Treatise on Social Theory: Substantive Social Theory*. Cambridge: Cambridge University Press.

Sachs, A. 1976, The Last Datable Cuneiform Tablets. In *Kramer Anniversary Volume*, ed. B. Eichler, pp. 379–398. Alter Orient und Altes Testament 25. Kevelaer: Butzon and Bercker.

Safar, F., M. A. Mustafa, and S. Lloyd 1981, *Eridu*. Baghdad: State Organization of Antiquities and Heritage.

Sahlins, M. 1960, Evolution: Specific and General. In *Evolution and Culture*, ed. M. Sahlins and E. Service, pp. 12–44. Ann Arbor: University of Michigan Press.

1963, Poor Man, Rich Man, Big Man, Chief: Political Types in Melanesia and Polynesia. *Comparative Studies in Society and History* 5:285–303.

1968, *Tribesmen.* Englewood Cliffs: Prentice-Hall.

Sahlins, M. and E. Service 1960 eds., *Evolution and Culture.* Ann Arbor: University of Michigan Press.

Sallaberger, W. 1988, *Das Pantheon von Kiš und Hursagkalama. Ein altmesopotamisches Lokalpantheon.* Diplomarbeit, Universität Innsbrück.

1999, Ur III-Zeit. In *Mesopotamien: Akkade-Zeit und Ur III-Zeit*, ed. P. Attinger and M. Wäfler, pp. 119–390. Orbis Biblicus et Orientalis 160/3. Freiburg, Switzerland: Universitätsverlag.

Salmon, M. 1982a, What Can Systems Theory Do for Archaeology? *American Antiquity* 43:174–183.

1982b, *Philosophy and Archaeology.* New York: Academic Press.

Sanders, W. 1974, Chiefdom to State: Political Evolution at Kaminaljuyu, Guatemala. In *Reconstructing Complex Societies*, ed. C. Moore, pp. 97–121. Supplement to the Bulletin of the American Schools of Oriental Research 20.

Sanders, W. and D. Nichols 1988, Ecological Theory and Cultural Evolution in the Valley of Oaxaca. *Current Anthropology* 29:33–80.

Sanders, W., J. Parsons, and R. Santley 1979, The Basin of Mexico: Ecological Processes in the Evolution of a Civilization. New York: Academic Press.

Sanders, W. and D. Webster 1978, Unilinealism, Multilinealism, and the Evolution of Complex Societies. In *Social Archeology: Beyond Subsistence and Dating*, ed. C. Redman, M. Berman, E. Curtin, W. Langhorne, N. Versaggi, and J. Wanser, pp. 249–302. New York: Academic Press.

Sanderson, S. 1990. *Social Evolutionism: A Critical History.* Oxford: Blackwell.

Santley, R. 1980, Disembedded Capitals Reconsidered. *American Antiquity* 45:132–145.

Scarborough, V. 2003, *The Flow of Power: Ancient Water Systems and Landscapes.* Santa Fe: School of American Research Press.

Schiffer, M. 1976, *Behavioral Archaeology.* New York: Academic Press.

1988, The Structure of Archaeological Theory. *American Antiquity* 53:461–485.

Schiffer, M. and V. Lamotta 2001, Behavioral Archaeology: Toward a New Synthesis. In *Archaeological Theory Today*, ed. I. Hodder, pp. 14–64. Oxford: Polity Press.

Schmandt-Besserat, D. 1977, *An Archaic Recording System and the Origin of Writing.* Syro-Mesopotamian Studies 1(2). Malibu: Undena.

Schmidt, K. 2000, Göbekli Tepe, Southeastern Turkey. A Preliminary Report on the 1995–1999 Excavations. *Paléorient* 26(1):45–54.

Schortman, E. and P. Urban 1987, Modeling Interregional Interaction in Prehistory. *Advances in Archaeological Method and Theory* 11:37–95.

Schreiber, K. 1992, *Wari Imperialism in Middle Horizon Peru.* University of Michigan Museum of Anthropology Anthropological Paper 87. Ann Arbor: University of Michigan Museum of Anthropology.

2001, The Wari Empire of Middle Horizon Peru: The Epistemological Challenge of Documenting an Empire Without Documentary Evidence. In *Empires: Perspectives from Archaeology and History*, ed. S. Alcock, T. D'Altroy, K. Morrison, and C. Sinopoli, pp. 70–92. Cambridge: Cambridge University Press.

Schwartz, B. 1985, *The World of Thought in Ancient China.* Cambridge: Cambridge University Press.

Scott, J. 1998, *Seeing like a State: How Certain Schemes to Improve the Human Condition Have Failed.* New Haven: Yale University Press.

Sebastian, L. 1992, *The Chaco Anasazi: Sociopolitical Evolution in the Prehistoric Southwest.* Cambridge: Cambridge University Press.

Seri, A. 2003, Local Power: Structure and Function of Community Institutions of Authority in the Old Babylonian Period. Doctoral dissertation, Department of Near Eastern Studies, University of Michigan.

Service, E. 1960, The Law of Evolutionary Potential. In *Evolution and Culture,* ed. M. Sahlins and E. Service, pp. 93–122. Ann Arbor: University of Michigan Press.

　1962, Primitive Social Organization. New York: Random House.

　1975, *Origins of the State and Civilization: The Process of Cultural Evolution.* New York: Norton.

Shanks, M. and C. Tilley 1987, *Social Theory and Archaeology.* Cambridge: Polity Press.

Sherwin-White, S. 1987, Seleucid Babylonia: A Case-Study for the Installation and Development of Greek Rule. In *Hellenism in the East,* ed. A. Kuhrt and S. Sherwin-White, pp. 1–31. London: Duckworth.

Sherwin-White, S. and A. Kuhrt 1993, *From Samarkhand to Sardis: A New Approach to the Seleucid Empire.* Berkeley: University of California Press.

Shils, E. 1975, *Center and Periphery: Essays in Macrosociology.* Chicago: University of Chicago Press.

Sigrist, M. 1992, *Drehem.* Bethesda, MD: CDL Press.

Simon, H. 1965, The Architecture of Complexity. *Yearbook of the Society for General Systems Research* 10:63–76.

Simons, W. 2001, *Cities of Ladies: Beguine Communities in the Medieval Low Countries, 1200–1565.* Philadelphia: University of Pennsylvania Press.

Simpson, G. 1961, *Principles of Animal Taxonomy.* New York: Columbia University Press.

Sinopoli, C. and K. Morrison 1995, Dimensions of Imperial Control: The Vijayanagara Capital. *American Anthropologist* 97:83–96.

Skinner, Q. 1978, *The Foundations of Modern Political Thought.* Cambridge: Cambridge University Press.

Smiley, Jane 1995, *Moo.* New York: A. A. Knopf.

Smith, M. 2003 ed., *The Social Construction of Ancient Cities.* Washington, DC: Smithsonian Books.

Snell, D. 1982, *Ledgers and Prices: Early Mesopotamian Merchant Accounts.* Yale Near Eastern Researches 8. New Haven: Yale University Press.

Soja, E. 2000, *Postmetropolis: Critical Studies of Cities and Regions.* Oxford: Blackwell.

Sollberger, E. 1967, The Rulers of Lagaš. *Journal of Cuneiform Studies* 21:279–291.

Sontag, S. 2003, *The Pain of Others.* New York: Farrar, Straus, and Giroux.

Spaey, J. 1990, Some Notes on KÙ.BABBAR/nēbih kezēr(t)i(m). *Akkadica* 67:1–9.

Speiser, E. 1952, Some Factors in the Collapse of Akkad. *Journal of the American Oriental Society* 72:97–101.

Spencer, C. 1987, Rethinking the Chiefdom. In *Chiefdoms in the Americas,* ed. R. Drennan and C. Uribe, pp. 369–389. Boston: University Presses of America.

1990, On the Tempo and Mode of State Formation: Neoevolutionism Reconsidered. *Journal of Anthropological Archaeology* 9:1–30.

Spencer, C. and E. Redmond 2001, Multilevel Selection and Political Evolution in the Valley of Oaxaca, 500–100 B.C. *Journal of Anthropological Archaeology* 20:195–229.

2003, Militarism, Resistance, and Early State Development in Oaxaca, Mexico. *Social Evolution and History* 2(1):25–70.

Spengler, O. 1918–22, *The Decline of the West*, trans. C. Atkinson. New York: Alfred Knopf.

Stahl, A. 1993, Concepts of Time and Approaches to Analogical Reasoning in Historical Perspective. *American Antiquity* 58:235–260.

Stanish, C. 2001, The Origin of State Societies in South America. *Annual Review of Anthropology* 30:41–64.

Stein, G. 1994, Economy, Ritual, and Power in 'Ubaid Mesopotamia. In *Chiefdoms and Early States in the Near East: The Organizational Dynamics of Complexity*, ed. G. Stein and M. Rothman, pp. 35–46. Monographs in World Archaeology 18. Madison: Prehistory Press.

1999, *Rethinking World-Systems: Diasporas, Colonies, and Interaction in Uruk Mesopotamia*. Tucson: University of Arizona Press.

Stein, G. and R. Özbal 2001, A Tale of Two Oikumenai: Variation in the Expansionary Dynamics of Ubaid and Uruk Mesopotamia. Unpublished paper, American Anthropological Association, December, 2001.

Stein, J. and S. Lekson 1994, Anasazi Ritual Landscape. In *Chaco Canyon: A Center and Its World*, photographs by Mary Peck with essays by S. Lekson, J. Stein, and S. Ortiz, pp. 45–58. Santa Fe: Museum of New Mexico Press.

Steinkeller, P. 1987a, The Administrative and Economic Organization of the Ur III State: The Core and the Periphery. In *The Organization of Power: Aspects of Bureaucracy in the Ancient Near East*, ed. M. Gibson and R. Biggs, pp. 19–41. Studies in Ancient Oriental Civilization 46. Chicago: The Oriental Institute.

1987b, The Foresters of Umma: Toward a Definition of Ur III Labor. In *Labor in the Ancient Near East*, ed. M. Powell, pp. 73–115. American Oriental Series 68. New Haven: American Oriental Society.

1989, *Sale Documents of the Ur III Period*. Freiburger altorientalische Studien 17. Stuttgart: Franz Steiner Verlag.

1993, Early Political Development in Mesopotamia and the Origins of the Sargonic Empire. In *Akkad: The First World Empire. Structure, Ideology, Traditions*, ed. M. Liverani, pp. 107–129. History of the Ancient Near East/Studies 5. Padua: Sargon srl.

1996, The Organization of Crafts in Third Millennium Babylonia: The Case of Potters. *Altorientalische Forschungen* 23:232–253.

2002, Archaic City Seals and the Question of Early Babylonian Unity. In *Riches Hidden in Secret Places: Ancient Near Eastern Studies in Memory of Thorkild Jacobsen*, ed. T. Abusch, pp. 249–257. Winona Lake, IN: Eisenbrauns.

Steponaitis, V. 1978, Location Theory and Complex Chiefdoms. In *Mississippian Settlement Patterns*, ed. B. Smith, pp. 417–453. New York: Academic Press.

1981, Settlement Hierarchies and Political Complexity in Non-Market Societies: The Formative Period in the Valley of Mexico. *American Anthropologist* 83:320–363.

Steward, J. 1955, *Theory of Culture Change*. Urbana: University of Illinois Press.

Stol, M. 1983, Leder(industrie). *Reallexikon der Assyriologie* 6:527–543.

Stone, E. 1977, Economic Crisis and Social Upheaval in Old Babylonian Nippur. In *Mountains and Lowlands: Essays in the Archaeology of Greater Mesopotamia (Robert Dyson Fs.)*, ed. L. Levine and T. C. Young, Jr., pp. 267–290. Malibu: Undena.

1982, The Social Role of the *nadītu* Women in Old Babylonian Nippur. *Journal of the Economic and Social History of the Orient* 25:50–70.

Struever, S. and G. Houart 1972, An Analysis of the Hopewell Interaction Sphere. In *Social Exchange in Interaction*, ed. E. Wilmsen, pp. 47–78. University of Michigan Museum of Anthropology Anthropological Papers 46. Ann Arbor: University of Michigan Museum of Anthropology.

Sugiyama, S. 1989, Burials Dedicated to the Old Temple of Quetzlcoatl at Teotihuacan, Mexico. *American Antiquity* 54:85–106.

nd, *Mass Human Sacrifice and Symbolism of the Feathered Serpent Pyramid in Teotihuacán, México*. Cambridge: Cambridge University Press.

Szlechter, E. 1963, *Tablettes juridiques et administratives de la IIIe dynastié d'Ur et de la Ire dynastie de Babylone conservés au Musée de l'Université de Manchester et à Cambridge an Musée Fitzwilliam, à l'Institut d'Etudes Orientales et à l'Institut d'Egyptologie*. Paris: Recueil Sirey.

Tainter, J. 1988, *"The Collapse of Complex Societies"*. Cambridge: Cambridge University Press.

Tambiah, S. 1985, The Galactic Polity in Southeast Asia. In *Culture, Thought, and Social Action: An Anthropological Perspective*, pp. 253–286. Cambridge: Harvard University Press.

Tanret, M. and K. Van Lerberghe 1993, Rituals and Profits in the Ur-Utu Archive. In *Ritual and Sacrifice in the Ancient Near East*, ed. J. Quaegebeur, pp. 435–449. Orientalia Lovaniensia Analecta 55. Leuven: Peeters.

Taube, K. 2000, *The Writing System of Teotihuacán*. Washington: Center for Ancient American Studies.

Tobler, A. 1950. *Excavations at Tepe Gawra 2*. Philadelphia: University of Pennsylvania Press.

Toll, H. W. 1984, Trends in Ceramic Import and Distribution in Chaco Canyon. In *Recent Research on Chaco Prehistory*, ed. W. J. Judge and J. D. Schelberg, pp. 115–136. Reports of the Chaco Center, no. 8. Albuquerque: Division of Cultural Research, National Park Service.

1985, *Pottery, Production, Public Architecture, and the Chaco Anasazi System*. Doctoral dissertation, University of Colorado.

Toynbee, A. 1933–54, *A Study of History*. Oxford: Oxford University Press. Abridgement by D. Somervell 1946, 1957.

Trigger, B. 1985, The Evolution of Pre-Industrial Cities: A Multilinear Perspective. In *Mélanges offerts à Jean Vercoutter*, ed. F. Geus and F. Thill, pp. 343–353. Paris: Editions Recherches sur les Civilisations.

1993, *Early Civilizations: Ancient Egypt in Context*. Cairo: American University in Cairo Press.

1995, Expanding Middle Range Theory. *Antiquity* 69:449–458.

2003, Understanding Early Civilizations: A Comparative Study. Cambridge: Cambridge University Press.

Tylor, E. 1881, *Anthropology: An Introduction to the Study of Man and Civilization*. London: Macmillan.

Valtz, E. 1991, New Observations on the Hellenistic Pottery from Seleucia-on-the-Tigris. In *Golf-Archäologie: Mesopotamien, Iran, Kuwait, Bahrain, Vereinigte Arabische Emirate und Oman*, ed. K. Schippmann, A. Herling, and J.-F. Salles, pp. 45–56. Buch am Erlbach: Internationale Archäologie 6.

Van De Mieroop, M. 1987, *Crafts in the Early Isin Period: A Study of the Isin Craft Archive from the Reigns of Išbi-Erra and Šū-Ilišu*. Orientalia Lovaniensia Analecta 24. Leuven: Departement Oriëntalistiek.

1992, *Society and Enterprise in Old Babylonian Ur*. Berliner Beiträge zum Vorderen Orient 12. Berlin: Dietrich Reimer.

1997, *The Ancient Mesopotamian City*. Oxford: Clarendon.

2004, *A History of the Ancient Near East, c. 3000–323 BC*. Malden, MA: Blackwell.

Van Dyke, R. 2004, Memory, Meaning and Masonry: The Late Bonito Chacoan Landscape. *American Antiquity* 69:413–431.

Van Dyke, R. and S. Alcock 2003 eds., *Archaeologies of Memory*. Malden, MA: Blackwell.

van Ess, M. 1991, Keramik. Akkad- bis der altbabylonischer Zeit. In *Uruk, Kampagne 35–37, 1982–1984: Die archäologische Oberflächenuntersuchung (Survey)*, ed. U. Finkbeiner, p. 91. Ausgrabungen in Uruk-Warka Endberichte 4. Mainz: Philipp von Zabern.

van Gijseghem, 2001. Household and Family at Moche, Peru: An Analysis of Building and Residence Patterns in a Prehispanic Urban Center. *Latin American Antiquity* 12:257–273.

Van Lerberghe, K. and G. Voet 1991, *Sippar-Amnānum: The Ur-Utu Archive*. Mesopotamian History and Environment Series III, Texts 1. Ghent: University of Ghent.

Veenhof, K. 1972, *Aspects of Old Assyrian Trade and Its Terminology*. Studia et documenta ad jura Orientis antiqui pertinentia 10. Leiden: E. J. Brill.

1994, Two *šilip rēmim* Adoptions from Sippar. In *Cinquante-deux réflexions sur le Proche-Orient ancien offertes en hommage à Léon De Meyer*, ed. H. Gasche, M. Tanret, C. Janssen, and A. Degraeve, pp. 143–157. Leuven: Peeters.

1995, Kanesh: An Assyrian Colony in Anatolia. In *Civilizations of the Ancient Near East*, ed. J. Sasson, v. 2:859–871. New York: Charles Scribner's Sons.

1997, "Modern Features" in Old Assyrian Trade. *Journal of the Economic and Social History of the Orient* 40:336–366.

1999, Silver and Credit in Old Assyrian Trade. In *Trade and Finance in Ancient Mesopotamia*, ed. J. G. Dercksen, pp. 55–83. Uitgaven van het Nederlands Historisch-Archaeologisch Instituut te Istanbul 84. Leiden: Nederlands Historisch-Archaeologisch Instituut te Istanbul.

2001, The Old Assyrian Period. In *Security for Debt in Ancient Near Eastern Law*, ed. R. Westbrook and R. Jasnow, pp. 93–159. Leiden: Brill.

2003a, Archives of Old Assyrian Traders from Karum Kanish. In *Ancient Archives and Archival Traditions: Concepts of Record-Keeping in the Ancient World*, ed. M. Brosius, pp. 98–123. Oxford: Oxford Studies in Ancient Documents.

2003b, Trade and Politics in Ancient Aššur: Balancing Public, Colonial, and Entrepreneurial Interest. In *Trade and Politics in the Ancient World*, ed. C. Zaccagnini, pp. 69–118. Rome: "L'Erma" di Bretschneider.

Verhoeven, M. nd, Ethnoarchaeology, Analogy and Ancient Society. In *Archaeologies of the Middle East: Critical Perspectives*, ed. S. Pollock and R. Bernbeck (forthcoming). Oxford: Blackwell.

Vidal, G. 1981, *Creation*. New York: Ballantine Books.

Vivian, R. G. 1990, *The Chacoan Prehistory of the San Juan Basin*. San Diego: Academic Press.

Vivian, R. G., D. Dodgen, and G. Hartmann 1978, *Wooden Ritual Artifacts from Chaco Canyon*. Arizona State Museum Anthropological Papers 32. Tucson: University of Arizona Press.

Vivian, R. G., C. Van West, J. Dean, N. Akins, M. Toll, and T. Windes 2003, Chaco Ecology and Economy. Unpublished paper.

Waetzoldt, H. 1971, Zwei unveröffentlichte Ur-III-Texte über die Herstellung von Tongefäßen. *Die Welt des Orients* 6:1–41.

1972, *Untersuchungen zur neusumerischen Textilindustrie*. Rome: Centro per le Antichità e la Storia dell'Arte del Vicino Oriente.

1987, Compensation of Craft Workers and Officials in the Ur III Period. In *Labor in the Ancient Near East*, ed. M. Powell, pp. 117–141. American Oriental Series 68. New Haven: American Oriental Society.

Walbank, F. 1993, *The Hellenistic World*, revised ed. Cambridge, MA: Harvard University Press.

Wallenfels, R. 1996, Private Seals and Sealing Practices at Hellenistic Uruk. In *Archives et sceaux du monde hellénistique*, ed. M.-F. Boussac and A. Invernizzi, pp. 113–129. Bulletin de correspondance hellénique, suppl. 29. Paris: Diffusion de Boccard.

Ware, J. 2001, Chaco Social Organization: A Peripheral View. In *Chaco Society and Polity: Papers from the 1999 Conference*, ed. L. Cordell, W. J. Judge, and J. Piper, pp. 79–93. New Mexico Archeological Council Special Publication 4. Albuquerque: New Mexico Archeological Council.

Watkins, T. and S. Campbell 1983, The Halafian Culture: A Review. In *The Hilly Flanks and Beyond: Essays on the Prehistory of Southwestern Asia Presented to Robert J. Braidwood*, ed. T. C. Young, Jr., P. Smith, and P. Mortensen, pp. 231–250. Studies in Ancient Oriental Civilization 36. Chicago: Oriental Institute.

1987, The Chronology of the Halaf Culture. In *Chronologies in the Near East*, ed. O. Aurenche, J. Evin, and F. Hours, pp. 427–464. BAR International Series 379(ii). Oxford: British Archaeological Reports.

Watson, P. J. 1992, A Parochial Primer: The New Dissonance as Seen from the Midcontinental USA. In *Processual and Postprocessual Archaeologies: Multiple Ways of Knowing the Past*, ed. R. Preucel, pp. 265–274. Carbondale: Center for Archaeological Investigations Occasional Paper No. 10.

Watson, P. J. and M. Kennedy 1991, The Development of Horticulture in the Eastern Woodlands of North America: Women's Role. In *Engendering Archaeology: Women and Prehistory*, ed. J. Gero and M. Conkey, pp. 255–275. Oxford: Blackwell.

Waugh, L. 1982, Marked and Unmarked: A Choice between Unequals in Semiotic Structure. *Semiotica* 38:299–318.

Webster, D. 2002, *The Fall of the Ancient Maya: Solving the Mystery of the Maya Collapse*. New York: Thames and Hudson.

Webster, D., A. Freter, and N. Gonlin 2000, *Copan: The Rise and Fall of a Classic Maya Kingdom*. Ft. Worth: Harcourt, Brace.

Webster, D. and S. T. Evans 2004, Mesoamerican Civilization. In *The Human Past*, ed. C. Scarre. London: Thames and Hudson (forthcoming).

Weiss, H. 1975, Kish, Akkad and Agade. *Journal of the American Oriental Society* 95:434–453.

Weiss, H. and M.-A. Courty 1993, The Genesis and Collapse of the Akkadian Empire: The Accidental Refraction of Historical Law. In *Akkad: The First World Empire. Structure, Ideology, Traditions*, ed. M. Liverani, pp. 131–155. History of the Ancient Near East/Studies 5. Padua: Sargon srl.

Weiss, H. and T. C. Young Jr. 1975, The Merchants of Susa: Godin V and Plateau-Lowland Relations in the Late Fourth Millennium B.C. *Iran* 13:1–17.

Wengrow, D. 1998, "The Changing Face of Clay": Continuity and Change in the Transition from Village to Urban Life in the Near East. *Antiquity* 72:783–795.

2001, The Evolution of Simplicity: Aesthetic Labour and Social Change in the Neolithic Near East. *World Archaeology* 33:168–188.

Wenke, R. 1997, City-States, Nation-States, and Territorial States: The Problem of Egypt. In *The Archaeology of City-States: Cross-Cultural Approaches*, ed. D. Nichols and T. Charlton, pp. 27–49. Washington, DC: Smithsonian Institution Press.

Westbrook, R. 1982, Old Babylonian Marriage Law. Doctoral dissertation, Yale University.

1989, Cuneiform Law Codes and the Origins of Legislation. *Zeitschrift für Assyriologie* 79:201–222.

Westenholz, A. 1984, The Sargonic Period. In *Circulation of Goods in Non-Palatial Context in the Ancient Near East*, ed. A. Archi, pp. 17–30. Rome: Ateneo.

Wheatley, P. 1971, *The Pivot of the Four Quarters: A Preliminary Enquiry into the Origins and Character of the Ancient Chinese City*. Chicago: Aldine.

White, L. 1943, Energy and the Evolution of Culture. *American Anthropologist* 45:335–356.

1947, Evolutionary Stages, Progress, and the Evaluation of Cultures. *Southwestern Journal of Anthropology* 3:165–192.

1959a, *The Evolution of Culture*. New York: McGraw-Hill.

1959b, The Concept of Evolution in Cultural Anthropology. In *Evolution and Anthropology: A Centennial Appraisal*, ed. B. Meggars, pp. 106–125. Washington, DC: The Anthropological Society of Washington.

1960, Foreword to *Evolution and Culture*, ed. M. Sahlins and E. Service, pp. v–xxi. Ann Arbor: University of Michigan Press.

Wilcke, C. 1969, Zur Geschichte der Amurriter in der Ur-III-Zeit. *Die Welt des Orients* 5:1–31.

1970, Drei Phasen des Niedergangs des Reiches der Ur III-Zeit. *Zeitschrift für Assyriologie* 60:54–69.

1973, Politische Opposition nach sumerischen Quellen: Der Konflikt zwischen Königtum und Ratsversammlung. Literaturwerke als politische Tendenzschriften. In *La voix de l'opposition en Mésopotamie*, ed. A. Finet, pp. 37–65. Brussels: Institut des Hautes Etudes de Belgique.

1974, Zum Königtum in der Ur III-Zeit. In *Le palais et la royauté*, ed. P. Garelli, pp. 177–232. Rencontre Assyriologique Internationale 19. Paris: Geuthner.

1976–80, Inanna. *Reallexikon der Assyriologie* 5(1–2):74–87.

1992, Diebe, Räuber und Mörder. In *Außenseiter und Randgruppen. Beiträge zu einer Sozialge-schichte des Alten Orients*, ed. V. Haas, pp. 53–78. Xenia 32. Konstanz: Universitätsverlag.

Wilcox, D. 1993, The Evolution of the Chaco Polity. In *The Chimney Rock Archaeological Symposium*, ed. J. M. Malville and G. Matlock, pp. 76–90. Rocky Mountain Forest and Ranger Experiment Station, Forest Service General Technical Report RM-227. Fort Collins, CO: Forest Service.

Wilhelm, G. 1990, Marginalien zu Herodot Klio 199. In *Lingering Over Words: Studies in Ancient Near Eastern Literature in Honor of William L. Moran*, ed. T. Abusch, J. Huehnergard, and Piotr Steinkeller, pp. 505–524. Atlanta: Scholars Press.

Wilkinson, T. 1999, *Early Dynastic Egypt*. London: Routledge.

Wilkinson, T. J. 2003, *Archaeological Landscapes of the Near East*. Tucson: University of Arizona Press.

Willey, G. 1979, The Concept of the "Disembedded Capital" in Comparative Perspective. *Journal of Archaeological Research* 35:123–137.

1992, Horizonal Integration and Regional Diversity: An Alternating Process in the Rise of Civilizations. *American Antiquity* 56:197–215.

Willey, G. and J. Sabloff 1980, *A History of American Archaeology*. San Francisco: W. H. Freeman.

Wills, W. 2001, Ritual and Mound Formation during the Bonito Phase in Chaco Canyon. *American Antiquity* 66(3):433–451.

Wilson, D. 1997, Early State Formation on the North Coast of Peru: A Critique of the City-State Model. In *The Archaeology of City-States: Cross-Cultural Approaches*, ed. D. Nichols and T. Charlton, pp. 229–244. Washington, DC: Smithsonian Institution Press.

Wilson, J. 1960, Egypt through the New Kingdom: Civilization without Cities. In *City Invincible*, ed. C. Kraeling and R. McC. Adams, pp. 124–164. Chicago: University of Chicago Press.

Winter, I. 1983, The Warka Vase: Structure of Art and Structure of Society in Early Urban Mesopotamia. Paper given at the American Oriental Society meeting, Baltimore.

1996, Sex, Rhetoric, and the Public Monument: The Alluring Body of Naram-Sîn of Agade. In *Sexuality in Ancient Art: Near East, Egypt, Greece, and Italy*, ed. N. Kampen, pp. 11–26. Cambridge: Cambridge University Press.

Winter, M. 1984, Exchange in Formative Highland Oaxaca. In *Trade and Exchange in Early Mesoamer-ica*, ed. K. Hirth, pp. 179–214. Albuquerque: University of New Mexico Press.

2001, Palacios, templos y 1300 años de vida urbana en Monte Albán. In *Reconstruyendo la ciudad maya: El urbanismo en las sociedades antiguas*, ed. Andrés Ciudad Ruiz, Ma. Josefa Iglesias Ponce de León, y Ma. del Carmen Martínez Martínez, pp. 277–301. Madrid: Sociedad Española de Estudios Mayas Publicación 6.

Withrow, B. 1990, Prehistoric Distribution of Stone Adzes on Hawai'i Island: Implications for the Development of Hawaiian Chiefdoms. *Asian Perspectives* 29:235–250.

Wittfogel, K. 1957, *Oriental Despotism: A Comparative Study of Total Power*. New Haven: Yale University Press.

Wobst, H. M. 1978, The Archaeo-Ethnology of Hunter-Gatherers or the Tyranny of the Ethnographic Record in Archaeology. *American Antiquity* 43:303–309.

Wolf, E. 1990, Facing Power – Old Insights, New Questions. *American Anthropologist* 92:586–596.

Wright, H. E. Jr. 1993, Environmental Determinism in Near Eastern Prehistory. *Current Anthropology* 34:458–469.

Wright, H. T. 1969, *The Administration of Rural Production in an Early Mesopotamian Town*. University of Michigan Museum of Anthropology Anthropological Papers 38. Ann Arbor: University of Michigan Museum of Anthropology.

1977, Recent Research on the Origin of the State. *Annual Review of Anthropology* 6:379–397.

1984, Prestate Political Formations. In *On the Evolution of Complex Societies: Essays in Honor of Harry Hoijer*, ed. T. Earle, pp. 41–77. Malibu: Undena.

Wright, H. T. and G. Johnson 1975, Population, Exchange, and Early State Formation in Southwestern Iran. *American Anthropologist* 77:267–289.

Wylie, A. 1982, An Analogy by Any Other Name is Just as Analogical: A Commentary on the Gould–Watson Dialogue. *Journal of Anthropological Archaeology* 1:382–401.

1985, The Reaction Against Analogy. *Advances in Archaeological Method and Theory* 8:63–111.

1992, Feminist Theories of Social Power: Some Implications for a Processual Archaeology. *Norwegian Archaeological Review* 25:51–68.

1993, A Proliferation of New Archaeologies: Skepticism, Processualism, and Post-processualism. In *Archaeological Theory: Who Sets the Agenda?*, ed. N. Yoffee and A. Sherratt, pp. 20–26. Cambridge: Cambridge University Press.

2002, *Thinking from Things: Essays in the Philosophy of Archaeology*. Berkeley: University of California Press.

Yasin, W. 1970, Excavation at Tell es-Sawwan, 1969: Report on the Sixth Season's Excavations. *Sumer* 26:3–20.

Yates, R. 1997, The City-State in Ancient China. In *The Archaeology of City-States: Cross-Cultural Approaches*, ed. D. Nichols and T. Charlton, pp. 71–90. Washington, DC: Smithsonian Institution Press.

Yener, K. A. 2000, *The Domestication of Metals: The Rise of Complex Metal Industries in Anatolia*. Culture and History of the Ancient Near East 4. Leiden: Brill.

Yoffee, N. 1977, *The Economic Role of the Crown in the Old Babylonian Period*. Bibliotheca Mesopotamica 5. Malibu: Undena.

1979, The Decline and Rise of Mesopotamian Civilization: An Ethnoarchaeological Perspective on the Evolution of Social Complexity. *American Antiquity* 44:5–35.

1988, Aspects of Mesopotamian Land Sales. *American Anthropologist* 90:119–130.

1993, The Late Great Tradition in Ancient Mesopotamia. In *The Tablet and the Scroll: Near Eastern Studies in Honor of William W. Hallo*, ed. M. Cohen, D. Snell, and D. Weisberg, pp. 300–308. Bethesda, MD: CDL Press.

1998, The Economics of Ritual at Late Old Babylonian Kish. *Journal of the Economic and Social History of the Orient* 41(3):312–343.

2000, Law Courts and the Mediation of Social Conflict in Ancient Mesopotamia. In *Order, Legitimacy, and Wealth in Ancient States*, ed. J. Richards and M. Van Buren, pp. 46–63. Cambridge: Cambridge University Press.

2001a, The Chaco "Rituality" Revisited. In *Chaco Society and Polity: Papers from the 1999 Conference*, ed. L. Cordell, W. J. Judge, and J. Piper, pp. 63–78. New Mexico Archeological Council Special Publication 4. Albuquerque: New Mexico Archeological Council.

2001b, Review of *Urbanization and Land Organization in the Ancient Near East*, ed. M. Hudson and B. Levine. *Journal of the American Oriental Society* 122:881–882.

2003, T. Patrick Culbert: An Appreciation. *Ancient Mesoamerica* 14:49–59.

Yoffee, N. and G. Cowgill 1988 eds., *The Collapse of Ancient States and Civilizations.* Tucson: University of Arizona Press.

Yoffee, N., S. Fish, and G. Milner 1999, Comunidades, Ritualities, Chiefdoms: Social Evolution in the American Southwest and Southeast. In *Great Towns and Regional Polities in the Prehistoric American Southwest and Southeast*, ed. J. Neitzel, pp. 261–271. Amerind Foundation Publication. Albuquerque: University of New Mexico Press.

Yoffee, N. and A. Sherratt 1993, Introduction: The Sources of Archaeological Theory. In *Archaeological Theory: Who Sets the Agenda?*, ed. N. Yoffee and A. Sherratt, pp. 1–9. Cambridge: Cambridge University Press.

Zadok, R. 1979, *The Jews in Babylonia during the Chaldean and Achaemenian Periods According to the Babylonian Sources.* Haifa: University of Haifa.

1984, Assyrians in Chaldean and Achaemenian Babylonia. *Assur* 4:71–98.

Zettler, R. 1987, Administration of the Temple of Inanna at Nippur under the Third Dynasty of Ur: Archaeological and Documentary Evidence. In *The Organization of Power: Aspects of Bureaucracy in the Ancient Near East*, ed. M. Gibson and R. Biggs, pp. 117–131. Studies in Ancient Oriental Civilization 46. Chicago: The Oriental Institute.

1992, *The Ur III Temple of Inanna at Nippur: The Operation and Organisation of Urban Religious Institutions in Mesopotamia in the Late Third Millennium B.C.* Berliner Beiträge zum Vorderen Orient 11. Berlin: Dietrich Reimer.

2003, Reconstructing the World of Ancient Mesopotamia: Divided Beginnings and Holistic History. *Journal of the Economic and Social History of the Orient* 46(1):3–45.

Index

Abada 31
Abu Hurayra 200
Achaemenid rulers, Achaemenids 112, 144, 155
achievement 27
actors, social 34, 35, 36, 102, 197
Adams, Robert McC. 19, 54, 148, 212
administrators 37
agency 113, 114, 182
'Ain Ghazal 202–4
Akins, Nancy 167
Akkade 37, 142
Akkadian 103
Akkadians 49
Alexander the Great 155
Algaze, Guillermo 212, 213
alternate trajectories 31
Amorites 49, 146–7, 150, 154
amphictyony 56
analogies and comparisons 188–95
analogy 5, 18, 28, 180, 181, 192
        ethnographic 23, 31, 196
Anasazi 163, 171
ancestors 37, 97
Andean prehistory 28
Anderson, Benedict 50
Anderson, David 25
Arabian coast 209
Aramaic 149
"Archaeology: The Loss of Innocence" 183
archaic states (see myths) 5, 13, 196–7, 228
arenas of power 198

assemblies 36, 61, 110, 111, 112
Assurbanipal 152
Assyrian family-firms 58, 150
Assyrian King List 147
Assyrians, modern 160
Australian Archaeological Association 184
Australian hunter-gatherer societies, Aboriginal
        societies 161–2, 177
autonomy (of local groups) 15
Axial Age 140
Aztec 171

Babylon 123, 127, 128
Baines, John 47, 52, 61
Bak, Per 169
bandishness 177
bands 6, 13, 17, 29
basic level theory 186
Bawden, Garth 28
beer hall 127
beguines, beguinage 119, 120
behavioral archaeology 185
Beld, Scott 51, 57
belief systems 6, 37, 56, 136
Belshazzar 160
Benedict, Ruth 9
Bernbeck, Reinhard 206
beveled-rim bowls 54, 101, 211
biblical times 194
big-man societies 27
Binford, Lewis 9, 185, 186

biology 28
Blanton, Richard 37, 177, 189, 191
Boas, Franz 9, 10
 Boasian particularism 9
Boltz, William 94–6
Bones 185
Book of Revelations 126
Bridges, Elizabeth 114
Bronson, Bennet 229
brothel 127
Button, Seth 157

Cahokia 30, 31, 174, 193
Calakmul 49
Caldwell, Joseph 9, 204, 205
Cameron, Catherine 165
Campbell, Stuart 207
capitals 37
Carneiro, Robert 14, 19, 25, 26
Carter, Elizabeth 127
catastrophe theory 134, 136
center and periphery 138–9
centralization, central authority 16, 17, 134, 136
 central leadership 3
Chaco Canyon 162–74, 193
 and Cahokia 230–1
 Chaco masonry 172
 Chaco old order 171
 Chaco phenomenon 167, 171
 Chaco rituality (*see* rituality)
 Chaco system 167
 Chaco system of roads 167–70
 Chacoan complexity 168
 Chacoan complexity and heterarchy 179
 Chacoan great houses 172
 evolutionary history 173–4
Chaco and Mississippian societies 174–7
Chakrabarti, Dilip 31, 51
Chaldean kings 128
Chaldeans 153, 160
Chang, K. C. 96, 97, 230
charismatic individuals 32
Charlton, Thomas 45, 49
Chetro Ketl 167
chiefdoms 6, 13, 17, 20, 22–31, 41, 44, 174, 176, 177, 188, 196, 209
 beneficent chiefdoms 14
 beneficent and redistributive chiefdoms 14
 defined 23
 matrilineal 23
 Mississippian 31
 Polynesian 31

Childe, V. Gordon 19, 60, 229
China 37, 45, 49, 50
 Anyang 43, 50, 51, 97
 dynastic cycle 96, 100, 194
 early civilization 60
 Erligang culture 96
 Erlitou 43, 50, 51, 52, 96
 evolution of the first cities and states 96–100
 Han dynasty 100
 literati 28, 37, 100
 Longshan 50
 Mandate of Heaven 99, 100
 pre-Shang 96
 royal burials 96
 Shang dynasty 50, 96–100
  kings 98, 99
  state 98
 unification 100
 writing 94–5
 Xia dynasty 96
 Yanshi 51
 Yinxu at Anyang 96
 Zhengzhou 43, 50, 51
 Zhou dynasty 50, 96, 98, 99
Churchill, Winston 44
Cipolla, Carlo 149
circumscription 26
cities 38, 42–62, 91, 212
city-hall 58, 111
city-seals 55, 56
city-state culture 46
city-states 17, 44, 45, 194
 Maya and Mesopotamian 194
civilization 13, 14, 15–19, 46, 134, 136
 definition of 17
Clarke, David 183, 205
Clastres, Pierre 161
climate change 32
collapse 1, 13, 15, 28, 29, 38, 171, 197, 198, 213
collapse of ancient Mesopotamian states and civilization 140–60
 Old Akkadian state 142–4
 Old Babylonian state 147–9
 Third Dynasty of Ur (Ur III) 144–7
collapse of ancient states and civilizations 131–60
collective memory 231
comparative method 193, 195
complex adaptive systems 3, 169, 230
complex systems, complex societies, complexity 16, 28, 41, 62, 91, 136, 198
community leaders 117, 212

Confucius 100
conical clans 24
conflict and consensus 15 (*see also* models)
        ubiquity of conflict 15
constraints on growth 15
consumption 208
contemporary ancestors 18, 22
contracts 102
Cordell, Linda 171, 172
corporate strategy 177
corporate-network model 178
councils (*see also* assemblies) 58, 111, 112, 176
        of Egyptians 112
        of great and small in Old Assyrian texts 111,
            150, 151
        of male citizens 110
countryside 61, 137, 197
Cowgill, George 38, 131, 137
craft specialists 35, 37
Creamer, Winifred and Jonathan
    Haas 23
cross-cultural comparison 23, 31
Crumley, Carole 35
Cuicuilco 48
cultural struggle 152
cultural-ecological adaptations 11
cycling 25, 26, 29, 132, 174
cylinder seals 54
Cyrus the Great 141, 155, 159

David (King) 37, 191
Darwin, theory of 21, 32
decision-making 36, 37
demographic implosion 54
dependants 35, 37, 39
deportations 152, 155
devadasis 127
Diakonoff, Igor 103, 111
differentiation (*see also* stratification) 15, 16, 32–3, 40,
    41, 42, 60, 91, 134, 136, 181, 194
        horizontal 32
        vertical 32
disembedded capital 189, 190
dispute-settlement arenas 112
disputes 111
division of labor 202, 212
Dombradi, Eva 109
domestication 201
domination 3
Domuztepe 206
down-the-line trade 202

dowry 117, 118
Doyel, David 23
Drennan, Robert 23–8, 168
Driver, Godfrey 106
dual-processual model 177
Durkheim, Emile 138

Eanatum 57
Earle, Timothy 23, 24, 26
early state modules 46, 48
Eastwood, Clint 116
Ebla 111
egalitarian 5
Egypt 45, 46–8, 194
        Abydos 47
        Amarna 43, 47, 57
        Hierakonpolis 43, 47
        Memphis 43, 47, 52
        Naqada 43, 47, 52
        New Kingdom 48
        Old Kingdom 48
        Ptolemaic 203
        Thebes 43, 47, 52
        Thinis 47
Eisenstadt, Shmuel 138–40
Elamites 104
elders 36, 112
        of Jews 112
elites 15, 35, 37, 39, 41, 42
        rural 61
Emberling, Geoff 206
emergent properties 200, 201, 204
empires 12, 45
Enga 22
Engels, Friedrich 10
Enheduana 142
Enshakushana 57
entrepreneurs 49
Erra Epic 125
Esarhaddon 152
ethnic groups, ethnicity 15, 36, 40, 41, 49, 146, 154,
        155, 156, 214
ethnoarchaeology 193
ethnographic examples 6
        ethnographic types 20
ethnolinguistic groups 208
Etowah 174
evolution 1, 4, 5, 6, 9 (*see also* neo-evolutionism)
        astrophysical 2
        biological 2, 4, 12
        civilizational ideology, of 17

cultural 8
cultural laws of 11
ladder of development 20
law of cultural evolution 9
law of evolutionary potential 13
multilinear 11, 12
of simplicity 92
pathways 161
social 8
socio-cultural 8
trajectories 197
universal 11
evolution of ancient states 6, 15
of ancient civilizations 15
new rules of the game 6
old rules of the game 6
evolutionary history 198, 199

factoid 6, 7–8, 44
facts 12
Fairservis, Walter 23
Feinman, Gary 19, 28, 177
feudalism 12
Finkelstein, Jacob J. 107, 123, 124
fire-eaters, jugglers, wrestlers 126
Flannery, Kent 18, 134–5, 136,
    189, 203
Forest, Jean-Daniel 210
Fortner, John 109
Foucault, Michel 184
Fowles, Severin 114, 173
free-floating resources 138, 139
Fried, Morton 7, 14
Friedman, Jonathan 10
Friedman, Renée 47
functionalist and adaptationist schools of
    thought 28

galacticize countrysides 50
Gallery, Maureen 125
Game of Archaeological Neologisms 181
Geertz, Clifford 50
Gelb, I. J. 111
Genealogy of Hammurabi 147
Giddens, Anthony 184
Gilgamesh, Gilgamesh and Akka 110, 111, 125, 160
    Epic 160
Gilman, Patricia 168
Göbekli Tepe 201
Godelier, Maurice 10
gods 37, 39

Goldenweiser, Alexander 9
Goodyear, Albert (see Raab)
Greece and Rome 194
Greeks, Greek 132, 155, 158
Griffeth, Robert 42, 46
growth model 229
Gulf War 160
Guti 144

Haas, Jonathan 8
Hacinebi Tepe 212
Hallan Çemi 200
Hallpike 16
Hammurabi of Babylon 58, 103–9, 123, 125, 127, 129,
    147, 148–51, 160
Hansen, Mogens Herman 45, 49
Harappa (Indus Valley civilization) 36, 45, 51–2, 194,
    228
    city-states 43, 52, 60, 229
    Harappa 43, 51
    Mohenjo Daro 43, 51
    tradition 60
Harris, Marvin 10, 11
Harris, Rivkah 117
Hawaii 22, 24, 30, 31
headman 110, 119, 148
Heidegger, Martin 184
Hellenism, Hellenistic rule (see also Seleucids)
    155–9
Henry, Donald 23
Herodotus 121, 122, 126
Herskovits, Melville 9
heterarchy 35, 179
heterogeneity 27
high-level theory 185, 187–8
high-modernist schemes 93
history 195
Hittites 147, 148, 151
Hoebel, E. Adamson 102
holistic change 28
Hopewell 204
Hopi town of Oraibi 114–15
horizonal integration 230
Hsu, Cho-yun 98
hunter-gatherers 229
Hurrians 49
hypercoherence 135, 136

Ibbi-Sin 145
ideal types 20, 46, 58
identity 16, 131, 137, 154

ideology 3, 5, 17, 28, 32, 33, 34, 39, 40, 42, 44, 62, 129, 174, 194, 197, 209, 214, 229
    high-modernist 92
    of domination 177
    of order and hierarchy 6
    of states, of statecraft, of governance, of centralization 3, 32, 39, 42, 115, 131, 140, 174
Ilushuma 149, 150
Indus Valley civilization (*see* Harappa)
inequality 27, 31, 35, 38, 40, 198
initial conditions 200
integration 32–3, 41, 42, 134, 136
interaction spheres 204–5, 230
Iraq 160
irrigation 11–12, 101, 102
Ishbi-Erra 145
Ishtar of Uruk 125, 126, 127, 128, 130

Jacobs, Jane 93
Jacobsen, Thorkild 55, 110
Janssen, Caroline 120
Jaspers, Karl 140
Jeffreys, David 47
Jerusalem 37, 160, 191–2
Jing, Zhichun 51
Johnson, Gregory 20
Jones, Rhys 162
Judge, James 168

Kantorowicz, Ernst 41
Kassites 49, 58, 147, 149, 151, 154
Katsina 171
Kauffman, Stuart 169
Katz, Dina 110
Kazane 206
Keightley, David 50, 96, 97, 98
Keith, Kathryn 61, 193
Kemp, Barry 47
Kenoyer, J. Mark 51, 52, 57
Kertzer, David 173
kezertu 116, 120
king lists 159
kinship 10, 16–17, 23, 26, 27, 29, 30, 32, 33, 34, 35, 37, 40, 41, 61, 62, 97, 110, 138, 147, 149, 202, 205, 209, 210, 214
Kirch, Patrick 27
Knight, Vernon 23
knowledgeables 98, 99
Kolata, Alan 52
Kowalewski, Steven 177
Kraus, Fritz Rudolf 106
Kuwait 160

laborers 35
ladder of progressiveness 5
Lambert, Wilfred 123
lamentation priest (at Sippar) 125, 126, 127
landowners 38
Landsberger, Benno 106
Langton, Chris 177
Larsen, Mogens Trolle 111, 149
Laufer, Berthold 8
law (true) 196
law and order 39
law of evolutionary potential 134
leadership, leaders 32, 33, 34, 36, 37, 42, 61, 62, 112, 194, 197, 214
    centralized 39
    of temple estates 36
    political leaders 38, 170
    principles 177
    religious leaders 38
    traditional 143
Le Corbusier 92
legal realists 102
legitimacy 17, 42, 61, 91, 155
Lekson, Stephen 162, 168, 171
Lenin 93
levels of archaeological theory 186
Levi, Giovanni 115
libraries 153
linearlization 134, 136, 137
list of professions 101
litigations 102
Liu, Li 50, 51
Liverani, Mario 110
Llewellyn, Karl 102
local community authorities, local autonomy, local groups 15, 28, 36, 110, 137, 139, 148, 192, 205
local resources 37
Lowie, Robert 9
Lugalzagesi of Umma 57

Machinist, Peter 100, 140
Maekawa, Kazuya 145
Mailer, Norman 7
Maine, Henry 10
maladaptation 134, 135
Mallowan, Max 207
Marxist theories 14, 138
Mathien, Joan 162, 167
Matthews, Roger 55
Maya 39, 52–3, 131
    city-states, small states 44, 45, 49, 53, 60, 177, 194

civilization and Maya states 44, 60
  collapse 134, 135, 136
  Copan 43, 53
  El Mirador 43, 52
  Nakbe 53
  Tikal (*see* Tikal)
  writing 48
McElmo phase 171
McGuire, Randall 27
McIntosh, Susan 161
McNamara, JoAnn 121
Mead, Margaret 9
meaning, systems of 34
Medes 152
Melanesia 27
mercantile activity (*see also* trade) 35, 149–51
merchant families (*see also* Assyrian family-firms)
  58, 150
merchants 117
Merodach-Baladan 160
Merton, Robert 20, 186, 187
Mesilim 57
Meskell, Lynn 47
Mesoamerica 167
Mesopotamia 11, 39
  Akkade 57, 58, 59
    collapse of 58
  Anu temple 54
  Assyria 149
  Assyria's Babylonia problem 152
  Assyrian national deity 56
  Brak/Nagar 43, 55, 211
  Choga Mami 206
  Choga Mami transitional 209
  city-states, small states, micro-states,
    statelets 44, 45, 49, 53, 198, 214,
    229
    evolution of 210
  civilization 44, 53, 60, 209
  collapse 53
  cultural identity 56
  Dilbat 116, 129
  Drehem 144, 145
  Eanna complex 43, 54, 211
  Early Dynastic period 56
  Eridu 54, 209, 210, 213
  god-lists 56
  Gawra 44, 209, 210
  Halaf 23, 101
  Hassuna 101
  Hassuna, Samarra, Halaf 205–9
  Isin 145
  Kanesh 58, 149

Karduniash 58
Kish 43, 57, 110, 123–8, 142, 211, 228
  and Hursagkalama 57
Lagash 43, 55, 57, 103, 142, 143, 145
  Girsu (Telloh) 43, 57, 211
  Lagash king list 55
  Tell al-Hiba 43, 57
land-sale documents, pre-Akkadian and
  Akkadian periods 111
Larsa 43, 58
later Neolithic 101
law codes 100–9
  Dadusha of Eshnunna 103
  Lipit-Ishtar 103
  Ur-Namma 103
legal pronouncements 94
Leilan 143
Maghzaliya 201
Marad 116
Mari 145
Mesopotamian and Aztec city-states 19
Neo-Assyrian capitals 192
Neo-Assyrian kings 58
Neo-Babylonian kings 59
Neo-Babylonian period 111
Nineveh 207
Nippur 56, 123, 211
Old Assyrian Assur 49
Old Assyrian city-state of Assur 58
  city-state government 58
Old Assyrian texts at Kanesh 111
Old Babylonian period 58, 61, 116–26
Port Tukulti-Ninurta 58
Puzrish-Dagan 144
Samarra 101
Sawwan 205, 206
Sippar 117, 125, 129
Standard Babylonian 56
stream of tradition 56
Sumerian King List 55, 56, 58, 59, 144, 197,
  213
tokens 94
transformation in the division of labor 54
Ubaid period 23, 31, 54, 101, 209–10
Umma 57, 145
Ur 56, 58, 211
  Ur III (Third Dynasty of Ur) 58, 59, 104,
    117, 144–7, 228
Uruk 43, 52, 54, 57, 60, 101, 110, 127, 128, 146,
  157, 158, 176, 211, 213
  and Kullab 57
Uruk expansion, Uruk colonies 54,
  212–13

Mesopotamia (*cont.*)
    Uruk period 23, 30, 54, 210–14
    Yarim Tepe 205, 206
Metcalf, Mary 167
Michalowski, Piotr 211
microhistory 115, 129
micro-states 17
middle-range theory 183, 184–7
Miles, John 106
military 37, 148
Millon, Rene 49
Milner, George 23
Mississippian polities, Mississippian chiefdoms 174–7, 209
Mississippian-ness 174
Moche 43, 52
models 6
    benefits and conflicts/coercion 14
    conflict 14
    on the middle-level 189
monocropping 93
Monte Albán 37, 189–92
Morgan, Edward 1, 5, 9, 10, 44
Morrison, Kathleen 45
Moundsville 174
myth, of social evolution, of the archaic state 2, 5, 44, 196–7, 231

Nabonidus 153
naditu 116–23
Naram-Sin 142
nation-states 13
Natufian 23
near decomposability 136, 137
Nebuchadnezzar II 153, 160
Neitzel, Jill 28
Nelson, Ben 170
Nemrik 200
new archaeologists 9
Nietzel, Jill 19
neo-evolutionism, neo-evolutionists 1, 4, 6, 7, 8, 9, 12, 15, 19, 21, 22, 26, 27, 28, 31, 32, 33, 38, 41, 45, 62, 100, 113, 134, 135–6, 173, 176, 180, 182, 188, 195, 231
    classification, flaws in 19
    evolutionist process 12
    failures of 6, 19
    general 12
    model 18, 21
    specific 12
    trees 18
    true believers in 20

network strategy 177
Nichols, Deborah 45, 49
Nissen, Hans 55
nomads 41, 60
nuns, medieval 119
Nyerere, Julius 93

Oates, Joan 206
old rules of the game 6
Oppenheim, A. Leo 56
oracle bones 98
oral history 194
order 34, 36, 39–40, 91
    and law (*see also* law and order) 62
oriental despotism 112

Paquime 171
palaces 228–9
Parsons, Talcott 5, 186
pathologies 135, 138
patrimonial bureaucracy 37
Patterson, Thomas 8
Pauketat, Tim 163
Paynter, Robert 28
peer-polities 44, 48
Pepper, G. R. 167
Peregrine, Peter 177
phase transitions 230
pilgrimages 91, 170
Pittman, Holly 212
Plog, Fred 171
Polanyi, Karl 24
polis 46
Polynesia 27, 29, 31
population growth and pressure 11, 12, 14, 26, 28, 32, 201–2
port authority (karum) 119
Possehl, Gregory 23, 51, 228, 229
post-processual 182, 184, 195
potter's workshop 207
Powell, Marvin 123
power 1, 3, 33–8, 197
    bottom-up aspects 2
    centralized 34
    competition for 198
    dimensions of 34, 38
    discourse about 34
    domains of 177, 194, 229
    economic 34, 35
    ideological 174
    ideologies of 16
    limited 29

local 36
  political 35, 37–8, 39
  relations of 6
  rules of 34
  social 35, 36–7
  sources of 34
  structures 14
  struggle for 6, 42
  varieties of 1, 35
Power, Eileen 120
pre-political 173
priests 37
prime mover arguments 14
prior probabilities 188
processual archaeologists, processual archaeology 9,
  184
profit 150
progress 1, 11
promotion 134, 136, 137
prostitution, ritual 122–6
pseudo-pressure 201
Pueblo Bonito 163–7
punctuated and holistic change 22, 26
purification priest 127

Qermez Dere 200

Raab, Mark and Albert Goodyear 185, 186
Rappaport, Roy 134, 135–6
Ratnagar, Shereen 51, 57
redistribution 24
reforms of Urukagina 103
relations of domination 32
relations of production 32
Rempel, Jane 155
Renfrew, Colin 22, 46, 134, 136
Rim-Sin 147
ritual caches 167
rituality 168, 170–1, 173, 177
rival claims to knowledge 7, 189
Roman empire 13
Rome 131
royal lineage 16
rules of the game 6
  academic rules 6
    rules of academic behavior 7
  new rules of the game 6
  old rules of the game 6
  substantive rules 6, 7
rules of social behavior 204
ruralization 52, 54, 61, 214
Russell, Bertrand 45

Sabi Abyad 206, 207
Saddam Hussein 160
Sahlins, Marshall 7, 12–15, 24, 27
Salado interaction sphere 171
salinization 102, 146
Salmon ruin 167, 168
Samsu-iluna 120
San 22
Sanders, William 20, 22, 26
Santa Fe Institute 169–70
Santley, Robert 189, 190
Sapir, Edward 9
Sargon (of Akkade) 37, 56, 57, 58, 142, 143, 144, 150
Schiffer, Michael 185, 186
Schreiber, Katharina 43, 52
Schwartz, Benjamin 98
Scott, James 92–4
sealand kings 123, 127, 128
seals 158
segmentation, social 36
segregation 134, 136
Seleucids (see also Hellenism) 155–9
self-organization (self-organized criticality) 169
Sennacherib 152
Service, Elman 7, 12–15, 134
settlement hierarchies 45
Shabik'eschee 162
shamans, shamanism 32, 97, 98
Shamash-shum-ukin 152
Shamshi-Adad 150, 151
Shoup, Daniel 157
Shulgi 144, 145, 147
Shutruk-nahhunte 104
silver 150
Simon, Herbert 136–7
simplicity 198
Sinopoli, Carla 45
site-size hierarchies 20
Smith, Adam 206
social change 131
social evolution 4, 29, 38
  and technological evolution 10
  Whiggish view 177
social evolutionary theory 1, 3, 6, 7, 197
social identity 16
social landscapes 44
social memory 40
social relations 32
social roles 3, 32, 114, 115, 131, 182, 198
social struggle 170
society-wide institutions 38
sociology of science 7

Southeast (American) 29
Southeastern ceremonial complex 174
Speiser, Ephraim 143
Spencer, Charles 25, 26
Spencer, Herbert 16
Spengler, Oswald 132, 133
spheres of interaction 96
stages 12, 13, 17, 18, 22, 28, 44, 134, 173, 180,
        188, 193
states 6, 15–19
        and non-states 16
        appearance of 39, 58
        class-riven 26
        coercive state 14
        date of origin 38
        definition of 17
        different from chiefdoms 25
        identifying the state 41
        the state 15
staple goods 24
Stein, Gil 23, 212
Stein, Gil and Rana Özbal 210
Steinkeller, Piotr 43, 57, 145
Steward, Julian 1, 5, 7, 10–12
storage 36
storage and redistribution 91
stratification 14, 15, 27, 40, 60, 181
        and social differentiation 3, 15
Struever, Stuart and Gail Houart 204
struggle 15
        for control of economic resources 38
        for control of knowledge, ceremonies, and
                symbols 38
        for political and economic power 38
        of armed forces 38
        political 33
Sugiyama, Saburo 49
Sumerian 101, 154
Sumerians 49
sumptuary rules 24
surplus 34, 35, 36, 39, 229
Susa 104, 127, 210
symbols
        central 36, 42
        of cultural commonality 37, 38
        of ideologies of state 39
        of kingship and unification 48
        of social integration 34
        of statecraft 44
systemic fragility 198
systems theory 113, 134, 135, 137

Tainter, Joseph 131
Tasmanians 162–74
Taylor and Ford 93
Tayma (Teima) 153
temple-estates 41
Teotihuacan 36, 43, 45, 48, 49, 50, 52, 60, 176, 177, 190,
        192, 229
        Street-of-the-Dead Complex 49
theatre-state 50
theocratic ruling class, theocracy 12, 24
        theocratic leadership 13
Theoretical Archaeology Group 184
theory, appropriate 182
theory, archaeological 183–95
theory, real 182
tholoi 206
Thomas, Carol 46, 49
Tiglath-Pileser III 152
Tikal 43, 49, 53
tin 150
Tiwanaku 43, 45, 52
Toll, H. Wolcott 167, 168
Toynbee, Arnold 132, 133
trade 35, 38, 41, 49, 96, 111, 130
trait-list 19
treaties 150
tribes 6, 13, 17, 29, 146, 149
Trigger, Bruce 50
Tukulti-Ninurta I 58
Tylor, Edward 1, 5, 8, 9, 12
types of societies 6, 7, 19, 23, 28
        culture types 11
        ethnographic 7, 20
typologies 5

urban interactions 197
urban flight 60
urbanization 60
        and ruralization (see also ruralization) 214
Ur-Namma 144
Uribe, Carlos 23
Utuhegal 144

valley-states of Peru 45
Varien, Mark 162
Vedas 194
Veenhof, Klaas 123
Vidal, Gore 122, 126

Ware, John 172
wards 110

warfare 14, 37, 49, 91, 96, 170
Wari 36, 43, 45, 52, 60
Watson, Patty Jo 23
wealth 35–6, 38, 39, 40
   stored 35
Webster, David 26, 52, 134, 136
Weber, Max 138
Weiss, Harvey and T. Cuyler Young, Jr. 212
Westbrook, Raymond 109
Wheatley, Paul 98
Willey, Gordon 189, 230
Willey, Gordon and Jeremy Sabloff 185
White, Leslie 1, 5, 7, 8–10, 12, 24
Wilcke, Claus 107, 110
Williams, William Carlos 113

Wills, Wirt 165
Wilshusen, Richard 162
Wilson, David 52
Wilson, John 47
Winter, Marcus 190
Wittfogel, Karl 11, 14
Wobst, Martin 192
world history 195, 197
Wright, Henry 20, 25, 26, 55
writing in China and Mesopotamia 94
   Mesopotamian 211
   official written langauge 101

Yates, Robin 50
Yoffee's Rule 41

Made in the USA
Lexington, KY
27 December 2013